EPHEMERATA

Odds and Ends of a Writing Life

F. Paul Wilson

Ephemerata

© 2024 by F. Paul Wilson
All rights reserved.

This is a work of fiction and non-fiction. Most of the people (living and dead), organizations, and events named within are real. They are mentioned only in passing so no one should have cause to be upset. However, should someone become upset…see that corner over there – the empty one? Head over there and wait for someone who cares. Go ahead. That's it…

Ebook – 1st edition published 3/29/17
- Revision 2.0 published 2018
- Revision 3.0 published 2019
- Revision 4.0 published 2020
- Revision 5.0 published 2021
- Revision 6.0 published 2024

Hardcopy publication - 2024

CONTENTS

Author's Note to the Sixth Edition - 4
Forewords, Intros & Afterwords - 6

Appreciations - 164

Memoirs - 216

Puffery - 320

The Byte Columns - 395

Fictions - 422

Reviews - 504

Opinion - 553

Timelime: The Secret History - 591

Bibliography - 600

AUTHOR'S NOTE

Ephemerata...is a neologism of my creation. It's supposed to sound like the plural of ephemera, but ephemera is already plural (*ephemeron* is the singular). So maybe "ephemerata" is pluplural. Anyway, it fits because I've got so damn much ephemera.

That's what happens when you start selling stories in 1970 and keep on writing. People begin asking you for an introduction or foreword or afterword to their anthologies and collections, and to comment on this or that for their magazine or fanzine. And then you read a book you like and want to tell people about it so you write a review. And then you're asked to write a column or two. You knew so-and-so – would you write an obit? Sometimes you write something simply because you feel like writing it and then don't have a place to publish it. And of course your publisher wants you to help flog your latest book and you can't say no to that.

After a while you wind up with scads of ephemerata. I've collected nearly 175,000 words of it here, and that's just the stuff I could find. There maybe be more of out there but I simply don't know where.

Reading through it all again, I'm surprised at the personal nature of a lot of the material. I'll never write an autobiography (writing a whole book about my prosaic existence would bore me to tears – maybe to death), but if you take the intros to all the stories in my collections, plus the more personal stuff here (the Byte columns, the travels, and other scattered bits) you've got a sketch. That's enough.

Up until now I'm published *Ephemerata* exclusively in ebook form. That's because it was a work in progress. I updated it with orphaned pieces that surfaced from the past or ones that were too new and had to remain exclusive to their original venue for a while. The nice things about ebooks is that readers simply reload the book into their reader and the new material appears. Magic.

No more. Time for a more permanent binding.

F. Paul Wilson
The Jersey Shore
March 2024

FOREWORDS, INTROS & AFTERWORDS

Seems apropos to start off with pieces designed to start off other books. Crikey, I've done a lot of these things. Here they are, presented in roughly chronological order.

No Flies on Frank - 9

The Sandman: Preludes & Nocturnes - 9

Dead End: City Limits - 12

Night Visions 9 - 16

Batman: Gothic - 21

Garden - 26

Cages - 28

Primum Non Nocere - 31

The Exorcist - 34

The Oldest Profession - 42

Andy Warhol's Dracula - 45

The Pirates of Venus - 47

The Distributor - 56

Fat - 59

Ship of Fools - 61

Taverns of the Dead - 62

Lipidleggin' - 66

Impaler - 67

Wolff and Byrd - 69

The Hounds of Skaith - 71

Robots Have No Tails - 79

The LaNague Federation Series - 85

Reunion - 87

Recalled - 91

The Leopard Couch - 93

Nothing As It Seems - 97

The Hogben Chronicles - 100

The Shaft - 103

Drive-In Creature Feature - 107

You, Human - 111

The Art of the Pulps - 115

Next Testament - 120

The Call of *Claimed!* - 124

What *Rocket to the Morgue* Means to Me - 133

Moonless Nocturne - 138

Hellstone - 143

Pines - 146

Blood of the Lamb – 149

Who is Sax Rohmer? - 152

Comic vs Abrahamic Horror - 158

For the John Lennon story in Dark Voices *(1990). Done in the style of the story, the intro is almost as long. Steve Jones paid me a bottle of domestic champagne.*

No Flies on Frank

Yes, it all comes bark to meow. I was 18 and a loyal Beatle fart with me own carpy of the brook In *His Own Write* by John Lemon of the famous sisters. "No flies on Frank" wars one of me flavored stones, along perhaps with "Angry Frank" to which it was maybe a sequin. Joycean Carrollean pre-Pythonesque minimalism some might squeak. In realty, "No Flies on Frank" is not very mulch a pleasured story, what with the red gore and purple violents and without munch of an end and no morals whatsoever. Almond lifelike you might say if you were inclined to peek.

***

This was the original 1991 intro to the first volume of Neil Gaiman's collected The Sandman. *It lasted until Karen Berger decided write her own. I have a feeling she thought my intro didn't approach the series with sufficient reverence. Probably right. I'm not known for reverence. But then, neither is Neil.*

The Sandman: Preludes & Nocturnes

Those Brits.

They've been making a habit of butting into our things, showing us up. All right, we did get the language from them but I don't care what they say, we're not paying royalties on it. That's not the subject, anyway. I'm talking about butt-inski Brits.

Take rock 'n' roll, for instance. We invented that. It's pure American, no question about it. Started it in 1955 or so and had it roaring great guns by '57. Of course, we did let it get run into the ground after that. I mean, what with Elvis shipped off to Germany with a crew cut, Jerry Lee in showbiz limbo because of his wife, Buddy, Richie and the Bopper smeared all over that cornfield in Ames, Iowa, Eddie Cochran dead, Gene Vincent crippled, Chuck Berry arrested on the Mann Act, and Little Richard a minister (could you believe it?), we spent a hell of a lot of time listening to the likes of "Hey, Paula" and "Take Good Care of My Baby" and such on the radio and believing we were hearing rock 'n' roll.

The Brits changed all that. They listened to our old rock records, started playing it the way it used to be played, put their own spin on it, and exported it back to America. The Beatles crafted these unforgettable pop gems while the Stones pointed us back to the roots of the whole thing. Everyone went nuts over it. The intrinsic vitality of the music, pent up for all those years, burst free in a torrent. Hey, man. Like, deja vu.

Yeah, well, they reminded us what it really was and showed us what it could be. Neither rock nor America has been the same since.

Years later, a quieter but equally revolutionary infiltration took place in the world of comic books. Comic books! Those are ours, too! We invented them back in the thirties with *Famous Funnies.* But it took the Brits to remind us where you could go with them.

Again, just like with rock 'n' roll, we had comic books fired up and going great guns in the fifties, but we let the Comics Code run them into the ground on us. Everybody remembers the old E.C. comics of the early fifties, even if born decades after they were killed off. Remember the above-ground comics of the sixties and seventies? Of course you don't. You've made yourself forget. Or tried to. While all those steroidal guys and buxom gals in tights were flying around with no visible means of support, blissfully immune not only to the effects of gravity but to those of momentum and inertia as well, the Brits were putting a hard edge on their comics. *Judge Dredd, Nemesis the Warlock, V, Marvelman (Miracleman* over here), *D.R. & Quinch.* Who was doing stuff like that on these shores? We liked it so much we surrendered *Swamp Thing* to Alan Moore. Swampy! In the clutches of a foreigner!

The rest was history. Like the British musicians in the sixties, Moore took a character and a setting that everybody thought was completely played out and breathed new life into it. Shortly thereafter, Jamie Delano, another Brit, followed with the John Constantine stories in *Hellblazer*.

Before anybody realized it, the Brits had taken possession of the DC Nether Realms. The place would never be the same. Aren't you glad?

Then Neil Gaiman – a third Brit – conies along with *Sandman*. Sandman – Death's younger brother, a.k.a. Dream, a.k.a. Morpheus, Lord of the Dream Realm – completed the spectrum of characters in DC's horror line. John Constantine is human, firmly embedded in the material world, Sandman is purely supernatural, one of the Endless, and Swamp Thing falls somewhere between.

And none of them flies or wears tights (thank-you, thank-you, thank-you).

Dreams. Are they merely unconscious ruminations and remastications of the events of the day, colored by our psyches and the combined weight of experience that shapes us, or are they scenes from another realm that we tap into and actually help shape while we're asleep? Neil Gaiman says it's the latter, and tells us of the time when the master of that realm was trapped on earth and had to go in search of the tools of his powers.

Oh, you'll love these stories. That is, you will if you have the power to suspend disbelief, if you've retained that child-like (that's child-*like*, not *childish)* ability to climb on an author's back and let him fly you to realms where all the rules are off, where school is out – was never in, actually – and everything goes.

Gaiman's *Sandman* dreams are wild, witty, and wicked, sly, and self-referential, wide-eyed with wonder and yet cynically post-modern. Afterimages linger...the living room (pardon the pun) in Rachel's house, and Rachel *herself* in bed, looking like Regan MacNeil at her worst, mumbling the lyrics to an Everly Brothers tune about dreaming... Sandman standing on a wharf in interstellar space... the stand-up gig in Hell...

And then we come to the centerpiece: the twenty-four hours in the All Nite Diner, very possibly one of the most gut-wrenching, deeply disturbing single issues of any title I have ever read. It has gore, sure, but that's mere trim. It strikes deeper than that. It shows people out of control, forced to be the worst they can be. The effect lingers long after you've closed the cover.

And that perhaps is the *sine qua non* of the best horror fiction. Anybody can splatter you with blood and other sundry precious bodily fluids. But they wash off, don't they? Just like mud. Just like spilled food and drink. Wash right off your skin without leaving a trace of their passing. Not the good stuff, though. Good horror gets past the skin. It seeps through and insinuates its way into the tissues, invades the circulation, spreads to all the vital organs, contaminates the nervous system, taking up residence behind the eyes so that nothing looks quite the same again. Ever.

The final story is my favorite, though. In it we meet the god Roderick Burgess was trying to bind at the start of the saga when he captured Sandman instead: Death. A gentle, strangely warm, and yet perfectly satisfying finish to *Sandman*.

Those Brits. I wonder what they'll tackle next.

***

For the 1991 anthology of the same name edited by Paul Olson and David Silva

Dead End: City Limits

Don't make eye contact.

At least not in The City. In most suburbs, and especially in rural areas, it's rude *not* to make eye contact. That and a little nod comprise a validation of another person's presence. It's part of a proper greeting.

Not in The City. Eye contact is a challenge, usually met with, "Whatchoo lookin at, fukkuh?" And sometimes you're lucky if that's the limit of the response.

That's not the way it was supposed to be.

The City. It started out as a place of commerce, often growing up around a convenient natural harbor. Traders came, seeking business; workers came, seeking jobs. And either they brought their families along or they started new ones. The resultant crowding called to those whose tastes and behavior were out of step with the norms of the provinces, and so the outcasts came, seeking anonymity and others of their kind.

And the predators came, seeking victims.

The City doesn't have a lock on predators. They're everywhere. You find them in rural towns and suburban malls, and at all levels in The City, from financial district boardrooms to the subways. But predators tend to concentrate in The City. It's only logical. All predators follow herds of prey. Used to be they skulked along the periphery. Nowadays it seems they're running the herd.

As a result, The City has become a sprawling nightmare.

It wasn't always like that.

I remember my adopted city, Manhattan, in the early to mid-sixties. I met it as a callow fourteen-year-old busing in from the Jersey suburbs to attend a Jesuit high school in the Chelsea district. In the morning I'd breeze through the Port Authority, grab the A train down to West 4th, where I'd transfer to the Sixth Avenue line and ride the D train up to West 16th Street, where Xavier was located. I'd come home a different route, taking the express D train up to 125th or 145th Street – the heart of Harlem – where I'd wait for an

Eighth Avenue train to whisk me up to 168th Street. I'd hang out at the White Castle in Washington Heights until my bus was ready to leave for Jersey.

Was I ever hassled? Occasionally, sure. But no more than I got hassled back home in Hackensack.

Would I want to ride those routes again today, especially the one home?

No way. Not even with a fully loaded Uzi. I mean, have you seen the PA lately? Heard what's going down in Harlem?

But people do run those routes, every day. They just don't make eye contact.

The City's not all bad. Really. The arts are perhaps most alive in the city. It's where everybody who's too far out or too original or too brilliant for small-town America winds up. Plus, there's the feeling that this is where it's at, no matter what particular "it" you're referring to. This is where things are happening, where the action is, where fortunes are being made and lost, where everybody's got a chance at the brass ring if you just know where to stand when it swings by.

And then there's the excitement, the rhythm, the incessant up-tempo beat of city life. Each city has its own, with New York's undoubtedly the most frenetic. But no matter what the city, the pace is heavier and headier than that in the environs.

Some people can't handle it for more than a minute, some can't go a day without it. Some can't take it as a steady diet but do crave a fix now and again.

You've simply got to learn to watch your back. You've always had to watch your back in The City. I learned that. I came of age in my city. I learned where I could get served underage on the Bowery (and the drinking age then was only eighteen) and knew who was selling illegal fireworks in the Village or Chinatown. I learned to spot trouble coming and make a detour, to sense when a situation might be deteriorating. I became streetwise. That's always been necessary for survival.

But what I sense now is different. There's a siege mentality in The City these days. The unspoken sentiment is that it's become ungovernable. The people who can afford to are leaving; those who can't are adding extra locks to their doors and are huddling all their belongings and loved ones close around them. You don't lay anything down, you don't leave anything – or anyone – you care about unguarded, even for a moment. At night you drag whatever you can inside your fortress – your car radio, your bike – and you chain down whatever you can't, including the trees and small shrubs in your yard. You do it because you've learned that nothing is too big or too small to steal. No crime is too low to be committed. And nothing is too trivial to kill for.

You can be killed for a fad.

Perfect example: As I sit down to write this, a news story from my city says another kid was killed last night for his 8-ball jacket. One of the local DJs has a running gag about buying 8-ball jackets as gifts for people he doesn't like. They're hot, those jackets – multicolored leather affairs with big black 8-balls centered on the back and the elbows. Wear one in the wrong neighborhood on the wrong day and you could be confronted with a demand to hand it over. Refuse, resist, you wind up dead like that kid last night. Next year, when it's passé, you'll be able to wear your 8-ball anywhere you damn well please and no one will give you a second look. But now it's like putting your life on the line.

Death by fad.

Only in The City.

Which is the only place the stories in this volume could happen. In The City. They may claim to be set in NY or Big D or LA or Chi or Frisco or Deeetroit. But that's just a cover for their *real* setting.

The City.

It embraces the best and worst of all cities. If you have your - own favorite or most-loathed part of any city, you'll probably find it here. It ain't pretty, but you'll soon discover there's one thing all these stories have in common, one thing each one of them forces you to do with its city:

Make eye contact.

**

For the 1991 Dark Harvest anthology.

Night Visions 9

Horror is dead.

Or if not dead, at the very least moribund and teetering on the edge of forever.

Or so we're told. We hear it from some editors, some publishers, and even some book sellers. We hear it from fanzine and prozine columnists and pundits, from self-proclaimed experts on the entire scope of publishing.

Horror is dead.

Sorry, no. Horror, like rock and roll, will never die. (Wait... maybe that's not such a good analogy. Judging by what's coming out of my radio speakers these days, rock may be deeper into a coma than horror fiction.)

No, not dead. But horror has been having some serious health problems lately, most of them related to its rapid (rapid, hell – *phenomenal)* growth during the 1980s. The problems have been mostly logistical.

Logistics. That's a military term most of us heard *ad nauseam* during Operation Desert Storm. It refers to procuring, maintaining, and transporting material, personnel, and facilities. In a nutshell: making sure the frontlines don't run out of the supplies they need to keep on fighting.

This is what Hussein couldn't do in Kuwait and southern Iraq.

This is what the publishers couldn't do in the bookstores in regard to the horror genre.

Horror got too big, too fast.

Think about it. In the Fifties, who was writing horror? Matheson, Bloch, and Wheatley, and that was about it. In the Sixties – Matheson, Bloch, and Wheatley, plus that bestseller by Ira Levin. The Seventies were launched with *The Exorcist*, followed by the movie, followed in mid-decade by somebody named King. In those three decades you could read everything – new and reprint – that was published in horror. *Everything.* I know. I did it. It got a little hairy by the end of the late Seventies with all those gerund titles, but I managed.

By the Eighties we were off to the races. I had to give up my omnivorish ways and become more selective.

And there's the rub. As I was becoming more restrictive in my choices (due to constraints on my reading time), the mass reading public was getting into the horror groove in a big way. And Stephen King's novel a year in those days was only whetting their appetites. More, more, more. Give us more. And when publishers see a demand, they rush to satisfy it. Nothing wrong with that. That's what a free market is all about: You want it? I'll see if I can get it for you.

Publishers started horror lines, horror imprints with neato horror logos. The market was booming, everything was selling like crazy. Trouble was, there wasn't enough good horror fiction to meet the demand. Publishers projected three horror slots a month – lead, middle, bottom. And when they didn't have the inventory to fill them, they went hunting. Hang around the bar at some of the more writer-intensive conventions and you'll hear some amazing stories: Writers getting calls from editors saying, "I've got this horror slot in April and it's gonna go begging if I can't find something to fill it. Can you get me a seventy-thousand-word giant-bug/evil-child/haunted-house/disturbed-burial-mound/vampire novel by the end of next week?"

Not a few damn fine writers took those offers. Why not? If they didn't fill the slot, somebody else would. The money might as well be in their pocket as in somebody's else's. And what the hell, they weren't going to use their own name anyway.

And that's okay. There are bills to pay and the bank doesn't care if the mortgage payment originated in royalties from a thousand-page treatise on the significance of porridge in the works of Charles Dickens or from *The Jellyfish that Plopped on San Diego*.

The important thing here is the publishing/editorial mind-set that was operating.

Filling slots.

That's not the way to develop a loyal audience.

Yes, I know all the arguments about the realities of modern bookselling, how the chain-store tail is wagging the publishing dog. Keep talking. The polls are closed and the results are in: too many second- and third-rate horror novels were shoved into the racks to fill the slots in the programs; those novels, a number of which should never have been published, were packaged to look like every other novel that had achieved a modicum of success in the preceding few months. The horror-fiction racks became a choice between Tweedledum and Tweedledummer. The readers get fed up with cloned covers outside and cloned fiction inside.

Horror fiction became fast food. Some of the publishers should have had golden arches over their doors. Predictably, the readers became tired of the assembly-line product. Cries of "Where's the beef?" arose. But even when the publishers managed to acquire some of the filet mignon we all know is out there, they plopped it into their regular hamburger boxes, dooming it to molder on the shelves.

Their logistics failed: they weren't getting the right stuff to the right people.

Boom became bust.

Which brings us to the *Night Visions* series.

Night Visions doesn't follow a schedule, doesn't worry about filling a slot. This is the ninth volume since 1984. The process is simple. Take two well-known writers and another talented but not-quite-as-well-known writer and turn them loose. Thirty-thousand words each, no holds barred.

If the purpose of horror fiction is to disturb and unsettle, then Thomas Tessier is certainly one of the all-time masters. I know of six novels he's done. There may be others. The ones I've read have been profoundly disturbing. His novella here, "The Dreams of Dr. Ladybank," is no exception. It probably should be labeled with one of those *Warning: Contains explicit scenes of sex and violence* stickers. And it is indeed disturbing – so deeply disturbing in some scenes that you are tempted to laugh to keep from screaming. *(Not* a happy sound.) His three characters, drawn from both extremes of the socioeconomic strata, are all sociopaths in one manner or another. As you breeze through his effortless prose you will come to loathe the upper-echeloner, a professional man of education, taste, and means; a natural response to the ultimate user: a very unique sort of psychic vampire. You will find your sympathies falling resolutely in step with the two low-lifes. Each is a hustler and a ne'er-do-well and a user in his own way, caring nothing for his fellow man, possessing nothing of value to offer human society. This is no little accomplishment for an author. Tessier makes it look easy. In less skillful hands the result easily might have been disastrous.

But Tessier is working on a deeper level here, exploring what is perhaps the ultimate horror – loss of control over your actions, your decisions, your everyday life. No matter who you are, you have a right to your own life. This is something so fundamental that we often take it for granted. And I believe it is at the heart of our fascination with the vampire. The vampire's victims find that not only have their lives been stolen, but their deaths as well. They walk the night eternally, ruthlessly sating an appetite they'd find repugnant in life. The two low-lifes in "Dr. Ladybank" do not rise from the dead, but they do have control of their lives siphoned away from them.

You will not soon forget this story.

James M. Kisner plays in another key entirely. Many keys, in fact. He can be grim, he can be touching, he can put you on with tongue firmly in cheek. After reading his five short contributions here, one can almost envision him sitting by a campfire, grinning wickedly and rubbing his hands together as he dreams up new tales to elicit laughter and raised hackles from his listeners.

Kisner is not as well known as Tessier or Hautala, but that's destined to change soon. He's not a new kid. He's the author of nine novels, has regular columns in Mystery Scene and *Pulphouse* magazines, has had stories in *Scare Care, Stalkers, Hotter Blood, Phantoms*, a number of the *Masques* anthologies, and many more, and has even taken up comic book scripting for titles like *Leatherface*. His current novel is *The Quagmire*. He's due for overnight world recognition any day now.

Kisner is a good choice to hold up the middle of this volume. Makes me think back to my involvement in *Night Visions 6*. Paul Mikol called early in 1987 and said he wanted Sherri Tepper and me for that particular number. Did I know of a relative newcomer I could recommend that I'd be comfortable sharing the volume with? A name immediately came to mind. I'd read his first three novels and knew he had something.

I said, "Ray Garton."

Paul said, "Who?"

"His latest novel is *Live Girls*," I said. "Pick it up and see if you want to publish him."

Paul called back a week later and said, "We've got to use this Garton guy. How do I get ahold of him?"

Well, finding Ray is a whole other story. But the point is, you've got to have a certain something to get into *Night*

Visions. They don't take just anybody. They're interested in quality. I didn't have to sell Ray to Paul. Ray, pretty much an unknown then (his first publisher, Pinnacle, was going down the tubes just as he was getting up to speed), sold himself with his work. He's anything but an unknown now.

The same with James Kisner. You may not know his name now, may not have read anything by him before, but I have a feeling these stories will whet your appetite for more. The man is a born storyteller.

Finally we come to Rick Hautala who likes to refer to himself as That Other Writer from Maine or That Other Writer Who Answers to "Rick", but he's overly modest. As the bestselling author of *Nightstone* – over a million-and-a-half copies in print at last count – and many other popular novels, he's about as close as you can get to a household name with a name no one can pronounce. Hautala apparently couldn't decide between writing a number of short stories or *a* single novella, so he chose the middle path. What we've got here is a series of four interconnected stories bridged by folk tales, all coalescing into a sequel of sorts to his novel, *Little Brothers*.

Quite frankly, "Untcigahunk" is a delight. I don't know anything about Micmac folklore, but if the Little Brothers aren't a part of it, they should be. And the three bridging folk tales, with their touching descriptions of the Old One and the creation of man and the Little Brothers, give Hautala's contribution a spiritual scope, a sense of breadth and depth too rare in horror fiction – hell, in *all* fiction – these days.

Night Visions 9 is proof that horror isn't dead. It's only taking a breather, recharging its batteries. It will be back full strength before you know it. Meanwhile, it's alive and well in the following pages.

***

Another graphic novel intro – this one to Batman: Gothic. *I believe Mike Hill commissioned this in the spring of 2001.*

Tonight's Blue-Light Special: The Soul

What's the going price for a soul?

Or let's get more personal: What's the price tag on *your* soul?

You needn't be religious to answer. You needn't believe in the traditional Christian soul or the Hindu *atman*, needn't believe that you harbor within you something as intimate as a piece of the deity or something so impersonal as an icy flake of eternity. You needn't buy into the supernatural at all to believe in the soul.

After all, maybe the soul is manmade. Maybe it develops within you as you grow, becoming the essence that determines who you are – your code of ethics, your dreams, your values. *You.*

Perhaps the soul is your integrity.

Whatever it is, your soul is so intimately bound to your being that it cannot be taken from you, at least while you live. No amount of abuse, harassment, threats, or torture can pry loose your soul. You can be robbed of your riches, your pride, your dignity, your beauty, everything but your soul. Like your integrity, no one can take that from you.

You must give it away.

Or sell it.

But selling your soul...is that relevant anymore?

I say yes. Now more than ever. Souls – or at least pieces of them – are being traded even as you read this: for a higher corporate gross, for a promotion, for a slot on the bestseller list, for a plum part in a hot film, for a first-string spot on the cheerleader squad, for a junior prom date, for a little glass vial filled with beige rocks.

You needn't sell your whole soul. Just a small chunk. Chip a piece off the rear corner. You'll never miss it, and hardly anyone will know it's gone. Haggle for the best price. Get the most you can for it. After all, souls don't come labeled with a UPC code. The price is up to you. Only you can decide to sell it, only you know what it's worth to you.

What if someone offers to buy the whole thing?

Better think about that. And first off, maybe you should check to see if you've got something left to sell. For all you know you could be one of the many among us who've bartered away their entire souls piecemeal and don't realize they've got nothing left to bargain with. But if you happen to have something left to sell, think well before you entertain that offer. Because you get only one soul and, like your integrity, once you've traded it away, it's damn near impossible to get back.

So if eventually you do decide to go through with the sale, you'd better get one hell of a good price for it.

For once you've handed it over, once you've sealed that deal, you become a lesser being. You become forever linked to the sort who trade in souls, and believe me, they're not the kind you want to invite over for dinner. Like it or not, you wind up hanging out with them.

Because no one else wants you around.

But why all this sententious talk of souls and deals for them?

Because it is upon such a deal that the tale within turns.

A tale aptly titled *Gothic*.

Gothic is a school of architecture that came to the fore in Western Europe between the 12th and 16th Centuries. But Gothic is more than thick granite walls, processions of pointed arches, rows of flying buttresses without and yawning, vaulted ceilings within.

Gothic is a state of mind.

It conjures visions of medieval times when we feared the dark not only because of the human threats that might lurk within the shadows, but because of its *in*human threats as well; a time when the Church squandered its treasure building huge, looming structures, the bigger the better.

Gothic is a dark, dour, gloomy state of mind.

Gothic is also a school of writing. The Gothic romance first appeared in the 18th Century. It was typified by a medieval setting or took place in a gloomy old castle or monastery. Walpole's *The Castle of Otranto* kicked off the trend in 1764; it peaked perhaps three decades years later with M. G. Lewis's *The Monk* and Anne Radcliffe's trend-setting *Mysteries of Udolpho*. None of those titles ring a bell? Try this one: *Frankenstein* by Mary W. Shelley. She borrowed the gloom and claustrophobic atmosphere of the Gothic romance and set her story in her own time.

Grant Morrison's tale in the following pages owes less to Radcliffe, who tended to end her novels with an explanation of the seemingly supernatural events she'd described, than to Lewis who filled his pages with blood-thirsty demons and chain-rattling spooks.

But the greatest debt here (acknowledged in the opening to Part Five) is to *Faust*, the German legend of the alchemist who sold his soul to Mephistopheles (You-Know-Who) in return for youth, knowledge, and power.

Thus my opening question: What is the price of a soul? What do you trade it for?

Grant Morrison's story tackles the next question: How do you buy it back?

Clearly, you must do something extraordinary.

In *Gothic*, Grant Morrison and Klaus Janson offer us a classic story of a Faustian bargain centering around not one but two examples of the Gothic school of architecture: a monastery – ancient and sunken, keeping hidden an ancient atrocity – and a newer piece, a cathedral built two centuries ago in Gotham, hiding an atrocity in the making.

A clockwork cathedral, a lithic time bomb, waiting to transfer a horror from the past to the streets of today.

The word *Shauerroman* perfectly fits this tale. It's a German term for the Gothic novel (literally, a "shudder-novel") and it just so happens that this particular

Shauerroman has been illustrated by an artist with a Germanic name: Klaus Janson. (Strange how things work, how seemingly random pieces seem to settle of their own accord into a cohesive whole.)

Janson's art in *Gothic* is, well, Gothic. Dark, moody, with long expressionistic shadows and extreme angles of perspective. He makes the dream sequences just surreal enough to keep you off balance, he plays up the Gothic aspects of Batman's *Wunderkammer*, the Bat Cave, and note how he renders the interior of a chemical plant like a cathedral – a Gothic cathedral.

The story bears rereading. This is no place for a full-blown exegesis, but allow me to mention a few points of special interest: Morgenstern's analepsis harkens back to Fritz Lang's *M*, and the rampages of Brother Manfred and his fellow capuchini carry echoes of the more controversial scenes from Ken Russell's *The Devils*. Yet amid all this darkness we catch brief flashes of humor – Alfred's dry wit, first manifested (at least to me) in *Year One*, is here more mordantly laconic than ever.

Gothic.

A perfect title for this story, this illustrated *Shauerroman*, combining as it does a Faustian bargain, a Gothic cathedral, a medieval monastery, a classic Gothic atmosphere of horrific gloom and mystery graced by moody, evocative art, all set here, now, in a city called Gotham.

And striding through its center is that most Gothic of all heroes, the one who has adopted a creature of the night as his motif.

The one whose soul has no price.

***

For Matt Costello's 2006 sequel to Wurm.

Garden

Loose ends...

I'm partly responsible for the existence of "Garden" (more on that later) so I couldn't very well refuse commenting on it. But before we get to "Garden," let me go back and touch a bit on the novel you've just read: *Wurm*. (At least I'm assuming you've read it. If not, get to it. This will make a lot more sense once you do.)

Wurm introduced Matt Costello to lots of people. That neato cover helped, I'm sure. But if you'd been keeping an eye on the reviews in our field, the name Matthew J. Costello was not new. His previous novels *Beneath Still Waters* and *Midsummer* received excellent reviews and word was out that here was a writer to watch.

Then came *Wurm* and that cover.

Great cover or not, if he'd spelled the title with an "O" I probably wouldn't have given it a second look. But *Wurm*...

Put an umlaut over that "U" and it could be a new headbanger group. (*Vuuuuuurm*) What did *Wurm* mean? Something more than a mere worm, surely. I was intrigued enough to part with a few bucks and risk precious reading time on a new (at least to me) talent.

I was well rewarded, as were you.

Wurm introduced me to the Matt Costello style (we can't just say "Costello style" because there's a Sean out there who's also very good), rife with staccato phrases, sentence fragments, one-word paragraphs, and ellipses which, in the wrong hands, can be more artifice than art, can cross the line into the land of the precious, the studied, the downright hokey. In Matt's hands it all works. The images splash cinematically against the brain's screen and the narrative pace never flags.

My lingering impression of *Wurm* is one of overwhelming grayness, of wanly lit days with the sunlight diffused through overcast skies stretched like muslin from horizon to horizon, and a feeling of impending doom, that everything was falling apart around me, and that death could be around any corner, might even walk through the door in the guise of your best friend...or your mother.

But *Wurm* is no mere *boo!* book. It's more than merely frightening; it reaches disturbing and then goes beyond.

Remember the walk on the ocean floor – the *empty* ocean? There's a deep-down creepiness there that arises not from author manipulation or creaky effects, but from the very concept at the heart of the scene.

Matt took chances. He went out onto the streets of Manhattan and turned them into a surreal nightmare. Who can forget those apocalyptic scenes crowded with human lemmings, and that zombie conga line, linked by a giant worm burrowing from person...to person...to person?

And then a means is discovered to counteract the worm, but not before it has wrought untold havoc on the world's oceans and on human civilization. The worm is beaten back, but it isn't beaten.

The novel was over, but the story wasn't. At least not as far as I was concerned.

I dropped Matt a line to tell him what a great job he'd done on *Wurm* and asked when I could expect to read the rest of the story.

He didn't know what I meant. What rest of it? *Wurm* is it.

But there are too many loose ends. The worms are still out there. And what about those things with the Tyrannosaurus feet that stepped out of the bodies in the TV studio?

Matt was unswayed. He had other writing projects, numerous irons in other fires. So every time I saw him thereafter I bugged him about it. Apparently I wasn't alone. Other readers wanted the rest of the story too.

So here it is: "Garden."

An antiphrastic title, to be sure. The apocalypse has come and gone and we're still here. Some of us, at least. Nobody won. The heated battles are five years gone but the cold war drags on. The world is sort of one big Mexico where no one can even *touch* the water, much less drink it.

Some old friends are back: Dr. Michael Cross, Father Farrand, and Martin the marine biologist who saved the planet. Remember little Jo Cross? She's now into puberty.

And the worms. The worms are back.

But then, the worms never really went away.

***

The intro to Cages, *a 1995 collection by my late telephone buddy, Ed Gorman.*

Twenty-One Excellent Reasons to Hate Ed Gorman

...if you're a writer.

Actually there are many more equally valid reasons to hate Ed Gorman, but the stories contained herein are ample cause for any self-respecting writer to loathe the man.

There. I've said it. And I'm glad. I think it's about time to hang out the dirty laundry: Any writer worthy of the designation hates every other writer who turns out a good story. We especially hate writers who can turn out good stories on a regular basis. And we *loathe* that rare writer with the audacity to produce outstanding stories on a regular basis in multiple genres.

Ipso facto, none of us can bear Ed Gorman.

If envy is the bread, then rancor is the butter of every writer who contemplates the works of his peers. And he hates the peer who spurns that leveling designation and spurts ahead at his own speed, upon his own course and, dammit, does well.

Oh, we compliment each other endlessly, and with gracious smiles present one other with awards, but in actuality we can't stand it when someone else gets a big advance, or hits the bestseller list, or knocks out a killer story. Ed hasn't joined the seven-figure advance club or hit the bestseller list (yet), but frankly, of all the things that make us crazy, those are the easiest to dismiss. ["I don't write that (*sniff*) commercial crap."] He *has*, however, hit the quality bullseye too damn many times for his own good. And that cuts to the quick.

To paraphrase Montresor: "The thousand injuries of Gorman I had borne as best I could...It must be understood, that neither by word nor deed had I given him cause to doubt my good-will. I continued, as was my wont, to smile in his face, and he did not perceive that my smile *now* was at the thought of his immolation."

Thus was I asked to write this introduction.

And now I'm free to talk about all of us who hate Ed Gorman.

Perhaps hate is too strong a word...abhorrence, loathing, and detestation are in the running, but for now, hate will do quite nicely.

You see, it's not fair that one man should be able to move from one style of writing to another, from one genre to another, with so much ease and fluidity. Some writers spend a lifetime mastering the tropes of a single genre. But not exhibitionist Gorman. He's up there in the highest reaches of the tent, swinging effortlessly from trapeze to trapeze -- and without a net.

Take "Moonchasers," for instance. Here's a mini-*Bildungsroman* that ranks with King's "The Body," McCammon's *Boy's Life*, and Bradbury's *Dandelion Wine*. What a sense of place. I mean, you can smell the creosote from those railroad ties.

Or "Deathman." Ed has been writing fine, fine westerns for years; not traditional Zane Grey types or ultraviolent shoot-em-ups, but his own unique brand that can perhaps be best described as sagebrush noir. I've read many of his western novels, and "Deathman" is a prime example of and excellent introduction to the Gorman western.

"The Brasher Girl" is straight-ahead weird fiction with no apologies – the kind of fiction he did so well as Daniel Ransom.

Then there's the post-bioholocaust science fiction of "Survivors" and the title story "Cages." In the former the reader has to watch the characters struggle through a physical and emotional nightmare. In the latter the story is the nightmare and the reader becomes part of it.

"One of Those Days, One of Those Nights" drops you off in the middle of a completely unexpected neighborhood. This is black comedy of the highest order, and I defy anyone to predict which way it's going to turn. Can't you see Quentin Tarrantino adapting this as is to the screen?

Then there's "The Beast in the Woods," which will tear your heart out. And the eerie "The Face."

But before I run out of space I must mention "The End of It All." This has got to be one of the most perfect noir stories of all time. I swear it would make James M. Caine join the Gorman haters. And don't you wish Bogey were still alive and Bacall hadn't devolved into such an old fool and both were still in their prime? Warner Bros. would buy the rights and film noir would live again.

So what have we got so far? Mystery, science fiction, horror, western, noir, coming of age, and black comedy. And that's less than half the book!

For the love of God, Gorman!

Any wonder why we get upset?

CAGES: Twenty-one reasons for writers to hate Ed Gorman.

Twenty-one reasons for readers to love him.

***

This was for The Pain Doctors of Suture Self General, *a totally crazy illustrated work by Alan Clark and written by him and some of his equally crazy friends in 1995.*

Primum Non Nocere

This all starts back in the summer of '94 when I bumped into medical thriller writer Steven Spruill in the hall at NECON. As he helped me off the floor (bumping into this man is like running into a steel door) he asked me if I'd been to the art show yet. When I said I hadn't, he told me to get right over there and see Alan Clark's new work – the most disturbing stuff he's ever done.

On my way directly to the art show (I always obey a six-foot-four block of granite with feet) I wondered about what Steve had said. *The most disturbing stuff he's ever done.* And he was talking about Alan Clark. I'd been admiring Alan's work over the years and it was *all* pretty damn disturbing. Especially those bucolic landscapes with the twisted pieces of wood that look like people or almost-people hung out to dry? Not exactly Maxfield Parrish. So I wasn't sure I was ready for the most disturbing stuff this loon's ever done.

And he *is* a loon. I think it's time we stop beating around the bush and tell it like it is: Alan Clark is more than a few French fries short of a Happy Meal. Yeah, I know he looks so innocent, that cherubic fellow with the clean-cut hair, easy smile, clear complexion, and bright eyes. No pony tail, dreadlocks, chin hairs, nostril rings, leather pants, fingerless gloves – none of the *artiste*-manqué affectations. Alan Clark tries to pass himself off as some plain old preppie dude with this slow, easy-going Southern drawl.

Don't be fooled for a minute. The staid, safe,

sane-looking guys are the most dangerous. The truly twisted ones, the *true* freaks, don't dress weird. They don't wear their aberrations on their sleeves. The guys and gals in the costumes are just actors. The real weirdos want to *hide* their psychopathy.

But the lunacy leaks out, man. No matter how they try to hide it, the madness creeps into their work. You've got to realize when you look at Alan Clark's paintings you're looking at the inside of his head.

How's *that* for a scary thought?

So I dutifully traipsed into the NECON art show and stopped dead. I was looking at "Blasted Femurs..." and "The Pain Doctors..." – the first of the paintings that form the backbone of this book. I was struck dumb. They were, quite simply, overwhelming.

Thankfully they're here in this book. I don't know what I'd do if I had to describe them.

Throughout that NECon I found myself returning again and again to the art room, standing before these paintings and staring at them. And each time I found some new marvel.

"Blasted Femurs..." was the most surreal of the pair, and that's saying something. It seems to be set in a surgical amphitheater, but the shadowy audience looks like it might have migrated from the cantina in *Star Wars*. It's the surgeons who grab your attention, however. None of them seems to be standing on the floor – and who can blame them, puddled as it is with blood and urine and body parts that never came from any human I ever met. One surgeon's body seems to dissolve into a double helix. And the patient...

I don't like to think about the patient.

Then there was the title piece: "The Pain Doctors..." Took me a couple of trips before I noticed the stars in the Grim Reaper's cloak – you're looking at eternity there – because I was too preoccupied with that swirl of greasy reddish smoke rising from the operating table. Where the hell is *that* coming from? One member of the gallery is a rat and others – along with a member of the surgical team – have bags over their heads. The anesthesiologist is strangling the guy he's breathing for and stealing his IV drip while one of the surgeons is holding the hand of the patient who's very obviously *light* on his anesthesia.

Phantasmagorical is the word – one of the words – for this scene.

And for this book.

This may not be how the practice of medicine and surgery *is* (at least not on any of the hospital staffs I've known), but I'm sure this is how it sometimes *seems*. To Alan Clark, anyway. And the members of the Bovine Smoke Society have augmented the visual experience with a story that is as phantasmagorical as the art.

The story takes all the genuine fears of being hospitalized – the loss of autonomy, the knowledge that people you barely know or have never met are making decisions about what you wear, what you eat, how far you can walk, whether you get to use a toilet or a bedpan. They're sticking needles in your arms and pumping god-knows-what into your veins. And they're shoving tubes into every orifice you've got. And then they take you to another room where they rob you of your consciousness and slit you open and rummage around in your innards and return you to your room with less than you left with.

This is not fiction – this is what *really* happens.

But that's not bad enough for the Bovine Society. They take all those real fears and push them to the limit in scenes that are alternately hilarious and disgusting.

How do I describe what you're about to experience? The closest I can come is that it's sort of like Hunter S. Thompson mugging Robin Cook. In 3-D. On the set of *Brazil*.

And on that set you'll meet a varied cast of misfits, among them the hapless Larry Lockjaw, the steadily diminishing Martha Ewing, the gravity-defying

Doctor Darling, the intrepid Alma Gloughton, the endlessly empathetic Dr. Myopiate, and of course, the man-u-tan.

Move over, *ER*. Make way, *Chicago Hope*. Here comes the staff of Suture Self General.

God help us all.

***

Written for the 25th anniversary edition. I'd done an earlier piece in 1988 for Horror: The 100 Best Books *which I incorporated into this.*

The Exorcist

From ghosties and goblins,
And long leggedy beasties,
And things that go bump in the night,
Good Lord, preserve us.
Old Welsh Litany

A bump in the night.

This is how it begins.

And not much of a bump at that. Little noises in the attic. Mice maybe? Or rats? No...something else has announced its arrival in the house where eleven-year-old Regan MacNeil lies sleeping, but not in a way that even hints at the enormity of what will follow.

Much like Harper & Row's initial take on William Peter Blatty's novel of demonic possession when they published it in 1971. They knew *The Exorcist* was a potential bestseller, and were probably hoping for *Rosemary's Baby*-league sales. No one was prepared for the runaway success of the hardcover, or for the blockbuster business the film would do, and I doubt that even the most optimistic executive in his wildest martini moments ever dreamed that they'd have to print twelve million copies of the paperback.

The Exorcist changed the face of publishing – suddenly houses that previously turned up their noses at anything that smacked of horror were actively seeking "the next *Exorcist*." William Peter Blatty wasn't ready to give it to them, so they looked elsewhere.

We all know what happened.

And Hollywood. Despite its graphic scenes, the Oscar-winning William Friedkin adaptation became one of the highest-grossing films of all time. Suddenly the majors and every independent that could rent a camera were cranking out horror films by the dozen.

We all know what happened.

So now it's a quarter century since *The Exorcist* was published. Hard to believe. Seems it was only a few years ago that I was sitting up into the wee hours reading it. I was in medical school at the time and hadn't been able to swing the price of the hardcover. But as soon as the paperback hit the stands, I was on it like the *Alien* face-hugger on John Hurt.

I was expecting a typical horror novel, another *Rosemary's Baby*, if I was lucky. I was not at all prepared for this novel about a tormented Jesuit priest in Georgetown confronting a pre-teenage girl who may – or may not – be possessed by a demon.

It blind-sided me.

I was raised a Catholic. I'd gone to a Jesuit high school and had graduated from Georgetown just a few years before. (I *knew* those fatal steps – damn near fell down them a couple of times myself after touring the M Street bars.) I'd already gone through the obligatory crisis of faith and come out the other side a devout agnostic. (But they say there are no ex-Catholics, only *recovering* Catholics.) Plus I was an avid horror fiction fan who'd already read everything in print and was hungry for something new.

I was a sitting duck for *The Exorcist*. And it got me.

With both barrels.

I remember devouring the book in great gulps, unable to put it down, but the first time I read the end of Chapter 3 in Part II is etched on my brain. It was late. Mary and our two infant daughters had gone to bed, so I was the only one awake in our tiny, chilly apartment, all dark except for the reading light over the living room sofa. I was about a third of the way through the book. Up to that point Regan had been exhibiting some odd behavior, but nothing that couldn't easily be explained away as pre-adolescent acting out. Oh, sure, someone had desecrated the local church, leaving notes in fluent Latin; a psychic at her mother's dinner party seemed disturbed by Regan, and then there was the vibrating bed, a proto-Magic Fingers, bouncing her up and down.

All strange, even creepy, but not horrifying. I confess I was a bit restless. I'd been expecting more.

But then Chris MacNeil, Regan's mother, gets word that Burke Denning, her director, has been found dead at the bottom of those steep, stony steps just under Regan's bedroom window. As the phone slips from her fingers, she sees Regan enter the living room on her belly, hissing, her tongue flicking in and out like a snake.

I just about lost it. I can't remember reading a scene before or since that has so disturbed me. I guess it was a result of being forced to spend all those hours in church, hunched on a pew, staring – for lack of anything else – at the statues in the sanctuary area. One of them always seemed to be the Virgin Mary, crushing a snake under her foot.

No question who the snake was.

And no longer any question as to the cause of the changes in Regan's personality. William Peter Blatty, who'd spent, I'm sure, as many hours as I in similar pews, was telling me that the Serpent had entered the garden and had usurped the body of an innocent child.

That did it. Mr. Agnostic, who believes in demons as much as he believes in angels – that is, not at all – found the apartment too dark and chilly to bear alone. He slammed the book closed, turned off the light, and ran – literally *ran* – down the hall to his bed where he snuggled shivering against his wife.

But I came back to the novel as soon as I awoke, and tore through it. The narrative momentum, the steadily mounting horror as the forces of good and evil gather to do battle in a child's bedroom gripped me in a clammy fist that did not let go until the final page. The power of it left me dazed and awed. I'd read all the masters of horror – the Arkham House and *Weird Tales* crews, the early Bradbury, Matheson – and some of them had shocked me, but as a rule I'd been able to finish the story and return to my quotidian existence unscathed. But this novel *disturbed* me. *The Exorcist* followed me around for days, weeks.

Certainly my personal history had a part in such an intense reaction. But I'm sure the *zeitgeist* contributed as well.

The Exorcist was a fitting cap to the Sixties. Many of us still play the music and look back fondly on edited memories of the sunnier of those days, but it was not a kind decade. Some of us lost men we looked up to as leaders, some lost faith in government, faith in the political process, faith in God. Some of us lost our minds. The whole damn nation lost its innocence.

And so then, in 1971, comes *The Exorcist*, with a Jesuit psychiatrist as its conscience. Fr. Damien Karras is embroiled in a crisis of faith. He has lost much of his faith in man, and now feels his faith in God slipping steadily from his grasp.

> ...in the world there was evil. And much of the evil resulted from doubt; from an honest confusion among men of good will. Would a reasonable God refuse to end it? Not reveal himself? Not speak?
> *"Lord, give us a sign..."*

The raising of Lazarus was dim in the distant
past. No one now living had heard his laughter.
Why not a sign?
...Ah, my God, let me see You! Let me know!
The yearning consumed him.

Even as he says Mass, he can't quite believe...

Against all reason, against all knowledge, he
prayed there was Someone to hear his prayer.
He did not think so.

Fr. Karras's spiritual torment struck a responsive chord
in a nation reeling from assassinations, a no-win war, urban
riots, and a generation in revolt.

But that was then...the early Seventies. This is the
Nineties. How does *The Exorcist* hold up in these days
of piercing, body-modification, and goth-industrial music,
of healing crystals, channeling, and soft-focus, warm-fuzzy
New Age spiritualism?

I wondered. I don't reread novels. So many good
books out there, so little time, why return to covered
ground? I had glanced through *The Exorcist* for an essay
I wrote in the Eighties, but I approached a full rereading
with dread. A quarter of a century had passed. I was
a different person from that medical student in 1972. I'd
written sixteen novels of my own since then, fully half of
them horror novels, and many of those influenced by my
cherished memories of Blatty's masterpiece. But memory is
so unreliable. What if I reread *The Exorcist* and hated it?

So...does *The Exorcist* hold up after a quarter of a
century?

Yes. Unequivocally. As long as man is inhuman to
his fellow man, as long as God remains hidden, as long as
intelligent men of faith question their faith, this timeless
novel will have a place on the bookshelves of the world.

In fact, it reads better the second time. I realize now

that I rushed that first reading. This is when story can do a disservice to style. I was so locked into the *What-happens-next?* mode that I missed many of the fine points. But now that I knew where the story was going, how it would end, I could relax and catch some of the scenery.

The Exorcist is a masterful novel, beautifully structured. Blatty is in complete control, setting up a series of crescendos – tiny, seemingly insignificant ones at first, and then letting them build, and build...

The reader is way ahead of the characters, of course. We *know* this child is possessed, so why not get on with it, get to the good stuff? But the really good stuff is in the build-up. Watching Chris MacNeil slowly backed into the realization that something is terribly wrong with her daughter; watching the doctors she consults flounder about as they try to piece together a rational medical explanation for the symptoms this child is exhibiting, finally coming up with a lame diagnosis of hysteria. They tell Chris that Regan *acts* possessed because she *believes* she is possessed; perhaps an exorcism will reverse the autosuggestion, making her *believe* she is cured. Chris rejects the idea.

And now we are slammed between the eyes with one of the novel's most unforgettable moments: Regan knocks her mother across the bedroom; through a haze of retreating consciousness, Chris sees Regan's head turn 180 degrees on her body and talk to her in the voice of Burke, the director who died of a broken neck from a fall from Regan's window.

It's as if the demon is saying, "*NOW will you call the damn priest?*"

Fr. Damien Karras gets the call. His job is to evaluate the situation and decide whether an exorcism is truly called for. And now it's doubting Damien's turn to wrestle with the manifestations in Regan's room. But Blatty has pulled a reverse. Damien's crisis of faith propels him to approach the problem of Regan from a new angle. The existence of a supernatural entity, whether good or evil, is evidence of transcendence, of an existence beyond the flesh. And if transcendent evil exists, why not transcendent Good... God? All the characters to this point have become mental contortionists in their efforts to avoid the idea of demonic possession. Not Damien...he *wants* to find the hand of the devil here.

And now Blatty really shines. Damien's conversations with the demon are simply wonderful. The casual malevolence of the entity is chilling. The demon speaks backward, teases him with complicated theological puns, torments him with his guilt about his mother's lonely death, time and again bringing him to the lip of the rational precipice where there can be no explanation other than the supernatural, then pulling back. A spiritual coitus interruptus, you might say. Blatty phrases it far more elegantly: "...he slowly watched blood turning back into wine."

The demon toys with them all, mixing lies and truth. Even Chris can't be *sure* Regan's head rotated on her body and spoke in that voice; she was losing consciousness at the time and could have imagined it. The demon's weapons are doubt, guilt, uncertainty, confusion. Potent weapons; they loose our spiritual moorings and set us adrift.

But why? Why is the demon here? As Fr. Merrin puts it: "...I think the demon's target is not the possessed; it is us... the observers..."

How true. For we come to learn that the demon's true target is not poor little Regan, not Chris, not even Karras. It's Merrin. They've met before, this priest and this evil entity, and last time Merrin won. So all this horror has been orchestrated to set up round two with Merrin. With the old priest's arrival – *"Merriiiiinnnnnnnnnn!"* – the stage is set for the final confrontation.

Merrin's presence has a profound effect on Karras. In the crucible of the exorcism rite, the old priest must battle not only the demon, but his own ailing heart. He knows he's choosing this poor child's life over his own, but that is why he's here, that is what he's about. His unwavering courage restores Damien's faith in man.

But what of his faith in God?

With Fr. Merrin's death, Karras flies into a rage, challenging the demon.

> "You're very good with children!...Little girls!... Come on, loser! Try *me!* Leave the girl and take me!"

We don't know what happens next. We shift downstairs to Chris's point of view as she hears shouts from the bedroom – two different male voices arguing – and then shattering glass.

And here is where the movie betrays the novel. I've spoken to many who've seen the film but not read the book, and the vast majority of them came away with the impression that "the demon made Father Karras commit suicide."

No. As Karras lies dying on those deadly steps below the bedroom window, Blatty gives us a look into his eyes which seem to "glow with elation." And later the priest who gave him last rites on the spot remembers "a mysterious look of joy in Karras's eyes...a deep and fiercely shining glint of triumph."

Perhaps his taunting of the demon to "take me" wasn't entirely altruistic. If he could *know*, if he could experience firsthand the hideous purity of the supernatural evil infecting Regan, then surely he could once again believe in the Ultimate Good. Before he died on those steps, Damien Karras had that experience – thus the elation, the joy in his eyes. And in the process, he removed the demon from the child, taking it with him through the window – thus the triumph.

Here's where you appreciate that the final nuance is in the title. You go through the novel thinking of Merrin as the title character, but it's all about Karras, who turns out to be the true exorcist.

Damien Karras resolved his crisis of faith by making faith superfluous. He found his answer. He *knew*.

The rest of us go on searching.

***

I remember writing this around the same time as "Ad Statum Perspicuum" (1990). It may have been intended as the intro for my Author's Choice Monthly *and I changed my mind. In 1998 I rewrote it for use as the introduction to* The Barrens & Others *but my editor nixed it as lacking sufficient gravitas for an intro. He was probably right. So here it is.*

The Oldest Profession

His name was Thurk. You've never heard of him. He lived in prehistoric times. I like to think of him as a blood relative; at the very least he's a spiritual progenitor. Bear with me while I relate a few key events in this extraordinary man's life.

Thurk was a member of a tribe of hunter-gatherers called the Wurks. Among his tribe Thurk had a reputation as a bit of a loafer. From the other tribe members' viewpoint, that assessment probably was not unjustified. But they didn't understand Thurk. They didn't realize that he was the first practitioner of the oldest profession.

No, not that one.

Take one typical day: Thurk should be hunting; instead he's sitting on a sunny hillside, enjoying the cool breeze and daydreaming. He isn't much into physical exertion or killing things, you see. So he starts picking a few berries but gets interested in the cloud shapes floating by instead. He starts hunting animal-shaped clouds instead of the animals themselves, picking out faces in the sky instead of berries from a bush.

He hears shouts and watches the other guys in the tribe chasing game on the plain below. He imagines himself a mighty hunter, stopping a charging sabre-tooth tiger with only his wits and a spear; he pictures all the startling moves he'd make, the wily strategies that would lead him to victory. And he fantasizes about what an important and respected member of the tribe that would make him.

Thurk daydreams on until he suddenly realizes it's getting dark. The whole day is gone and he hasn't caught a thing – *again*. (Trust me, this isn't the first time.)

So Thurk hurries back to the cave where he finds the whole tribe sitting around the fire, chowing down on bronto steaks and mastodon stew or whatever they ate in those days. And he's *starving*. He stands there with his empty eating bowl and asks if anybody's got some extra.

The cave fills with derisive laughter. Thurk's done it again – gone out in the morning and come back at night empty-handed. Serves him right for doing nothing all day. What a loser.

"But I wasn't doing nothing," Thurk says. "I was telling myself a story about a mighty hunter and his greatest hunt."

"Yeah? Who's the hunter?"

"Why..."

Now, in Thurk's fantasy, the mighty hunter was Thurk. But Thurk is no dummy. He knows that if he says he was the mighty hunter they'll laugh him right out of the cave. So he glances around and sees Gurk, the best hunter in the tribe, tearing into a somethingsaurus haunch.

"It was Gurk."

Suddenly all ears around the fire prick up, especially Gurk's. To prove he wasn't doing nothing, Thurk begins to tell his story of the ferocious sabre-tooth tiger that was killing off members of the tribe, one by one, and how the mighty Gurk stalked the fearsome beast to its lair and–

Suddenly Thurk's stomach rumbles and he looks around and sees all these grease-smeared faces staring at him. He looks down at his empty eating bowl and says, "Never mind."

But as he turns to go he hears the tribefolk saying, "But what happened? What happened next?"

Then he hears Gurk say, "Whoa, Thurk. Where y'goin'?"

Thurk says, "I'm hungry, man. I've got to go find something to eat."

And Gurk says, "Sit yourself down over here and help yourself to my saurburgers. And while you're munching you can finish that story. Hey, you! Outta the way and let my buddy Thurk through."

So as Thurk chows down on a load of Gurk's food, it occurs to him that something's happening here. He's not sure yet what's going on, but he likes it. He has their attention. They're waiting for him to continue. They're *hooked*. He finishes the story of Gurk killing the sabre-tooth with only his spear, his wits (this *was* fiction, after all) and raw courage. When Thurk is done, Gurk slaps him on the back and shoves another saurburger at him, and then all the tribefolk drop little bits of food into his eating bowl.

(Thurk doesn't realize it, but he's just received history's first literary royalties.)

As Thurk is finishing up, full-bellied for the first time in his life, another of the mighty hunters, Murk, sidles over and hands him a roasted rabbit. He says, "Yo, Thurk. Take dis. An' tomorrow night, if you should happen to tell a good story about me, you'll get another just like it. Know what I'm sayin'?"

Thurk knows indeed what Murk is saying.

(What he doesn't know is that he's just received the first royalty advance.)

Being no dummy, Thurk realizes he's stumbled onto an amazing discovery: people are willing to feed him for doing the same thing he's been doing for nothing all those times when he should have been hunting. So Thurk becomes the first practitioner of the oldest profession – storytelling. Soon he's traveling from tribe to tribe, campfire to campfire, telling and retelling his tales.

I've tried to continue Thurk's tradition. Don't ask me how I fell into his profession; I haven't a clue. I do know that I began writing down my stories at age seven, but I don't know why I do it, and I don't understand how I do it. I simply know that I *must* do it.

So I thank you for inviting me to your campfire. Ready? Listen up...

***

Knowing I was a big fan of his Anno Dracula, *Kim Newman asked me to intro this 1999 novella. I was delighted to accommodate.*

Andy Warhol's *Dracula*

I confess: *Anno Dracula* blindsided me. Way back in 1992 when Simon & Schuster (UK) sent me an advance copy for comment, I'd expected something along the lines of *Night Mayor* and *Jago*, both of which I'd enjoyed. Neither of those, however, had prepared me for the quantum leap in style and substance of *Anno Dracula*.

I took the bait of the first chapter wherein Dr. Seward murders a vampire streetwalker in a style I recognized immediately. When Inspector Lestrade appeared in the following chapter, the hook was set and I was reeled through the rest of the book at breakneck pace, running across characters from Stoker, Doyle, Wells, Rohmer, Stevenson (I still recall that wonderful scene with Drs. Jekyll and Moreau arguing about human nature), and others. The Victorian London of *Anno Dracula* was a seamless blend of the real and the fictive, in which notable historical figures mingled and interacted with famous characters who had lived only in print.

Less celebrated and some downright obscure characters abounded as well. Lord Ruthven, Graf Orlok... the roster of cameos and references lengthened until I realized that Kim Newman had penned, in a very real sense, a literary novel. But his referential base was not the canon of English literature taught in schools, it was *our* canon, *our* literature, the colportage we devoured on buses and subways and under the covers with a flashlight at night. The more deeply immersed you are in our thing, the more old friends you will find in *Anno Dracula*.

Rarely have I felt so at home in a novel. (*The Exorcist* is the only other challenger, but for entirely different reasons.)

But more wondrous from a writing standpoint was the way he fleshed out the characters – history's, other writers', and his own – making them live and breathe on the page, sometimes more so than in their source fiction. Kim Newman's skill with characters turned what in lesser hands might have been a merely clever parlor game into a full-blooded novel.

I wrote back to Simon & Schuster and said, "Isn't it about time to quit referring to Kim Newman as a 'promising horror writer'? He's here folks. He's arrived. *Anno Dracula* is incontrovertible proof."

I have also said, in private conversation and on convention panels, that *Anno Dracula* should be the litmus text for anyone applying for an editorial position in the fantasy and horror fields. A prospective editor who doesn't get it, who can't identify most of these characters (probably only Kim knows them all) should be considered culturally deprived (remember, this is *our* culture) and banished to the romance department.

The timeline of this alternate universe was extended with *The Bloody Red Baron*, "Coppola's Dracula," and *Judgment of Tears*. And now we have "Andy Warhol's *Dracula*."

The great Lord Dracula is finally, really, truly dead, but his legacy lives on. Europe is loaded with vampires, yet the New World's blood remains largely untainted. Time for one of Dracula's get to expand the frontiers and stake his claim to new territory.

The choice of late '70s Manhattan is inspired. Those were the days when it was Disco/Punk City, where life began to flow only after sundown, and didn't ebb until first light. And who better to anchor the tale than the lord of the glitterati, with his cadaverous grin, his dead white skin and wasted frame... Count Warhola himself.

Moving like a wraith in an ever narrowing gyre around the very solid Andy Warhol is Ion Popescu, a vampire transplant from Romania, reborn here as Johnny Pop. Being of and from the Old World, Johnny is a perfect lens through which to view American soi-disant culture. His haughty disdain and barbed comments about New Yorkers in general, and the art and disco scenes in particular, are dead on.

The underlying theme of tainted blood, and Johnny poisoning his own milieu – literally peeing where he lives – brings to mind Gaetan Dugas, the Canadian flight attendant widely considered the Patient Zero of the AIDS epidemic... another international man who brought an insidious gate crasher from an old continent to the new one, and effectively pulled the plug on the decade-long party of the '70s.

But you need not delve that deep (this is about 70s Manhattan, after all, where superficiality was a badge of distinction), or delve at all – revelations leap at you from every page. You nod in recognition, you smile in wonder (in envy, if you're a writer) at the marvels of interconnectedness and correspondence between Johnny Pop's '70s and the decade the rest of us survived.

I will keep you no longer. Turn the page. See for yourself.

***

I don't know what possessed the editors of Bison Press at the University of Indiana to approach me in 2001 to write this intro, but they did. As a kid I'd plowed through about 90% of ERB's fiction but had never written anything about him. The Venus series was far from my fave but I gave it a shot. In researching it I learned a lot about the man himself – perhaps more than I cared to.

The Pirates of Venus

The serial version of *Pirates of Venus* began its six-issue run in *Argosy Weekly* in 1932, twenty years after the debut of the author's first novel, *Under the Moons of Mars*. At the time, Edgar Rice Burroughs appeared to have the world by the tale.

Consider: MGM's *Tarzan the Ape Man*, the first Tarzan "talkie," starring Maureen O'Sullivan and an Olympic swimmer named Johnny Weissmuller, was well on its way to becoming one of the most popular and profitable movies of the year.

His publishing venture, ERB, Inc., had just released its third title (*Tarzan Triumphant*) and, despite dire warnings from supposedly knowledgeable sources that he'd be courting disaster by self-publishing, was turning a profit.

The Tarzan daily comic strip illustrated by Rex Maxon was syndicated in over two-hundred-and-fifty newspapers, and the brilliant Hal Foster, later to create Prince Valiant, had started illustrating the color Sunday page.

The Tarzan radio show had just debuted, sparking via its sponsors a surge of merchandising that encompassed everything from Tarzan statuettes and spears to Tarzan chewing gum.

In addition to his ranch, he had a new beachfront home in Malibu.

The town of Tarzana, named after his ranch, had been incorporated with its own postmark.

But typical of Burroughs's life, every silver lining had its cloud. Never satisfied with the considerable income from his writing, he had spent the preceding decade looking for ways to parlay that money into even larger profits; in one venture he'd converted part of the Tarzana ranch into the El Caballero Country Club which recently had gone into default and foreclosure; Apache Motors, an airplane engine company he'd underwritten, went under, taking his entire investment with it. He'd had a recent run of medical problems, including multiple surgical procedures for bladder obstruction. And to top it all off, his marriage was crumbling.

Despite all this, Edgar Rice Burroughs, at age fifty-seven, was in the middle of one of the more productive periods of his writing life, completing seven novels plus half a dozen murder mystery shorts, a novella, and sundry articles in a two-and-a-half-year period. After finishing a pair of back-to-back Tarzan novels (*The Triumph of Tarzan*, *Tarzan and the City of Gold*) he decided to invent a fresh landscape for a new series of adventures. He'd already conquered Africa, the Earth's core, various lost continents, and Mars, so he turned his eye toward the morning star, Venus.

Otis Adelbert Kline, ERB's most successful imitator, already had swashbuckled Venus by then with *Planet of Peril* and *Prince of Peril*, but that didn't deter Burroughs. Neither did the current scientific evidence about the planet.

We know now from the Magellan, Mariner and Venera missions that the clouds wreathing the second planet consist of droplets of concentrated sulfuric acid; the atmosphere below is carbon dioxide with a fairly uniform temperature in excess of 700^0 K / 1000^0 F; the photos sent back show a bleak, barren surface. But even back in the 1930's most astronomers declared Venus an inhospitable world. Sir James Jeans, one of the most respected cosmologists of the day, postulated that although the atmosphere might contain a little oxygen, there was by no means enough to sustain higher life forms.

Undaunted, Burroughs set his sights on Venus and began spinning his tales.

At first glance, *Pirates of Venus* and its sequels might

appear to be a rehash of the John Carter Mars novels. Not so. They have their own distinct character, in both their tone and their protagonist, Carson Napier. When one looks at what was happening in Burroughs's life at the time, it's plain that Carson Napier, much more so than John Carter, Tarzan, or David Innes, was a conscious reflection of his creator.

True to the Burroughs formula, Carson Napier is a wealthy, capable man of good family (like John Carter, Virginian blood flows in his veins; like Tarzan he can learn a new language in three weeks) but he's also brash, impulsive, and doesn't always fully think things through as carefully as he should. (In a later story Carson says, "I must be the prize incompetent of two worlds.") Look at how he winds up on Venus: by trying to rocket to Mars.

He builds a giant torpedo in Mexico, aims it at Mars (not, you will note, at where Mars will be when he reaches its orbit, but directly at that little red dot as it rises above the horizon) and shoots himself into space. He hasn't accounted for the moon's gravitational pull either, and it's not long before he's headed straight toward a fiery death in the sun. Fortunately the planet Venus gets in his way and he parachutes to safety. (Well, relative safety, since no one is safe for long in a Burroughs tale.)

This creates a motif for the rest of the novel, and the entire Venus series as well: unlike Tarzan or John Carter who always seem to be in control, or when presented with a new set of dangerous circumstances soon have the situation well in hand, Carson seems to be playing by ear, and at times he appears to be tone deaf. Most of Burroughs's heroes *make* things happen, but things tend to happen *to* Carson Napier.

The novel's wry tone is set in the opening chapter which offers a glimpse not only into the offices of ERB, Inc., but into the life of the author himself. As narrator of the chapter, Burroughs never mentions himself by name, but he does name and converse with his real-life amanuensis, Ralph Rothmund. He mentions being distracted by "the annoying details of a real estate transaction that was going wrong." And when Burroughs has what he thinks is a hallucination, Rothmund repeats a warning about the after-effects of the narcotics taken during the course of "your last operation." No question about it: Burroughs is venting his workaday concerns in front of his readership. (But not necessarily his true character: He tells Napier, "I detest business and everything connected with it." Odd statement from a writer known to challenge publishers' word counts and haggle over a quarter cent in word rates; a man in the process of building an empire out of his literary properties.)

The purpose of the opener, as in so many of Burroughs's novels, is to assure the reader that what he is about to read is true, and to establish a rationale for how the author learned of the extraordinary exploits related in the pages that follow (a hoary Victorian conceit that Burroughs used time and again). In it Carson Napier, born of a British father and American mother in India where he learned certain mystic arts, demonstrates his ability to speak to Burroughs's mind and project telepathic images (which makes one wonder if ERB had been tuning into that hot new radio drama, *The Shadow*). Carson wants someone "of sufficient intelligence and culture" with "a reputation for integrity" to relate the details of his trip to Mars. As mentioned above, he winds up on Venus instead, but nevertheless contacts the author telepathically across the tens of millions of miles to recount his adventures. Thus Napier tells Burroughs, Burroughs repeats the story into his Dictaphone (he was dictating most of his fiction at this time), after which the account is transcribed by Rothmund who sends it on to the publisher.

We follow Carson as he bails out of his torpedo and plummets through the planet's double layer of clouds until his parachute snags on a branch of one of the giant trees of Amtor, as the natives call the planet. The trunks of these can reach a thousand feet in diameter as they soar miles into the clouds. They're home to a race of civilized humans known as the Vepajan who've carved their homes into the boles of the trees. After rescuing Carson from a one-eyed, lobster-clawed predator, the Vepajans take him in and teach him their language.

During his schooling Carson learns that, because of their planet's perpetual cloud cover, the natives have no concept of astronomy. They believe Amtor to be a huge disk afloat on a sea of molten metal and rock. Out near the rim of the disk is Strabol, the hot country (what we'd call the equator); Karbol (one of the poles) is the circular cold country at the center of the disk, and Trabol, the temperate country where most of the population lives, lies between the two extremes. Since no one has crossed the hot country and survived, the Vepajans have no evidence to contradict their floating disk theory, and cannot conceive of a spherical world. In one of the novel's more humorous exchanges, Burroughs takes an amiable swipe at Einstein as Carson's Vepajan teacher explains away obvious inherent discrepancies in the maps of Amtor by invoking the great scientist Klufar's "theory of relativity of distance."

Burroughs used the Amtor setting to explore a theme that must have been especially attractive at this point in his life: he was looking his sixtieth birthday in the eye; he'd been hospitalized recently for an obstructed bladder; and a younger woman, Florence Dearholt, soon to be the second Mrs. Burroughs, had caught his eye. Perhaps as a result of all this he made the Vepajans virtually immortal. Not because of a genetic trait or an effect of the planet itself, but due to a serum they had perfected a thousand years before. It's not merely an anti-aging preparation, but protects from disease as well. They offer Carson a dose and he accepts. Burroughs no doubt longed for the same opportunity.

But Carson soon discovers that Amtor is not quite the Garden of Eden it appears. He learns that the island nation of Vepaja is at war with the Thorists. Long ago, it seems, the Vepajan society occupied a huge territory, but they were a stratified monarchic society, and a group of dissidents calling themselves Thorists engineered a revolt by promising the lower classes "no masters, no taxes, no laws." But after a bloody revolution that sent the decimated upper classes into exile, the masses discovered they'd been duped into "exchanging the beneficent rule of an experienced and cultured class for that of greedy incompetents and theorists."

It requires no profound exegesis to read Marxists for Thorists, especially if you're familiar with Burroughs's politics. Conservative doesn't quite do justice to his place on the Left-Right spectrum. Perhaps a couple of sentences from *Pirates of Venus* will lend a better idea. At this point in the story Carson has been fomenting rebellion among his fellow captives on a Thorist prison ship; his rebel group calls itself the Soldiers of Liberty.

> (Kiron) did not say Soldier of Liberty, but "kung, kung, kung," which are the Amtorian initials of the order's title. Kung is the name of the Amtorian character that represents the K sound in our language, and when I first translated the initials I was compelled to smile at the similarity they bore to those of a well-known secret order in the United States of America.

This is not to say that he was a card-carrying fascist, because many of his novels skewer dictatorships of all stripes with equal relish, but his views were unquestionably well right of center.

But even if Burroughs were a more liberal sort, his depiction of the Thorists as villains might simply have reflected what he was reading in his daily papers: Russia in the early 1930s had been wracked by one famine after another, millions in the Ukraine were dying of starvation, and its infrastructure lay in ruins; it was about to embark on its second Five Year Plan which no one expected to be any more successful than the first. Clearly the Bolsheviks had botched it.

So had the Thorists. The egalitarian society they'd promised never came to be; instead their people lived under the iron fist of a military dictatorship, with spies everywhere to ferret out anyone who might be plotting a counterrevolution. In our first look at a group of Thorists, they are described by Carson as "coarser, more brutal" than any Vepajans he has seen. The individuals in question have invaded the tree kingdom to kidnap the beautiful princess living next door to Carson. Why? It seems that during the revolution, the Thorist zealots killed or drove out the best and the brightest of the old order; the long-term effects of this brain drain has caused their society to deteriorate to the point where they must abduct Vepajans not only to update their scientific knowledge, but to upgrade their gene pool as well.

Which opens another door in the Edgar Rice Burroughs psyche: Welcome to the Eugenics Suite.

For years Burroughs had been an outspoken proponent of eugenics, a philosophy advocating the forced sterilization of criminals and "mental defectives." It was around the time he was writing the early Venus novels that he penned an essay called "I See a New Race." It envisions an America of the future where peace and prosperity reign because for generations "criminals, defectives, and incompetents" have been sterilized, thus removing their "tainted" genes from the population. He never found a publisher for it.

In *Pirates of Venus* Burroughs dips his toes in the eugenics pool, but he takes a swan dive into the deep end with the sequel, *Lost on Venus*, which strands Carson and the Princess Duare in Havatoo, a society governed entirely by the principles of eugenics.

By the time Burroughs died in 1950, the Venus series totaled four volumes – *Pirates of Venus, Lost on Venus, Carson of Venus,* and *Escape on Venus* – but they read like one very long novel, each taking up where the other left off. This can be frustrating when, as in the case of *Pirates of Venus*, a book has no conclusion: The last page leaves Carson facing certain capture by the Thorists; he may be happy in the knowledge that the Princess Duare returns his love, but none of the plotlines is resolved. Readers were not kept long in suspense, however. The first installment of *Lost on Venus* – already written by the time *Pirates* saw print – appeared a few months later in the March 4, 1933 issue of the same magazine, *Argosy Weekly. Lost* rejoins Carson Napier only minutes after the close of *Pirates* and, thankfully, provides some closure, with Carson flying the Princess Duare back toward Vepaja in a homemade plane. (The no-conclusion problem was remedied temporarily in 1963 when Dover Books reprinted *Pirates of Venus* and *Lost on Venus* in a single volume, joining the tale of Carson Napier's first few months on Venus into a continuous narrative.)

Burroughs didn't return to Venus until 1938 when *Carson of Venus* was serialized like its predecessors in *Argosy*. He was at work on the fourth Venus book in December, 1941, when World War Two exploded and his role as war correspondent cut down his fiction output. *Escape on Venus* didn't see print until 1946. If you've browsed Burroughs's titles you may have seen a book called *The Wizard of Venus*, but it's not a novel. The title story is a 1941 novelette that went unpublished in ERB's lifetime; in 1970 it was resurrected from a trunk and cobbled together with "Pirate Blood," an unsold eugenics broadside in story form from the 1930s.

Although it started off well, the Venus series deteriorated along the way into a succession of capture-and-escape novelettes (indeed some segments were published as self-contained stories before inclusion in the books) strung together by the slimmest of narrative threads. But *Pirates of Venus* and *Lost on Venus* remain milestones in the Burroughs oeuvre. You hold the inaugural volume. Here begin the adventures of Carson Napier, Burroughs's most flawed hero, and the character closest to his true self. The journey through *Pirates of Venus* is an excursion through the author's head.

So let's not waste any more time...

***

In 1999, the now-departed Mike Baker asked me to pick My Favorite Horror Story *and write an intro to it. Well, no question what that would be: "The Distributor" by Richard Matheson. (I loved it so much I returned to Mr. Gordon in "Recalled.") But I didn't see how I could do the intro justice without spoilers. So I came up with the idea of both a foreword and an afterword.*

The Distributor

(first section – to precede the story)

It's a rare story that won't go away. Most are forgotten as soon as you turn the page; some linger for a while, then join their brethren in the void. But every so often you encounter one with a special, mysterious quality that encodes it into your synapses, making it a part of you. We all have our own set of special stories. Here's one of mine.

But first, a little background. I was thirteen when I decided to write horror fiction. That was in 1959 – a banner year for me. I discovered Lovecraft in Donald A. Wolheim's *The Macabre Reader*, and then went out and bought everything good ol' H.P. had in print. When I exhausted him, I started in on the rest of the old masters: Bloch, Howard, Derleth, Long, Hodgson, Leiber, and whoever else I could find. The reading exacerbated a lifelong writing itch, one I'd started scratching in second grade. Now I began to believe I could write this stuff. Not at age thirteen, but later on. I could do it. I *would* do it. But for now, I'd keep reading.

When I ran through everything overtly horrific in print, I started on the Alfred Hitchcock collections. And so in that same year, in *13 More Stories They Wouldn't Let Me Do On TV*, I came across Ray Bradbury's "The October Game," which left me gasping and convinced me I had to write horror fiction. I *had* to do to other people what Ray Bradbury had just done to me.

Here's the point to all this me-focused stuff: All along I wanted to write horror fiction; all along I was convinced I could do it. No question about it: "Someday I'll do this."

Then, two years, later I picked up a paperback called *Shock* by Richard Matheson. I'd read Matheson's work before, had been deeply touched by "Born of Man and Woman," and suitably impressed by many of his other stories. Here was a guy who delivered. And *Shock* was okay. Lots of interesting stories – sf, social commentary, suspense – but not much horror.

Then I came to the last story. "The Distributor" stopped me dead. All along I'd been telling myself, "I can do this."

Now I was muttering and mumbling, "No way can I do *that*."

I don't know how it is with other writers, but most of the time when I finish a story or novel, I may be pleased, I may even be impressed, but somewhere in the back of my mind I'm thinking, *I can do that*.

Every so often, though, you come across a piece of fiction that blows you away, not just because you've been hanging onto every word, but because when you're done you have to admit, *I couldn't do that*.

That's what makes certain stories special to me; those are the ones I admire most: the ones I lack the talent or insight or command of the language to write myself.

"The Distributor" is one of those. And now it's your turn to read it. What I have to say on the other side of the story will make a lot more sense once you've experienced "The Distributor."

(see afterword at end of story)

(afterword)

Yeah, I know. Pretty damn unsettling. First published in *Playboy* in 1957 and look what's happened to the country since. "Mr. Gordon" (or whatever his real name is) and his fellow distributors have been busy, busy, busy.

Maybe it's a little dated. What used to be scandalous is now daily fodder for today's talk shows (more evidence of Mr. Gordon's handiwork?), but change maybe fifty words, substituting incest and pedophilia – not too many people anxious to wave those flags yet – for a couple of passé taboos, and the story is right up to date.

Why did I say *I can't do that* after reading "The Distributor"? Not because I couldn't sit down and imitate it – I couldn't have *originated* it.

Did you notice the utterly flat affect? "The Distributor" is an epiphany in that sense. All horror fiction I'd read until then pulsed with vibrant emotion – rage, hate, fear, lust for revenge. "The Distributor" has none of that. And that's what makes it so horrifying.

Note Matheson's perfect pitch. The story is a parade of simple declarative sentences (hell, he uses fewer adverbs than Elmore Leonard) with only an occasional off-the-wall adjective to let us know "Mr. Gordon" is well educated. We spend the entire story in Mr. Gordon's point of view but experience no emotion; we witness only the surfaces of events. This is one of the most effective uses of minimalist technique you will ever see.

Mr. Gordon doesn't hate the residents of Sylmar Street.

Nothing personal here. They're just people and this is just another town along his distribution route. It's just a job, folks.

Just a job.

But who does he work for?

That's Matheson's final coup. If he'd revealed that Mr. Gordon worked for the CIA or the KGB, or even some invented secret organization or cult, "The Distributor" would have migrated to short story limbo long ago. But he didn't. Who is behind this? Where is their home office? What is their agenda? *Why are they doing this?*

I wanted to know in 1961.

I still want to know.

***

For R.C. Matheson's Dystopia *collection. He's known for his brevity. I admire that.*

Fat

People hate it on their bodies – if they can't exercise or diet it off, they have it sucked off. They avoid it in their food – things labeled "Low Fat!" or "Less Calories!" (ah, the mainstreaming of lumpen grammar) fairly leap off supermarket shelves.

But when it comes to fiction, people don't seem to mind fat. In fact they seek it out.

"Yeah, I think I'm gonna go home and curl up with a nice fat novel."

Why a *fat* novel instead of a *good* novel? Since when is corpulence a literary virtue? Is it a matter of economics, like buying the giant economy size? Is it tactile, the feel of that thick spine against the palm? (And even if the book itself has modest dimensions, open the cover and too often you're in adipose city.)

Let's face it: Not every *mot* is *bon*.

So much fiction seems like Beef Wellington served by a chef who thinks the outer pastry is the thing, and leaves you cutting through layer after layer of dough in search of the meat.

It's not always the writer's fault. The editor/publisher/ bookseller axis encourages writers to chew more than they bite off, to the point where lean prose seems an endangered species.

Which, after an admittedly chubby preamble, brings us to the work of Richard Christian Matheson, who has managed to sidestep the oleo trend. His income from script work insulates him from market pressures in prose, so he can write any way he wants.

And apparently he wants to write lean. Perhaps that's fallout from the very script work that unfetters him.

Whatever the reason, I find the conciseness bracing. Many of his pieces fall into the vignette category: he takes an idea, a character, a situation, an event and probes it, explores it, and then moves on. He doesn't inflate it to something it was never meant to be. He moves on. Reminds me of the Pythons – when a skit idea had run its course, they didn't try to graft on an ending or a framing device that would have it all seem to make sense in a larger context; they simply said, "And now for something completely different." And moved on.

But despite its economy, RC's work isn't minimalism. The minimalist (continuing the culinary motif) tends to toss a bunch of vegetables and seafood on the table, say, "Bouillabaisse," and expect the reader to do all the cooking. RC is his own sous chef. And he knows the art of reduction.

"Vampire," for instance: Fewer than 200 skillfully chosen words (177 to be exact – I counted them) and yet, it's all there. Or "The Barking Sands" – a dysfunctional family history captured in a couple of thousand words. Or the hilarious "Cancelled"...I *know* that guy. And then there's "Red"...blows me away every time I read it. And I've read it multiple times. Because it's short.

Consider: What can usually be stated in the fewest words? What tends to be revealed in inverse proportion to the verbiage used to depict it?

Truth.

***

The author, Bryan Glass, asked me to read this 2001 graphic novel Ship of Fools *and intro it if I liked it. I did and I did.*

Booking Passage

Atlanta is cool.

Not the city...the psycho-savant poet-sociopath in *Ship of Fools* who makes a fashion statement with her straitjacket. So is Shiro, the green-skinned alien with the two prehensile dreadlocks dangling from the back of his head. In fact, there's not a single dull character aboard. Perhaps because they're all so grossly dysfunctional, including Lloyd the android.

But *SoF* emphasizes the fun in dysfunctional. The storyline bears about as much resemblance to the Catherine Anne Porter novel as the film of *I Know What You Did Last Summer* does to the young adult novel it was based on. It shares far more with Sebastian Brant's fifteenth century satirical poem *Das Narrenschiff* (which translates as *The Ship of Fools* and was illustrated by Dürer himself) – a satire about a shipload of people looking for paradise.

They all die.

Not quite *everybody* dies in the Glass-Oeming version, but not for lack of trying. Acrobatic murder and creative mayhem abound, challenging the combined body counts of

John Woo, Tobe Hooper, and George Romero, who are all obvious influences. So is Robert Anton Wilson (no relation). But the sheer exuberance of the action and attendant character interplay make the carnage not only tolerable but exhilarating.

If I had to describe *Ship of Fools* in just a couple of words, I'd say it's anarchic and autotelic.

Anarchic for obvious reasons: on this ship, school's out, all the rules are on hold, and anything goes, not only within the story, but in the telling as well. Startling shifts of point of view, jumping from typical comic book cinematic into a character's head where he's having an argument with his hand, or she's cozied up to her chainsaw after beheading everyone in the room.

Autotelic because it exists for its own sake, without excuses, without remorse.

Ship of Fools, a juggernaut of mayhem in a buttoned-down universe, looking not for paradise, simply for freedom.

Hop aboard and hang on for dear life.

***

Back in 2002, Kealan-Patrick Burke asked me to contribute to his anthology Taverns of the Dead, *but I couldn't squeeze out time for a story. So he asked me to do the intro.*

Step Up to the Rail, My Friends

I so wanted to be in this anthology, really I did. But when mid-January found me still cranking on a novel that had been due December 1, I knew I'd never make the deadline.

But I can talk about the book. And, of course, about taverns – or bars or pubs or whatever you wish to call it them.

Taverns…empires rise and fall, religions come and go, ideologies and political philosophies wax and wane, but the tavern remains a fixed star in the human social firmament. Even when pursed-lipped, tight-assed, self-righteous ninnies try to eradicate them, taverns keep popping back. Sort of like Gopher Bash. You know, that game where you take a mallet and keep hammering a plastic gopher back into its hole only to have it pop up out of another. How appropriate that Gopher Bash is most often found in bars.

There's an old Scottish proverb: *They talk of my drinking but never my thirst.* And it's because of a thirst for something other than drink that the tavern exists and perseveres. It's not simply the consumption of ethanol in all its various and wondrous permutations that attracts you – let's face it: if inebriation were the sole objective, it would be quicker and far cheaper to buy a bottle and drink at home – but for the embrace of kindred souls (who also happen to like to consume ethanol in all its various and wondrous permutations). Camaraderie… it's a potion far more potent and alluring than distilled spirits.

For that reason, a good neighborhood tavern is a rare thing, a place to be nurtured and cherished. There's the feel of the bar's mahogany under your elbows (or, if you've overindulged, the pressure of the pine floorboards against your cheek), the give of the leather on the chairs and stools and booths, the drama and pageant of foam rising in a draft pint of lager or stout, the smell of what's been spilled, the rattle of the cocktail shaker, the murmur of conversation, the green glow of a football game on the TV screen, the smoke layered in the air.

Where everybody knows your name… it's more than a theme song, it's the foundation of what makes a tavern work. But you don't need everybody knowing your name to feel at home, just a few of the regulars to nod and wave as you step through the door will suffice. And there aren't many things better than the bartender timing the preparation of your favorite drink – your "usual" – so that it's coming in for a three-point landing on the bar as you slide onto that stool or lift your foot to the brass rail.

Every neighborhood bar (as opposed to hotel bars or railway station bars, or the bars in chain restaurants like Applebee's and TGIF) has a unique character. It's not often apparent to the casual visitor, but hang around and you'll see that certain places tend to attract the morose drinkers, others the rowdy kind, and almost every bar has a tale-teller – sometimes a teller of tall tales, sometimes simply a silver-tongued raconteur. Basically a guy who fills the silences.

Some bars become gathering places for fringers – people who don't have an easy fit with the mainstream. That's why certain sections of towns have gay bars, leather bars, biker bars, S&M bars, and so on, spanning the gallimaufry of human diversity.

And, as you'll see in *Taverns of the Dead*, some bars attract patrons who edge into *non*-human diversity.

A little history of this subgenre: Ever hear of Gavagan's Bar? During the early 1950s L. Sprague deCamp and Fletcher Pratt told us tales about the strange goings on in that noble establishment (collected in 1953 into *Tales from Gavagan's Bar*). On the other side of the Atlantic, Arthur C. Clarke didn't feel deCamp and Pratt should have all the fun, so he started chronicling the equally strange doings in a hard-to-find London pub called The White Hart (collected in a 1957 volume called – surprise – *Tales from the White Hart*).

In the 1970s Spider Robinson revitalized the weird tavern genre with his tales from Callahan's Crosstime Saloon (available in a half-dozen or so volumes). Today the tradition is being carried on by writers such as Tina Jens with her tales from the Lonesome Blues Pub on Chicago's north side, and Peter Crowther's stories – one of which resides within – set in a most oddly named Manhattan walk-down, The Land At The End of the Working Day.

Which brings us to the volume you hold. Gathered in

Taverns of the Dead are tales not by one author, but many; not about one bar, but sundry. Some of the tales revolve around the tavern itself, others use the place as a launching pad. But whatever the circumstances, a tavern is a wonderful place for tall tales, is it not? As the ethanol from those brewed hops and malt, that fermented grape juice, or that single malt Scotch seeps through the intestinal membranes and into the bloodstream, through the liver and onward to the brain, the tongue is loosened, and tales are told, tales which might never reach other ears if the teller were a teetotaler.

Some of those tales are true, some are not. In the case of *Taverns of the Dead*, let's hope not.

When Kealan told me about the concept for the anthology, I thought, *Nice idea*, but saw the risk that too many stories would be the same. Not to worry. I haven't yet read all the stories (as I write this, they're not all finished), but of the dozen or so available to me, I've found no two alike. None of the taverns, real or fictional, are alike either. Most are located on this side of the Atlantic, but a fair number sit on the far side; some are trendy (Christ, remember fern bars?), some are glitzy, some dowdy, some sinister, and some aren't really there. Some of the barflies are old friends, who may or may not wish you well, and the same might be said of the strangers who wander in. And whatever you do, don't assume you can trust the bartender. Even the drinks are suspect: Do you really want to try a pint Shoggoth's Old Peculiar?

Maybe you do.

Whatever your tastes, now's the time to sit back and, to get into the spirit, dip into this book with a drink in hand, or at least within easy reach.

Bottoms up.

***

I wrote this intro to my own story in July, 2003. I don't recall the occasion. The story itself was first published in 1978, and seemed a little far out then – my tongue too firmly in my cheek, so to speak. But our politicians have made it come true. As one of my readers recently commented: "It went from science fiction to documentary since the time FPW wrote it."

Lipidleggin'

1977. Teddy Kennedy was pushing hard for a British-style national health insurance program -- very similar to the Canadian-style, single-payer proposals some of our esteemed leaders played footsie with during much of 1994. NHI seemed to have a lot of support then. I'd already aired my views on the idea of government-controlled health care in the April 1975 issue of *Analog* with a guest editorial titled, "And Now, From the People Who Brought You Vietnam and Watergate..." It was time to approach it in fiction.

The idea for "Lipidleggin'" hit me as I was driving past packed parking lots at McDonald's and Burger King, imagining all those folks inside washing down Big Macs and Whoppers with milkshakes, setting up their coronary arteries for bypass grafts. I asked myself how, under a national health insurance plan, would a Teddy Kennedy remedy the problem of America's high-cholesterol diet? Most likely he'd do what any self-respecting politician would do: He'd outlaw it. Makes sense: Cholesterol prohibition not only protects citizens from harming themselves, but reduces the cost of health care as well. And the public would back him. Face it: If your taxes keep rising to pay for an endless stream of coronary bypass grafts, you're going to get a little touchy with people who don't take care of their arteries.

Kennedy's national health insurance push fizzled, which should have reduced "Lipidleggin'" to obsolescence, as much an artifact of its time as all those post-atomic holocaust stories of the fifties. Not so. Fifteen years later the NHI corpse was resurrected by Hillary Clinton who spent millions gathering input from 500 experts on how to put the government in control of the national healthcare system. The document was hilarious. Even the most strident members of the media's Hillary claque were hard pressed to defend, much less comprehend, the mishmash she delivered.

And now we're told that healthcare reform is dead. Don't believe it. No way will politicians – Republican or Democrat – be able to resist the temptation to manipulate a seven-billion-dollar sector of the economy. And if you think the idea of outlawing high-fat foods is too farfetched, remember that our elected officials don't have to abide by the laws they pass for us hoi polloi – they've exempted Congress from the Equal Pay Act, the Age Discrimination in Employment Act, the Occupational Health and Safety Act, and the National Labor Relations Act, just to name a few. Be assured, eggs Benedict and filet mignon will always be available in the Senate dining room.

So whenever your suspension of disbelief is threatened, try to recall all those senators sitting and listening straight-faced as Meryl Streep lectures their committee on the imminent dangers of alar, and afterward warmly thanking her for opening their eyes to this terrible threat.

These clowns are capable of anything.

**

Another graphic novel intro, this one in 2008 by William Harms.

Impaler

You hold in your hand the inaugural compilation of *Impaler*, brimming with dread and mayhem but sprinkled with tantalizing questions as well. An ancient horror has arrived in New York to wreak havoc on the populace. In its wake comes a man from the past, a warrior sworn to battle this evil, an evil he has faced before. But this is no knight in shining armor. He bears a load of moral baggage. Somewhere in the past he struck a bargain, and we witness him using evil means to fight this vampiric threat.

Evil…the word gets bandied about – the Evil Empire, the Axis of Evil – and can mean different things to different people. Here in the West we think of the Islamic fascists as evil; but when they look at us, they see the Great Satan. Your perception of evil often depends on where you're standing.

To members of certain religions, particularly among those in the Judeo-Christian-Islamic axis, evil has a name. Be it Satan, Lucifer, the Devil, the Serpent, evil is a force in the world, existing independent of humanity as it corrupts human action.

To secularists, on the other hand, evil is born in the human heart and exists solely as the result of human action.

But no matter where you've unpacked your bags along the believer-skeptic spectrum, everyone agrees that merely causing harm is not enough. Evil must involve intent.

The Ebola virus can cause untold harm, wiping out entire villages in days. But is it evil? It's simply doing what comes naturally. And what comes naturally for a virus – which, as a mere strand of RNA wrapped in a protein coat, does not meet the criteria for being alive – is pretty much the same for every other organism: Continue its existence and make more of its kind. But a virus can't divide or spawn. It must hijack the cells of another organism and retrofit the nuclear machinery to replicate itself. In the process, the cells are destroyed, but that's no more evil than a lion killing and devouring a wildebeest.

Of course, a virus can be *used* for evil – imagine someone contaminating a water supply with Ebola – and that brings us back to intent.

Which in turn brings us to the vampire.

The vampire exists on the borderland. It's an intrusion

of the supernatural into the real world. In Christian mythology, Satan's purpose is not to do evil, but rather to cause humans to commit evil acts, thus jeopardizing their souls. Not so the vampire. The vampire causes death, but worse, in so doing it creates others like itself.

But are vampires evil?

In many ways they aren't that much different from a virus. Like Ebola, vampires aren't living creatures, can't spawn, and need a host to increase their population. When they sink their teeth into a pulsing carotid and drain the lifeblood, aren't they simply doing what vampires do?

Certainly they do harm, but their intent, at least in the traditional sense, is survival of themselves and their species.

Is that evil? I'll let you decide.

The vampires you'll meet in the following pages are not quite traditional. And their purpose appears to be more than simple preservation of their species. *Impaler* teases us with hints that they are being directed by a malign intelligence – the beast – with perhaps a larger purpose. An *evil* purpose. We're also left wondering about the man from the past – *"the price you paid"… "you condemned yourself for nothing"* – and his methods. Can the evil the city faces be countered only by more evil?

I'm intrigued. I want more. So will you.

***

Batton Lash and his wife Jackie Estrada are longtime friends. Batton creates Wolff & Byrd and Jackie publishes them. I love these comics for many reasons (as explained below), so when they asked me to write an intro to this 2008 collection, The Soddyssey and Other Tales of Supernatural Law, I immediately agreed. You can't go wrong with…

Wolff & Byrd

I don't like lawyers.

With good reason. Between 1996 and 2008 I've been sued three times for no cause. In each case those suits eventually resulted in a summary judgment dismissing all claims with prejudice (which means that's the end of it – they can't be reopened).

Notice I said "eventually." Before each of those dismissals I had to plod through years of interrogatories and depositions. And even though the cases were all proven to be without merit, my malpractice premiums went up.

The plaintiffs' attorneys had cast wide nets and didn't give a damn who they hauled in. It cost them next to nothing to send out extra subpoenas. Like buying extra lottery tickets. Hey, who knows? Maybe one will pay off. And in the end I had no recourse against them, so they went their merry ways, free to do the same again and again.

So I repeat: I don't like lawyers.

But I do like Wolff and Byrd.

I like the stories, mainly because they're *stories* – they start, go someplace, and then end in a way that's relevant and adds symmetry to what has gone before. You don't see that enough in comics these days. Hardly at all. They've become soap operas. Sure, *W&B* has some longer arcs and recurring clients, but they act as bridges between the stories without *becoming* the stories.

Another joy of the series is its use of the English language. Barton Lash does not write down to his readers. His love of language is evident on every page. And that's fitting. Alanna and Jeff are lawyers; their weapons are words, so we expect them to use them well. And they do. Their aim is true. Their repartee is bright, clever, and witty. Wordplay abounds. (The Laws of Gravidity... The Statue of Limitations...ha!) I don't know about you, but I love whimsical wordplay, and even a bad pun is better than no pun.

But I take special pleasure in the cultural references peppered throughout the stories. (Dennis Miller, eat your heart out.) I'm not talking about the inspiration for "The * Files" – that's be obvious; no, I mean the origin of the names of the two FBI agents, and the town of Ft. Charles, NJ. Doesn't that judge in "I'm Carrying Satan's Baby!" look familiar? Did you have any doubt who Dr. Skratzsch might be when you heard his name and saw the acronym for Doctor's In-utero Services? (Keeping up here?) And consider the cast of "Personal Injuries and Guardian Angels" – the characterizations are spot on, although I do miss a certain raspy-voiced valet.

Wolff and Byrd's relationship rings true. They're rounded characters with distinct personalities and lives outside the plots; they care about each other both personally and professionally.

But I like Wolff and Byrd most of all because they tend to do the right thing. They take on the system on behalf of the outcasts, the "different" ones, the rejects… the *monsters*, if you will. They defend the sanctity of the individual and (as long as he, she, or it doesn't initiate force) the right to be different.

Yeah. Wolff and Byrd…they could make me almost like lawyers.

Almost.

***

In 2009 my old buddy Pierce Watters tapped me for this and I was glad to do it. I couldn't resist the Randian opening line.

The Hounds of Skaith

Who is Eric John Stark?

I'll get to that in a bit. First a little about Leigh and me.

We never met in person (she was terminally ill by the time I attended my first SF convention), so I have no personal anecdotes for you.

But we did meet in the pages of her novels, early on

in the 1964 back-to-back Ace Double containing *People of the Talisman* and *The Secret of Sinharat* (both Eric John Stark novels), and later in *The Book of Skaith* (an omnibus edition of *The Ginger Star*, *The Hounds of Skaith* and *The Reavers of Skaith* from the Science Fiction Book Club).

I remember back then thinking how similar the novels were to Edgar Rice Burroughs's Martian series. Now, decades later, having reread them to write this piece, I'm struck by the glaring differences. Leigh Brackett is so much better.

Don't get me wrong. I'm not here to snark on ERB. The work he produced during the first dozen or so years of his career stands out for its vitality, originality, and energy. I wouldn't send a newbie genre writer to Burroughs for style, but for pacing and narrative drive, he's hard to beat. (Only Robert E. Howard's Conan stories challenge him there.) But after the mid-1920s, ERB's work devolved into a formula of repeated captures and escapes (reaching its nadir with the Carson of Venus series) that made every novel feel like the previous.

The Skaith novels share ERB's muscular protagonists and headlong pace, but Leigh Brackett's style is head and shoulders above.

Witness Alderyk's comments to Stark:

> "You are the future standing there, a strange thing, full of distances I cannot plumb. A black whirling wind to break and scatter, leaving nothing untouched behind you..."

ERB couldn't have dreamed of dialogue like that. Or consider:

> All night long the werewinds laughed and gamed in Yurunna, and the Yur looked up with their copper-colored eyes like the eyes of dolls and saw deadly roof tiles spin like autumn leaves, shied down at them by the fingers of the wind. Chimneys tumbled. Old walls swayed and shook until they

toppled. The dark was full of clatterings and clashings.

You find descriptions ranging from the brilliantly direct ("When he smiled he was handsome, as a sword is handsome.") to the disturbingly oblique (as when the Tribesmen found the screaming slugs of the Yur young and "made a silence in the place.")

Made a silence... what a unique and brilliant way to describe slaughter.

Her treatment of the titular hounds is no less skillful. They – Gerd especially – become characters in the novel, but never overly anthropomorphized. Though they remain alien, with their own set of rules and ingrained priorities and prohibitions, I came to care about them. I learned just how much I cared during the invasion of Ged Darod as they headed for a showdown with their old houndmaster. Which way would their loyalties flow? And if they defied the houndmaster, would they survive? I tell you, Brackett had me worried, a testament to her skills.

But this novel isn't about the hounds, it's about Eric John Stark, a jagged stone tossed into the seemingly tranquil pool of Skaith.

Skaith is a unique planet with a fascinating history. Its geopolitics and social order have been shaped by its deteriorating climate.

The politics of climatology... the climatology of politics. How much more topical can you get? Obviously Leigh Bracket has her finger on the pulse of the zeitgeist.

Except that she died more than three decades ago.

It's worth noting that she wrote the three *Book of Skaith* novels in the 1970s, a time when the scientific community was abuzz with concern about the creeping changes they'd detected in Earth's climate, whispered fears about the possibility of a new ice age due to global cooling.

That's right: global *cooling*.

And that's what Skaith is doing. Cooling. Its sun, known variously as the ginger star or Old Sun, is dying. All stars die. Some go out with a bang, burning off their hydrogen in a single burst as a nova or supernova. Some expand to multiples of their original size, becoming red giants. Others simply fade.

The ginger star is fading, dimming, delivering progressively smaller consignments of life-giving light and warmth to its only inhabited planet, Skaith.

I can't say for sure that the seventies' concern over global cooling is what inspired Brackett's world building here, but it's an engaging conceit, and amusing to toy with.

Will Dourant once said, "Civilization exists by geological and climatological consent, subject to revocation at any time." Leigh Brackett brings that concept to rich life in the Skaith novels.

Once the planet sported a thriving, globe-spanning civilization, described as "rich, industrialized, urbanized and fruitful." But as the ginger star dimmed, the climate cooled – most noticeably, at first, near the poles. As growing seasons in the higher latitudes contracted, formerly hardy crops died before fruiting, and finally refused to germinate. If this wasn't enough to drive populations closer to the equator, the relentless encroachment of the expanding polar ice caps sealed the deal. Glaciers aren't arable.

Imagine the population of Canada fleeing the cold into the warmer climes of the US, or all of Scandinavia and Finland migrating into Germany and France and Poland.

Take it further. Imagine, generations later, the population of the upper US (which with then include all those displaced Canucks) moving into the Sunbelt, or hordes of Australians pushing into the Philippines and Southeast Asia.

Imagine the crowding, the chaos, the social upheaval. Imagine the inevitable violence as the displaced populations vie with the natives for land, for food and water, for life.

The ancestors of Skaith's current population did not have to imagine it. They lived it. The societies in the higher latitudes north and south crumbled, sending their citizens in search of better climes. The Wanderings and the Great Migrations caused social upheavals on a global scale.

The men who became the Lord Protectors saw what was coming. With a steadily shrinking mass of arable land, unable to produce enough to feed all the hungry mouths, many would have to go without. Some would have to die. The strong would live on, the weak would be buried...

Or perhaps not buried. In such times, no source of nourishment could be allowed to go to waste. They would be consumed. Survival of the fittest, nature's first imperative, would become the law of the land. Hunger would become the Great Thinner of the human herd.

Somehow the Lords Protector were able to step in and establish order before the thinning went too far. Though they failed to prevent the fragmentation of the previous civilization, somehow they managed to head off complete chaos. Their rules: "Succor the weak, feed the hungry, shelter the homeless – striving always toward the greatest good of the greatest number."

Sounds like a bed Karl Marx could sleep in.

The Lords Protector no doubt took control with the best intentions. Daniel Webster put it well: "Good intentions will always be pleaded for every assumption of authority... There are men in all ages who mean to govern well, but they mean to govern. They promise to be good masters, but they mean to be masters."

That pretty much describes the Lords Protector.

Though most collectivist dreams and schemes start out with the best intentions, they are by and large utopian. And Utopia, as we all know, is a fiction. A perfect civilization requires a perfect citizenry. Humans can be pretty damn impressive in what they can think and do, but perfect? I haven't met one yet.

The individual is an inconvenience in a collectivist society – the welfare of the group is paramount, which is why it's called "collectivist." That being the case, certain leveling measures must be put into effect. After all, if this is going to work, we must all be equal (except, of course, for those making the rules). All the pegs must be the same height, therefore those who lift their heads for a better view must be hammered down until they are even with the common denominator.

So how did the Lords Protector go about feeding the hungry and sheltering the homeless? By using the tried-and-true leveling techniques of fraud and force. The fraud lay in setting themselves up as supernatural beings, "undying and unchanging." As such they could decree that the producers must give up a share of the fruits of their labors. The gullible producers, duped into believing they must please these super beings, did just that. But not all were gullible, and so to assure compliance from the skeptics, the Lords hired mercenaries.

Yeah, Karl from-each-according-to-his-abilities-and-to-each-according-to-his-needs Marx would have loved the politburo – I mean, the Lords Protector.

The result was a fragmented society with a relatively limited group of producers feeding a large rabble of freeloaders known as Farers. The productive members couldn't complain too loudly because they'd become virtual slaves to the Wandsmen who enforced their "contribution" to the greater good. And the do-nothing Farers were loyal to the Wandsmen and the Lords Protector because they put food on their plates.

When you rob Peter to pay Paul, you rarely hear a complaint from Paul.

It's an effective political ploy, with plenty of antecedents here on Sol III: Make a large segment of the population dependent on the current regime for daily bread and comforts, and you create a loyal constituency resistant to any change of regime.

So for centuries the civilization they designed functions according to the Lords Protector's plans. And then the starships land and threaten to change everything. The Lords have been in control because they're supposedly super beings, the be-all and end-all, but suddenly here's something they could not possibly have foreseen. Their comfortable cosmology, with them as the center of the universe, is challenged. And so is their primacy.

Knowledge of the existence a star-spanning culture offers options, and an entrenched power structure needs to discourage options. Your only choice is to be a good member of the collective.

Worse, options engender dreams... and dreams are even more threatening. It can be dangerous to let people dream. The Lords Protector had no worries about the Farers. Why should they dream? They were suckling for free on the collective's teat. But the producers – the farmers, the builders, the artisans – they would dream, and those dreams would be of something brighter than their current state. Skaith's collective would collapse if these folk realized how much better off they'd be in a socioeconomic system that allowed them to trade the fruits of their labors with other free men.

If the producers shrugged off their yokes and moved off to the stars, who would feed the Farers? Who would feed the Wandsmen and the Lords Protector?

True to form, the Lords threw up a blockade around Skeg, the city where the starships landed, to prevent any dreamers from leaving. (Odd how Berlin comes to mind – it still had a wall when this was written.)

Threatening though all this might be to the status quo, the prophecy made it worse: A Dark Man would come from the stars. "A wolf's head, a landless man, a man without a tribe" who would destroy the Lords Protector and the Citadel where they dwelled.

And then a man named Erik John Stark, a black-skinned orphan without a homeland, debarks from a star ship.

Who is Eric John Stark?

Even if he's not the man of the prophecy, he's a wild card. And there's nothing an entrenched power structure fears more than a wild card. So the Lords Protector, already agitated by the arrival of the space ships, did what entrenched power always does when it feels threatened: They struck out at Stark.

Bad move.

Not because Stark was a unique individual, a mercenary, product of a harsh upbringing that had made him tough and resourceful, and earned him a warrior's heart.

But because they didn't have to.

Stark wasn't on Skaith to change the world, simply to find Simon Ashton – something he'd never accomplish, because only a select few on Skaith knew where he was being kept. Stark's fruitless search finally would have forced him to conclude that Simon was dead.

Eventually he would have left and returned to Pax.

Game over. The Lords Protectorate win and life on Skaith continues as before.

Fortunately, the arrogance of power often bears the seeds of its own downfall.

They tried to kill him. And in the course of that attempt he learned that Simon was still alive. They gave him hope, they gave him a mission, and worse, they pissed him off.

The Dark Man prophecy was nothing more than an assemblage of words, and would have remained just that if the Lords had simply left him alone. But by attacking Stark they spurred him to action and he *became* the Dark Man.

By the end of book one he has fulfilled the prophecy.

But he's only begun to fight.

***

Pierce must have liked the Skaith intro because he immediately asked me to do the same for one of my fave collections of all time, Robots Have No Tails. *And I so enjoyed writing about Kuttner that I suggested collecting his Hogben stories. That opened one unholy can of worms, but more on that later.*

...but they do have tales...

First things first: Who is Henry Kuttner?

Good question. Even though New Line recently released one of his best-known stories, "Mimsy Were the Borogroves," as a feature film (*The Last Mimzy*), the reading world has pretty much forgotten the man. Back in 1953 his story "The Twonky" was filmed starring Hans Conried, and his "Vintage Season" was adapted into a Jeff Daniels vehicle known variously as *Timescape* or *Grand Tour: Disaster in Time*. Luminaries of the SF and fantasy field such as Ray Bradbury, Richard Matheson, Marion Zimmer Bradley, and Roger Zelazny all cite him as a major influence on their work.

Yet mention his name anywhere outside a World Science Fiction Convention and World Fantasy Convention and the reaction is too often, "Henry Who?" (In fact, in a sad commentary about the collegial state of the genres, many of the attendees at those conventions might offer the same response.)

Forgotten... but not by people like me and the folks behind *Planet Stories*. We remember.

A case could be made that it's partially Kuttner's own fault for publishing under (by my most recent count) seventeen pseudonyms. "Vintage Season" and "Mimsy Were the Borogroves," easily his most-anthologized works, were published, respectively, as by Lawrence O'Donnell and Lewis Padgett. Most of the pseudonymous stories were written in collaboration with his wife, Catherine Moore, who had earned a reputation in *Weird Tales* under the gender-neutral name, C. L. Moore. In fact, she and Kuttner met after he wrote her a fan letter thinking she was a guy.

The stories here in *Robots Have No Tails* – possibly the most beloved of his oeuvre – were not written under his own name. He used his Lewis Padgett pseudonym, but that may not have been his original intent. He had another story, the extremely clever "Nothing But Gingerbread Left," under his own name in the same issue of *Astounding Science Fiction* that carried the first of these. It's an unwritten editorial law that if author has more than one story in an issue – a common occurrence in the pulp era – he may use his real name on only one.

A look at the 1942 run of *Astounding*, just one of the pulp magazines Kuttner wrote for, gives you an idea as to why he needed pseudonyms. Of the twelve issues, he's in ten, with two stories in both January and March. (In the latter, "Clash by Night" was written with C. L. Moore and is listed as by Lawrence O'Donnell.)

You could say he's forgotten because he died young – at 42 of a heart attack – and didn't live to fulfill his potential. But I don't think so. I've read that he and Moore felt burned out in the early 1950's. They weren't unique in that regard. Many writers from the pulp era suffered from a similar malady. They were paid by the word and under constant pressure to keep cranking them out to keep food on the table and a roof overhead. Hundreds of writers were eaten alive in the pulp jungle.

Kuttner and Moore decided to get educated. Both earned undergrad degrees in psychology from USC, and Kuttner was headed for an MA. He wrote some excellent short fiction in the fifties that, stylewise, was miles above his work in the preceding decade. But his output had slowed by then. He tried his hand at murder mysteries but that didn't work out. Novels weren't his thing. His strength was in the short form. I've heard he didn't write the last couple of mysteries that appeared under his name. He'd lost the fire that keeps a writer pounding those keys.

And then he was gone.

Another possible reason he's off the radar these days is because he didn't stick to one genre. He wrote horror (his first published story was "The Graveyard Rats" and he was part of the Lovecraft circle), sword and sorcery (the Elak of Atlantis series), science fiction ("The Twonky" and "Two-Handed Engine"), whimsical fantasy ("A Gnome There Was" and "The Misguided Halo" in *Unknown Worlds*), and unclassifiables such as his stories of the mutant hillbilly Hogben family.

(I will note here that I found all of the above unforgettable.)

Ray Bradbury has suggested that Kuttner's low recognition factor is due to its lack of polarizing qualities. Well, it's true he wasn't pushing a social, political, economic, or technological agenda. His prose wasn't edgy, and he offered no literary pyrotechnics. He didn't file high-profile lawsuits, didn't write in store windows, didn't issue manifestos. He simply told stories.

And there might be the rub.

Storytellers get no respect. Or at least not nearly as much as they should.

So let's examine some of those stories he told. The ones collected here are known as the Gallegher stories, named after their tipsy protagonist, Galloway Gallegher (more later on that name), and number only five. What is it about them that would induce Gnome Press, an early and renowned science-fiction and fantasy specialty publisher, to devote a volume to them back in 1952? Four of the five were almost a decade old then, tucked away in moldering back issues of *Astounding Science Fiction*. But somebody remembered. *Robots Have No Tails* was published and soon became a collector's item. Twenty-one years later, Larry Shaw, editor of Lancer Books, remembered too, and reprinted the collection as part of the imprint's Science Fiction Library. And now, three and a half decades after that, thanks to Paizo editors Erik Mona and Pierce Watters...they're back again.

Henry Kuttner and C. L. Moore were said to have had a unique collaboration style: One would type away until he or she ran out of gas or had to take a break, and then the other would settle into the still-warm seat before the typewriter and pick up where the first had left off, sometimes in midsentence. In her introduction to the Lancer edition, Moore stated that although she and Kuttner collaborated on almost all the Lewis Padgett fiction, she had no recollection of contributing a single word to the Gallegher stories, thus justifying the single byline.

The first four stories, "Time Locker," "The World is Mine," "The Proud Robot," and "Gallegher Plus" were written in 1942 before Kuttner entered the army. The final entry, "Ex Machina," wasn't published until 1948. All were bought for *Astounding Science Fiction* by the father of modern science fiction, John W. Campbell, Jr. I have to wonder... if Campbell had decided to turn down the *ASF* editing gig and continue instead his successful writing career (among his many gems was the basis for John Carpenter's *The Thing*, "Who Goes There?"), would these stories have been published? Campbell had a sense of whimsy – he was simultaneously editing *Unknown Worlds*, a magazine acclaimed for its whimsical fantasies – that I'm not sure was shared by other SF editors of the time. The Gallegher stories are, at their very least, whimsical, and might even be called screwball comedies – I know I can't read "The Proud Robot" without being reminded of the martini-gulping Nick and Nora Charles of the *Thin Man* films.

And that brings up an issue that needs to be addressed in regard to these stories: the milieu in which they were written. Screwball comedies were in their heyday in the latter thirties and early forties. In addition to the six *Thin Man* films that span the screwball era, Nick and Nora Charles starred in a weekly radio show that ran throughout the forties. So very likely their tipsy adventures were part of the background music of the Kuttner household.

Tipsy, however, doesn't begin to describe Gallegher's usual state. He's a lush, a tippler, a boozer, a drunk... let's say it: an alcoholic. Heavy drinking is very un-PC now. We are no longer allowed to laugh at a drunken person. But we used to – all the time. Foster Brooks made a career out of it, Red Skelton's Willy Lump was always plastered. Even hangovers were funny. Nick and Nora's cure was "a little pick me up."

So, a little advice: If you've been infected with political correctness by the state school systems and the establishment mass media, try to put that aside while you read these stories. Gallegher has no dependents, doesn't drive drunk (doesn't even own a vehicle, as far as I can tell), and the only damage he does is to his own liver. And since he lives way in the future, they've probably got a fix for that. Turn it off and let it go... because without booze, there ain't no Gallegher stories.

That's right. The recurring MacGuffin of the series involves the consumption of mass quantities of ethanol. You see, Gallegher is an inventor, but not a very good one – sober. When blind drunk, however, he's a genius. The trouble is, when he sobers up he has no idea what he's done, or why, or for whom. Inevitably someone who's paid him an advance shows up looking for the solution to his problem. Gallegher has no clue as to who the man is or the nature of his problem, and of course he can't ask because he's supposed to know. What ensues is a science puzzle story wrapped in a screwball comedy inside a future milieu.

Except for "Time Locker," the first of the series, in the January 1943 issue of *Astounding*.

I consider it the least of the Gallegher stories for a number of reasons, the most obvious being Gallegher's relegation to something of a supporting role. The point-of-view character here is a crooked lawyer. Yes, it's a science puzzle, but lacking the anarchic zaniness of the stories that followed. It did, however, establish Gallegher as a hard-drinking inventor who wasn't always sure of what he'd created.

"The World is Mine" appeared five months later in the June issue and set the tone for the rest. Gallegher's grandfather from the wilds of Maine is his foil here, the most madcap of the series, wherein Gallegher is accused of murdering himself.

"The Proud Robot" followed in October and is the best known, funniest, and fits most snugly into the screwball formula. It introduces the narcissistic robot, Joe, who becomes a continuing character and a constant source of irritation for his creator. Their clever banter, Joe's air of superiority and conviction that he's partnered with someone beneath his station, all the farcical goings on, plus the copious amounts of alcohol consumed, make this a classic screwball comedy.

"Gallegher Plus" (which happens to be Gallegher's name for his drunken alter ego) appeared in November and carried on the madcap tradition.

The final story, "Deus Ex," did not appear until six years later the April 1948 issue, but doesn't miss a beat. Grandpa is back, Joe is into philosophy, and Gallegher is again accused of murder. Just another day in the life of a drunken inventor.

As Ray Bradbury noted, these stories are anything but polarizing – unless you've got something against entertainment. The puzzles posed sometimes have ingenious solutions, sometimes not, but it's the journey that matters. If they have an underlying message, it's faith in the human mind's ability to know, to learn, and to solve problems. They're delightfully amoral tales whose philosophical underpinnings are empiricism and pragmatism, but what else would you expect from a scientist, drunk or sober?

Are they some of the best SF ever written? Hell, no. They show many of the failings of hastily written pulp fiction. The writing is slapdash at times, suffering from polyadverbosis and digressions that would give Poe fits. The science is often suspect, the extrapolations occasionally sloppy. All would have benefited from a week or two of marinating in a drawer before careful revision. But neither Henry Kuttner nor Lewis Padgett nor Lawrence O'Donnell nor any of his other pseudonyms had that luxury. Pulp writers were paid a penny a word (less in the down markets, two cents if they had a following), sometimes on acceptance, too often on publication. To maintain a living wage and a reasonably steady cash flow, writers were backed into sending off pencil-edited first drafts.

According to C. L. Moore in her intro to the Lancer edition, the scientist's name in the first story was "Galloway," a fact Kuttner had forgotten by the time he began writing the second. He probably hadn't kept a carbon of "Time Locker" and couldn't check the magazine because the story hadn't been published yet, so he went from memory. The error was remedied in the third story by referring to the protagonist as "Galloway Gallegher."

But none of that in any way diminishes the wacky inventiveness and entertainment value of these tales.

So sit back, relax, and enjoy them for what they are: products of their times, prismatic glimpses into the early 1940s through a future imagined by one of the most inventive writers of the period.

***

This celebrated the moment in 2010 when all the LaNague novels and short stories became available as ebooks on Amazon. (More details available in the Byte columns.)

The LaNague Federation Series

Galactic Empires are a joke.

At least I've always thought so. So when I started writing science fiction I looked for something different. I wanted to set my stories against a single consistent coherent background – my own Future History (a la Heinlein and Niven) – because even as a novice I recognized the enormous benefits to both writer and readers. Half a dozen stories set in an interesting Future History acquire a scope and sense of depth unattainable by an equal number of unlinked stories.

And besides, I had an ax to grind.

When I sketched out the LaNague (rhymes with "the plague") Federation future history, my world view – *Weltanshauung*, as the literary folks like to say – differed radically from anything being published at the time. I figured I'd be saying something that wasn't being said by anyone else. And even if I was an unknown and a beginner, maybe readers would take notice.

Barely a quarter of a century out of the womb, I knew there was something gravely wrong with statism. I was unable to perceive any functional difference between state socialism, communism, and fascism. Different rhetoric maybe, but the end result was the same: state control of the schools, the media, the means of production, and ultimately the quality of life – all at the expense of the individual.

So I swiveled in the political current and swam not rightward or leftward, but *outward*. I based the socioeconomic tenets of my LaNague future history on a laissez-faire model. It makes more sense than an empire. An empire needs absolute control if it's to function in an empirish way. That's all but impossible over interstellar distances, even with an FTL drive. What's needed is a freer, looser form of government, one dedicated to preserving the diversity of humanity, allowing it to develop along the myriad possible paths open to it, yet carrying a big club to break up the fight when one segment takes a swing at another.

This then shall be the whole of the law: Go where thou wilt, do what thou wilt, but initiate no force.

The books were not politically correct then, and are certainly not now, but they found an enthusiastic audience, grabbing SF readers first, then moving beyond. A novel in the series won the first Prometheus Award; two other titles won Prometheus Hall of Fame Award; another was named on the recommended lists of the American Library Association and the New York Public Library. KYFHO, the acronym that sums up the sociopolitical philosophy I created for *An Enemy of the State*, took on a life of its own and refuses to die – Google it and you still get thousands of hits.

I'm thrilled that now, for the first time in the decades since I began writing them, the five novels and five short stories of the LaNague Federation series are available at the same time in the same place. The result is a giant *roman à thèse*. Some of the props are creaky, especially the references to computers. (Who would have imagined they could get so small and so fast so soon?) But the ideas are what count here, and they remain as fresh and relevant now as ever. Perhaps more so. Human freedom and personal self-determination are ideals that don't age.

So, for those of you who can still dream, here is how it could happen, here is what it could be like. You and I will never see it, but maybe someday... somewhere...

***

In 2007, Peter Crowther asked me to do an intro to Reunion, *an upcoming Rick Hautala novella. I'd known Rick for almost forever, so I agreed. When completed, I saw that it needed to be an afterword instead. No problem. The novella was finally pubbed in 2010.*

These Are the Good Old Days

Only Rick Hautala could have written *Reunion*.

But he couldn't have brought if off back in the eighties when he was writing *Nightstone* and *Little Brothers*, nor in the nineties between the likes of *Ghost Light* and *The Mountain King*.

Certainly he could have brought off the kids, the Maine setting, the intense emotions and internal conflicts – all staples of his work – but I believe Rick had to wait until now to be able to do full justice to one of the themes of "Reunion."

I say that because I can't see anyone on the uphill side of fifty producing a work with the same mature sensibilities. There's a melancholy here, a long – and perhaps longing – view from the bridge of years. A perspective that can't be achieved through reading or imagination, but gained only through the joys and pains of experience.

The Finns are known to be a melancholy people. Rick is a Finn and, though rarely without a smile, he has a melancholy core. He can't help it. It's in his DNA. "Reunion" is proof.

Consider our protagonist(s). The twelve-year-old boy Jackie and the fifty-something John. Neither of them can be called a barrel of laughs.

Jackie worries more than an average twelve-year-old boy. He should be laughing, enjoying himself, feeling immortal. But he has a dour – dare I say, melancholy? – core that won't allow him to let go.

Then there's John. Not exactly a happy camper either. Though we'll eventually learn that his concerns run much deeper, he appears at first to be caught up in a typical midlife crisis: The man in his fifties looking back on his life and hearing the old Peggy Lee tune, *Is that all there is?* A looming high school reunion only exacerbates the feeling. He knows he won't be able to resist comparing his own life accomplishments with his classmates'. It's human nature.

But worse, John already feels like a lesser light. "What

the fuck have I accomplished?" pretty much says it all.

The question of *when* all this is happening rises.

I especially like the sly hints. Within the first half dozen pages you start to get a feeling that something's off: Two kids camping out and (one of them, at least) planning some mischief? Why aren't they being shuttled to soccer games and ballet lessons, or karate or lacrosse or computer camp, or a basketball or tennis clinic? Why are they on their own and allowed to be simply...kids? (What a concept.)

Then Jackie's mother drops a stealth bomb about the temporal setting. (I say stealth because if you're not paying attention it could slip right by you.)

"Maybe I should give you a dollar and send you downtown on your bike to fill up the gas can. As long as you bring me back the change and don't spend it on candy and soda."

Huh? A dollar for gas and...there's *change*?

What's going on? (Or, as we say online: WTF?)

Then Jackie drops and even stealthier bomb of his own: "My dad stays up late every night to watch Jack Parr."

Really, how many people today remember Jack Parr? If you're under forty, you probably don't, and the reference will slip right past you. But we boomers remember the crazy host who put *The Tonight Show* on the map.

Holmesian deduction leads to the conclusion that the setting's either late 1950s or very early 60s.

Later on, in case you haven't been paying attention, Jackie comes right out and tells us it's 1960 for him, but it's 2006 for John.

Both, however, are headed for a rendezvous at the same cookout, and neither enjoying the journey.

But John's not going for a dose of self-flagellation; he plans to meet his twelve-year-old self.

Is there anyone who doesn't wish he or she could go back in time and give their younger self a bit of advice? Of course not. There are few more appealing fantasies.

If only I knew then what I know now...

But a writer with lower mileage on the life odometer might have had a character say something like, "Buy Microsoft." Or "Don't marry him." Or "Don't let her go."

Not Rick. Sure, John needs to warn his younger self about a matter of life or death, about the dangers that await Jackie and his friend Chris that night.

And yet, when the moment comes, what is the first thing out of his mouth?

"I want to tell you ... that this ... I don't know how to put it, but this is your time ... this is what is called the 'time of your life.' "

Not about the doom awaiting Chris on the trip back home, but about the way his younger self is spending his childhood.

"You have to enjoy this time...I mean *really* enjoy it. You have to savor every minute, every second of it because before you know it, it's going to be gone."

Odd, don't you think?

But perhaps not so odd. Because we're in Jackie's point of view at that moment, we can't know John's mental and emotional state. We can only infer from his words, his expressions, and the way his voice breaks. Perhaps he has carefully rehearsed what he's going to say to Jackie, but then the sight of his younger self blows all his plans out of the water. He's so overcome with a sense of loss, with an unplumbed longing for all that he didn't do and didn't enjoy in that time of his life, that instead of a warning he blurts out advice.

This is potent stuff, revealing of the character and, perhaps, the author. Perhaps it applies to all of us.

And that's sad...sad to think that someone feels he has no Good Old Days to look back on. Because it's never over till it's over. No matter what time of your life you're in right now, someday *these* could be the good old days.

***

If you've been reading these in order, you can probably skip this one. Been there, done that. It's a rehash of my early intro for "The Distributor." I cannibalized it a dozen years later to intro my sequel to the Matheson story when I reprinted "Recalled" in the 2011 collection, Quick Fixes – Tales of Repairman. *It's here because...well, just because.*

Recalled

It's a rare story that won't go away. Most are forgotten as soon as you turn the page; some linger for a while, then join their brethren in the void. But every so often you encounter one with a special, mysterious quality that encodes it into your synapses, making it a part of you. We all have our own set of special stories. "The Distributor" is one of mine.

But first, a little background. I was thirteen when I decided to write horror fiction. That was in 1959 – a banner year for me. I discovered Lovecraft in Donald A. Wolheim's *The Macabre Reader*, and then went out and bought everything good ol' H.P. had in print. When I exhausted him, I started in on the rest of the old masters: Bloch, Howard, Derleth, Long, Hodgson, Leiber, and whoever else I could find. The reading exacerbated a lifelong writing itch, one I'd started scratching in second grade. Now I began to believe I could write this stuff. Not at age thirteen, but later on. I could do it. I *would* do it. But for now, I'd keep reading.

Here's the point to all this me-focused stuff: All along I wanted to write horror fiction; all along I was convinced I could do it. No question about it: "Someday I'll do this."

Then I picked up a paperback called *Shock* by Richard Matheson. I'd read Matheson's work before, had been deeply touched by "Born of Man and Woman," and suitably impressed by many of his other stories. Here was a guy who

delivered. And *Shock* was okay. Lots of interesting stories –
sf, social commentary, suspense – but not much horror.

Then I came to the last story. "The Distributor"
stopped me dead. All along I'd been telling myself, "I can do
this."

Now I was muttering and mumbling, "No way can I do
that."

I don't know how it is with other writers, but most of
the time when I finish a story or novel, I may be pleased, I
may even be impressed, but somewhere in the back of my
mind I'm thinking, *I could have done that.*

Every so often, though, you come across a piece of
fiction that blows you away, not just because you've been
hanging onto every word, but because when you're done you
have to admit, *I couldn't have done that.*

That's what makes certain stories special to me; those
are the ones I admire most: the ones I lack the talent or
insight or command of the language to write myself.

"The Distributor" was first published in *Playboy* in
1957 and look what's happened to the country since. "Mr.
Gordon" (or whatever his real name is) and his fellow
distributors have been busy, busy, busy.

Maybe it's a little dated. What used to be scandalous
is now daily fodder for today's talk shows (more evidence
of Mr. Gordon's handiwork?), but change maybe fifty words,
substituting incest and pedophilia – not too many people
anxious to wave those flags yet – for a couple of passé taboos,
and the story is right up to date.

Why did I say *I can't do that* after reading "The
Distributor"? Not because I couldn't sit down and imitate it –
I couldn't have *originated* it.

Notice the utterly flat affect. "The Distributor" is an
epiphany in that sense. All horror fiction I'd read until
then pulsed with vibrant emotion – rage, hate, fear, lust for
revenge. "The Distributor" has none of that. And that's what
makes it so horrifying.

The story is a parade of simple declarative sentences (hell, he uses fewer adverbs than Elmore Leonard) with only an occasional off-the-wall adjective to let us know "Mr. Gordon" is well educated. We spend the entire story in Mr. Gordon's point of view but experience no emotion; we witness only the surfaces of events. This is one of the most effective uses of minimalist technique you will ever see.

Mr. Gordon doesn't hate the residents of Sylmar Street. Nothing personal here. They're just people and this is just another town along his distribution route. It's just a job, folks.

Just a job.

But who does he work for?

That's Matheson's final coup. If he'd revealed that Mr. Gordon worked for the CIA or the KGB, or even some invented secret organization or cult, "The Distributor" would have migrated to short story limbo long ago. But he didn't. Who is behind this? Where is their home office? What is their agenda? *Why are they doing this?*

I wanted to know in 1961.

I still want to know.

So as a tribute to Matheson and his story, I wrote "Recalled." I took the same story as "The Distributor," but flipped it on its head and made it my own.

Its simple presence here gives away the twist, but I think you'll enjoy it anyway.

***

I met Tom Roberts at the 2011 Bouchercon in St. Louis. He was manning a dealer-room table for his small press, Black Dog Books, which was reprinting some of Sax Rohmer's early short fiction, and we had a nice discussion about his Dr. Fu Manchu character. Later that year he contacted me about doing the intro for The Leopard Couch and Other Stories. *An important moment for me because it introduced me to the mysterious*

Madame de Medici and triggered my ongoing affair with the lady.

The Leopard Couch

"Stories of the Fantastic and the Supernatural" indeed.

All but two of this baker's dozen of strange tales were first published in the teens of the last century. A pair have already celebrated their centennial, and the rest will soon follow.

A century ago...what a wondrous time for fiction lovers. That single decade witnessed the advent of John Carter in *A Princess of Mars*, *The Gods of Mars*, and *The Warlord of Mars*, all serialized in *All-Story Magazine*, plus the first half-dozen Tarzan novels. And of course, from 1914 to 1917, starting in *The Storyteller Magazine*, Sax Rohmer gifted us with the first three novels featuring the paradigm of Yellow Peril and the crowning achievement of his career, Dr. Fu Manchu.

I confess to ignorance of Sax Rohmer's short fiction, even though I've had two collections sitting on my bookshelves for decades. In fact, I read my first tales just last year in this volume's predecessor. So how, you ask, does such a Rohmer ignoramus come to write the introduction to a collection like this? Good question.

In 2011, as I was browsing through the booksellers' room at the St. Louis Bouchercon (an annual gathering of mystery writers and their readers), I happened across the wonders of Black Dog Press stacked upon a table. The Rohmer collection, *The Green Spider*, was among them, and I segued into a discussion with its publisher, Tom Roberts, about Yellow Peril fiction in general and my longtime admiration for the nuances of Rohmer's Fu Manchu character in particular. Long story short, a few months later he read "Sex Slaves of the Dragon Tong," my homage to that branch of pulp fiction, and knew I wasn't just blowing smoke.

So he contacted me about writing the intro to the collection you hold in your hands.

Oddly enough, although their author made his bones with the infamous Dr. Fu Manchu, none of these thirteen tales takes place in the good doctor's homeland. The closest we come to China is Burma in "The Valley of the Just." Five stories are British through and through, but the rest – more than half – are all tales of Egypt.

"The Haunted Temple," "The Red Eye of Vishnu," "The Curse of a Thousand Kisses," and "In the Valley of the Sorceress" all take place in the land of the Pharaohs. "The Hand of the White Sheikh" finishes in London, but its first half is set in Cairo. "The Leopard Couch" and "That Black Cat" may take place in England, but their plots turn on Egyptian artifacts.

Another confession: I know nothing of the author's personal life beyond the fact that Sax Rohmer is a nom de plume and that his real name is Arthur S. Ward. After all, I'm here to talk about the man's fiction, not the man himself. But I'll go out on a limb and state that he traveled to Egypt and was fascinated with the place.

I feel safe on that limb because of the loving detail he pours into the Egyptian settings of these tales. Such a profound sense of place is possible only when the author has been there – more than once, I'll venture. Perhaps that's the reason the Egyptian stories stand out from the others. And preeminent among the Egyptian stories are "The Haunted Temple" and "The Red Eye of Vishnu," both featuring the mysterious Madame de Medici.

Who was she, and from whence did she come? She was steeped in mysticism, spoke intimately of the strange writings of Eliphas Levi, and quoted Pythagoras and Zarathustra with the same facility wherewith Swynnerton quoted Kipling. She had tremendous intellectual fascination, and made him feel as a child

*at one moment; in the next the wondrous eyes would
look into his own, and they were the luresome eyes of a
ghâzeeyeh, setting his blood more quickly coursing.*

Yes, who is Madame de Medici and whence did she
come? Many of the stories here are notable for what they
don't say, and the madame's are two excellent examples of an
author dropping hints for his readers and leaving them to fill
in the blanks. The technique is a tightwire – withhold too
much and the reader comes away dissatisfied, may even feel
cheated. But strike just the right balance and you'll leave the
characters and their stories reverberating through reader's
brain.

If I am correctly reading Rohmer's hints, Madame de
Medici might be an ancient Egyptian goddess, or the avatar
of one. He never tells us for sure. Her agenda is as obscure as
her origin. In "The Haunted Temple" her last words are, "…
perhaps I learnt that a poor dying shred of soul yet survives
within me. Perhaps I relented – even at the eleventh hour." *A
poor dying shred of soul…* now there's an image full of portent.

Contrast the fate she arranges for Roy Swynnerton in
that story to the fate of the "poor little brown man" from
Kathmandu in "The Red Eye of Vishnu." Worlds apart.

I don't know how many stories Rohmer wrote
featuring the enigmatic Madame de Medici, but I hope more
are hiding somewhere. If they exist, someone please find
them and put them between covers. You have at least one
guaranteed customer here.

As for the rest of the stories, this collection offers
wonderful variety – from psychic detectives to haunted
mansions, even haunted valleys. Much of the weird fiction of
Rohmer's time presented a mystery or a fantastic occurrence
that appeared to have a supernatural origin but in the end
was revealed as something with a mundane explanation.
Not so these tales – at least the majority of them. After all,
sometimes a ghost is a ghost and a demon is a demon.

A note about the prose: if you like lengthy, adjective-strewn sentences, well, you're in for a treat. If not, keep in mind that Rohmer was writing in the style of the times. Hemingway had yet to appear on the scene to show writers how to clean up their act.

My advice: settle back and savor these little time capsules from nearly a century ago. And keep your eye out for Madame de Medici. I'm delighted to read about her, but not sure I'd want to get on her wrong side.

***

I had an epiphany writing the intro to Nothing As It Seems. *I realized I was wasting my time and decided to stop doing intros for collections by authors like Tim Lebbon. Tim needs no introduction – not then, and certainly not now. These small presses have a fetish for introductions. I'm off introductions unless it's about something that grabs my interest or by a newbie I want to push in your face.*

The Many Voices of Tim Lebbon

Tim Lebbon's got voice.

Not vocal talent. *Voice.*

Every January I participate in a writers bootcamp where fledgling authors submit their latest to a group of grizzled vets (that would be me) who dismantle the works and examine all their components to see which need refining and which aren't needed at all. You must be readable to get in; the aim is to make you publishable.

Somehow it always falls to me to explain voice.

Google "literary voice" and you'll come across a gallimaufry of definitions. Newbie writers can often recite the definition but few can put it into practice. The better veteran writers have stopped thinking about it but practice it with every sentence.

So what is "voice?" I hate hard-and-fast definitions

when it comes to good writing, preferring to follow Justice Potter Stewart's approach when he was asked to define pornography: "I know it when I see it." I don't present myself as an expert on literary voice, but I know it when I see it. And I miss it when I don't see it.

The easiest, most proletarian definition: It's the *personality* of the prose.

Whose personality? Depends.

In nonfiction, we're almost invariably referring to the *author's* personality. The easiest examples are Tom Wolfe's essays on culture in the 60s and 70s with their snarky asides and ubiquitous exclamation points. You feel as if he's sitting next to you, speaking in your ear. Unfortunately his fiction uses the same voice. You can't read *Bonfire of the Vanities* without hearing Wolfe shouting from every page.

What I tell the bootcamp grunts: Every story has its own voice; it's up to the writer to listen for it and adapt his narrative accordingly. Every character within a story should have a distinct voice so he or she can speak to the reader in a voice consistent with his or her personality and life experience.

Tim Lebbon knows voice, and uses it with skill and aplomb. I offer this huge collection of his shorter fiction as proof.

"Just Breathe" is told in a child's voice; Tim had to be especially convincing with Nia's voice to make the story's twist work. In "the God of Rain," the voice of Francis (I don't know why he used the male spelling) is clearly that of a dotty widow. "Bleeding Things" is told in the frantic voice of someone who has been undone by the stresses of war and the shrapnel in his brain. The voice that relates "The Body Lies" is not Tim Lebbon's – he's not the cold, petty, hateful fellow who invites his neighbors to see what he's found in his basement.

I confess a weakness for Tim's world of Noreela – its shifting landscapes, its strange cultures and creatures –

so I particularly liked "Chanting the Violet Dog Down." I was struck by the Mourner's uneasy mix of empathy and overriding sense of duty.

You'll notice that the narrators Tim uses to tell his stories are not always reliable. We are sharing what they are seeing, but are they really seeing what they say they are? Do you believe Holly in "Falling Off the World," or Jack in "Making Room"? I'm not sure I do. But then again, this is Lebbonville, so anything can happen.

Or the nameless narrator of "Meat." He's real, the famine is real, but I'm not so sure about Probert. Is it Probert chasing him across the ravaged countryside, or merely an avatar of his own guilt? I mean, who really killed and ate Angeline?

A bit more about "Meat," if I may. I was struck by its many similarities to a novel I'd read half a dozen years before: Cormac McCarthy's "The Road." Both share the mysterious, unexplained apocalypse, the barren, devastated landscape, the collapse of civilization, the cannibalism. Tim Lebbon copies no one, but I couldn't explain why he would write a novella so similar to an international bestseller. The answer became clear when I compared the copyright dates: both were published in 2006.

And yet for all their similarities in the circumstances afflicting the characters, the two tales could not be more different in style, tone, and, yes, voice. McCarthy uses flat, affectless prose that sets a mood of weary acceptance; his narrator seems beaten down despite setting out on a last desperate journey with his son. Tim's narrator, on the other hand, is in a constant state of panic as he flees his murderous nemesis. The prose is charged with emotion.

For me the two stand-outs of the collection are "Slaughterhouse Blues" and "The Reach of Children."

"Slaughterhouse Blues" is based on the Nick Cave song, "O'Malley's Bar." A number of very good songwriters possess voices which – to me – sound like fingernails on a chalkboard.

Tom Waits immediately comes to mind. Nick Cave is another. I tried to listen to his recording of "O'Malley's Bar" but didn't make it past the two-minute mark (it's a *long* song). So I Googled the lyrics. The song is an extended, step-by-step recounting of the details of a mass murder, all from the psycho killer's point of view. Not much story there, just madness and a catalogue of cold-blooded murders. A more conventional writer would have delved into the killer's past and tried to shine a light on what drove him to slaughter his neighbors. Tim flips it around and invents a survivor. "Slaughterhouse Blues" is her story, not the killer's. You will not soon forget it. Or her.

I don't think anyone will argue that the collection's pièce de résistance is "The Reach of Children." In it, Tim returns to his recurring theme of dealing with loss. It has a child's point of view and we struggle with ten-year-old Daniel who has just lost his mother and appears to be losing his father as the man crumbles before his eyes. As if the poor kid doesn't have enough to deal with, Tim insinuates a mysterious box into Daniel's life. I'm not easily unsettled – I like to think I've written my share of chilling stories, so I know how they work – but when Daniel first taps on that box, and something taps back, I experienced a genuine *frisson*.

You have many treats ahead of you here. Go now and savor them. And listen to the voices.

***

Neil Gaiman did the introduction, I did the afterword. Sounds simple, doesn't it. But it took Pierce Watters, publisher Tom Monteleone, Neil, and yours truly (starting with my comment to Pierce after writing the intro to Kuttner's Robots Have No Tales*) from 2009 to 2013 (including a Kickstarter campaign) to make* The Hogben Chronicles *a reality.*

The Hogben Epiphany

How odd that Neil and I should be initiated into the Hogben cult via different editions of the same collection (although a decade or so apart). The cover of his edition of *Ahead of Time* had "a man with a bowler hat with his back to us, and a sort of a fairy hiding behind him, looking at us." Mine was the original Ballantine paperback with a Richard Powers wraparound that looked like this:

I'd never heard of Henry Kuttner but what self-respecting preteen sci-fi/monster-movie nerd could resist a cover like that?

I was heavily into SF then. I'd cut my teeth on EC comics along with the Tom Swift Jr. and Rick Brant series, then graduated to adult SF with William Sloane's *Space, Space, Space*. Put a monster or a spaceship (better yet, both) on the cover and I was *there*. All the SF I was reading was deadly serious – scientific problems with scientific answers, Earth threatened by aliens, nuclear-wasted futures – you know the drill. I found this Kuttner guy's stories in *Ahead of Time* pretty much in that vein... until I came to "A Pile of Trouble."

What the hell was this? The story was crazy, it lacked scientific rigor, it was ridiculous, it was...funny. And I *loved* it.

Later I came across another collection: *No Boundaries*. Well, I knew the Kuttner name now so I picked it up and what do you know – the Hogbens were back in "Exit the Professor." And again I loved it. In *Bypass to Otherness* I found "Cold War" and "See You Later" in *Return to Otherness*.

I experienced what I now call the Hogben Epiphany (I say "now" because back then I didn't know what epiphany meant): science fiction could be silly, whimsical, *funny* and still be good SF. Of course lots of older folks better versed in SF and fantasy, who'd read Campbell's *Unknown/Unknown Worlds* back in the forties, knew that, but for me it came as a revelation.

I wanted more Hogbens but everyone I asked said Kuttner had written only four of them, and who was I to doubt?

But they were wrong.

Decades later, enter Pierce Watters asking me to write the introduction to *Robots Have No Tails*, a collection of Kuttner's Gallegher and Joe stories (written under his Lewis Padgett pseudonym), tales that crossbred SF and the screwball comedies of the forties. I eagerly agreed and suggested a companion collection of all four Hogben stories. Pierce said he'd heard somewhere that there was a fifth.

If only we'd had the Internet back when I was a kid. A Google search quickly revealed that the first Hogben story, "The Old Army Game," had seen print in the November 1941 issue of a magazine called *Thrilling Adventures*. No problemo. Moldy issues of the *Thrilling* line of pulps were for sale all over. All I had to do was pick up a copy, scan the story, and we'd be set to go. For the first time ever, all the Hogben stories would nestle side by side in chronological order between a single set of covers.

Not so fast. Even knowledgeable collectors who thought they'd heard of that particular pulp had never seen a copy. I looked everywhere – pulp dealers, pulp collector groups, pulp conventions. No luck. It became an obsession, my Holy Grail. I was going to find that story.

It took years (I won't bore you with the details), but finally I laid my hands on "The Old Army Game" and at last we had all the Hogbens. Along the way Pierce learned that Neil Gaiman shared a passion for the Hogbens and would gladly write an intro. Pierce cleared the stories with the Kuttner estate and we were ready to roll.

Or so we thought. But even with Neil on board, the publishers we approached had a problem with the collection's brevity. I mentioned this to Tom Monteleone whose Borderlands Press had published both Neil and myself in the past. Turned out Tom is a charter member of the Hogben cult (also introduced via "A Pile of Trouble") and said he'd be honored to do it. I put Pierce in touch with Tom and...

So, this collection you've just read is truly a labor of love (and, okay, maybe a little OCD too). We hope you like the Hogbens as much as we do. We hope you're thinking *I'm glad they did this.*

We know we are.

***

Okay, I said I wasn't going to do another author intro after Lebbon, but this was a rewrite of an intro I'd already written for the novel many years before it's US publication got, well, the shaft. When Centipede Press decided to do a deluxe new edition, David asked me to dig it out and revisit it, which I did.

The Shaft

I first read *The Shaft* in ARC form around 1990. MacDonald had published it in England and the novel was on its way to America. Or so the author thought. The book has had, as the cliché goes, a long, strange trip.

I haven't known David Schow forever, but that's the way it feels (intended in the best possible way). I'm fuzzy on the exact occasion we met but I think it was when we were both speakers at the Dimension Awards ceremony put on by *Twilight Zone Magazine* back in the mid-eighties. We've stayed in touch. I've taken him to strange little NJ Pine Barrens eateries when he comes east, and he takes me to Hollywood dives when a book tour brings me to LA. I wrote a story for his *Silver Scream* anthology, and not too long after that he sent me a copy of *The Shaft*.

I'm not sure what I was expecting, but it sure as hell wasn't what I got.

> *Dope. That was how Bauhaus looked – strung out to the max. Blood and brain cells were dying by the millions in there. His mind was slamming shutters. Closed: Sorry We Missed You. His head would burst like a cantaloupe from the internal pressure.*

Welcome to David J. Schow's Druggy World, where everyone and everything is narcotized, amphetaminized, caffeinized, and desanitized. Where even the architecture is stoned. And where everything is thoroughly scrutinized through the Schow microscope.

This man must sound *El Deguello* when he sits down to write: No quarter. No prisoners. No deals. If the only other Schow fiction you've read is *The Kill Riff* or *Internecine*, you might not be prepared for *The Shaft*. Chronologically it falls between those two, but *The Shaft* is so much more visceral, so much darker – the perfect marriage of horror and noir. However, if you got off on "Jerry's Kids Meet Wormboy," well, then, okay. You know the territory.

> *The attacker possessed no actual face to speak of. But it grinned... The stress of the grin pulled loose a dripping gob of cheek and chin which smacked the floor with a meaty splash, exposing gapped yellow teeth.*

The Shaft offers a much more intense, moody, in-your-face style than the others, an acute sense of place, and a subversive use of the weather as a claustrophobic device. The prose is about as dense as you'll see in a post-World War Two horror novel. Trust me, this takes time, effort, care, and most of all, talent. The book is packed with imagery – *intense* imagery. Visions that other writers would spend paragraphs exploiting, Schow effectively brings off in a single line or two.

> *Tougher now, to moon over Amanda. She was gaining a sepia tint, spoiling on the shelf of his memories.*

When you turn to another novel after reading *The Shaft*, the prose will seem impoverished.

The action is set in the heart of a Chicago winter and revolves around a decaying apartment building known as the Kenilworth Arms. The point of view shifts between drug dealers (Cruz, Bauhaus, and Emilio), a Texan on a spongy rebound from a love affair (Jonathan), his caffeine-addict friend (Bash), a prostitute (Jamaica), and various residents of the building, including a cat who walks through walls. (A tip of the Schow hat to Heinlein?) The plot winds through the seamiest back alleys of Life in These United States.

Schow hasn't updated the setting, leaving it as a time capsule of low-end urban life in the late-eighties. For most folks back then the Internet was just a technogeek word, cellphones were rich folks' toys (and the size of bricks), and a certain cable station still played music videos.

> *MTV rages away on the video screen. Sedative rock, clichéd to snoozeland. Guitar rapists with big hair, throttling their penile fretboards and making faces as though what they are doing is **really hard**.*

But it's the characters that make *The Shaft* truly daring. They're richly-detailed and warty – not a bunch of Ken and Barbie dolls begging to be taken to heart and cuddled. These folks demand acceptance on their own terms, not the reader's. Which is a gutsy move on Schow's part. He had to know it wasn't going to work with all readers – especially not with all editors, if any. *The Shaft* breaks lots of rules, flies in the face of much of the accepted current wisdom of publishing. Perhaps that's why it took so long to find a US publisher. (We're talking decades here.) But I knew some editor this side of the Atlantic – most likely one without a corporate presence looming over his or her shoulder – would reprint the book.

That is, if the DEA doesn't get to Schow first.

> *He let the mix burn, then cocked and shot an aftersniff, pinching his nostrils shut alternately... Some mystery additive was numbing his nasal tissues; not the anesthetic freeze of pure coke, but more likely the psychoactive saltiness of procaine, or the coffee boost of benzocaine.*

I mean, the guy's got to be a cokehead, right? Not only a user, but a dealer too. Gotta be. *The Shaft* demonstrates too much intimate knowledge of the scene. He *must* be involved. Or so you'd think. Despite his well-known disdain for the drug culture – he's seen too many friends tumble off that cliff – he might soon find the DEA parked outside his house.

Some may have a problem with the Schow ethic of the unflinching eye, feeling a little judicious obliquity now and again doesn't hurt. On occasion I might count myself in that number. We've all blown lunch. Does anyone want to watch someone else blow theirs, up close and in color?

But the vitality of the prose more than compensates for the occasional excesses. (You did say you'd read "Jerry's Kids Meet Wormboy," didn't you?) *Vitality* is an apt descriptor, in more ways than one. Everything is alive in *The Shaft*. The weather is a character, and so is the Kenilworth itself. The building shifts, it twists, it chews and swallows. And at regular intervals, moist fleshy slits open in its softening walls, vaginal orifices daring you to return to the womb.

Long out of print in its original British edition, *The Shaft* has now landed on American shores. I believe you will find the long wait more than worthwhile. Because it's more than a book – it's an experience. So turn the page and live it.

***

In June of 2016, when Eugene Johnson and Charles Day asked me to do an intro to their anthology about drive-in theaters and movies, I couldn't resist.

Drive-In Creature Feature

Park-In Theaters...that's what they were called at first. The first official, free-standing, permanently located Park-In opened in 1933 in – where else? – my home state of New Jersey. They multiplied slowly through the thirties, limped through the gas rationing of WWII, but surged to new popularity with the post-war motorization of America, especially during the 1950s.

They became known as Drive-Ins and were great for families. A mother and father could take the whole gang to a Disney movie or a western or even a Doris Day rom-com without hiring a babysitter. If the kids (usually admitted free under a certain age) got bored, they could fall asleep on the back seat. For teenagers, it allowed them some privacy, and the phrase "passion pit" entered the American lexicon.

No wonder the drive-in numbers grew to 4-to-5,000 screens at their peak in 1960. They were cool.

What else helped drive their growth during the 50s? Monster movies, of course. Movies with *big* monsters – what the Japanese call *daikaiju eiga. I count 40 or so big monster epics released during that decade. What kicked off this blitz of daikaiju eiga (besides nuclear testing paranoia)? If you say The Beast from 20,000 Fathoms*, you're almost right. For the true answer you've got to consider what film helped get *Beast* green-lighted. I'll give you a hint: It had been a monster hit two decades earlier.

That's right. *King Kong.*

After its initial release in 1933, RKO rereleased *Kong* every 4-6 years or so. But when, in 1952, they presented it for the fifth time (a censored version with no chomping on natives or cops or undressing Fay Wray), they added advertising on that new-fangled thing called TV. It grossed $4M. This was unheard of. A twenty-year-old film grossed almost as much on rerelease as it had on all its previous releases combined? Crazy!

That very same year Warner Bros started production on a giant monster film called *The Monster from Beneath the Sea.* The script included scenes of a huge dinosaur rampaging through Manhattan, just like *Kong.* Was the greenlighting a coincidence? I don't think so. The film was released the following year as *The Beast from 20,000 Fathoms,* the same title as the Ray Bradbury story that inspired it. Following the example of *Kong*'s rerelease the year before, they saturated the few existing TV channels at the time with the *Beast* trailer.

That was when Li'l F learned that he was a *daikaiju* fan.

I was only seven, yet to this day I clearly remember the moment I first saw that trailer (in black and white, of course). It opens with an A-bomb explosion, then a series of avalanches, followed by a glimpse through an Arctic snowstorm of a huge dinosaur. But this trailer doesn't play coy. It shows you the creature demolishing a lighthouse (the centerpiece of Bradbury's story) and then rising from the East River to wreak havoc on the streets of Manhattan – crushing cars, knocking down walls, panic everywhere. Big white letters fill the screen:

THE BEAST!
THE BEAST!
THE BEAST FROM 20,000 FATHOMS!

I lived in Hackensack, NJ, a few miles across the

Hudson River from Manhattan. We received a total of six TV feeds at the time (cable TV was at least a quarter century away): CBS, NBC, ABC, WNEW, WOR, and WPIX. After seeing that trailer – we called them "previews" back then – I began frantically switching channels (manually, of course) to see if I could find another station playing the *Beast* trailer. Eventually I found one. And another. I watched with my face pretty much pressed against the screen. (Think the face-hugger and John Hurt's space helmet.)

Lil F was in love.

I had to see this movie. *Had* to. And I had no doubt that I would. Just a few months previous I'd gone to the Oritani Theater with a friend to see the new Martin and Lewis film, *The Caddy*, so no problem going to see *Beast*. Right?

Wrong. I'd gone to see *The Caddy* in the cool weather. This was summer, and summer was polio season. Polio is a virus that can cause a condition called poliomyelitis or "infantile paralysis." Most polio-infected people don't even know they have it; some get flulike symptoms and get over it. But an unfortunate 1% experience varying degrees of paralysis, the most serious involving the phrenic nerve. Without the phrenic nerve, you can't move your diaphragm, and if you can't move your diaphragm, you can't breathe. These poor kids wound up in big cylindrical chambers called iron lungs. (Think of spending all day, every day, lying in something like an MRI scanner.)

Polio stopped being a problem with the arrival of the Salk vaccine in 1955, but before that, movie theaters were considered dangerous. When you packed kids together in an enclosed space, you put them all at risk for polio. Later generations have no idea (polio has been controlled for over half a century) and many members of my generation – the first wave of boomers – have forgotten the plague mindset involving movie theaters in the early 50s.

So, no way was I going to see *Beast*. I was crushed.

(Don't forget, this was before VCRs and DVDs and DVRs. The only way you got to see a film after its theatrical release was hit or miss on a Saturday afternoon double feature at the local theater. Maybe.)

But I was rescued by...the Drive-In.

After weeks of constant pestering, I convinced my father that I couldn't catch polio in the family car, so he relented and took my brother and me to the local drive-in to see *The Beast from 20,000 Fathoms*.

After impatiently suffering through animated dancing hot dogs and juggling bags of popcorn, we finally got to the feature. A glorious night, an epiphany in black and white. I confess to puddling up a little when they killed the beast. Even at that age I realized it was only being true to its nature.

Spurred by the success of *Beast* (I'm guessing here), the Japanese shot *Gojira* and released it the following year. (It would take two years before an Americanized version of *Godzilla* reached US shores.)

In 1954 my dad took me to *Them*. After that, with the polio scare over, I returned to the indoor screens for the likes of *It Came from Beneath the Sea, Tarantula, The Black Scorpion, The Deadly Mantis*, the laughable *The Giant Claw*, the very cool *Twenty Million Miles to Earth, The Blob*, and so on.

But when I got my driver's license at seventeen, it was back to the drive-ins, sometimes with my girlfriend, sometimes with a bunch of guys and a couple of six packs for a gorefest. I remember the members of my garage band piling into a car to go see *A Hard Day's Night*.

But technology, domestic / international politics, and simple economics were conspiring to sound the death knell of the drive-in. The oil crisis of the 70s made everyone stingy with their mileage; they'd watch TV rather than waste gas going to a drive-in. And for anyone owning one of those relatively new VCRs, the decision to stay home was a no-brainer. To make matters worse, the oil crisis also spurred a national shift to daylight savings time, forcing drive-ins to start their shows an hour later, cutting off much of their traffic for family films. Add to that the inexorable rise in the value of their land with the attendant higher property taxes and the writing was on the wall.

Result: From a peak of nearly 5,000 screens in the early 60s, the number had fallen to less than 350 by 2014. All the beloved drive-ins of my youth are now either strip malls, flea markets, or garden apartments. Despite recurrent talk of a resurgence, I'm not holding my breath. The digital projectors necessary to show new releases these days cost a bundle and aren't feasible for a single-screen theater.

But do not let your hearts be troubled. Eugene Johnson has called on some of the best writers in the world to hold up mirrors to those films we loved. Some of the writers here are simply talented fans of drive-ins and creature features, and some have actually written those features.

I thought I had only memories of those days. Now I have these stories as well.

And so do you.

**

I first met Michael Bailey at one of the Borderlands Bootcamps and knew right away he was going somewhere. First off, he's a very talented writer. But beyond that, he has an entrepreneurial streak that led him to start his own small press and edit anthologies. His skill as an editor matches his skill as a writer. You, Human is a fine anthology.

Humanness

Define *humanness*.

Notice I didn't say *human*, because then you can get away with saying *Homo sapiens* and leaving it at that.

Humanness is the quality of being human, and pinning that down is a lot tougher. Because humanness isn't limited to a given set of 46 chromosomes. Some people have 47 chromosomes, some have only 45, but we still consider them *Homo sapiens*, still consider them human, because they have humanness. But what of a comatose patient in a persistent vegetative state? Human, sure, but where is the humanness?

Or look at chimpanzees. We share 98 % of our DNA with them. What if we spliced in some genes we've associated with human creativity and gave them a hyoid bone so they could speak? They still wouldn't be human, but they might be able to acquire humanness.

I think we can all agree that consciousness, self-awareness, and sentience – the capacity for subjective feelings and perceptions – are indispensable to humanness. The comingling and interaction of all three lead to sapience – the capacity to act with reason and judgment. Apes and dolphins are considered sentient, but not sapient. Sapience builds civilizations.

Of course, to act without any semblance of reason and judgment is perfectly human as well. Because, just as having access to data does not make one intelligent, simply having the capacity for wisdom does not make one wise. Consider our approach to death. Humans fear it and go to remarkable extremes to delay it, yet the vast majority of humans deny the finality of death, believing – entirely on hearsay, without a shred of hard evidence – that some part of them will go on for eternity. What is this pervasive belief in our transcendence? Hubris? Wishful thinking? Or, as the believers say, a natural response to the spark of the divine within us all? Whatever the truth, only humans possess it.

Humanness should not be confused with *humaneness*. Humaneness is a quality that involves tenderness, compassion, and sympathy. These are often considered "human" qualities and those people who don't possess them are called "inhuman." Which is hardly fair considering how the capacity for wreaking havoc on one's fellows is very much a human trait. "Man's inhumanity to man" ignores how, throughout history, humans have focused their unique tool-making skills on fashioning the most ingenious devices for damaging other humans. Few traits are more human than cruelty.

Or slavery. *Homo sapiens* is the only species on Earth that enslaves its own kind.

Or hatred. Animals can have fearful avoidance reactions related to instinct or past experience, but only humans seem capable of hate. Or revenge.

This is where the mind-brain dichotomy becomes important. The brain can exist without the mind (e.g., the persistent vegetative coma mentioned above) but the mind is totally dependent of a functioning brain. Humanness resides in the mind. The brain is ruled by two drives: self-preservation and survival of the genome. The mind can't help being influenced by those drives, but it can sublimate them to more refined – one might even say, "higher" – purposes.

The brain has no empathy, no respect for others, no sense of mine and not-mine. A male brain sees a healthy female of child-bearing age and nudges the body to grab her and impregnate her with its seed. Without a mind, that is exactly what the body would attempt to do. But with a functioning mind on board, filtering the body's impulses, most of the time that's not what happens. The mind is capable of empathy, but empathy is not a default state. If the mind's empathy isn't developed enough to consider how the woman might feel about such treatment, maybe it is at least cognizant of the penalty for rape. But if the mind possesses only rudimentary impulse control, then a sexual assault follows. (I'm simplifying, of course, since it's well established that the procreative drive is only one motive for rape.)

The health of the brain, the functionality of its neural

network, the levels of its various neurotransmitters, all have effects on the mind, and thus on one's humanness. You are your chemicals. But that's a can of worms better left sealed.

Better to move on to the dilemma of humanness and artificial intelligence. AI is all around us – our laptops, our tablets, the ubiquitous smartphone. They solve problems, communicate and interact with each other in countless ways at the speed of light. In recent experiments, linked computers have been observed to deceive each other, while supercomputers have, under certain conditions, been known to lie to their human operators. But they have yet to show self-awareness, consciousness, sentience.

Notice I said "yet." No one who works in the field these days and mentions the singularity – the emergence of cybernetic consciousness and self-awareness – talks of "if." They talk of "when." Vernor Vinge predicts it will happen by 2030.

So the question is: When the singularity occurs, will the mind that results demonstrate humanness? Why not? Humans designed and built and programmed it, did they not? But is being like us a good thing? We know it can be. We know of love, courage, heroism, risking one's own life to save another's.

But we also know how appalling and mind-numbingly awful we can be.

So why can't this cyberintellect be taught to be humane? Would it even need to be taught? The cliché is a coldly analytical, emotionless, self-serving intelligence ruled solely by logic. And on the surface that makes sense, since binary code doesn't leave room for empathy. But there's another kind of code, an ethical code, and it's not something we associate with troglodytes, but we do associate with humans, even close to the gutter humans like Dashiell Hammett's Sam Spade. Here's what he had to say in *The Maltese Falcon*:

"When a man's partner is killed he's supposed

to do something about it. It doesn't make any difference what you thought of him. He was your partner and you're supposed to do something about it."

That's a code, a combination of duty, self-respect, and a fundamental need to restore balance to a situation that's been knocked off kilter. If Sam Spade can come up with an ethical code, why can't a high-functioning, self-aware cyberintellect develop something similar?

We have no answers at the moment. And until we do, we can explore the question by telling each other stories about the things that define us as humans, that make us what we are and who we are. Fiction is perhaps the most effective way to illuminate the human condition.

For *You, Human* Michael Bailey has collected a richly varied assortment of fictions by seasoned fantasists as well as newcomers whose tales will have you searching out more samples of their wares (as I've already done).

The stories range from the bizarre to the deceptively prosaic, from a sly wink to a jolting shock, from dark to uplifting, rhapsodic to hardboiled, hopeful to despairing. Not one of them could be described as mimetic. They're all weird in one way or another, containing elements that do not exist in the real world – at least not yet. And that's a good thing, because the weird is what makes them effective. Looking at ourselves through warped glass or reflected in a distorted mirror often reveals the truth behind the façade, the face behind the mask. You'll find the fictions that follow engaging and insightful as they challenge you to contemplate their skewed views on the human condition.

Which means they're all about you, human.

***

In March 2016, Bob Weinberg emailed me about writing a foreword to a book of pulp art he and others were working on. I love the pulps, so I agreed. His health had been failing for years and, tragically, he died six months later. But the book went on, with his name on it.

The Art of the Pulps

"All life is only a set of pictures in the brain, among which there is no difference betwixt those born of real things and those born of inward dreamings, and no cause to value one above the other." H. P. Lovecraft

I love the pulps. The prose might be uneven (okay, execrable at times), but it has its rough charms. And no matter what the genre – SF, horror, detective, western, romance, masked avenger – the authors barrel you through the story at headlong velocities. I've been a fan since my teens, when the pulps were already long out of business and little more than a memory. They belonged to my father's generation, but they called to me across the decades.

I was thirteen when I read Wollheim's *The Macabre Reader*. I noticed that some of my fave stories in that beloved paperback had been originally printed in something called *Weird Tales*. I'd seen an ad in the back of *The Magazine of Fantasy and Science Fiction* from a local guy who was selling copies, so I went to visit him. He turned out to be legendary collector and pulp art aficionado Gerry de la Ree.

Gerry took me on a tour of his house and his enormous pulp collection. My first view of those covers was an electrifying epiphany. Love at first sight. They spoke to me. He had *Weird Tales* and lots of other pulps for sale at prices too rich for my pocket, but I was happy to hover there and drink in the images. He sold me some water-damaged copies for a pittance (which turned out to be the equivalent of giving a sample of crack to a potential junkie). I took them home and pored over their covers, amazed that back in the day images like this could be had for a measly dime.

As far as those images go, despite Lovecraft's opinion,

I've always found a *huge* difference "betwixt those born of real things and those born of inward dreamings." I much prefer the dreamings.

You could say most art is a mix of images born of real things filtered through inner dreaming. Less so with the likes of Vermeer and van Musscher, more so with the Impressionists or, say, Robert Williams.

The art you'll see here, the cover paintings and interior illustrations of the pulp magazines, relied heavily on "inward dreamings." The science fiction pulps, for instance, depicted fantastic technologies, bizarre spaceships, improbable bug-eyed aliens, flying buzz saws cleaving through aircraft, midriff-baring space suits and the like that never were and most likely never will be. They showed us the future, not the way it *might* look, but the way we *wished* it would look – chock full of bright colors and cool gadgets.

The pulp artists illustrating the more contemporary titles – the mystery, hero, and shudder pulps – were no slouches with the "inward dreamings" either. The scenes they depicted were as fantastic and as unlikely as those concocted by their science fiction brethren, although a little more twisted. With the shudder pulps especially, we prayed that no one would be subjected to the horrors adorning their covers.

After that early exposure I became a pulp collector. I have some complete runs – *Unknown Worlds, The Avenger, Famous Fantastic Mysteries*, and a few others – plus a large, seemingly random selection of single issues from a wide variety of titles. What prompted me to buy those random issues? The cover art.

As I became more familiar and better versed in pulp art, I began noticing how certain illustrative elements would crop up again and again on the covers of my favorite genres. It became a sort of game for me: How many elements could I find in each painting?

Sometimes you're faced with an image you can't resist.

Take this 1936 issue of *The Spider*, for instance. I wasn't a fan of this particular masked avenger (I preferred the Shadow) but this cover spoke to me because it combined so many tropes of pulp cover art in one scene that I simply had to have it.

Consider the composition. We have an intervening hero (this time a masked avenger) entering from a secret passage through a trapdoor to confront a crooked politician, an ethnic mobster, and a representative of the insidious Yellow Peril in order to save a helpless damsel in bondage. We have blood, filthy lucre, a dagger, plus guns and gunfire. The only tropes missing are nudity (*The Spider* covers tended to keep their females clothed), a skull or skeleton, and a wild-eyed madman.

I want you to remember those elements as you page through the hero, horror, and crime/detective covers in this wonderful collection. Here's your checklist:

An intervening hero
A secret passage / trapdoor
A crooked politician
An ethnic mobster
Yellow Peril
A damsel in distress
Some sort of bondage
Skull / skeleton
A madman / mad scientist

Your choice of blood, lucre, and weapons

Partial or complete nudity (shielded by strategically placed objects)

See how many *you* can find.

The sports, western, and romance pulps had their own sets of cover tropes, I imagine, but they never held my interest long enough for me to tease them out. Really, who could pay them any mind when they sat cheek by jowl with another pulp genre, the air-war pulps, screaming for your attention?

The air-war pulps provided another treasure trove of bizarre "inward dreamings." The heroes were WWI aces like Dusty Ayers and G-8, but it very soon became apparent that, to keep up with their more outré competitors, the aces needed to be pitted against adversaries more colorful than mere "huns" like the Red Baron and his Flying Circus. And so, in issue after issue, G-8 faced giant bats, flying zombies, sky leopards, giant birds, monster flying heads, manned flying bombs that presaged the kamikazes of the next war, and of course, the machinegun firing "Skeletons of the Black Cross." As you'll see within, the story concepts pushed the reader's suspension of disbelief to the limits while the artists had a ball bringing them to life on the cover. I kid you not, *Zeppelin Stories* even featured a story titled "The Gorilla of the Gas Bags" with suitably iconic art.

If you come away with nothing else, *The Art of the Pulps* should leave you feeling *good*. As you make your way through these pages, you'll encounter varying degrees of artistic talent – some highly imaginative practitioners, some more prosaic in their approach, but all *fun*. Most of these artists looked on their pulp work as ephemeral and disposable, displayed on newsstands for two weeks to a month and then tossed to make way for the next issues. They never dreamed they'd receive the beautiful, reverential, glossy-stock treatment accorded them here by Doug Ellis, Ed Hulse, and Bob Weinberg, all experts in the field and collectors themselves. I think those artists would be delighted to know their work lives on.

Before you move on, let me share one of my all-time favorite pulp covers. Its trope count from the list I gave you is only two (blazing gun and lucre) but it's so brilliantly conceived that it needs no more. And check out the header on the poster: humor too. Gotta love it!

***

This was originally commissioned by Clive Barker's people as an introduction to the third and final volume of a comic book / graphic novel series called Clive Barker's Next Testament. *They decided to kill the introductions, but Mark Miller, who'd been writing the series with Barker and was adapting it to a novel, asked to use my introduction. Well, sure. The intro is based on the graphic novels, but since Mark was scripting them, they are a perfect fit.*

Next Testament

I'm not on Clive's speed dialer and he's not on mine, but we go back quite a ways. Like thirty years or so.

I think it was 1984 and I was in London for some reason – the paperback of *The Keep* or something to do with the film, or maybe touching base with my UK publisher (Hodder & Staughton / NEL back then). I'm not sure. I do remember connecting with an editor at the time and he takes me 'round to some place where this new writer is signing his books. Seems Sphere had simultaneously published three collections of his short stories – *Books of Blood* 1-2-3.

Really? Three books at once? On the same day? By a newbie? I'd never heard of such a thing even with writers who were household names.

Well, the editor introduces me to this handsome, charming fellow named Clive Barker (really, how many names are more British than that?) and we all chat a bit, and then Clive goes back to signing. He's got quite a crowd around him, mostly pretty young women who look like secretaries and such on their way home from work. And after he signs their books, they don't leave, but hang around, staying as close to him as possible.

And I say to the editor, "Well, there's a fellow who won't be lonely tonight."

He sighs and says, "Someone really ought to tell them that they haven't got a chance in hell of going home with him."

Oh? Oh.

I promptly forgot about Clive (as I'm sure he did about me) until his name popped up a few months later at the World Fantasy Convention in Ottawa. I'm sitting next to Ace editor Ginjer Buchannan (Putnam / Ace was my US publisher at the time) listening to a panel that includes Stephen King (this will turn out to be his last WFC) who says something like, "I've seen the future of horror and it's Clive Barker."

I'm thinking, *Clive Barker...wasn't that the guy I met in London... the guy with the three books at once?* Then I become aware of this flurry of activity beside me as Ginjer frantically searches through her bag.

"What's the matter?"

"Pen! I need a pen!"

I forget if I gave her mine or she found one, but next thing I know she's scribbling Steve's remark on her program.

I give her a questioning look.

She grins and says, "We have North American rights to *Books of Blood*."

Oh? Oh.

Since then it's been reading his books and seeing his movies and paths crossing at an occasional convention (I remember him and Poppy and me on a panel before a packed room at the 1997 DragonCon).

And now, *Next Testament*...

...in which Yahweh / God / Allah – depending on whichever version of The Book you prefer – manifests the full breadth and depth of his magnificent psychopathy. In polite conversation, when the subject matter veers into religion, I often refer to the Old Testament God as "a bit cranky" and leave it at that. That's why I was so glad to see Clive quote one of my favorite Richard Dawkins passages:

"The God of the Old Testament is arguably the most unpleasant character in all fiction: jealous and proud of it; a petty, unjust, unforgiving control-freak; a vindictive, bloodthirsty ethnic cleanser; a misogynistic, homophobic, racist, infanticidal, genocidal, filicidal, pestilential, megalomaniacal, sadomasochistic, capriciously malevolent bully."

Dawkins is not overstating his case. Have you read the Old Testament? Check out this tidbit from *Deuteronomy*:

"However, in the cities of the nations the Lord your God is giving you as an inheritance, do not leave alive anything that breathes. Completely destroy them – the Hittites, Amorites, Canaanites, Perizzites, Hivites and Jebusites – as the Lord your God has commanded you."

And then there's the ever-entertaining, fun-filled *Leviticus*:

"If, however, the charge is true and no proof of the girl's virginity can be found, she shall be brought to the door of her father's house and there the men of her town shall stone her to death."

Christians will later spend volumes extolling God's "love."

Wick, the name God the Father gives himself in Clive's *Next Testament*, is a cleaned up and more colorful version (literally and figuratively) of the God of the Old Testament. And he has the nerve to be ticked off at the flaws in humanity. How could such a flawed deity (reread Dawkins's perfectly accurate description of those flaws), omniscient and omnipotent though he may be, expect anything he created to be perfect?

And how many times have we seen the worst of Wick's flaws manifest themselves in the worst of us?

Wick's most telling quote from this installment of *Next Testament*:

"I fucking hate free will."

That pretty much says it all. That's God the Father in a nutshell. Disobedience is what most often triggers the Old Testament God's rages – he sets down a rule, expecting to be obeyed, and then we blithely ignore it. Does he care if the rule is arbitrary or just plain silly? No! He's God, goddammit! But when we blow him off and do our own thing instead, he loses it.

The worst examples of humankind have an instinctive loathing of free will as well. The Hitlers, Stalins, Pol Pots, Kim Jon Uns, and Ahmadinejads; the statists, the collectivists, the fascists, the ayatollahs – they hate anyone who dares to be different, anyone who stands out, anyone who rises above the common denominator. Uniformity and conformity. Dress the same, eat the same, live the same, believe the same.

Although he doesn't seem so at first, Wick is a nuanced character. Those nuances are what made *Next Testament* work for me. As the story progressed I came to realize that Wick – God the Father – hates himself.

Bear with me.

At the outset he appears simply psychopathic. If

Lord Acton's maxim ("Power corrupts and absolute power corrupts absolutely") holds true, you could expect no less from an omnipotent being. But as we get to know Wick and see how he despises the flaws in humanity, we realize it's not only because he thinks we've let him down, it's because he comes to recognize that all those shortcomings we exhibit are reflections of his own flaws. He hates us because he sees himself in us.

Yes, he's all-powerful and all-knowing but – let's face it – he's a creep. And he knows it.

A self-loathing Yahweh / God / Allah – what a concept.

Clive also manages to find a practical purpose in the Holy Trinity: It's a system of checks and balances, for which the surviving humans in *Next Testament* can be very grateful.

All right. I've rattled on enough. Time for you to hop on and ride *Next Testament* to its apocalyptic finale.

***

After The Leopard Couch *was pubbed (with my intro) Tom Roberts asked me to introduce his pairing of two novels by Francis Stevens (a female write using a male name, common in those times):* Claimed! and Avalon. *Once I'd read* Claimed! *I pretty much forgot about the second, and it's evident why.*

The Call of *Claimed!*

I had heard of Francis Stevens (nee Gertrude Barrows Bennett) but had never read her (didn't even know until recently that Stevens was a pseudonym). The publisher asked me to read the two novels herein with an eye toward writing an introduction. He thought both the protagonist and the Lovecraftian overtones in *Claimed!* would appeal to me. Intrigued, I agreed to have a look.

"Lovecraftian" indeed.

Claimed! concerns a small box, six by twelve inches, made of strange green stone, adorned with a crimson inscription in an unknown language – an inscription that always winds up on the underside. The inscription translates: *To the great deep. To the abyss.* If you stare long enough, you can lose yourself in those green swirls, and proximity causes strange dreams. A sailor found it on an island that had recently risen from the sea in some cataclysmic upheaval, an island of strangely shaped rocky prominences. The box's original owner turns out to be a godlike being older than mankind, and he wants it back. The protagonists head to sea where they encounter this being and barely escape with their lives.

Now consider H. P. Lovecraft's "The Call of Cthulhu." What I remembered off the top of my head: A raving sailor, the sole living occupant aboard a derelict ship, is discovered clutching "a horrible stone idol of unknown origin" with an inscription in an obscure language that translates: *In his house at R'lyeh dead Cthulhu waits dreaming.* We learn that the sailor and his fellows encountered an island recently heaved up from the sea, an island of huge edifices canted at non-Euclidean angles. There he encounters the model for the statue, a godlike being older than mankind, and barely escapes with his life.

My first thought as I was reading *Claimed!* was that the author had been heavily influenced by "The Call of Cthulhu"... until I checked the copyright date. *Claimed!* had been serialized in *Argosy Weekly* in 1920, a full six years before H. P. Lovecraft wrote "Call." And Lovecraft has been quoted as placing Francis Stevens "among the top grade of writers."

Had *Claimed!* inspired "The Call of Cthulhu?"

I didn't trust my memory, so I pulled out the Lovecraft piece and reread it. The similarities are significant, but so are the differences. *Claimed!* is a science fantasy of the A. Merritt school (in fact, for years a number of critics suspected that Stevens was a Merritt pseudonym), with occult overtones. "Call" is horror fiction through and through. *Claimed!* is far more character driven, with a traditional three-act structure. In "Call" the first-person narrator is little more than a collator of stories and events from around the globe, leading to a world-shattering revelation. And then of course we come to the matter of style. Both authors overwrite in the fashion of the day (Hemingway had yet to put his stamp on American fiction) but Stevens's practical prose pales before HPL's frenzied adjectival barrage. Love it or loathe it, HPL had staked out his stylistic territory and was fearlessly exploring it.

Compare how the two authors contemplate a similar subject.

The most merciful thing in the world, I think, is the inability of the human mind to correlate all its contents. We live on a placid island of ignorance in the midst of black seas of infinity, and it was not meant that we should voyage far. The sciences, each straining in its own direction, have hitherto harmed us little; but some day the piecing together of dissociated knowledge will open up such terrifying vistas of reality, and of our frightful position therein, that we shall either go mad from the revelation or flee from the light into the peace and safety of a new dark age.

vs

It is rarely indeed that the mind of any man is exposed to the full shock of a great event or catastrophe. Fear is necessarily limited by the powers of perception and imagination. In the face of an event too monstrous, imagination grows numb, perception halts, and the mind is shut in as it were by a protecting cyst of sheer incomprehension.

I hope I don't need to tell you who wrote what.

Intrigued, I combed though both pieces and assembled the similarities in a table:

"The Call of Cthulhu" (1926)	*CLAIMED!* (1920)
"The bas-relief was a rough rectangle less than an inch thick and about five by six inches in area; obviously of modern origin. Its designs, however, were far from modern in atmosphere and suggestion; for, although the vagaries of cubism and futurism are many and wild, they do not often reproduce that cryptic regularity which lurks in prehistoric writing. And writing of some kind the bulk of these designs seemed certainly to be"	(Leilah's Uncle Jesse buys) "an oblong, bluish-green box about a dozen inches long by half as many wide, highly polished, but severely simple of workmanship. Its sole decoration was a single short line of characters belonging to some foreign language, which had apparently been incised across the top with an engraver's tool and the lines filled in with scarlet enamel."
(Atlantis and Lost Lemuria referenced)	"That is my honest belief in respect to the green box, Blair. That enshrined in it is a secret, indeed—a secret of the ancient peoples, who were wiped from the earth when the cities of Atlantis fell before earthquake and flood."
(Inspector	"Instead of

Legrasse presents a) "terrible object, yet centuries and even "thousands of years seemed recorded in its dim and greenish surface of unplaceable stone"…"its very material was a mystery; for the soapy, greenish-black stone with its golden or iridescent flecks and striations resembled nothing familiar to geology or mineralogy."	the regularly banded variation of hue peculiar to that stone, this had a curious, unevenly clouded effect; and if one looked long at any part of it, the blue-green color of that part seemed to deepen, grow greener and, at the same time, more transparent, so that presently one's vision penetrated far— far and deep. *But, great God, how deep!* Down—down—through miles of transparent green."
"The characters along the base were equally baffling; and no member present, despite a representation of half the world's expert learning in this field, could form the least notion of even their remotest linguistic kinship. They, like the subject and material, belonged to something horribly remote and distinct from mankind as we know it."	"I have seen an inscription in hieratic Egyptian which somewhat resembled this."
"They	"'Because I am older

worshipped, so they said, the Great Old Ones who lived ages before there were any men, and who came to the young world out of the sky. Those Old Ones were gone now, inside the earth and under the sea"

than life—because all the life that is was created within me—I in my own being am also alive.'"

"Several among his mongrel prisoners had repeated to him what older celebrants had told them the words meant. This text, as given, ran something like this:

"In his house at R'lyeh dead Cthulhu waits dreaming."

"It consisted of two short phrases set in quotation marks, and Vanaman judged they were meant for alternative translations of the inscription.

Moodily, he folded the letter and thrust it back in his pocket.

"To the great deep. To the abyss."

"'I was weary of men, and slept. Till, stirring in a dream, it came to me that the sacred thing flung away by Azaes was again in the hands of a mortal. Give it me now, that I may rest and once more forget your race and its ingratitudes.'"

"The great stone city R'lyeh, with

(The ten red cities sink beneath the waves)

its monoliths and sepulchres, had sunk beneath the waves"	
"He talked of his dreams in a strangely poetic fashion; making me see with terrible vividness the damp Cyclopean city of slimy green stone – whose *geometry*, he oddly said, was *all wrong*"	"'wakin', walkin' dreams of red cities'"
"Geologists, the curator told me, had found it a monstrous puzzle; for they vowed that the world held no rock like it."	(no one can identify the green stone of the box)
"On April 12th the derelict was sighted; and though apparently deserted, was found upon boarding to contain one survivor in a half-delirious condition and one man who had evidently been dead for more than a week. The living man was clutching a horrible stone idol of unknown origin"	(a sailor brings the box home from the sea)

"The *Emma*, in ballast, had cleared Auckland on February 20th, and had felt the full force of that earthquake-born tempest which must have heaved up from the sea-bottom the horrors that filled men's dreams." "Then, driven ahead by curiosity in their captured yacht under Johansen's command, the men sight a great stone pillar sticking out of the sea, and... come upon a coastline of mingled mud, ooze, and weedy Cyclopean masonry" "Johansen and his men were awed by the cosmic majesty of this dripping Babylon of elder daemons, and must have guessed without guidance that it was nothing of this or of any sane planet."	"Approaching at last the island referred to on my last entry of the 16th... The island proved to be perhaps five miles in circumference, being of an irregular, oval shape... Near the center, the rock has been flung up in ridges, forming rectangular and other shapes quaintly reminiscent of the ruins of old buildings. From where we stood, the illusion of ruins was nearly perfect, and indeed —who knows?—we may today have looked upon the last surviving trace of some ancient city, flung up from the abyss that engulfed it ages before the brief history we have of the race of man began."

The parallels are incontrovertible. One might even say that HPL took the gallon contents of *Claimed!* and distilled them down to a quart, added a generous dose of horror while upping the threat to humanity by a factor of ten, then christened it "The Call of Cthulhu."

But did he do it consciously?

I won't go there. My gut says no. He'd published "Dagon" in an amateur press magazine almost a decade before – a story about a land mass thrust up from the sea, inhabited by a huge loathsome creature worshipping at a carved monolith. *Claimed!* was Stevens's last novel before she retired from writing and was never reprinted until long after both authors were dead. So unless HPL saved those 1920 issues of *Argosy Weekly*, he would have no access to the novel at the time he wrote "Call" six years later.

How then to account for the parallels?

I couldn't believe I was the first to notice this, so I consulted friend, fellow writer, and weird literature expert Darrell Schweitzer. He informed me that the mythos aficionados have not been able to link HPL to the "top grade of writers" quote. It originated in a letter to *Argosy Weekly* signed by Augustus T. Swift of Providence, RI; many assumed he was Lovecraft, but further investigation deemed that unlikely. Darrell also pointed out that Lovecraft claimed to have stopped reading the pulps in 1917 and never once mentioned Francis Stevens in any of his voluminous letters and critiques.

So we have a good case against *Claimed!* influencing "The Call of Cthulhu." And yet... and yet...

The mysterious box in *Claimed!* is suspected of being a relic the times "when the cities of Atlantis fell before earthquake and flood," and Rick Lai reminded me that in 1920, within months of the novel's serialization in *Argosy*, Lovecraft penned "The Temple," a short tale about a doomed German U-boat sinking into... Atlantis. In addition to the Atlantis connection, "The Temple" involves a statuette that functions as an inciting factor, just like the box in *Claimed!*

Look, I know from personal experience that an author

doesn't need an older work open on his desk to have it influence him. When *Dagon* asked me for a piece on the first HPL story I'd ever read, I went back to "The Thing on the Doorstep" and realized with a shock how much it had influenced my story "Ménage à Trois" and the related novel, *Sibs*. Another instance: Upon reviewing some old Richard Matheson stories before writing a pastiche for *He is Legend*, I realized to my horror that Carly, the misshapen killer in my "Faces," was the little girl in Matheson's "Born of Man and Woman" all grown up. I'd had no idea at the time.

So isn't it a possibility, however remote, that H. P. Lovecraft read *Claimed!* in 1920 and then forgot about it? Isn't it possible that its subconscious echoes influenced "The Call of Cthulhu" six years later?

It's not a trivial question, because "The Call of Cthulhu" influenced the entire Cthulhu Mythos. "Call" is the bedrock on which Lovecraft and hundreds of others have built an entire library of work, inspiring films, music, videogames, and millions upon millions of words of fiction and criticism.

Perhaps you hold the stimulus for all that in your hands. *Claimed!* could be the spark that ignited an entire subgenre of fantastic fiction. Read on and see for yourself…

***

Otto Penzler of Mysterious Press started a new imprint called Penzler Books and its first project was the Classic American Mysteries series. He wrote the introductions to the first dozen or so. (And who better? The man's a walking encyclopedia of the mystery genre.) But he tapped me to do this one, for reasons made clear below.

What *Rocket to the Morgue* Means to Me

For the longest time I thought it was "Boo-SHAY." I'd seen the name "Anthony Boucher" a lot: On the masthead of *The Magazine of Fantasy & Science Fiction,* for instance, and I'd read his *Far and Away* and *The Compleat Werewolf* collections of SF and fantasy fiction. I was studying French in school, so it seemed natural to use the French pronunciation. Only when I attended my first Bouchercon did I learn to pronounce it "BOW-chur."

Bouchercon is an annual gathering of mystery readers, writers, and collectors, and I was confused as to why they'd name it after a sci-fi guy. But to these folks, Anthony Boucher was a mystery guy – he not only wrote mysteries, he reviewed them for the San Francisco *Chronicle, Ellery Queen's Mystery Magazine,* and the New York *Times.* Oh, and he helped found the Mystery Writers of America. So, yeah, he was a mystery guy too.

Rocket to the Morgue combines both these passions.

When Otto Penzler, the esteemed publisher of this line of classic mystery novels, emailed me saying he thought I'd be "a great choice" to write an introduction to *Rocket to the Morgue,* I wondered why. I'd never heard of the novel and I'm not known as a mystery writer. I started in science fiction, moved into horror fiction, and for the last quarter century or so I've busied myself with weird thrillers. But it was Otto, and it was Boucher, and the novel had "rocket" and "morgue" in the title, so I said I'd give it a read.

Am I ever glad I did.

A little background: the man born William Anthony Parker White did most of his writing under the name Anthony Boucher; in the early 1940s his Boucher pen name adopted the pseudonym "H. H. Holmes" (which is, in turn, the pseudonym of a late 19th century serial killer) to write mysteries, including *Rocket to the Morgue.* (Confused? Wait...)

Rocket is set in 1941 Los Angeles, less than a year

before the USA entered World War Two. It can be categorized as a locked-room mystery, but it's so much more than that. It's a firsthand peek into the innards of what came to be known as the Golden Age of Science Fiction, written by a man who hung out with the writers who forged that age and became household names within the genre. Not only did he know those writers, he peopled the novel with thinly disguised versions of them.

But I knew none of this when I opened the copy Otto sent me.

The first chapter is a prosaic domestic scene that introduces the detective protagonist, Lt. Terrence Marshall. He's soon faced with a locked-room stabbing that defies explanation. Baffled, he turns to an unorthodox consultant: a nun. Sister Ursula lives in the convent of the Sisters of Martha of Bethany and helped Lt. Marshall solve another locked-room mystery in their previous outing, *Nine Times Nine*. Sister Ursula, the daughter of a policeman, possesses a brilliant analytical mind that's attuned to crime solving, and is a fascinating character in her own right.

The suspects are many and, of course, each has a convincing alibi. But about those suspects...

The next chapter drops us, *in medias res*, into a clichéd space opera starring Captain Comet and his robot companion Adam Fink –

Hold on. Captain Comet sounded an awful lot like Edmond Hamilton's Captain Future from that period, and I remembered a whole series of stories by the Binder brothers about a robot named Adam Link.

Turns out Boucher has us watching over the shoulder of pulp writer Joe Henderson as he types out his latest novel while talking to his agent, M. Halstead Phyn, specialist in SF and fantasy.

Interesting...was this a tip of the hat by Boucher?

Then, in a progression of vignettes, we meet various pulp writers, all of whom have reason hate a certain Hilary

Foulkes, ruthless executor of his father's huge literary estate. All typical mystery fare until Boucher drops a roman-à-clef bombshell:

It happens during the opening of the novel's second day when a character drops the name "Don Stuart," editor of two magazines, *Surprising Stories* and *The Worlds Beyond*.

I almost drop the book.

Don A. Stuart was the pseudonym of John W. Campbell under which he wrote the timeless *Who Goes There?* (adapted into *The Thing from Another World* and John Carpenter's *The Thing*). In 1941, under his real name, he was editor of not one but two magazines: *Astounding Stories* and *Unknown Worlds*.

No question: Boucher is talking about John W. Campbell – my mentor.

You see, decades later, when I was trying to break in, Campbell was the only editor who told me *why* he was rejecting my stories. His rejections became my only writing course. I made my very first sale to him in 1970.

Imagine my shock to see Boucher's characters talking about this Don Stuart fellow – knowingly and with respect as the editor who was forcing science fiction to grow up. Which is exactly what Campbell did, starting in 1937, as editor of *Astounding*.

From that point on I began putting the characters under a microscope. Half the fun of the novel (at least for me) was sussing out who was who.

No question that one of the early major suspects, Austin Carter, is Robert A. Heinlein, known as "the dean of science fiction." The detective interviews him in Carter's office where the writer has a wall chart to keep track of all the interrelated stories he pens under his own name. Fact: In 1941 *Astounding* published a chart delineating the course Heinlein's "Future History" stories.

The scene also gives insight into how the pulp writers played the game. The average pay rate was a penny a word, with an occasional bonus of a quarter of a cent to half a cent per word. Austin Carter explains his use of multiple pseudonyms:

"So whatever's outside the series is by Robert Hadley—that is, in a one-cent market or better. I don't like to hurt the commercial value of those names, so whenever I sell a reject for under a cent, it's by Clyde Summers."

Fact: Heinlein did just this with his pseudonyms "Anson MacDonald" and "Lyle Monroe" (who have cameos in the novel).

Elsewhere, in conversation with the character named Joe Henderson – seen earlier writing Captain Comet space operas – someone mentions "annihilating galaxies left and right." Well, the writer who penned the deliberately juvenile Captain Future novels was Edmund Hamilton – or rather, Edmund "World Wrecker" Hamilton, as he was known.

As for agent M. Halstead Phyn, specialist in SF and fantasy, he might be Julius Schwartz, but I'm going with Forrest J Ackerman, an agent and a fixture around the LA science fiction community at that time.

The only writer character I had no feel for was Matt Duncan. He may well represent a real person, but I know too little about him to make a guess.

So, Boucher has Heinlein, Hamilton, and Forry Ackerman on stage, with John W. Campbell in the prompt box.

But who does writer "D. Vance Wimpole" represent? He's got crimson hair and blue eyes and can dash off a thirty-thousand word novella like most people scratch out a shopping list. He's also a cad, a conniver, and a pathological liar.

There's only one answer: L. Ron Hubbard. Before he invented Dianetics and Scientology, L. Ron Hubbard was a redheaded, prodigiously prolific writer, known for the speed at which he could compose, who sold to a wide array of SF, fantasy, adventure, and western pulps. His reputation was that of a chronically broke womanizer who wouldn't know the truth if it bit him on the nose.

An amazing cast. *Rocket to the Morgue* made me very happy. In fact, it made me want to run up to every science fiction fan I know and shove a copy at them, shouting, "You have *got* to read this!"

The mystery element made me happy too. I'm usually pretty good at sussing out the perp, and I thought I'd solved the second death (yes, there are two), but I was wrong. I like when a book fools me.

If you're not into science fiction, or if you think science fiction began with *Star Trek* or *Star Wars*, ignore all my backgrounding and simply enjoy *Rocket to the Morgue* as the murder mystery Anthony Boucher intended it to be. But if you're a well-read fan, or simply interested in the history of the genre, a double treat awaits.

***

This is how not to do an introduction. Hank Schwaeble asked me to intro his second collection and I agree because Hank I go back a ways. But as I was rereading it to include it here, I realized that this wasn't about Hank and his work...it was all about me (as you'll see if you read it). Embarrassing. I wouldn't have submitted it if I'd realized. Sorry, Hank. You deserved better.

Moonless Nocturne

Short fiction...it's different. It requires a different skillset – a different *mindset* – from the novel. I know excellent novelists who can't write a short story worth a damn. Conversely, I know short story wizards who are totally flummoxed by the long form. When I was starting out – shortly after the Permian extinction – I counted myself in the latter category.

I've always written. I can remember penning stories – haunted house and ghost stories, naturally – as far back as the second grade. But in my early twenties I set myself the goal of becoming a published author. I saw no way of making a living as a writer – not at a pay rate of a few cents a word – but I loved telling stories and wanted to make writing a part of my life.

With absolutely no guidance, without ever taking a writing class or attending a workshop, I began writing short stories. No horror market existed at the time so I sent them off to the SF magazines and collected a pile of rejection slips. But I was not to be deterred. I was going to make this happen. I kept submitting and soon started selling. Five cents a word when I was lucky, otherwise three cents. Sometimes nothing when the magazine folded before it sent the check.

I wanted very much to write a novel, but found the prospect of sustaining a coherent narrative for that long positively daunting. My first "novel," *Healer*, was in fact a succession of novelettes and short stories about the same immortal character strung out over 1200 years. Next came *Wheels Within Wheels* which was just as fragmented with flashbacks and side stories. My first real novel is my third, *An Enemy of the State*.

But I kept writing short stories because I loved the discipline, the focus, and the tradition.

Speaking of tradition, the short story is a very American form of fiction that finds its origins in Edgar Allan Poe. According to Poe, a short story can be read in less than an hour and must leave a powerful impression. It should strive for a "unity of effect," and by that he means that every word in the story is directed toward its *dénouement which* should land with an impact "unattainable by the novel."

His form of short story became immensely popular in the US, leading eventually to the pulp magazine era in the first half of the twentieth century. People who've researched that period say that at the height of their popularity in the mid-1930s, an amazing total of 150 pulp titles fought for newsstand space. We're talking general fiction, romance, western, mystery, SF, horror, "spicy" fiction, crime, sports, war, aviation, and on and on. Consider that each title published an average of ten stories per issue (some fewer, some more, but even the hero pulps with a "novel" every issue contained backup short stories) and some of these, like *Argosy* and *All-Story*, were published *weekly*.

Think about that: a short-fiction market in the neighborhood of 1,500 stories per *month*, every month. Of course, if Sturgeon's law holds true, 90% of those stories were crap. But I think I can safely say that if you couldn't place a piece of your fiction then, you'd never sell – anywhere, any time.

Things are different now. Short fiction is undergoing a bit of a resurgence in popularity at the moment but the market to *sell* it (as opposed to self-publish it) has contracted dramatically. The novel is the most popular length for thriller fiction (and under that umbrella I include political thrillers, horror thrillers, science thrillers, and so on), but the short form exists.

Case in point: Back in 2006, the International Thriller Writers put together an anthology called, surprisingly, *Thriller*, a who's who of the thriller genre: Lee Child, Brad Thor, Preston & Child, Rollins, Lescroart, etc. All great novelists, but some not so comfortable with the short form. I'm happy to say, though, that in her review for the *NY Times*, Janet Maslin singled out my story for special mention because it had "a beginning, middle and ending, as well as some neat tricks in between."

This does not mean I'm a better writer than my friends in *Thriller*, it simply means that I cut my teeth on short stories and was at home with both the long- and short-form thriller. Many of them were not.

Unlike Hank Schwaeble who is at home with any length, it seems, a fact of which I remained unaware until I read *Moonless Nocturne*.

I've known Hank a long time. We would run into

each other again and again at a convention in Rhode Island called NECon; in 2010 we taught a writing class together at the Pen-to-Press Writers Retreat in New Orleans. Oh, and we both like blues guitar. But I'd read only his novels before now. (If you haven't read his Jake Hatcher novels, you need to remedy that.) Somehow his shorter works and I never intersected. His previous collection, *American Nocturne*, also slipped past me. So *Moonless Nocturne* came as an oh-so-pleasant surprise.

This is a truly outstanding collection. I say that not because I was asked to write the intro, but because it's true. First, you have such a variety of time periods – the '30s, the '50s, the '80s, present day, even the future – along with an amazing array of settings: Chicago, Houston, Mississippi, Georgia, Florida, Africa, and more.

He starts you off with "The Yearning Jade," a classic noir that could have come from the pages of the rightfully venerated *Black Mask* magazine where the likes of Dashiell Hammett, Raymond Chandler, Cornell Woolrich, and others found their hardboiled voices. On further consideration, it might have felt right at home in the old *Weird Tales* under Farnsworth Wright as well.

"Household" is unlike any haunted house tale you've ever read, but nowhere near as frightening as "Everything not Forbidden." I found the latter the most disturbing piece in the collection, creating a deep unease that lingered long after I'd finished it. Lingers with me still, in fact. This is a future I don't want to happen. I wish I could say it's a future *no one* wants to happen, but that's not true. *That's* the scariest part: not the inevitable singularity that will present us with a self-aware artificial intelligence, but our fellow human beings who are all too willing to sacrifice their agency for a patina of security.

The next tale, "A Shifty Bargain," is almost comforting by comparison, despite the Faustian bargain at its heart. As a fan since my teens, I find any story with the blues at its heart irresistible.

I see "Haunter" as a companion piece to "Household," except it's not a house being haunted but a person. I think I would have flinched a few times if I were telling this story. Hank doesn't, not once, and that's what makes it such a wrenching piece.

"Deepest, Darkest" stars Hank's recurring character, Jake Hatcher, in an uncharacteristically non-urban environment: Africa. It could have been a straight action-adventure piece, but Hank isn't going to let you get off with something so simple as that. Be prepared for multiple dark twists and turns before he cuts you loose.

"Psycho Metrics" is another period piece (the 1980s) that looks for all the world like a cop procedural and turns out to be something else entirely. Leading to "Payday," in which you know something's coming but you just don't know what. The only story in the book I might venture to call "fun."

"Zafari!" closes the collection by transporting us once again to Africa for a zombie hunt. You think zombies have been done to death? So did I, but Hank brings some fresh ideas to the "science" behind the walking dead.

I've saved comment on the noirish title novella, "Moonless Nocturne," for last. This truly delicious piece moves the timeframe to the late 1950s and is my favorite in the collection. When you can mix cold war paranoia with murder and a hardboiled private eye slinking through the underbelly of a corrupt city, then add a soupçon of either the supernatural or possibly alien technology, you've got me – hook, line, and the proverbial sinker.

"Moonless Nocturne" presents a perfect example of Poe's "unity of effect:" no narrative wanderings, no aimless digressions; everything in the story points toward the dénouement.

You are poised on the bank of a globetrotting, time-travelling collection of bizarre thrillers. Dive in and start swimming.

***

Steve Spruill asked me to do the intro for the limited edition of one of his early novels. I couldn't say no, but I wondered...

Hellstone

Does it hold up? That's the big question when approaching a beloved book for a reread after a long interval.

As a rule, I don't reread books. The way I see it, there are too many good books I haven't read to waste time rereading ones I have. On occasions when I have reread a beloved book, it didn't always hold up. In fact, the reread ruined whatever fond memories I'd harbored for it. (Some do hold up. *The Exorcist*, for example, not only held up perfectly, it left me with an even greater appreciation of William Peter Blatty and his masterpiece.) I had no worries about the prose holding up, because Steven Spruill has always been a meticulous writer, but would the story still work for me?

So it was that I approached a reread of *Hellstone* with no little trepidation. The author had asked me to write an introduction and I agreed, but in the back of my mind was the worry that it might no longer appeal to me. I remembered little about the story beyond the fact that it involved the Loch Ness monster and that I'd enjoyed it back in 1981.

Hellstone is the author's third novel, the first two published as part of Doubleday's science fiction line, and this one marketed as horror by Playboy Press (which was having success in the genre with John Farris and others). But would it still work for me? After all, I'm not the same person I was forty-plus years ago – no one is. My tastes have changed. Also, I've been an instructor at a writers bootcamp for the last sixteen years and the experience has transformed me into someone who mentally line edits everything he reads.

Full disclosure: Steven Spruill and I go waaay back. Our friendship predates *Hellstone*. We met in 1977 at Disclave, a Washington, DC, science-fiction convention. My editor at Dell had arranged a launch party for the paperback reprint of my first novel, *Healer*. Steve stopped by and introduced himself as a fellow author who'd soon have his own first novel reprinted like mine. As we talked I learned that we'd both sold our first novels to Sharon Jarvis at Doubleday; he was trained as a clinical psychologist and I was in family medicine, so we found we had a lot in common. A friendship developed and, since we had similar literary tastes, we eventually became beta readers for each other's latest efforts. In 1997 we went so far as to collaborate on a crime thriller, *Nightkill*. We have, as they say, a history. So I had very good reasons to want to like *Hellstone* the second time through.

A lagniappe of the reread was that I remembered so little about the plot and characters, it was like finding a new book. I know from personal experience how time and technology can wreak havoc upon a thriller: Many of the problems my characters faced in a couple of novels written in the nineties could have been so easily solved (or at least vastly mitigated) by the simple presence of a smartphone. There's very little of that in *Hellstone*. Oh, you might wonder in passing why the characters are using analog recording technology like magnetic tape rather than going digital, but it has no effect whatsoever on the story. As for the specifics of Jonas Honig's camera, back in 1981 I knew next to nothing about optics and camera technology (what is an F-stop anyway?) and even less now. Knowing Spruill's obsessive nature, I'm certain he did a deep dive into researching the technology to make sure he was well informed on the topic and got the terminology right. But I wouldn't know. I still don't know. It all could be arrant bullshit, but that's not what matters. What matters is that he *sold* me. Twice. He sold me back in 1981 and he sold me again decades later. I totally bought into the technology then and I buy into it now. I have no doubt that Honig designed and built a camera that could see through the mucky waters of Loch Ness and expose Nessie at last.

I'd also forgotten about the novel's impressive sense of place – so spot on that you might think it had been written by an Inverness native. Spruill was only a tourist there, but truly soaked up the landscape. His descriptions are filled with love and awe of the terrain. The action is so inextricably woven into the loch and the stony hills surrounding it that the locale itself becomes a character. Urquhart Bay and the ruins of Urquhart Castle all seem so familiar after reading *Hellstone*.

The plot is complex. Not just good guys vs bad guys, but good guys vs bad guys and even worse guys – plus whatever lives in the loch. (And that's not a spoiler because it's clear from the get-go that there's something there. The question is: *What?*) Not only are you tasked with solving the mystery of the loch, but also discovering who's friend and who's foe. He had me fooled to the end.

But even the best plots and the most twisty-turny mysteries fall flat without solid characters. Plots happen to people, and complex, three-dimensional characters have always been one of Spruill's strong points. The two main protagonists, Jonathan Gant and Jonas Honig, are both driven men, but fueled by different needs and running in divergent directions. Add in Honig's beautiful wife, Sandra, another in the long line of Spruill's strong females, and you've got a combustible concoction just waiting for the inevitable spark.

Another thing I'd forgotten about *Hellstone* was how intense it is. The stakes and the body count keep mounting higher and higher, ratcheting up the suspense until it all explodes in a bloody finale.

Hellstone has been out of print for four decades – really and truly out of print – suffering the fate of most paperback originals in the 1970s and 80s: Printed, shoved into racks in drugstores and mall book chains, then yanked from those racks to make room for the publishers' new round of titles, to end up pulped or used as sanitary landfill. No reprint edition. No ebook edition once it became feasible. And that's a shame, because this is a gripping thriller. A lost gem. Thank you, Centipede Press for making it available again.

To answer my opening question: Yes, *Hellstone* holds up beautifully.

And lucky you. You get to read it for the first time.

***

This the afterword of the Gauntlet special limited edition of Brake Crouch's Pines.

Pines

(I'm going to assume you've read *Pines* – this is the *After*word, after all. Unless you don't mind spoilers, I suggest you read the novel before proceeding further.)

Let's start on the personal side: I've known Blake Crouch for a baker's-dozen years now. Seems longer. Joe Konrath introduced us at the Baltimore Bouchercon in 2008, and at first glance I thought he was John Lennon's clone. Seriously. Check out the Beatles' "Hey, Jude" video and that was Blake's look back in those days. Same color hair of similar length, same center part, same wire-rimmed glasses, same complexion. John was 29 for "Hey, Jude" and Blake was 30 when we met. Uncanny, I tell you.

He's since cut the hair and grown a beard and no longer looks a bit like Lennon. But back then, at first look...whoa!

Over the years we wound up at many of the same writer gatherings – Bouchercons, Murder and Mayhem in Muskego, things like that. Blake, Joe and I, along with Ann Voss Peterson, became a quartet who closed many a hotel bar with our heartfelt rendition of "Paperback Writer," carrying it into the lobby at the top of our lungs (where we were often gently told to "Shut the fuck up!").

But no matter how many songs sung together, how many times you've been told to cease and desist from such songs, how many beers or joints you've shared, nor all the subsequent hours spent bullshitting about life, liberty, and the pursuit of bestsellerdom, you never truly know a fellow writer until you've collaborated with them.

Blake and I have collaborated.

Back in 2010, Blake and Joe Konrath concocted an idea for a collaborative horror novel called *Draculas*. Jeff Strand was going to make it a threesome. They asked me if I wanted to come on as a fourth. I knew and liked all these guys so I said sure, why not? There's a limited first hardcover edition of *Draculas* in the works which I'm sure will include loads of background info, so I'll skip the details here and simply say that Blake added a bit of business to one of the maternity ward scenes that, quite frankly, shocked the hell out of me. The gross-out was something that would cause barely a blink if it came from Joe or Jeff, but Blake? (For those who've read *Draculas*, I'll say "kangaroo mother," and leave it at that.) So I thought, If Blake of all people is letting loose like this, I'll have to see him and raise him. Which I did.

After my work on *Draculas* was done, I felt the need to read some of Blake's solo fiction, so I picked up *Abandon,* a novel he'd published a year before. And was mightily impressed. This guy takes no prisoners, folks.

As a result, I snapped up *Pines* upon publication in 2012. The novel starts off with a creepy, *Twin Peaks* vibe (he freely acknowledges the show as an inspiration), which is all fine and good, but then it gets creepier and creepier, and you start questioning what is real and what isn't. I mean, if the crickets aren't real, what else is fake? And when you try to escape you're attacked by murderous, ravenous mutant bipeds that clearly want you for dinner.

Now you're totally disoriented. What the hell is going on?

But Blake isn't through screwing with your head yet. He introduces you to a man named David Pilcher who reveals the mind-blowing secret behind the town of Wayward Pines: It's the last town on Earth, and its inhabitants are the last humans on Earth. You thought you were living in the 21st century? Think again. You spent 1800 years in suspended animation. The world you knew is gone and those mutants that attacked you are what's become of the human race. Pilcher saw the end of humanity coming and developed the suspended-animation technology to save a few hundred people and resettle them in the future where they can restart the human race from the relative safety of Wayward Pines.

I was blown away not only by the audaciousness of the premise, but by the effectiveness of its execution. Anyone can come up with an off-the-wall idea, but only a few have the ability and the balls to sit down and develop it into a coherent narrative *and make it work*. Patrick Lee might be the only other author I know who can match Blake in that arena.

Next thing I knew, M. Night Shyamalan was developing it as a TV series that would cover all three novels in 10 episodes. It went on to become the #1 scripted show of 2015.

Sometime in 2013, I believe, Blake called me to tell me that Amazon was creating a Kindle World for his *Wayward Pines* trilogy. Kindle Worlds was a now-defunct project that provided a venue where fans of authors – mostly those pubbed by Amazon's imprints – could write fanfic and get paid for it. Immediately upon reading *Pines* I'd told Blake how much I liked it, and so he wanted to know if I'd be interested in contributing a story to help kick off the *Wayward Pines* Kindle World.

I'd pretty much given up writing short fiction by then, but this was Blake and this was the *Pines* sandbox. I couldn't say no. But I didn't say yes, either. At least not right away, because I didn't know if I had a *Pines* story in me. I told him I'd see if I could come up with something worthy.

What I came up with was "The Widow Lindley," which is set right after *Pines* and before its sequel, *Wayward*. And it was worthy. At least I thought so. And Blake agreed.

We'd collaborated on *Draculas* and later, in a different way, we also collaborated on "The Widow Lindley," because the story wouldn't exist – could *not* exist – if Blake hadn't written *Pines*.

Next up from Blake was *Dark Matter*, another audacious premise that tells a heartfelt love story that spans the multiverse of quantum mechanics. You don't see how romantic love and quantum theory can work together? Blake makes them work. So well that Sony made a pre-emptive seven-figure bid on the screen rights before he'd even finished the first draft. Then he was back on TV with his Letty Dobesh novellas as the basis of *Good Behavior* on TNT, starring Michelle Dockery. In 2019 he gave us the mind-bending time-travel tale, *Recursion*. I still don't know how he kept the paradoxes of that story straight.

I can't wait to see what this guy comes up with next.

***

Written for the unpublished limited edition of Thomas Monteleone's bestseller.

Blood of the Lamb

By the end of Chapter One you understand why Hollywood hitmeisters Don Simpson and Jerry Bruckheimer were all over *Blood of the Lamb* like ticks on a deer. Talk about high concept: You've got the clone of Jesus Christ for starters, but on top of that you've got spectacular miracles, a sociopathic Jesuit, a mad nun with terrifying visions, a Vatican hitman, sex, murder, torture, explosions, floods, and other assorted apocalyptic goodies including (perhaps) old Scratch himself, all tied to a millennial theme.

Yeah, I know: It was raining millennial books for a

while. But this one was published back in 1992, far ahead of the deluge.

I picked up *Blood of the Lamb* shortly after its release and was struck by the change in Tom's style. I was familiar with his science fiction voice, his horror voice, and even the Wise Guy demotic of his hilarious scorched-earth "M.A.F.I.A." columns. But this was different. This was something new.

Tom and I go back a ways—to the mid seventies when we were slogging away on our early novels and determinedly scratching out short stories for the sf and fantasy magazines. We weren't instant friends then, but we read each other's work and over the years we kept crossing paths at various Lunacons, NEcons, Disclaves, and Balticons (where he eventually was ruled *persona non grata*). Tom's lifestyle in those days had a higher chaos quotient than mine, but the more we talked, the more we found we had in common—how we were raised, politics, tastes in books and music. The final bonding ritual took place one night in Baltimore when we sampled the wares of just about every bar in Fell's Point —from And The Horse You Rode In On to Bertha's to The One-Eyed Cat and beyond. (I say "beyond" because things got fuzzy after Black Bush on the rocks at The One-Eyed Cat. One thing I do remember about that night was meeting the extraordinary Elizabeth who soon would transform Tom's life.)

Over the years I've found Tom to be a good-natured soul with an easy laugh, an excellent listener, and a great raconteur. On the flip side, his politics and social views could be called radical by some and he has zero tolerance for bullshit, with no qualms about sounding the alarm when he sniffs some out.

Oddly, as his lifestyle has stabilized with his marriage to Elizabeth, his writing has become edgier.

Which brings me back to my discovery of the new Monteleone voice. The writing in *Blood of the Lamb* was full-tilt international thrillerese with echoes of Ludlum and Puzo, but cleaner, leaner, with more telling imagery. I'd never heard this side of Thomas F. Monteleone, but here he was, rattling out those terse sentences at breakneck speed as if he'd been doing it all his writing life.

I think that sort of versatility is the hallmark of a true storyteller. A fair number of writers have only one voice; no matter what kind of story they're telling, one sounds pretty much the same as last, or the next. (Right now I'm sure you can reel off half a dozen names who fit this particular shoe.) Many of these writers are excellent, exceptional talents, the kind who come to mind when we capitalize the W —Writers whose reputations derive from their voice; they're deservedly proud of it, it's part of them, it pretty much defines them. Therefore their voice dictates the story. (At least it does for the smart ones, who won't touch a theme or character or situation that might clash with their voice; others less wise plunge ahead, often with disastrous results.)

But for a storyteller it's different: the needs of the story dictate the voice. And for Tom, the voice that worked in *Seeds of Change* would have been dead wrong for the Bradburyesque tone of *The Magnificent Gallery*, and neither was suitable for *Blood of the Lamb*. The style he settled on is neither too gosh-wow nor too ornamental—it's spare, propulsive, perfect.

Blood of the Lamb is a Catholic novel in the sense that it involves Catholic mythology and the Church hierarchy, with numerous scenes set in that tiny sovereign state in the heart of Rome known as the Vatican—scenes so tellingly detailed you'd swear the author must have lived or worked there in a former life. But it's not Catholic to the degree of *The Exorcist*. You had to be raised Catholic to catch and appreciate all the subtleties and imageries layered throughout that novel. With *Blood of the Lamb* you don't need any sort of Christian background to feel the full impact of the story of a man cloned from a sample of what is believed to be Jesus Christ's blood, trying to come to grips with the powers springing to awesome life within him as he navigates his thirty-first year.

Yes, you'll have questions about that sample of blood, and Tom answers them in a very elegant manner. You may even question, as I do, why Father Carenza seems to look more like a young Al Pacino rather than Dustin Hoffman. (Still waiting for an answer to that one, Tom.)

If I had a gripe with *Blood of the Lamb* back in 1992 it was that it didn't really end. We witnessed a gloriously suspenseful mini-apocalypse in the City of Angels, but the story wasn't over. We had questions: Was Carenza really cloned from the blood of Jesus, or from someone— or some*thing*—else? After all, is divinity carried in DNA? Is Carenza even human? Something wondrous and powerful and frightening is afoot in the world. Who? What? Why? And where is all this going? In fact, we sensed that the really good parts were just about to get cranking, but we'd run out of pages.

Lucky you. You're spared that gripe. Because now Tom has added lots of pages after the LA debacle—a whole novel's worth called *The Reckoning*.

But first you must start decades ago... in Rome... as a young, ill-fated Jesuit embarks on a secret mission...

***

Written for The Little Yellow Book of Perilous Stories

Who is Sax Rohmer?

Good question.

He was born on February 15, 1883 with the name Arthur Henry Ward. As a descendant of Irish General Patrick Sarsfield, he added that to his name at age nineteen and sold his early fictions as A. Sarsfield Ward.

But whence the name "Sax Rohmer"? In an interview, he claimed he came up with his famous nom plume by combining words from ancient Saxon: the word "sax" means "blade" and "rohmer" means "roamer." He used both A. Sarsfield Ward and Sax Rohmer interchangeably in his writing until the pseudonym gained international recognition.

He published his first stories at twenty years of age and kept up a stream of fiction and non-fiction (and even a clutch of popular songs) until an Ouija board supposedly set the course of his life when it spelled out "CHINAMAN" as the key that would seal his fortune. Though quite prolific (forty some-odd novels and volumes of short stories) he will ever be remembered as the creator of the infamous Dr. Fu Manchu.

> Imagine a person, tall, lean and feline, high-shouldered, with a brow like Shakespeare and a face like Satan, a close-shaven skull, and long, magnetic eyes of the true cat-green. Invest him with all the cruel cunning of an entire Eastern race, accumulated in one giant intellect, with all the resources of science past and present, with all the resources, if you will, of a wealthy government – which, however, already has denied all knowledge of his existence. Imagine that awful being, and you have a mental picture of Dr. Fu-Manchu, the yellow peril incarnate in one man.

The first Fu-Manchu story, "The Zagat Kiss," appeared in *The Story-Teller* magazine in the October 1912 issue. It totaled less than seven thousand words but it set the template for the series with its combination of adventure and sinister intrigue. The agents of the Western World are mere pawns of an evil Oriental genius who deals exotic death to those to oppose him. (Indeed, Dr. Fu-Manchu became known as "the Lord of Strange Deaths.") Nine more monthly installments followed, which were then collated into the novel, *The Mystery of Dr. Fu-Manchu* (retitled *The Insidious Dr. Fu-Manchu* for the US).

Coincidentally, *A Princess of Mars* was also serialized that same year, a routine practice of the time: A novel would be serialized in a periodical and then reprinted in book form shortly thereafter, allowing an author to get paid twice for the same story.

The book was an instant smash and was followed by *The Devil Doctor* in 1916 (*The Return of Fu-Manchu* in the US) and *The Si-Fan Mysteries* in 1917 (*The Hand of Fu-Manchu* in the US). After the initial trilogy, Dr. Fu-Manchu went on hiatus. But by no means was his creator idle. Rohmer kept up a steady stream of fiction during the intervening years – fourteen novels and four short story collections – until he was ready to tackle the Devil Doctor again.

The Daughter of Fu Manchu appeared in 1931, displaying all the familiar tropes of the series, but now the good doctor's name was no longer hyphenated. Rohmer would continue the series until it totaled fourteen volumes by his death in 1959.

Fu Manchu had a lively film career as well, played by the likes of Warner Oland, Boris Karloff, and Christopher Lee, among others. But, singularly, only H. Agar Lyons, the actor to first play him in 1925, portrayed him as Sax Rohmer described him – without a mustache. The "Fu-Manchu mustache" is a misnomer: Dr. Devil Doctor was clean-shaven. And the movie scripts? Just what you'd expect, with Fu Manchu portrayed as a clichéd, mustache-twirling (see what I did there?) pulp villain. Anyone with even a passing acquaintance of the character knew his literary persona was richly nuanced.

To speak to that point, permit me to delve into my personal history with the character. I'm old enough to remember catching an episode or two of a TV series called

The Adventures of Dr. Fu Manchu on the tube back in the mid-1950s. I also remember not being impressed.

But in 1961, as I was browsing a paperback spinner rack in a variety store, I spotted a copy of the Pyramid edition of *The Insidious Doctor Fu-Manchu*. I checked the copyright page to see when it was written (pretty savvy for a fifteen-year-old, right?) and the 1913 date gave me pause. I'd read the "classics" of weird fiction like *Frankenstein* and *Carmilla* and *Strange Case of Dr Jekyll and Mr Hyde* and found them a slog to get through. But I was desperate for something weird, so I plunked down my 35 cents and started reading.

I quickly became enthralled by this evil genius. I bought each new reissue in the series as soon as it appeared. The novels delivered on the promised thrills and chills and "strange deaths," but the character orchestrating these intricate plots was a revelation. Dr. Fu Manchu answered to an organization known as the Si-Fan, what might viewed as a collective of Tongs – Chinese criminal societies ruling the underworld. (Later he would rule the Si-Fan.) But he was not concerned with the more mundane vices that funneled riches into the Tong coffers. The doctor had his eye on loftier goals. The first was to banish foreign influences from Chinese soil. After that... "to crush what the West calls civilization." And he would pursue that goal by whatever means necessary.

So far, a clichéd pulp villain, right? But as you got to know the good doctor, you started to recognize certain quirks in his personality. Here's this guy trying his damnedest to kill you by the foulest means imaginable because you dare to threaten his latest scheme, but... he will never lie to you. Yes, he's a fiend, but you can take his word to the bank. If he says you are free to go, you can turn your back and walk away. His personal honor means more to him than anything else.

But his eccentricities didn't stop there. For instance, he sends Shan Glenville, one of his later adversaries who bested him, a large emerald and a string of one hundred pink pearls as a wedding gift, with a note saying, "I bear you no ill will... you are an honorable man; and I wish you every happiness."

I was only a teenager (albeit one already well versed in imaginative fiction) but I'd never encountered an antagonist like Fu Manchu.

Indeed, there seems to exist a codependency between Fu Manchu and his protagonists Nayland Smith and Dr. Petrie. These two Brits seem rudderless without their raison d'etre.

Finally, with the reprint of *The Wrath of Fu Manchu*, I had exhausted the entire Fu Manchu canon. The rest of the Sax Rohmer oeuvre failed to grab me, not even Sumuru, the distaff version of the Devil Doctor.

Although tempted to write my own Fu Manchu fiction, I knew I wasn't ready. But that didn't mean I didn't think about it. Sometime in 2004 Joe Lansdale provided the perfect excuse when he asked me to contribute to his anthology *Retro Pulp Tales*. I wasn't sure of Fu Manchu's copyright status, so I identified him as "The Mandarin," head of San Francisco's Dragon Tong in 1937, but there's absolutely no doubt as to his identity. I had so much fun that I returned to the milieu twice more and collected the triptych under the most lurid title imaginable: *Sex Slaves of the Dragon Tong*.

Now flash forward to 2011, to the St. Louis Bouchercon. In the dealer room, the Black Dog Books table drew me in with the cover for a forthcoming Sax Rohmer collection. Tom Roberts runs the press and we hit it off talking of Rohmer and all things pulp. Tom asked me if I'd care to write an introduction to a collection of Rohmer's earlier short fiction, the upcoming *The Leopard Couch*. I told him to send me the contents and I'd see.

By and large, I was unimpressed by most of the stories, couched as they were in lengthy, adjective-strewn sentences. But two stories from 1916 stood head and shoulders above the rest: "The Haunted Temple" and "The Red Eye of Vishnu" blew me away. Both concerned this enigmatic woman named Madame de Medici.

I am baffled as to why Madame de Medici fascinates me. Perhaps it's the way Rohmer introduces her, perhaps it's the way she winds through the stories like some exotic serpent. She is timeless in her wisdom, ageless in her beauty, and inscrutable in her agenda.

Who is she? If I am correctly reading Rohmer's hints, Madame de Medici might be an ancient Egyptian goddess, or the avatar of one. He never tells us for sure. In "The Haunted Temple" her last words are, "...perhaps I learnt that a poor dying shred of soul yet survives within me. Perhaps I relented – even at the eleventh hour." *A poor dying shred of soul...* now there's an image full of portent.

I asked Tom where I could find more de Medici stories and he told me Rohmer had written only one other: "The Black Mandarin," published years later.

The Madame haunted me to the point where, just like with Fu Manchu, I could not resist adding to the canon. I assigned her a central role in my Sherlock Holmes pastiche, "The Adventure of the Abu Qir Sapphire." More than that, the reveal of her true identity in the acrostic clues made her a major player in my Secret History of the World.

She appears again in "Infernal Night," a story I wrote with Heather Graham for the *Face Off* anthology. We kept her on the periphery and gave her only two scenes, but she's a pivotal character. (You may notice that, although nearly a century has passed since the events of "The Black Mandarin," Madame de Medici remains as young and captivating as ever. Hmmmm.)

But I wasn't through with her yet. I had to give her a star turn in a Repairman Jack novel: She saves Jack's life in *The Last Christmas.*

So, *The Little Yellow Book of Perilous Stories* treats you to the very first Fu Manchu story, as well as the Madame de Medici triptych. The Devil Doctor is renowned the world over, but Madame de Medici is known to only a few Sax Rohmer fans who have read beyond the Fu Manchu tales, or are true aficionados of pulp fiction.

Enjoy.

***

This was published in Weird Tales *in 2023*

Cosmic vs Abrahamic Horror

There was this Catholic boy who discovered cosmic horror at age thirteen and it changed his life. He'd been a devoted fan of horror films and fiction until then – the vampires and werewolves and giant monsters – but this was something new. Cosmic horror didn't spark the half-century-plus writing career that followed, but it certainly influenced it. And though he'd answered the call of the Void and left his old beliefs behind, he never lost his love of old school horror, which he came to categorize as Abrahamic.

The Abrahamic religions – Judaism, Christianity, and Islam – are the most prevalent on Earth, accounting for approximately 55% of believers in any of the world's many religions, and 90-plus percent of believers in Europe and the Americas, where much of the world's horror fiction is written. All three have their origins in the Old Testament which is the wellspring of western Gothic literature.

When I say *Abrahamic* I'm including many of the ancient religions, for it's clear that the Old Testament incorporated many concepts from the Zoroastrians (angels, demons, the seven days of creation among them), as well as the Mesopotamians' *Epic of Gilgamesh* (the Garden of Eden and the Great flood) as it fused the polytheistic pantheons of Greece, Rome, and other lands into a single all-powerful deity. Even casual study reveals a panoply of antecedent religions represented in bits and pieces.

Abrahamic sensibilities involve an orderly cosmos ruled by a provident Creator who watches over the domain He created because He *cares*. And because He cares, He has expectations of his creations. He demands certain behaviors, such as worshipping Him, and proscribes others, such as killing, stealing, and lying. He gets cranky if His rules are broken, and can be ruthless to the point of genocide. But in the end this is an *ethical* god who decides what's right and wrong.

Vengeance and retribution are major factors in much of Abrahamic horror fiction. After all, what is more Biblical than retribution? "'Vengeance is mine; I will repay,' says the Lord." Ghost / haunted-house stories usually involve vengeance, as do tales of transgressions into forbidden places. A rule has been broken causing an imbalance in the scales which must be corrected.

Once those scales have again been balanced we can go back to our lives. The circle is no longer broken. It is mended. We have symmetry again, and the human mind finds few things more satisfying and reassuring than symmetry.

The Bram Stoker-inspired vampire is obviously Abrahamic due to its fear of the cross. Its cousins, the zombies, however, are a heterogeneous group and don't fall automatically into one group or the other. The classic Haitian zombie is unquestionably Abrahamic, as are zombies that result from viruses or nuclear/electromagnetic radiation, because their depredations are a form of retribution. The Romero zombies from *Night of the Living Dead* however are somewhat problematic. Their cause might be the briefly mentioned Venus probe, but the voice on the radio tells us that scientists and the military are at a loss as to the cause. Corpses rising from their graves for no discernible reason and posing an existential threat to the living smacks of cosmic horror.

But as a rule, the hoariest and most familiar horror clichés like haunted houses or cabins in the woods or the sites of a prior atrocity or native burial mounds are steeped in Abrahamic tradition. You have transgressed by wandering into a territory claimed by another and so a toll must be exacted.

The slashers and serial killers – Freddy, Jason, Michael Myers, and their kin – are perhaps the narrowest and most earthbound horror tropes, lacking all breadth and wonder, yet the vengeance motif draws even them under the Abrahamic wing. They play God in a way, exacting a price for past transgressions against them or transgressions currently in progress (e.g.: promiscuous sex). Eventually the slashers get their comeuppance for playing God, thus restoring the precious balance (until the inevitable sequel).

To my mind, two milestones of modern Abrahamic horror are Levin's *Rosemary's Baby* and Blatty's *The Exorcist*. Both involve the intrusion of Biblical evil into our world. Why is it intruding? To corrupt us via doubt and fear so we'll abandon the Creator. But again, *why*? Simple: because we *matter*.

And there beats the heart of Abrahamic horror: *The individual human matters*. The Creator cares about what we believe and how we act. And the very fact that we matter earns us a special place in the cosmos. That exceptionalism, however, makes us the target of the Enemy, who has had many names through the millennia, but whatever it's called, its purpose is to corrupt and defile the Creator's work.

The Exorcist is perhaps the most disturbing example of purely Abrahamic horror because the Enemy is targeting an innocent. Why? Simply *because* she is innocent. Retribution is not a factor here. She is victimized not because of some transgression but because she has *not* transgressed. This is why demonic possession – the defilement of an innocent in order to sow doubt and dismay among the Creator's faithful – occupies one of the darkest corners of Abrahamic horror fiction.

Cosmic horror, on the other hand, does not recognize

innocence. Nor does it recognize any value in an individual human. As a species, perhaps: We're playthings as a collective, but as an individual you're largely irrelevant. That is, perhaps, the core horror: facing your irrelevance. You can't transgress, because your actions, whatever they might be, do not matter. Because *you* don't matter. You won't find people displaying Black Lives Matter banners in the realm of cosmic horror because it's a land where No Lives Matter. When you get down to it, the only transgression possible for you in that land is being born: the sin of existence. You might not be responsible for your conception and birth, but that doesn't mean you won't suffer for it.

Abrahamic horror tends to exalt logic. There's cause and effect, things happen for a reason – you may not always know that reason, but you can be sure it exists. Cosmic horror often doesn't make a whole lot of sense. You may think you know the rules but you'll soon learn that there aren't any, not really. It's a realm of strange geometries, absent symmetries, and paradoxical physics.

The sanity of the ordered Abrahamic cosmos is gone. The comforting scenario of a benign, caring Creator watching from above, His evil counterpart plotting below, while you wander through the middle ground, struggling toward you eternal reward – that's all gone as if it never was. The cold, dark cosmos is inhabited by inscrutable and inexplicable beings with their own agendas; some inimical to us, many others indifferent, but that indifference doesn't make them any less dangerous. In many cases we fall victim to them simply as collateral damage... because *we don't matter.* Cosmic horror paints a portrait of human insignificance. And as for balancing the scales, no scales exist. What good are scales when there was never any balance to begin with? Chaos reigns.

At its most basic, the distinction between Abrahamic horror and cosmic horror boils down to a very simple dichotomy: Abrahamic horror is spiritual; cosmic horror is materialistic. The possibility of rescue and redemption abounds in the Abrahamic, but does not exist in the cosmic. And hope? Fughedaboudit. Thomas Ligotti is one of the most influential purveyors of this view.

But even Ligotti tips his hat to the work of H. P. Lovecraft's circle and its mythos, the cycle most people consider the crux of cosmic horror. Those stories were written in the early 20th century, a time when science was pushing the Abrahamic sensibilities of an orderly cosmos further and further beyond the horizon of credibility. As physicist Steven Weinberg says, "The more the universe seems comprehensible, the more it also seems pointless." The tales of the Lovecraft Circle consigned the moaning, chain-rattling tropes of Gothic horror to the trash bin. They dismissed the Abrahamic religions without so much as a by your leave and replaced them with cold, hard materialism (despite the persistence of many in the circle in referring to the entities they created as "gods").

But the work of the Lovecraft Circle was presaged at the turn of the century by Arthur Machen's *The Great God Pan*, which can rightly be viewed as a paradigm of cosmic horror.

If you take the title literally and assume Machen is referring to the pagan deity from the Greek pantheon, you chain the tale to the traditions that influenced the Old Testament, thereby consigning it to the Abrahamic camp and robbing it of its immense power. Yet if you approach it with the idea that he's not talking about the cloven-hooved being in Barnard's famous sculpture, but an unrelated entity existing in another realm that was perhaps glimpsed by ancient humans who pigeonholed it into a more comfortable and manageable identity, then the story soars. So much is implied, so much left to be inferred, all of it unsettling in the extreme.

Cosmic-Abrahamic hybrids exist, of course. In fact they're quite common. The scholar who ventures too close to the abyss or opens a passage to the Other Side and pays a hideous price are a dime a dozen.

Abrahamic horror is not going away, nor should it. The rise of scientific knowledge gave elbow room to another, more materialistic view that competed but did not supplant it. Both approaches have their place, and the Abrahamic will go on as long as there are those who believe, just as its antithesis will persist as long as there are those who don't.

F. PAUL WILSON

APPRECIATIONS

*Varied pieces on books, bands, stories, and
people real and imaginary.*

Mary S. Wilson – 165

Richard Matheson - 177

Stringbean and the Stalkers - 181

Dallas Mayr - 184

Hannibal Lecter - 187

The Hunter - 191

Day of the Jackal - 195

'Salem's Lot - 198

No Reply - 202

How a G-Major-6 Made Me a Beatles Fan - 204

The Thing on the Doorstep - 206

Thomas F. Monteleone - 213

Mary S. Wilson

Back in 1999 I sat down and interviewed my mother for this biographical sketch. Written as an adjunct piece for an anthology called Mothers and Sons *that I don't think ever happened.*

Tata

My mother never fully understood me.

It was the monster thing. For some reason, I was born hardwired for scary stuff. I can't explain how or why, but I've always had a thing for monsters, would conjure them up in the most mundane situations.

For instance, when my father was out of the country – which was frequently – Mom would often ask me to lock the front door before heading up to bed. But for me, closing the door wasn't just a minor chore – it became a life-or-death mission because of this slimy, many-tentacled *thing* oozing up the front steps and reaching for the doorknob and I had to get there and turn the lock before the thing got inside. So I'd pound across the living room at top speed, do a flying leap at the door, slam my body against it, and turn the lock – just in time.

Mission accomplished, I'd slump to the floor, panting, heart racing, because for those few seconds I truly believed that all our lives depended on my getting there and turning that bolt in time.

And then I'd look up and see my mother staring at me over the top of her magazine wondering what in the name of God is wrong with this boy.

Where did the monster thing come from? Certainly not from my home or family. In my formative years not a single thing even remotely monsterish entered my staid, middle-class, church-going, two-parent, three-child, one-dog, Scotch-Irish, Roman Catholic American environment. I watched the usual kid TV of the day where you could find a rocket ship or two, but nothing that could be considered a monster.

Maybe it came from my father, because he seemed to understand, but no way from Mom... I know she worried about me. She'd never met anyone like me. Even as grown man, married, a father and a grandfather, she'd say, "Why do you have to write that stuff? Couldn't you write something *nice*? Like a romance?"

But that's fine with me. She was a great mother, the old-fashioned full-time homemaker, always there for me and my younger brother and sister. She reigned over a warm home where we all knew we were valued and precious, and where we all felt safe and secure... except perhaps at dinnertime. Dinners in our house tended to be an adventure because Mom always served two choices: *Take It*, or *Leave It*. We never had a Cheerios or Wheaties option for dinner.

She was always experimenting with new recipes and spices that my father would bring back from his trips to the far corners of the globe, and she'd keep trying and trying until she got it right. (Unfortunately, as soon as we said we liked something, that was it – we never saw it again.)

But Mom never talked much about her background.

Every couple of Easters we'd pile into the family car and spend six hours on the road to Massachusetts so we could spend a few days with her Aunt Mamie and Uncle Dick. Somewhere along the way I gathered that Aunt Mamie had raised her, but not much else sank in. I was a typical self-centered kid. Mom was Mom. She was here and that was all that really mattered; where she came from and how she got here didn't seem important.

So when I was asked to write this piece about her, I realized how little I knew about my mother's formative years. To correct that we'd sit down together at home, or I'd take her out to lunch, and we'd talk, and she'd write things down, and gradually the pieces began to take shape, began to snap together to form a picture.

The first revelation was that no one called her Mary as she was growing up. People called her Tata.

Mary Elizabeth Sullivan never really knew her parents. Never had much of a chance. Born on June 15, 1916 in Medway, Massachusetts, she was effectively orphaned at the tender age of 18 months. I say effectively because only her mother was deceased – from pneumonia while pregnant with the child who would have been Mary's first sibling; her father was still alive and well, but he left her in the care of her maternal grandparents, the Butlers, in West Medway. Then he returned to his own family in Hyde Park and vanished from her life.

She was enfolded in the arms of the Butler household, mostly in the care of its two teenage girls – her aunt Grace, and her cousin Mamie Dolan, another motherless child. (West Medway mothers didn't seem to fare so well in those days; Mamie's had dropped dead when she was six weeks old and she'd been living with her grandparents for nearly twenty years.) Uncles Emanuel and Jack Butler also pitched in to help with the homeless toddler.

They called her Tata. She's not sure why. ("Probably because it was one of my first words and I'd say it over and over.") And of course, this being Massachusetts, it was pronounced "Tah-dah."

The Butler house was a good size, but a bit crowded as you can imagine. It became a constant in the shifting landscape of Tata's extended family. The town around it exerted considerable influence on Tata's early life. In many ways West Medway was a world apart. Somewhere beyond its horizon the twenties were beginning to roar, but West Medway barely heard a buzz.

The town in those days was a Currier & Ives sort of place stuck in the middle of the farmlands of Norfolk County, Massachusetts. Route 495 rushes along nearby now, but back then it was horse and buggy country, the classic small town where everybody knew everybody, where everyone looked out for each other, and the thought of locking the door when leaving the house never crossed anyone's mind.

"People had cars, but rarely used them around town. I used to walk to school, or to my friends' houses, and of course I walked to the store for food."

But sometimes the food came to her – and not just the milk man.

"I remember the green grocer would come around twice a week to take orders, then deliver them later. Same with the butcher, and on snowy winter days I'd love to stand by the window and watch for him to arrive in his horse-drawn sleigh."

When it was too far too walk, she took a street car. The nearest movie house was ten miles away in Milford. "I remember going to the silent movies – "The Perils of Pauline," "The Sheik" with Rudolph Valentino, "Robin Hood" with Douglas Fairbanks."

The Butler house was often filled with people, music, and laughter. Neighbors were always stopping in. Sometimes Aunt Lizzie would come by with one of her homemade mincemeat pies. ("Everybody loved Lizzie's mincemeat pies – that was because she loaded them with brandy.") The adults would sit around the kitchen table, drinking beer, eating Lizzie's pie, telling jokes, and soon Mamie was on the piano and everyone would be singing.

West Medway was pretty much a WASP enclave where the Presbyterians moved in their own circles, leaving most others out. Not so much a prejudicial matter as the simple fact that much of their social life revolved around their big white-steepled church in the center of town, granting them more in common with each other than with the minorities in town. And so it transpired that the town's Jews and Irish Catholics wound up being neighbors and best of friends.

"But the thing we could never understand about our Jewish friends was why they buried their dead so quickly. A death was a big gathering occasion in town. If someone in the neighborhood died, word got around in a flash; ovens were lit, put-up foodstuffs were brought down, and the whole neighborhood got to work."

Before they could turn around, the deceased's family home would be crammed with fresh loaves of bread and pies and casseroles from up and down the block.

"They waked you at home in those times, you know, and the Irish wakes would last a good three days; and then after the burial everybody would be back to the house once again for more food and drink. Especially drink."

When Tata was six years old, her Aunt Grace married, and Tata moved in with her and Oscar Hamm, her new husband. As years passed, Grace had children of her own who became Tata's playmates along with other cousins. She grew up doing all the Norman Rockwell things like taking piano lessons and marching in the Memorial Day and Fourth of July parades with her Girl Scout troop.

"I dreamed of becoming a dancer, and I really wanted lessons, but Grace said no. I had to take piano lessons instead."

But it wasn't all Norman Rockwell in the Hamm household.

"I used to get whacked around by Grace's husband Oscar."

Tata was about ten then, and when her Uncle Jack heard about this, he moved her out of there. With the death of her grandparents, Jack had become her legal guardian.

Tata went to Erie, Pennsylvania, to live with her Aunt Mamie who had moved there after marrying Dick Kenny. This proved to be a radical change of environment.

"I don't remember any affection from Grace. Nor from my Uncle Jack. He'd buy you something, or take you on a trip, but never think about putting an arm around your shoulder or giving you a hug. Mamie was just the opposite. She couldn't love you enough. She never had children of her own so I think she lavished all her affection on me. I had to get used to that. Sometimes I think I hurt her feelings because I didn't know how to respond."

Mamie and Dick placed Tata in the St. Benedict Academy for Girls, but the Great Depression soon put an end to that.

Mom can't quite say the Depression went unnoticed by the folks in West Medway, but she doesn't remember it as the looming presence it became in other parts of the country, perhaps because the town's rural location had integrated a certain amount of self-sufficiency into its lifestyle.

The area was virtually town one big orchard, and almost every home devoted a fair percentage of its yard to a vegetable garden. Every household spent much of the growing and harvest seasons "putting up" or "canning" fruit and vegetables.

"I could never figure out why we called it 'canning.' We never once used a can; Mason jars were the thing."

"I remember stirring steaming pots of blueberries to make preserves and jams, and layering the tops of the jars with paraffin to seal them."

This was the way they'd always lived, and it served them well in the Depression. Perhaps they bought less meat, but no one in town was going hungry – your neighbors would never allow such a thing. Maybe there were fewer cars around, and less money for gas, but you walked everywhere anyway, so who noticed?

For a rural high school girl during the Depression, college was out of the question, so Tata made sure she took business courses at Medway High. But it wasn't all work. There was the radio, of course.

"Sunday nights we'd all sit around and listen to Jack Benny at seven, Charlie McCarthy at seven-thirty, and Fred Allen at eight."

Like any other self-respecting teenage girl of the time, she thrilled to the voice of Bing Crosby on his weekly radio show, but there was another she liked even better: Russ Columbo, the "Romeo of Radio."

"Russ Columbo had a beautiful voice and could have been bigger than Bing Crosby if he'd lived longer."

And of course there were movies – and now they had sound. "I loved the musicals, of course. But I remember seeing "*Dracula*," and hurrying home as fast as I could afterwards. I slept with Rosary beads around my neck for weeks!" (Little did she know that *Dracula* would be her first-born's favorite movie, one he'd watch dozens of times.)

During those years she found an outlet for her desire to sing and dance in the school's drama club and in the town's annual Minstrel Show. After graduating, she worked as a secretary for a real estate office and the local bus company, but stayed active in amateur theater, eventually snagging the lead in "Father Knows Best."

No longer Tata by the late thirties, Mary Sullivan left Medway for Worcester to work for the Worcester Street Railway. The Depression seemed to be on the wane, but sabers were rattling in Europe, and the Japanese had invaded China. War was in the air.

Finally, on a sunny Sunday in December, 1941, it came. And it changed everything. The protective bubble that had insulated West Medway from the Roaring Twenties and the Great Depression burst. The real world crashed in with a vengeance.

"Kids who had never flown on a plane were becoming pilots and fighting over Europe. Kids who had never seen the ocean or sailed on a ship were being assigned to carriers. Women worked in factories as riveters or made army uniforms. It was the greatest coming together as a nation we will ever see."

Mary did her part, volunteering with the Red Cross, typing up reports on local enlisted men who had been injured or needed assistance (thankfully, volunteers didn't have to type the death reports). It was at the Red Cross office in 1943 that she met an army lieutenant named Frank Wilson who was teaching logistics to army personnel at Clark University in Worcester. The university provided quarters for the enlisted men, but not the officers, so he'd stopped by the Red Cross to see if they could help him find a place. They sent him to Mary Sullivan.

She was taken by this young man who'd arrived here from Scotland with his parents at age eight, become an American citizen, and put himself through night school to earn a degree in accounting. He'd been on the verge of acquiring his CPA when he the army drafted him in early 1941. He'd had two months left on his hitch when Pearl Harbor was attacked.

A relationship began between the Orphan and the Immigrant. They dated while he was stationed in Worcester, and later at nearby Fort Devon. They were parted when the army transferred him to New Orleans, but always stayed in touch. Frank's accounting background and knowledge of logistics had made him more valuable stateside than overseas, so they shipped him around the country. But by 1944 the war had reached a crucial point. The armed forces needed every able-bodied man on the line, and Frank was expecting his traveling orders to the Pacific theater any minute.

But he wanted to marry Mary Sullivan before he left.

So they got engaged.

By proxy.

In September, 1944, while Frank Wilson was stuck in New Orleans, Mary Sullivan traveled alone to Union City, New Jersey, to meet his parents for the first time.

"It was a terrible trip. The big nor'easter of 1944 had been through the day before, washing out bridges and tracks. My train had to be diverted so many, I arrived in Grand Central Station four hours late."

Frank's parents were supposed to be there to meet her, but they had already been back and forth between north Jersey and Manhattan twice, looking for her. After a series of bus and taxi rides, she finally arrived at the Wilson apartment in Union City.

"They saw me standing outside their door with my suitcase and welcomed me with open arms."

Frank's parents, Francis and Nellie, along with Nellie's sister Ina, had been worried sick about her. But now that she'd arrived, it was time to celebrate.

"Out came the Manhattans – they loved their Manhattans, you know – and we all sat down and had a few."

Mary was utterly charmed by this poor but proud couple with their thick Scottish burrs and Old World manners,

"After a while, Frank's father stood up, made a little speech, and presented me with the ring. Frank's mother was crying, Ina was crying, and I think I was teary too."

She was engaged now but she didn't know when she'd see her fiancé again – if ever.

"You felt as if you had no control over your lives – people you didn't know and had never seen were deciding your fate."

In an abrupt about face, the army changed its mind and transferred Frank to an ordinance unit in Cleveland.

He managed to wrangle a thirty-day leave before he was transferred, but the couple wasn't in the clear yet. They had to obtain a special dispensation from the Catholic Church to get married because it was the middle of the Lenten season. That came through, and they set the date for Saturday, February 10, 1945, at St. Joseph's Church in West Medway.

But once again the weather barged in to make things as difficult as possible.

"A day or two before the wedding, New England was hit with one of the worst blizzards of the decade. The day of the wedding we had mountains of snow all over the place, cars were stuck on the roads, and the trains were all delayed."

And worst of all, trays of chicken á la king were sitting in the Worcester Country Club kitchen, waiting to be picked up and brought to Aunt Mamie's house where the reception was to be held, but no car could get to it.

"Frank and I were beginning to wonder if we were ever meant to be married."

But Mary was still working for the Worcester Street Railway at the time, and her boss – who was invited to the wedding – sent one of the company plows to the country club to retrieve the food and deliver it to Mamie's.

Finally, the ceremony. Not a large, fancy one. In fact, they couldn't be married before the altar, but had to gather in the priests' rectory because, due to the wartime oil shortage, the church proper was heated only on Sundays.

"I think my mother-in-law was beginning to suspect I was a Protestant because we weren't being married in the church."

And then the reception at Mamie's house. The two families hit it off wonderfully. "After dinner, Mamie took to the piano, and Dick did a soft-shoe, and Frank's father began singing. He had a wonderful voice. I loved that man."

After a brief honeymoon they had to part because Frank's leave was up. Mary couldn't quit her job at the Worcester Street Railway until her replacement was trained, and Frank was reassigned to Washington, DC. So one weekend she'd travel south to stay with him, and the next he'd travel north to be with her. In April, 1945 he was transferred back to Ohio where Mary joined him. The Orphan and the Immigrant moved into their first home, a furnished apartment in Cleveland.

Frank was finally discharged in December, 1945, and they moved back east. Mary was pregnant with her first child by then, but no housing was available anywhere. Every GI who had been discharged was back home and looking for a place to live. Every apartment had a waiting list, and houses were being snapped up before ground was broken. So Frank and Mary had to move into his parents' tiny apartment in Union City.

In May of 1946, Francis Paul Wilson, Jr. (yours truly) was born, joining the leading edge of the great postwar Baby Boom, and Mary Sullivan Wilson became Mom.

Yes, my first name is Francis, but I've never been called Francis or Fran or Frank. We already had one Frank in the house, so they called me by my middle name. I'm told I was trouble even before I was born. The obstetricians were overworked due to the baby boom, with the obstetrical wards filled beyond capacity. They let me gestate a little too long, and my nine-and-a-half pound birth weight made for a long and very difficult delivery (my mother rarely missed a chance to complain about the size of my head, usually at the most inopportune time). But both of us survived the ordeal

In 1946 my folks bought a house in Hackensack, NJ (named after an Indian tribe) in a neighborhood filled with other newly married GIs, all with kids of their own. My brother Peter was born there in 1948, and little Mary came along in 1952. (Yes, we were Peter, Paul, and Mary before there was Peter, Paul & Mary.)

In her own way, my sister Mary carried on the Tata tradition: As a toddler she pronounced "hello" as "lu-lu." Inevitably she became known as "Lulu."

While all this was going on, my father took a job as a CPA with one of the big six accounting firms, but soon was recruited by Charles Pfizer, Inc., a chemical and pharmaceutical company. He helped get its international division up and running, and remained there the rest of his working life (something almost unheard of these days). His job with Pfizer International kept him on the run, traveling the world to set up a global corporation. At first he was mainly flying to Panama and Brussels, but as the division expanded its reach, he'd be off to India, Thailand, Manila, and all along the Pacific Rim. All of which meant that he wasn't around a lot, and much the burden of raising the three of us was shouldered by my mother.

A woman from a more sheltered background might have felt sorry for herself. But Mom had been Tata, don't forget. The loss of her parents, life in a succession of homes, the Great Depression, and World War Two had taught Mary Sullivan Wilson resilience and self-reliance.

And so it went. We typified an American family struggling through the decades, surviving hernias, tonsillectomies, appendectomies, and the like.

But the big worry in the early fifties was polio.

It's hard for those who didn't live through the epidemics of the post-war 1940s and early 1950s to appreciate the havoc wrought by poliovirus in its heyday. Most of the time it caused a mild flu-like syndrome and three days later you were fine. But if you were among the unlucky ten per cent in whom it invaded the nervous system, you could wind up in an iron lung. Or paralyzed for life. Or dead.

And the overwhelming majority of its victims were children. AIDS paranoia is small stuff compared to polio: No reckless behavior, no dirty needle, no tainted transfusion, no unsafe sex required. Polio targeted kids, and usually hit them while they were doing normal kid stuff.

Mom was terrified that someone might sneeze on one of us in the supermarket and a week later Pete or Lu or I would be in an iron lung.

The fifties rolled on, and the Wilsons with them. Later in the decade, Mom, the veteran Bing Crosby and Russ Columbo fan, was utterly baffled by the appeal of a raucous new music called rock 'n' roll. The long hair of the sixties brought equal bafflement, but the big terror of that decade was the war in Vietnam. Fortunately I was in medical school and Peter was turned down because he was underweight.

The seventies and eighties brought marriages and grandchildren and Dad's retirement, allowing them the time to travel the world.

And by the nineties, Tata was no more. The last person who had ever called her that is long gone. But she lived on as Mom and as Nana. She and Dad divided their time between homes in Florida and New Jersey. They have five grandchildren, and one great-grandson.

She's proud of all of us. Lu is a systems analyst, Peter is an attorney, and I'm a writer-physician. I still practice medicine two days a week, but the rest of the time I spend writing. Much of what I write involves monsters of one sort or another.

Mom is proud of my success as a writer, but she still doesn't get the monster thing.

[Addendum: Mary Sullivan Wilson died in 2012 at age 96.]

***

I wrote this in 2008 for The Richard Matheson Companion. *I meant every word. Still do.*

The *SHOCK* of Recognition

My first knowing contact with Richard Matheson's fiction came in the summer of 1961. I say *knowing* because I'd had many previous contacts without connecting them to his name. (Like any kid, credits on TV or in the movies existed to be ignored, a penance you paid before getting to the good stuff, the stuff you came for.)

While browsing the paperback rack of the local drugstore, looking for something to read, a book caught my eye. It had a cool cover very similar to my beloved Ballantine SF paperbacks (later I'd learn the artist's name was Richard Powers) but it was the title that made me snatch it from its slot.

Shock!

Could this be another horror anthology like *The Graveyard Reader* or *Deals with the Devil*? I couldn't get enough of those. But no, this was by just one guy name Richard Matheson. Never heard of him.

Still...it was titled *Shock!*

So I checked out the back cover where, instead of telling me about the contents, it asked questions.

HAVE YOU EVER WONDERED –
Who is really at the other end when you pick up
a ringing phone and hear a soft, breathing silence?
Why do quiet little men suddenly go berserk?
Where do dirty jokes come from?
Why do traffic cops seem so anxious to catch you speeding?
How do national safety councils get their
holiday casualty figures?
Why is Los Angeles County growing so rapidly – so purposefully?

Huh? This didn't sound like horror. Or even SF. The bottom of the back cover called it "a collection of fiction fantastique," whatever that was. Well, the rack held nothing else of interest so I plunked down 35 cents and took it home.

Am I ever glad I did. Of course I eventually would have discovered Richard Matheson, but I'm glad it was sooner rather than later.

Shock! was a revelation. To this point in my experience, what little horror fiction I could find had been peopled with eccentric professors or intrepid explorers or mad scientists. This guy Matheson's stories concerned everyday people in everyday lives in everyday towns and cities – people I might know, people who might live next door, people like – *gasp!* – my folks.

A few of the stories left me cold – like the one about the relentless growth of LA County – because I had no frame of reference for them. But the rest were creepy and disturbing. (One of them, "Dance of the Dead," recently showed up on Showtime's *Masters of Horror*.) I read them in order, and that turned out to be a good thing because the last piece in the book was "The Distributor."

I've gone on at length in *My Favorite Horror Story* about my love affair with "The Distributor," so I'll not repeat myself here. I will say that I remember being a bit disappointed at the ending because it offered no closure. Like most people, teenagers especially, I liked stories with a beginning, middle, and an end. This one didn't really end. The guy in the story simply packed up and moved on to the next town. Who did he work for? Why was he causing all this trouble?

Dumb story.

But I found myself thinking about it when I went to sleep and again when I woke up. Who...? Why...? I must have missed something. So I read it again. And again.

I'd already had my I-want-to-write-horror epiphany years earlier after reading Ray Bradbury's "The October Game," so perhaps I was subconsciously on the lookout for techniques to disturb readers. Bradbury's story is filled with emotion and slowly growing menace, and then ends with a karate chop to the throat that leaves you gasping.

"The Distributor" takes a different tack. It is utterly devoid of emotion and leaves you unsettled and scratching your head.

I learned something from Richard Matheson then. I realized a story that leaves readers wondering will follow them around long after they've closed the cover. But beware:

It's a delicate balance. Leave too many questions and you have angry, dissatisfied readers who feel the author has let them down. Leave just enough uncertainty and the story will cling like a bad debt.

Shock! proved to be a tipping point. Thereafter everywhere I looked I saw Richard Matheson's name. I'd spot it in *Thriller* and *Twilight Zone* credits (Oh my God, he wrote that one about the demon on the wing of the plane!), rerun movie credits (*The Incredible Shrinking Man*), and on new movies as well (*The Pit and the Pendulum* and *Master of the World*).

But it was the written word I craved.

Shock! sent me on a Matheson hunt. *Shock II* and *Shock III* wouldn't be published for years, and hardly anything of his was in print. I did find a used copy of the *Shores of Space* with the terrifying "Little Girl Lost." Then Bantam reprinted an earlier collection, *Third from the Sun*, wherein I found the horrifying and heartbreaking "Born of Man and Woman," parts of which I stole decades later for my own "Faces." (Unconscious theft, I swear. When I reread "Born of Man and Woman" sometime in the mid-90s I realized what I'd done. The story still moves me. So let me cop my plea: My guess is that "Born of Man and Woman" left an open, festering wound in my psyche, and perhaps the only way I could heal it was to write about the adult that poor, deformed child would become.)

So I owe you, Richard Matheson. Not just for "Faces," but for showing this would-be writer that horror need not drip ichor, need not befall eccentrics seeking Forbidden Knowledge in ancient ruins. It could happen next door, or be found simply by peeking behind the veil of everyday reality. I owe you too for demonstrating again and again that what you don't say can be as important as what you do say.

Thank you.

***

This dates back to 1998. I wrote it for a Jersey Shore giveaway rag called Shore View *as both an appreciation of my favorite blues band and as liner notes for the group's CD ("Hey-Hey").*

STRINGBEAN AND THE STALKERS
(at Ragin Cajun, Belmar, NJ)

The reactions run from "God, what are these guys doin' playing *here*?" to "How long has this been going on and why hasn't anybody told me about it?"

To answer the second question: It's been going on every Sunday night since mid-1996. As for the first question: Damned if I know. But I don't ask questions. I say nothing and just hope they never stop playing *here*.

Here is Ragin' Cajun, a funky little 50-seat restaurant in an old converted house on Rte. 35 across from the marina in Belmar, NJ, around the corner and down the road apiece from the legendary Jason's. That's right, a restaurant – not a bar, not a night club – and it doesn't even have a liquor license (it's BYO). What it does have is the best Cajun food this side of the Delta; that's the draw Monday through Saturday. But on Sunday nights, owner-chef Tracey Orsi provides another reason to be there: Stringbean and the Stalkers.

A typical Sunday night...

The Ragin' Cajun crowd is an eclectic bunch, spanning the shore's social strata: yachtsmen and fishermen wandering over from the marina, sun worshippers trekking from the beach, bohos and bikers, matrons and mademoiselles, Deadheads and demimondaines.

You can count on Ken Sorensen, aka Stringbean Walker, setting up early in a corner of the front room. After all, it's his group. He's tall, tan, and lean with sun-streaked blond hair. You see him and you think, Hell, with the beach only half a dozen blocks away, this must be a surfer band. Then he unpacks all these Hohners from his little black doctor bag and arranges them on the mixer box. When he fits one into the Strnad mike and clips that into the harp rack around his neck, you start to get the idea you're not going to hear Dick Dale covers.

Then Sonny Kenn starts setting up his gear. It's the Gibson hollow body tonight, but sometimes it's a white Strat. With his slicked back hair and long sideburns, Sonny could step onto the set of *Grease* and blend right into the cast. Okay, you think, so it's gonna be rockabilly.

The bassist is usually Dave Meyers, and he's got this serene air, this beatific smile. So maybe we're gonna do a Woodstock thing?

The drummer tends to be whoever doesn't have a gig somewhere else, and his kit rarely goes beyond brushes, snare, high hat, and ride. And if he's late they start without him. When the clock hits seven, Stringbean and the Stalkers launch into their opener, Jimmy Reed's mournful, languid "You Don't Have to Go," and then all questions are answered:

It's a blues thing.

Kenny Sorensen plays a sweet, sweet harp. He's played a lot with Billy Hector and opened for the likes of B.B. King, James Cotton, and Dickie Betts. He *owns* that harp: it wails, howls, moans, raves, rants, and sometimes you'd swear it was an accordion. You just know he wore out the grooves on his Sonny Boy Williamson and Little Walter records as he was growing up, but Charlie Musselwhite and John Mayall are in there as well. Watch closely you notice he's fingerpicking a counterpoint melody on his Guild acoustic as he blows.

Jersey Shore blues legend Sonny Kenn is on lead and he's one of those rare guitarists who knows how to accompany a harmonica. Plus, he's got so many styles tucked away in his repertoire that no song sounds the same twice. One time it could be Jimmy Rogers, then Elmore James, or Scotty Moore, or Buddy Guy or something completely out of left field. (Hell, I *know* I've heard him sneak Link Wray into a jam.) But those are simply influences – Sonny sounds like Sonny Kenn, which means any which way he pleases.

This is the real thing, Delta and Chicago blues, roots music played with exquisite skill and feeling, but without slavish aping of the originals. Serious blues by guys who are serious about the music but not overly serious about themselves. They toss in country blues for kicks (how about "Birmingham Daddy" from *Gene Autry Sings the Blues*?) and borrow from the Grateful Dead and Bob Dylan when it suits them. (After hearing Stringbean and the Stalkers' take on "I Shall Be Released" I can no longer listen to the original.)

Look up "laid back" in *Webster's Colloquial Dictionary* and I do believe it says, "See Stringbean and the Stalkers." No showboating here. No windmill strums, no agonized expressions to show how *really hard* it is to wring those notes from your ax. Everyone's sitting, either on chairs or amps, and playing low (after all, the waitresses do have to take dinner orders). The music is up front, not the players. They tend to keep it down tempo, the songs leaning toward the likes of "Honest I do," "Long Distance Call," and "The Sky is Crying," but eventually the Prozac kicks in and they shake up the place with a smoking version of Elmore James's "Mother-in-Law Blues" or an extended version of the Dead's "Deep Ellum Blues" (where the jam often strays into "East-West" territory).

Stringbean's pretty much laid back about his personnel as well. You never know who's going to sit in. Chris Baron of the Spin Doctors, Buddy Cage of New Riders, Marc Muller from the Shania Twain band, they've all taken turns from time to time. When Neil Thomas isn't on the road for zydeco band Loup Garou, he trains down from NYC and brings his accordion. Sometimes it gets a little crowded. In addition to the core four, I've seen a squeeze box, a mandolin, a second lead guitar, and a 300-pound Irishman playing lap steel all crammed into that corner of the front room. And the music was *amazing*.

No matter what the mix, the crowd is into it – the regulars and the lucky newcomers who saw the bright red flaming crawfish on the sign and decided they could do with a little Cajun cooking tonight. It's back to the weekly grind tomorrow, but for now...wine and beer are flowing, jambalaya and etouffee are steaming on the table, Stringbean's on the harp, and all's right with the world.

***

I knew Dallas (who writes as Jack Ketchum) for what seemed like ages (he died in 2018) and was happy to do this for the 2010 World Horror Convention's program book.

Dallas Mayr: An Appreciation

"Good news, Paul. Dallas Mayr is going to be on our quad."

So said Doug Winter as we threaded the underpasses along the Merritt Parkway in Connecticut. This was sometime in the early-mid nineties as were headed for Rhode Island and NECon.

(For those unfamiliar with Camp NECon, it's a summer con for horror folk; over the years it has rotated through a number of college campuses, but in every case we campers stay in the dorms.)

I remember saying, "Dallas Mayr? Who the hell is Dallas Mayr? And why is that good news?"

"He writes as Jack Ketchum."

I said, "*The Girl Next Door* Jack Ketchum?"

Doug nodded.

My first thought was – and I wasn't the first to think it – why someone would switch a cool, stand-out name like Dallas Mayr for the pedestrian Jack Ketchum.

My second was that I wasn't so sure I wanted to sleep next door to the author of one of the most disturbing books I'd ever read.

I forget who recommended *The Girl Next Door*. Doug, maybe. Even so, when I saw that cheesy cover, I almost moved on. I mean, if a short-skirted, bobby-socked, saddle-shoed, ponytailed, pompom-waving cheerleader with a skull face captured the essence of the novel within, I wanted no part of it. Gimme a break.

But the recommendation had been strong enough to push me past the cheesy wrappings and plunk down my money.

Right now you're expecting me to say something like, *And boy am I glad I did.*

Well, I'm not so sure. That I'm glad, I mean. Of course it's always a treat to find a well-written book with solid characters and an engrossing plot – a description that fits perfectly *The Girl Next Door*. And if it's a horror novel, so much the better.

But *The Girl Next Door* was more than I'd bargained for. No comfortable supernatural forces here. (I say "comfortable" because in most cases your conscious and/or subconscious finds it easy to distance itself from the supernatural because it's, well, not real.) *The Girl Next Door* turned out to be an unflinching stare into the abyss of human evil. It doesn't take place in a neverland, and it has no ghosts and goblins and things that go bump in the night. It happens next door, to real people. For all I knew, similar appalling events could have been going on in my neighborhood while I was reading the book and I wouldn't have had a clue.

Plus, *The Girl Next Door* offers no redemption.

I can't remember a more disturbing book. Ever. I guess that was why it stayed with me – is still with me.

And that was why I wasn't ready to start tossing confetti and donning funny hats because this fellow, Ketchum or Mayr or whoever he was, was staying in the same quad. I mean, NECon is all about fun, and how much fun can you expect from a guy with that bleak a view of humanity?

What can I say? When I'm wrong, I'm *really* wrong.

Dallas Mayr the man bears no resemblance to Jack Ketchum the author. Dallas is well read, erudite, witty, articulate, sophisticated, quick to laugh, and a great raconteur. He's written – under various pseudonyms – just about everything a freelancer can write. In the early seventies he wrote ad copy. His fiction career began in 1976 (as Jerzy Livingston) with a short story titled "The Hang Up." For the next half-dozen years Jerzy paid Dallas's bills by writing fiction, non-fiction, book and record reviews for the likes of *Swank, Stag, Genesis, Penthouse, Creem, High Society,* the Franklin Library, and on and on.

Really, how many authors can say they've sold to everything from *Porn Stars* to *Classic Decorating and Home Crafts Magazine?*

In 1981, after Ballantine published Dallas's first novel, *Off Season,* Jerzy began to wither, his precious bodily fluids transferred to Jack Ketchum,

Some people say *Off Season* is more disturbing than *The Girl Next Door.* In fact the *Village Voice* damned it as violent pornography – and that was the expurgated version! I came to *Off Season* later and, no question, it is disturbing. But it didn't get under my skin like *The Girl Next Door.* (For which I am thankful.)

Three years later he did *Hide and Seek.* And three years after that came *Cover,* and then he began hitting his stride: *She Wakes, The Girl Next Door, Offspring,* and so on. You know them.

But do you know the man?

Do you know that he used to be an agent for the Scott Meredith Agency?

Do you know that he's been an actor? (I remember watching TV a few years ago and on comes this commercial for some college, and there's freakin' Dallas playing a professor shilling the school.)

Do you know that he can sing – *really* sing – and his Anthony Newley impersonation is so dead on you'd think he was channeling the guy?

And do you know he has the worst, girly bat swing in

the history of softball? (Trust me. I've seen it.)

Dallas is envied by his fellow writers for what we perceive as a rock-star lifestyle: drinking, women, drinking, smoking, drinking...

He tells me he's quit smoking. Hope so. We want him around a while longer. I don't think he's quit women. How could he? They won't leave the poor guy alone. And Dallas certainly likes the women – preferably alert and breathing, but he's been known to make exceptions.

But that's Dallas's convention lifestyle. Is that the real Dallas Mayr? Deep inside is he a sad, lonely man crying out for a wife, a house, two kids, and a dog?

Nah.

The real Dallas's life probably falls somewhere between the convention Dallas and his recurring character – my favorite – Stroup.

For me, one of the best things about NECon is knowing that Dallas will be there and we can hang out. One of the best things about this year's World Horror Convention is that he'll be here, walking among you.

Don't be afraid to approach him. He's a legend but genuinely friendly and truly accessible. Especially if you buy him a drink.

Just don't ask him to demonstrate his softball swing. Please.

***

This little ditty about my most memorable villain from the 1980s was commissioned by Wattpad and DC Vertigo to psyche readers up for Vertigo's Survivors' Club. *It gave me a chance to sound off about how I thought the Hannibal character had been ruined.*

Lessons Learned from Taming a Monster

Hannibal "the Cannibal" Lecter first entered public

consciousness as a supporting character in Thomas Harris's 1981 novel, *Red Dragon*. When we meet the oddly brilliant homicidal psychopath, he is serving multiple life sentences in a state hospital for the criminally insane. The novel involves the twist of using one serial killer to help catch another, but what elevates it above the general procedural-thriller genre is the deep, unobstructed view it offers into the heart of human evil known as Hannibal Lecter.

Lecter is not simply brilliant; he's also a psychiatrist. He has studied the human mind, knows how to manipulate it, bend it, and twist it to his advantage. He can spot your tells, sense your fears, your darkest secrets, and use them against you.

In the 1988 sequel, *The Silence of the Lambs*, Lecter graduated from supporting role to center stage and became a household name. Here he functions as a dark god to whom supplicants must pay obeisance.

Throughout both novels Harris confronts us with two species of evil. One belongs to the serial killers, Francis Dolarhyde and Jame Gumb; their evil, though appalling, is all too human, born out of rage and madness. The other evil is, however... something entirely other.

Lecter's evil is a distilled essence, a malevolence of such hideous purity that it seems almost supernatural. It transcends madness. It feeds on pain. When people in the world outside the asylum are faced with a horror they cannot comprehend, they seek insight from Lecter, the font of evil. And he bargains with them-for petty privileges, for a taste of their pain. We watch him through the supplicants' eyes as he sits in his cell and figuratively reaches between the bars to lacerate their minds and hearts with his verbal scalpels.

Gradually you come to understand that he's not quite human. In his eyes, we are nothing - another species, another genus, perhaps - lower life forms to be toyed with and disposed of at his whim. Fortunately we've gained the upper hand: We've bottled this evil... for now.

Lecter's influence over *Lambs* is pervasive. Each page is goose fleshed with the chill of his presence. The result is unforgettable.

But it gets worse. As if all the foregoing weren't enough, the man is a cannibal. He *eats* his victims. But not with the vicious rending of the flesh like Jeffrey Dahmer. No, he prepares gourmet meals of various human organs. He brags at one point that he sautéed someone's liver and served it "with fava beans and a big Amarone." (They switched to Chianti in the movie because most people wouldn't recognize Amarone as a heavy red wine.)

As practiced in many primitive tribes, cannibalism was a means of incorporating a fallen enemy's strength into one's self - could be interpreted as an honor, although a dubious one at best. For Lecter, though, it's not simply a matter of culinary preference, but an expression of icy contempt for his victims: We are lambs, swine, and kine to be slaughtered at whim - for simple rudeness or some other seemingly inconsequential offense to his rarified sensibilities.

Why? How? we asked ourselves back in the eighties. What turned this brilliant, cultured, educated man into such a monster?

Thomas Harris offered no answers. For the next eleven years Hannibal Lecter remains an enigma, a malevolent force of nature: He is what he is and he does what he does and that's it.

I admired that. My first bestseller, *The Keep*, was published the same year as *Red Dragon* and I'd painted its supernormal antagonist with an equally unusual palette. In the late 80s, when I began adding to the mythos I had created, I took the lesson of Hannibal Lecter to heart: I never explained Rasalom. He too existed almost as a force of nature; he simply was what he was and did what he did.

I know it sounds like heresy, but I wish Harris had left well enough alone and forgotten about Hannibal Lecter after those first two books. I wish he had moved on to something else. Lecter had escaped by the end of *Lambs* and was out in the world, killing and eating people who offended him. I thought - and still think - that was the perfect place to leave him.

But no. In 1999 Harris published *Hannibal* in which the eponymous character is pursued by one of his earlier victims, a mundanely evil pedophile named Mason Verger. Even when captured, Lecter is always cool and in control. He manages to thwart all Verger's plans and rescue Clarice Starling in the process. Yes, a wonderful Grand Guignol of a novel, but we're left with the problematic spectacle of...

Hannibal Lecter - superhero.

Sorry...not for me.

It gets worse. The series finished off with a prequel, *Hannibal Rising*, wherein we're treated to all the horrors and spectacular abuse Li'l Hannibal suffered during his formative years. *No wonder he's so screwed up.*

No-no-no-no-NO! I deny those last two books! They ruin Lecter for me. They reduce him from a force of preternaturally pure evil to a tawdry, tedious product of childhood abuse.

No-no-no-no-NO! (he repeats) I do *not* want to understand him! I want him to remain a mystery.

So I've done by best to erase books three and four from memory, but I've taken their lesson to heart: In fiction as well as life, familiarity breeds contempt.

When shaping a character, don't over explain, not even to yourself. Leave your reader with something to think about. The best characters, the ones who linger in memory, are those who retain a subtle air of mystery, where no one knows the whole story. Characters truly come alive when readers are compelled to fill in a few blanks on their own.

That's the lesson of Hannibal Lecter. Now get back to work and put it to use.

***

Written in 2012 for Books to Die For *edited by John Connolly and Declan Burke. Payment: 1 bottle of Midleton Irish Whisky.*

The Hunter by Richard Stark

As a Lee Marvin fan, I couldn't miss *Point Blank.* And being an aspiring writer at the time (we're talking 1967) I always kept an eye on the credits for the name of the screenwriter. This film had three but was "based on the novel *The Hunter* by Richard Stark."

Who the hell was Richard Stark and how did he get *The Hunter* made into a film?

I went on the hunt myself and found a movie tie-in edition. I didn't know that Richard Stark was a pseudonym for Donald Westlake and wouldn't have cared if I had – Westlake was a relative newbie then. I plunked down fifty cents and started reading.

Whoa! I'd thought the movie gritty and violent, but that was kindergarten fare compared to the novel. The protagonist, Parker, capitalizes the *anti* in anti-hero. Parker Who? Who Parker? We never know. He has aliases, but most of his cronies, his wife included, know him only as Parker. He even thinks of himself as simply *Parker.*

Set in the early sixties (published in 1962), *The Hunter* opens with:

When a fresh-faced guy in a Chevy offered him a lift, Parker told him to go to hell.

He's in the process of walking across the George Washington Bridge toward Manhattan – a penniless, raw-boned man in ill-fitting clothes, a man with a major chip on his shoulder, a man with a purpose, but we don't know what. By the end of the day he's scammed his way into a new suit, a hotel room, and eight hundred bucks in cash. Along the way, he skates a subway turnstile, bums a dime from "a latent fag with big hips," is needlessly cruel to a diner waitress, forges a license, and empties some poor s-o-b's bank account. And that's just chapter one.

All right…this is the bad guy, right? When do we meet the *good* guy?

Don't hold your breath.

The next chapter opens with Parker looking down at a beautiful blonde he's just slugged and knocked to the floor.

As shocking as the scene was, this neophyte writer was struck by the economy of the transition. A page later, intervening events are backfilled in a couple of sentences, but Stark spares us the trip from Parker's hotel to the apartment house, as well as entering the apartment and (most importantly) delivering the punch. Instead he plops us *in medias res*.

The woman is Lynn, Parker's wife. We learn she betrayed him after a heist and left him for dead to run off with Mal Resnick, one of the heist crew.

"I was never a whore, Parker," she said. "You know that."

"No. You sold my body instead."

We learn Parker's mission: Get his hands around Mal Resnick's throat and squeeze the life out of him.

The next morning he finds Lynn dead of an overdose and his only emotion is anger that he now has to dispose of her body. He spends the day with the corpse, drinking and watching TV. The whole while, his wife is never "Lynn," but simply "her" or "she." He's severed *all* connection. Once night comes, he dumps her body in Central Park. He doesn't want Mal spotting a photo of her in the paper, so he slashes her dead face until it's unrecognizable.

Whew.

In the course of his search for Mal, we learn that Parker and Mal and a crew massacred a dozen or more South American revolutionaries who'd come north with $90k to buy guns. We also learn that Parker was planning (surprise!) to kill Mal and take his share, but Mal got to Lynn and forced her to shoot him. They left Parker's body and set the house on fire.

Parker wasn't dead, of course. He pulled himself from the burning building, but before he could start pursuit he was jailed on a vagrancy charge. Finally he killed a guard, escaped, and headed for New York.

The story switches to Mal's side. He now has a managerial position in the Outfit (read: Organized Crime). He'd bungled an assignment a while back, resulting in a big loss to the Outfit, but used the proceeds from the gunrunner heist to pay off the debt. Now he's sitting pretty... until he hears that some tough guy is asking questions, looking for him. Who? When he learns Lynn has disappeared, he knows it has to be Parker, back from the supposedly dead.

After some cat and mouse, Parker tracks him down, gets his hands around Mal's throat... but eases back. Where's the money? When he learns Mal gave it to the Outfit, Parker gets a list of names from him, *then* strangles Mal.

End of story? No. Parker decides that killing Mal isn't enough. Half of that $90k was rightfully his and he wants it back. To do so, he's going to have to take on the Outfit. Well, why not?

Now things get a bit surreal, but *really* interesting. Everything that's happened so far has been about settling debts. Lynn and Mal owed him. Other people who died simply got in the way. Now, the way he sees it, the Outfit owes him. And what is owed must be paid. Simple as that, as he explains to one of the Outfit's bigwigs:

"The funnies call it the syndicate. The goons and hustlers call it the Outfit. You call it the organization. I hope you people have fun with your words. But I don't care if you call yourselves the Red Cross, you owe me forty-five thousand dollars and you'll pay me back whether you like it or not."

Throughout the novel, Parker reveals only what's necessary. But as he makes his moves against the mob, we sneak a peek inside. His lifestyle until now has been living in luxury resort hotels, financed by one or two juicy heists a year. That pattern was changed by Lynn's betrayal and he's now caught in a new pattern of collecting on debts. The $45k will allow him to return to his old pattern. This is his true mission: restore the old lifestyle.

I don't want to spoil the resolution for those who haven't read it, but I will tell you it doesn't end like any of the film adaptations. In fact, the final chapter has a tacked-on feel.

Only years later did I learn that *The Hunter* was intended as a one-off, but Westlake / Stark's editor suggested he change the ending to allow for more Parker novels. Was Parker killed in the original? Jailed? Sadly, Donald Westlake is no longer around to answer.

But what is it about Parker that created an audience for twenty-four novels and eight films? (Three based on *The Hunter* alone: *Point Blank, Full Contact, Payback*. None of the films has the real Parker – Hollywood can't resist infusing him with empathy; Brian Helgeland's *Payback: Straight up: The Directors Cut* comes the closest – and he was fired from the film because of that.) Parker has no respect for life, liberty, or the pursuit of happiness except his own. He's a sociopath who steals and kills without remorse. He has no code, no honor, even among his fellow thieves, as witnessed by his plan to kill Mal and take his share of the heist.

Yet clearly in *The Hunter* he is the wronged party (just marginally so) and we wind up rooting for him. Perhaps it's Parker's single-mindedness and relentless efficiency that draw us.

I remember tearing through *The Hunter* and wanting more-more-more, and going out to find them. During the reread to write this, the 1962 period offered a few smiles: ten cents for a cup of coffee; eighty-five cents considered extravagant for a roast beef sandwich; Mal "splurging" thirty-two bucks on a Midtown hotel suite.

I hit some speed bumps I hadn't noticed before.

Stylewise, the writing is crisp and terse enough to overcome a surplus of passive voice. Try as I might to suspend disbelief, Lynn's betrayal of Parker, despite Mal's threats, doesn't wash. Also, the novel seems padded in spots, most blatantly in Mal's dalliance with the prostitute, and in Parker's surreptitious invasion of the Outfit's hotel only to discover what the reader has known for quite a while: Mal has moved out. Knowing Parker's elaborate B&E will not lead to a confrontation robs the sequence of all sense of anticipation.

These are quibbles against the big picture of a writer taking a major risk in creating a murderous sociopathic protagonist with a supporting cast that includes not a single decent, trustworthy human being. And making it *work*.

The Hunter: a violent, twisty, oft-imitated tour de force crime novel that was sui generis in its time.

***

Written in 2010 for Thrillers: 100 Must Reads *edited by David Morrell and Hank Wagner.*

Day of the Jackal

Frederick Forsyth's first novel (that last bit bears repeating: *first* novel) put a new twist on a number of spy-thriller conventions. Although not a true spy novel, it's structured as one: Its titular character, a professional assassin, functions very much like a spy – forging new identities, moving secretly from country to country, dealing with traitors. It's also very much a procedural, leading the reader in great detail through the intricate measures the Jackal takes to avoid detection, and all the methods his pursuers employ to track him down.

The novel, set in 1963, also takes the unprecedented step of making Charles de Gaulle his target.

Excuse me? Charles de Gaulle was not assassinated;

he died of natural causes the year before the novel was published. So unless this takes place in an alternate universe, the Jackal is doomed to failure. How can you possibly build suspense – let alone maintain it for the length of an entire novel – when the reader knows from the get go that the plot is going to fail?

In the hands of Frederick Forsyth, it doesn't matter. He makes it work.

The novel was inspired by the real-life assassination attempt on de Gaulle in 1962 after he endorsed independence for Algeria. A group of French militants calling itself the OAS waged a campaign of terror against it. A fellow named Jean Bastien-Thiry was executed for masterminding the plot.

The novel opens with Bastien-Thiry's execution and a recap of the failed attempt on de Gaulle. Shortly thereafter, a remnant of the OAS hires a professional assassin known only as the Jackal to finish the job. Wisely the Jackal tells his employers nothing about his plans, and just as wisely, Forsyth tells the reader nothing as well. Instead, he does what all good storytellers do: He *shows*. We follow the Jackal, whose true identity we never know, through England, France and Belgium as he researches de Gaulle, sets up false identities, and purchases the weapon he'll use for the assassination. Slowly, piece by piece, we see the plan begin to take shape.

On the other side, the French police have tumbled to the fact that the former OAS reprobates are up to something. They capture a bodyguard named Kowalski and brutally interrogate him (believe me, he'd pray for waterboarding instead the electric wires attached to sensitive parts of his anatomy) to extract what he knows, which isn't much beyond the name "chacal" (French for jackal). Eventually, a doggedly persistent French cop, Inspector Claude Lebel, is set on the trail of this nameless, faceless killer. He traces the Jackal to an apartment in England occupied by a man named

Charles Calthrop (note what the first three letters of those two names spell) but misses him.

Now the cat-and-mouse game begins in earnest, with the Jackal receiving tips from an OAS contact in the French government that help him stay one step – sometimes less than that – ahead of Lebel.

In contrast to Robert Ludlum, who published his own first novel (*The Scarlatti Inheritance*) that same year, there's little passion in Forsyth's prose. The affect is generally flat, with the Jackal showing scant or no emotion. He isn't a radical firebrand; there's no pleasure for him here (other than, perhaps, the satisfaction in bringing off this nearly impossible feat), no emotional or ideological stake. It's simply a job – a challenging one, yes, but still a job.

Forsyth writes in what I call movie mode. We witness the action from outside; rarely are we allowed into the hearts and minds of the characters. This should make for an uninvolving read but in Forsyth's hands it's curiously compelling. The torture scene is a perfect example. Its matter-of-fact presentation is utterly chilling.

Unlike the characters in James Bond-style novels, the Jackal is no bon vivant. He doesn't high roll in casinos or dally in five-star hotels. He's more at home in the underworld, the demimonde of gun runners and forgers. He even has an interlude in a gay bar.

Whether we're following the Jackal or the police, Forsyth renders the locations in exquisite detail. Never do we question that the author has spent time in these places. And it is perhaps this attention to detail that empowers the Herculean suspension of disbelief necessary to overlook the historical contradiction so central to the plot. Everything is so real, the Jackal is so skilled, so expert at his profession that, yes, never mind what history says, this man just might be able to assassinate de Gaulle.

And as we read on (perhaps to one's dismay, perhaps not), we find ourselves rooting for the Jackal. He may be a cold-blooded killer, but his foes are equally ruthless. And he's the underdog, a man on a high wire with no safety net, single-handedly facing down the combined police forces and intelligence networks of Western Europe. Every time the authorities start closing in, you can't help hoping he outwits them... again.

In the end the story distills to a battle of wits between the Jackal and Lebel, and along the way the two men develop a grudging mutual respect.

The final scene between the pair is delivered in Forsyth's typical affectless style:

Lebel stared into the eyes of the other man...

"Chacal," he said. The other man said simply, "Lebel."

After that it's a matter of who can shoot first.

***

I wrote this for a French collection of essays on King's work: Le Livre des Livres de Stephen King *back in 2006. It remains my fave King novel.*

'Salem's Lot: Mutant Makes Good

We were born in the forties in the first wave of the baby boom. We were raised through the fifties by stay-at-home moms and WWII Two vets in family units of 2.3 children, a dog, and two cats. We witnessed the advent of rock 'n' roll and our Elvis remains young, slim, and twangy. We went to school with the neighbor kids – where we all learned the duck-and-cover move in the event of nuclear attack – and played with them after school and on weekends.

But we weren't like them. Not really. Sure, we liked baseball and watching Friday night wrestling on our tiny black-and-white TVs. But somehow it wasn't enough. We didn't know what was missing, but we knew we felt incomplete.

Then we got our first glimpse of the cover of a horror

comic – for me it was *Witches Tales* #25 – and experienced a galvanizing thrill. But in 1954 Frederick Wertham's *Seduction of the Innocent* was making waves about horror comics, convincing our parents they'd twist our minds. Ha! We were already twisted. We were *born* twisted.

So horror comics were banned from many of our houses. No problem. We bought *Tales from the Crypt* or *Vault of Horror* and stuck them inside *Donald Duck* covers, or hid them in the garage.

And then we saw our first monster movie trailer on TV – most likely *Beast from 20,000 Fathoms* or *Godzilla* – and it was love at first sight.

Sure, they were popular movies, and millions upon millions of kids went to see them. But they didn't *live* for those moments.

We did.

We combed through *TV Guide* for titles of movies that had horror potential. The Betamax was three decades off, so we couldn't simply pop in a favorite movie and watch it. If we found an interesting title playing at two A.M., we couldn't record it. No, we had to set our alarm clock, get up, and sneak downstairs to catch it.

When the first issue of *Famous Monsters of Filmland* hit the stand we snatched it up and read and reread it until the staples fell out.

We celebrated when we found the rare anthology that contained horror stories. Reading our first Lovecraft was almost sexual. And when Universal released its horror library to TV, we were in heaven.

Tom Monteleone has labeled us *mutants* and it's as good a handle as any. We were wired in ways that deviated from the norm.

Since then the world has changed. The VCR makes seeing the classic and not-so-classic horror films easy. Monsters and vampires have been mainstreamed. I mean, breakfast cereals named Frankenberry and Count Chocula –

can you believe it?

Back then, thanks to Roger Corman and others, we had plenty of low-budget fodder to keep us in the movie houses. But as for horror fiction... not much happening.

Sure, we found an occasional collection like *Cry Horror* or *The Macabre Reader*, but they were mostly reprints from *Weird Tales* and the like. Arkham House books cost more and were pretty much the same. We'd hunt down Poe and M.R. James, and classics like *Dracula* and *Frankenstein*, but besides occasional publishing aberrations like *The Haunting of Hill House*, where was the new stuff?

Then, in 1967...*Rosemary's Baby*. An oasis in a desert of blah that had its moments, but no sock on the jaw. The imitations that followed were mostly awful.

It took four years for our next fix, a gut punch called *The Exorcist*.

Then in 1974 came *Carrie*, a novel about a telekinetic adolescent by a newcomer named Stephen King. I read the paperback in 1975 and it was... okay. I dug the pyrotechnics but teenage angst wasn't my bag.

I liked it enough, though, to order his second novel, *'Salem's Lot*, when I saw it listed in the Literary Guild circular.

Nothing in the book club blurb or the flap copy hinted at vampires. Maybe because, with no such thing as a horror genre back then, Doubleday thought the word "vampire" on the jacket would hurt sales. Looking back I feel fortunate that I was able to come to *'Salem's Lot* with no idea of what I'd find.

Though the flap copy mentioned a stranger "with a secret as old as evil," it took a while before what might be supernatural evil revealed itself. Oh, there were hints when Straker bought the Marsten house, and portents with the dog spiked on the cemetery fence, but the early parts seemed more concerned with human evil – I still remember the sick jolt of reading about Sandy punching her ten-month-old baby.

King told us about the junkyard man, detailed Bonnie's affair, the Glick family dynamics, Crockett's wheeling and dealing... all these characters. Was this going to turn out to be some kind of dark soap opera?

Then "darkness enfolded" Danny Glick... followed by the "unspeakable" scene in the cemetery.

Now I was into it. This wasn't your mother's *Peyton Place*.

The anemic Danny Glick dies in his hospital room... and the epitaph on Hubert Marsten's tombstone: *God Grant He Lie Still.*

Ooooh, is this going where I hope it's going?

And then the epiphanic scene.

I knew nothing of this Stephen King guy except that the flap said he lived in Maine with his wife and kids. No jacket photo, so for all I knew he could have been fifty-sixty-whatever years of age.

King was a stranger until I came to section 5 of Chapter Six: *The Lot (II)* where we find Mark Petrie gluing the arms on an Aurora glow-in-the-dark Frankenstein monster. He has a whole table of the models, including Dracula, the Mad Doctor, and Mr. Hyde.

Just like I had when I was Mark's age.

With a sudden burst of joy I knew all about Stephen King. I remember thinking, THIS GUY IS ONE OF US!

If joy seems an inappropriate response, let me explain.

Rosemary's Baby had been written by a guy born in the 1920s, a playwright best known for "No Time for Sergeants" – a *comedy*.

William Peter Blatty was also a child of the 1920s. A mundane novelist and comedic screenwriter – *A Shot in the Dark*, for chrissake.

But here was someone from *my* generation referencing a shared mutant past. A bestselling author – and he was a member of the club.

Stephen King was a fellow mutant.

I'd just sold my first novel – sf because no horror market existed then – and the idea that one of us was already making it big was more than heartening and inspiring, it was goddamn electrifying.

And I knew right then that he wasn't going to let me down by jimmying up a real-world explanation of all the weirdness he'd been describing. My fellow mutant would deliver.

And deliver he did. *'Salem's Lot* is a classic not just of vampire fiction, but of the whole horror genre. I gobbled every word. There are so many reasons to love this book, but the mutant epiphany in Chapter Six cast it in stone as my favorite King novel.

Mutants rule!

***

I love this song. And when I love a song or a story, I try to figure out why. Posted on the website and Facebook 12/13/17

No Reply

Recorded 9/30/64
Released 12/4/64 on *Beatles for Sale*

I just listened to "No Reply" maybe ten times in a row. It's been my fave Beatles tune since the day I heard it. I never tire of it. Quite a shock to learn it was not written for The Beatles.

When I looked up "No Reply" on beatlesbible.com, I learned that John had written it for a guy named Tommy Quickly who shared their manager, Brian Epstein. I knew Lennon and McCartney had written songs for Peter & Gordon and Billy J. Kramer and the like, but those tunes never seemed fit for The Beatles anyway. "No Reply," however...

Lennon says he was inspired by "Silhouettes," the old hit by The Rays, but his take is much darker.

Check out the lyrics and their rhyme scheme:

Verse 1	Verse 2 & 3
This happened once before	I tried to telephone
I came to your door	They said you were not home
No reply >>>	That's a lie
They said it wasn't you been	'Cause I know where you've
But I saw you peek through	I saw you walk in
Your window >>>	Your door
I saw the light! >>>	I nearly died!
I saw the light! >>>	I nearly died!
I know that you saw me hand	'Cause you walked hand in
'Cause I looked up to see	With another man
Your face >>>	In my place

I'm a fan of inter-verse rhymes and use >>> to highlight them here. ("Your window" and "Your door" don't rhyme, of course, but they thematically unite the verses in that they both divide him from his lover.)

The arrangement is spare, mostly acoustic, with Ringo's offbeat playing perfect for the verses. Those verses are all sung by Lennon except for the lines "I saw the light!" and "I nearly died!" where McCartney's harmony packs a wallop of shock, anger, and anguish.

Lennon (as he often did) said he wrote the whole thing, while McCartney says John arrived as usual with the song lacking a vocal bridge – what he likes to call "the middle eight." So who to believe? I choose Paul. The verses are dark with hurt and anger – pure John. The bridge however picks up tempo, is all in harmony, adds handclapping, and closes with:

"And I'll forgive the lies that I
"Heard before when you gave me no reply."

What's that I hear? A chance for redemption? The verses carry not a whiff of forgiveness – too much hurt and anger there. But the bridge lets a ray of hope peek through.

And that's gotta be McCartney.

There. I've put down everything I know and feel about "No Reply" in the hope of figuring out why I like it so much. I still don't know

***

How a G-Major-6 Made Me a Beatles Fan

The Beatles' "She Loves You" had its initial US release in September of 1963 and flopped so badly it never made it to my radio. By contrast, when "I Want to Hold Your Hand" was released 3 months later, it sold 750,000 copies in the first three days (New York City alone was selling 10,000 copies an hour). Demand was so great that Capitol had to pay its record rivals Columbia and RCA to press extra copies for them.

Despite all that, "I Want to Hold Your Hand" was not a hit with me. I was drumming in my own garage band then, accompanying the likes of "Walk Don't' Run," "Rawhide," "Ghost Riders in the Sky" and other instrumentals, and developing an ear for what I liked and why I liked it. The melody of "I Want to Hold Your Hand" didn't gab me and I thought the lyrics were hokey. My younger sister, however, was an instant fan. Soon the twelve tracks on *Meet the Beatles* were echoing incessantly through our house. Though they didn't make me a fan, some of the songs grew on me.

I finally heard "She Loves You" upon its re-release in March of '64 when it zoomed to number one on the charts.

Ba-dum-ba-dum (on the floor tom)
She loves you yeah-yeah-yeah!
She loves you yeah-yeah-yeah!
She loves you yeah-yeah-yeah-YAAAAAH!

Whoa! That last *YAAAAAH!* What was *that?*

As I said, I was a drummer. I hadn't taken up guitar yet. I didn't know chords and such. But I knew what I liked and I liked that *YAAAAAH!* I couldn't remember ever hearing anybody sing something like that.

So I listened – really listened – to the rest of the song, wanting to hear it again. But alas, although they sang *yeah!* plenty of times, no *YAAAAAH!*...until the very end: an extended, echoey *YAAAAAH!* to close out the song.

Yes! I loved everything about the song – the tempo, the harmonies, the way the drummer switched from the hi-hat to the floor tom on the choruses, its overall exuberance. It made me *happy*. But I especially loved that *YAAAAAH!*

"She Loves You" wasn't on either of my sister's albums (she had *Introducing the Beatles* on the Vee-Jay label by then too) so I went out and bought the single and played it over and over to hear that strange *YAAAAAH!* I began listening more closely to the albums and appreciating the way these guys put their songs together.

Then they released the buoyant, contagious "Can't Buy Me Love" followed by "A Hard Day's Night" with its clang of an opening chord that no one on the whole bloody planet had ever heard before and I became thoroughly and permanently hooked.

But the tipping point had been that *YAAAAAH!* on "She Loves You." What made it so special? I later learned it's a G-major-6 chord and it almost didn't make it into the song (or so I'm told).

Apparently in the initial "She Loves You" mix, that last *yeah!* had John, Paul, and George harmonizing to a simple G-major chord, singing G-B-D. But George Harrison wasn't happy with finishing the song that way. He petitioned their producer, George Martin, to let him go back and overdub an E note above the basic three. Martin didn't like the idea but finally relented. As a result, the G-B-D *yeah!* became a G-B-D-E *YAAAAAH!*

And not only made the song as far as this listener was concerned, but led him to become a Beatles fan.

Like they say, it's the little things.

That's my story and I'm sticking to it.

***

This involves the first H. P. Lovecraft story I ever read, a story that changed my life. I've scribbled many bits and pieces about "The Thing on the Doorstep"—I believe I wrote the first for Dagon, *a British fanzine that folded before it could publish it – but this is the definitive version published in* Windy City Pulp Stories *in 2015.*

The Thing on the Doorstep

"The Thing on the Doorstep."

What a title, conjuring a gallimaufry of images, all of them unsettling.

This was my first Lovecraft story, the one that started me down the road to ruin. Had I but known...

Never mind.

According to the de Camp biography, this was one of H.P.'s last stories, written in longhand in August of 1933, but not typed up until the winter of 1934. After *Weird Tales'* rejection of "At The Mountains of Madness" (due more to its length than to its story values), he was apparently so unsure of himself and of what he perceived to be a waning talent, that he did not have the courage to send "The Thing on the Doorstep" off to *Weird Tales* until the summer of 1936 – two years after he'd written it. Farnsworth Wright, no dummy, snapped it up immediately.

Good thing he did. H.P. had less than two years to live.

The story was finally published in 1936.

Twenty-three years later it found me.

Donald A. Wollheim is to blame. He started me on Lovecraft. In 1959 I was just a kid, a mere thirteen years old when he slipped me my first fix. I was a good kid up till then, reading Ace Doubles and clean, wholesome science fiction stories by the likes of Heinlein, E.E. Smith, Poul Anderson, Fred Pohl, and the rest. But he brought me down with one anthology. He knew what he was doing. He called it *The Macabre Reader* and slapped this lurid neato-cool Ed Emshwiller cover on it. I couldn't resist. I had to open it, look for pictures (there weren't any), and check out the table of contents. I hadn't heard of any of the authors, but the titles – good Lord, the titles were fabulous. "The Crawling Horror" by Thorp McClusky, "The Opener of the Way" by Robert Bloch, "The Curse of Yig" by Zelia Bishop, "The Hollow Man" by Thomas Burke, "The Hunters from Beyond" by Clark Ashton Smith, "It will Grow on You" by Donald Wandrei, and others. But the title that really promised to bring the horror home (literally and figuratively) was "The Thing on the Doorstep" by someone who didn't use a first name, just initials – H. P. Lovecraft. I bought it. I read it. And that was it. The beginning of my end.

You've got to understand where I was coming from. This was the late Fifties. No one was publishing horror fiction – *no one.* We had plenty of horror to watch – Universal had sold its horror library to TV and Hammer was putting out some great Technicolor remakes – but after you'd read the original *Dracula* and *Frankenstein*, and the too-rare Bradbury or Matheson collections, what was left? Forry Ackerman's *Famous Monsters of Filmland* was the only thing coming out on a regular basis and that was all pictures. I wanted to be scared, to be chilled, I wanted to gasp, wanted my skin to crawl.

The Macabre Reader did it all. Here were the stories I'd been looking for. Creepy tales – dark, eerie, intense, the emotions jumping right off the page – like nothing I'd ever read before. But the one that grabbed me by the throat was "The Thing on the Doorstep."

I was dragged into the story by the opening line ("It is true I have sent six bullets through the head of my best friend, and yet I hope to show by this statement that I am not his murderer."), captivated by the setting ("...witch-cursed, legend-haunted Arkham, whose huddled, sagging gambrel roofs and crumbling Georgian balustrades brood out the centuries beside the darkly muttering Miskatonic"), blown away by the dense prose that tossed off words like eldritch and foetor and Cyclopean and nacreous, that casually mentioned strange, forbidden books and towns like Innsmouth (where even Arkhamites fear to go) as if I should be familiar with them.

All this was old hat, I suppose, to Lovecraft devotees, and must have been par for the course for *Weird Tales* regulars in the Thirties, but it was a revelation for me.

"The Thing on the Doorstep" delivered on the up-close, breath-clogging horror that *The Macabre Reader*'s cover had promised, but it also served as my Cthulhu Mythos primer, my introduction to what would come to be known as Cosmic Horror.

The story

Since this seems to be something of a forgotten Lovecraft story, let me refresh your memory.

The narrator, Daniel Upton, tells us of his longtime friend, the brilliant, precocious Edward Pickman Derby, a young man of good family who was born in frail health and overly coddled by his parents. He has "Poe-like talents," immerses himself in weird literature, and while still a teenager publishes a book of poems – "collected nightmare-lyrics" – called *Azathoth and Other Horrors*. He enters Miskatonic University in Arkham at 16 and graduates at 19. He's a withdrawn sort and remains single into his late thirties – "more through shyness, inertia, and parental protectiveness than inclination."

Then Derby meets and falls for Asenath Waite, of the Innsmouth Waites, who is "dark, smallish, and very good-looking except for over-protuberant eyes." Asenath is the daughter of Ephraim Waite, a deceased wizard, and has a talent for hypnotism; such a deep talent that her subjects have come away with the sensation that they'd actually changed places with Asenath while under her spell. Asenath has been heard to say that she wishes she were a man because the male brain has unique cosmic powers. Edward Derby and Asenath marry, and slowly a change comes over our friend Derby. He starts acting out of character – he never learned to drive yet with increasing frequency he's seen handling Asenath's Packard like a race car driver.

During his third year of marriage, Derby is found wandering in the Maine woods, rambling about "the pit of the shaggoths" and how his wife switches bodies with him, locking her own body in the library while she wears his and attends foul rites; but she occasionally loses contact, and when that happens he suddenly finds himself back in his own skin, confronting mind-numbing horrors.

But months later Derby comes to our narrator and tells him that he has sent Asenath away, that he found some spells of his own that he used to lock her out of his body before she could take it over for good, which had been her plan since marrying him. He's free.

But instead of recovering, Derby continues to deteriorate, screaming about how she's trying to take him over again, and that she really isn't a she, but old Ephraim himself! He says the aging wizard took over his daughter's body and poisoned his own. For years now Ephraim has been inhabiting Asenath's body, but all the while he's longed to be back in a male body – and he is taking Edward's!

Edward is finally committed to Arkham Sanatorium where he raves on for weeks...and then is abruptly sane again. But our narrator is alerted now, and he's got a pretty good idea that the suddenly rational mind in his friend's body does not belong to Edward Derby.

Now the real horrors begin.

Our narrator gets a midnight phone call but all he hears is "a sort of half-liquid bubbling noise – 'glub... glub...glub-glub.'" Two hours later there's this shabby, dwarfed, humped, foul-smelling...*thing* standing in the shadows on his doorstep. It wears a low-pulled slouch hat and is draped in an oversized overcoat the narrator recognizes as Edward's. The thing says, "glub...glub." A pencil protrudes from one of the sleeves; and stuck on it is a note written in something that resembles Edward Derby's hand. The note tells the final truth.

Edward writes that he lied about sending Asenath away; the truth is that during one of the increasingly rare moments when he controlled his own body he crushed her skull with a candlestick and buried her in the basement of their home. But Asenath – or actually old Ephraim, for that's who was inhabiting Asenath's body – could still exert control from the grave. He continued to pry into Edward's body, and eventually succeeded in making the final switch while Edward was confined in the sanatorium. Edward suddenly found himself inhabiting Asenath's rotting corpse. He clawed his way out of the basement floor, and has now come to our narrator for help. Since he's inhabiting a rotting corpse, he can't speak and can barely write. So our narrator must save him. He must go to the sanatorium and shoot the man who is calling himself Edward Derby. For he is not Edward Derby. He's really Ephraim Waite.

The narrator faints, but eventually does as he's bid,

thus bringing us full circle to the story's opening hook. The final paragraph describes the nature of the *thing*.

"What they finally found inside Edward's oddly assorted clothes was mostly liquescent horror. There were bones, too – and a crushed-in skull. Some dental work positively identified the skull as Asenath's."

Blown Away

In order to write the above, I reread "The Thing on the Doorstep" for the first time since 1959. All that I clearly remembered from back then was the lurid image of that putrescent *thing* on Daniel Upton's doorstep, and an intense craving for more of this sort of fiction.

Today I see a lot more. I see striking parallels between Edward Derby's social, intellectual, literary, and family history and those of his creator, H. P. Lovecraft.

I remain amazed at Lovecraft's toss-offs – the hints he drops with such apparent carelessness. Other writers would be tempted to dwell on them, or repeat them, but H.P. drops them once and then goes on. He knows what he's doing, though. The toss-offs have a cumulative effect that works in the subconscious, depositing thin layers of eeriness on everything until nothing seems quite safe or sane anymore.

Here are a few from "The Thing on the Doorstep":

1) Edward Derby "was a close correspondent of the notorious Baudelairean poet Justin Geoffrey, who wrote *The People of the Monolith* and died screaming in a madhouse in 1926 after a visit to a sinister, ill-regarded village in Hungary."

2) Asenath "was Ephraim Waite's daughter – the child of his old age by an unknown wife who always went veiled."

3) One of Asenath Waite's servants is "a swarthy young wench who had marked anomalies of feature and seemed to exude a perpetual odor of fish."

But most of all, I'm struck by the intricacies of the plot, and by the subtle kinkiness of Edward marrying – and presumably bedding – a woman housing the personality of a man. Edward's body was being usurped by Asenath, but Asenath wasn't really Asenath because she'd been kicked out of her body by her father, Ephraim. We're dealing with a hideous form of child abuse *cum* transsexualism here. Talk about kinky! But the implications of this clever double-switch went right over my teenage head. (Although perhaps not completely. I'm more than a little taken aback by the switch aspect of the story: My novel *Sibs* hinges on an uncomfortably similar switcheroo. I remember congratulating myself on being such a clever fellow to come up with that final twist. But now, upon rereading "The Thing on the Doorstep," I realize the seed was planted decades before by old H.P. himself.)

The Legacy

But after the image of the *thing* faded, the heart of the tale that lingered in my teenage mind long after I'd finished the story: the concept of another reality impinging on ours, knowledge of which could drive you stark raving mad; a dimension of perverse logic and bizarre geometry, full of godlike creatures with unpronounceable names, aloof and yet decidedly inimical.

"There are black zones of shadow close to our daily paths, and now and then some evil soul breaks a passage through."

My thirteen-year-old world did not seem quite so safe and sane, my reality seemed a tad less real.

After that first fix, I started mainlining Lovecraft. The local pushers – excuse me, *book dealers* – introduced me to Arkham House and I nearly died of an overdose. Eventually I went cold turkey and kicked the habit. (Well, not completely. Occasionally I'll reread a favorite story. I can handle it now. Really.) But the Cosmic Horror concept still fascinates me. I used it in *The Keep* and I used it in "The Barrens," and it's the engine that powers the larger arc of the Repairman Jack novels.

Thanks, H.P.

**

Thomas F. Monteleone

When Tom presented this award to me back in 2008, he covered how we grew up living parallel lives even though we lived 100 miles apart and had never met. I didn't want to reprise that, but I did want to mention how long I've known this gavone.

My first SF con was a Disclave on CT Ave in DC, Jim Frenkel put on a little Friday night party for the launch of the mass market paperback of *Healer*.

This stranger comes up to me and asks what the F stands for. I give my usual forthright response: "Francis, but I never use it." He points to the F on his *Thomas F. Monteleone* badge and says "Francis – I never use it either. Looks like we both got 'F'd by our parents." And that was the start of a long friendship.

But when did this happen? How long ago? The same weekend *Star Wars* opened. May 25, 1977 – **exactly 40 years this past Monday!!!**

There are no coincidences, folks. This is the work of the Otherness.

I'm gonna hit you with some data now, because I want you to understand and appreciate how much this man deserves the Lifetime Achievement Award, and how overdue he is to receive it.

He sold his first fiction to *Amazing Stories* in 1972 – which means he's been a pro for 45 yrs.

In 1976 his first novel *Seeds of Change* kicked off the Laser Books SF line with a print run of half a million. Can you imagine today your 1st novel with 500-600,000 copies going out?

The MAFIA column started 1976. It's survived the

demise of five magazines – risen like a phoenix from their ashes. I'm not saying they died *because* of MAFIA. I'm just... sayin. CD has somehow survived. And truthfully, when you open an issue of CD, if MAFIA isn't the 1st feature you turn to, it's the second, right?

Borderlands Press started in 1990 with a collector's edition of Joe Lansdale's *Magic Wagon*. Horror fiction is in the throes of its Permian extinction and he's starting a small press specializing in horror. He survived and thrived, publishing over 100 titles (8 of them Stoker winners). Just a sampling of the authors he's published: Barker, Bradbury, Ellison, Etchison, Farris, Gaiman, Grant, King (*père et fil*), Kuttner, Lansdale, McCammon, Morrell, Moore, Simmons, Straub, Strieber, Vachss, Tessier, Wagner, and many more.

He started the highly acclaimed and award-winning *Borderlands* anthology, now continuing with his daughter Olivia at the helm.

In 1992 his *Blood of the Lamb* became a NYT bestseller and a Notable Books of the Year.

Newer writers like Brian Keene began referring to him as *Il Padrone* – the Godfather. Because anyone who needed help or a favor pertaining to the craft could go to Tom and he'd never turn them away. His generosity toward young writers is legend.

In 2004 he compiled all that advice into *The Complete Idiot's Guide to Writing a Novel* which was a runaway success, going through multiple printings and later a revised 2nd edition.

The following year he and Elizabeth started a practical application of the *Guide* called the Borderlands Press Bootcamp for writers -- which continues annually to this day, providing guidance and impetus for a whole crew of successful writers who claim that they wouldn't be where they are in their careers of not for the Bootcamp.

Along the way he won a slew of Bram Stoker awards in

multiple categories.

Collection

Anthology

Non-Fiction

Novel

He even won the *Gabriel Award* for Best Teleplay, Public TV – "Mister Magister" on *American Playhouse*

SO...here we have a bestselling novelist, an award-winner for fiction, nonfiction, and editing, a man who's been a teacher and mentor to a whole generation of writers in and out of the genre.

What are we gonna do with this guy? We're gonna give him long overdue formal recognition for his contributions to the field. And to that end I'm proud to present HWA's Lifetime Achievement Award to Thomas Francis Monteleone.

MEMOIRS, CLOSE ENCOUNTERS, OBITS

These are pieces from here and there, often published on my website just so I could nail down a significant memory that might interest other folks.

The Beast from 20,000 Fathoms - 217

The Dirty Dick's Affair - 226
Laura Nyro - 230

Look What They've Done to My Song, Ma - 235

The FTL Newsfeed Saga - 238

Ron Paul - 242

Shelly Berman - 243

1990 - 224
LA Diary: 1997 - 287

LA. Diary: 2002 - 290

"Pelts" Shoot: 2006 - 296

The Origin of the Signalz - 302

John W. Campbell, Jr. - 306

Kay Nolte Smith - 313

Poul Anderson - 315

Little Richard - 316

David G. Hartwell - 317

At NECon back in 1994 (a lot of work trails back to that annual convention) I was reminiscing with Steve Bissette about my childhood travails and machinations to see The Beast from 20,000 Fathoms. *He asked me to write it up for the third issue of his (then) new* Tyrant *comic. I don't think he ever published it. Gauntlet Press finally released it as a chapbook giveaway with a Repairman Jack limited edition. I partially reprised it the* Drive-in Creature Feature *intro.*

The *Beast* and Me

The second most often asked question I hear (besides "Where do you get your ideas?") is "Why horror?" That one often is followed by its close affiliates, "Why not write something *nice*, like a romance? Or a coming-of-age novel? Or something literary?" Stephen King has the best answer: "What makes you think I have a choice?"

My usual answer is that writers do best when they write the kind of book they'd choose to read, and I don't choose to read those kinds of books. Maybe they're too close to real life. I mean, I *have* a real life, and after dancing cheek to cheek with reality all day, I want something different, something that fulfills the promise of fiction. And since I don't do drugs, I look for books that offer something a little more interesting than reality. Not saying there's anything wrong with those barely-fiction books, I'm simply saying I'm not wired for them.

The new slang for discussing nature and nurture is hardware and software. Our genetic make-up is the hardware, our environment provides the software. Not the best analogy, but it makes its point.

In my case (maintaining the metaphor) I was hardwired for monsters and other scary stuff.

Can't explain how or why, I was simply born that way. Factory-equipped, you might say. But it wasn't apparent at birth. In fact, I didn't find out myself until I was seven years old. Until 1953 not a single thing even remotely monsterish had entered my staid, middle-class, church-going, three-child, two-parent, one-dog, Scotch-Irish, Roman Catholic American environment. I watched *Howdy Doody*, of course – even got on the show and sat right next to Buffalo Bob – and I especially loved *Captain Video* and *Tom Corbett, Space Cadet*. But, except for the occasional ghost or witch costume arriving at the door on Halloween, nary a monster in sight.

Looking back, though, I can recall early hints that something might be amiss in my circuitry. For instance, when my father wasn't home – a frequent occurrence because he worked for the international division of a major corporation – my mother often would ask me to lock the front door before heading up to bed. A simple task for another kid, but for me, locking the door suddenly became a life-or-death mission because something truly awful (I had no idea what it might be, just that it was up to no good) was creeping up the front steps and reaching for the doorknob and I absolutely had to get there first and turn the lock before it got inside. So I'd pound across the living room at top speed, do a flying leap at the door, slam my body against it, and turn the lock – just in time.

Mission accomplished, I'd slump to the floor, panting, heart racing, because for those few seconds I truly believed that all our lives depended on my getting there and turning that bolt in time.

And then I'd look up and see my mother staring at me over the top of her magazine and wondering what in the name of God is wrong with this boy.

So the circuits were there, ready and waiting. All they needed was a jolt of the right kind of energy to open them up. That came in June of 1953 when TV delivered a monster into my living room.

But unknown to me, the stage for this awakening had been set the year before by *King Kong*.

Few people remember that the classic 1933 film was re-released in 1952 with a massive television ad campaign. The result was phenomenal: $3,000,000 at the box office – quadruple its first-run take two decades before.

Three megabucks doesn't sound like much these days – it's Nick Cage's hairspray allowance in his recent contracts – but Hollywood of the fifties sat up and took notice.

The message was clear: Big Monsters = Big Bucks.

The following year Warner Brothers picked up an independent production called *The Monster from Beneath the Sea* with special effects by a Willis O'Brien protégé named Ray Harryhausen. The Warners changed the title to that of a Ray Bradbury short story from the *Post* and *The Beast from 20,000 Fathoms* became one of the largest grossing movies of 1953.

With good reason: the ad campaign was superb. Taking a cue from the success of the *King Kong* re-release, Warner Brothers saturated the airwaves (not so hard to do in those days since there weren't nearly so many airwaves in use) with *Beast* 's coming attractions trailer. I don't remember seeing the *Kong* ads (a good indication that we didn't have a TV in 1952) but I do I ever remember the trailer for *Beast*. Whoever pieced together that sixty-second run of film must have had little seven-year-old F in mind. It tripped *all* my circuits – circuits I didn't even know I had.

Remember the face-hugger in *Alien*, the way it came out of the egg and into John Hurt's helmet? If so, you've got some idea of the sudden intimacy between little F and the family TV screen when I first saw the *Beast* trailer.

F. PAUL WILSON

This is what I mean by hardwired: Those images did something to me, something akin to a religious epiphany. My entire being responded instantly to the sight of Harryhausen's monster stomping through Manhattan's financial district and sending all these screaming, terrified New Yorkers tripping and falling over each other in panicked flight from it.

It was...beautiful. I think it was love. Or like coming home... and I hadn't even known I'd been away.

I wanted it. Do you understand? I *had* to see that movie. My parents said no way, Jose. (Not in those words, exactly, but the message was just as clear.) The reasons were many: I was too young, the movie was too scary, they'd have to take my little brother, too, (a mere five at the time) and the two of us would be up all night every night for weeks afterward with nightmares.

Hey, no problem. I had it all figured: Mom could take Peter to a Martin & Lewis movie while dear old dad took me to *Beast*. No nightmares, I promise. After all, I was starting second grade in September. And even if I did get nightmares about giant scaly monsters, I wouldn't complain. I wanted nightmares about giant scaly monsters. Hell, I *craved* nightmares about giant scaly monsters.

I thought I had them, but then they pulled their ace card:

Polio.

Most of you probably don't remember the polio epidemics of the post-war 1940's and early 1950's, and so you can't imagine the havoc wrought by poliovirus in its heyday. You think AIDS paranoia is something? Small stuff compared to polio. You have to *work* to catch HIV. I mean, there's got to be intimate contact and an exchange of bodily fluids. Not so with polio. You could be standing with your mother in the check-out line at the local supermarket... someone nearby sneezes... *boom!* you've caught polio.

What did polio do? Ninety per cent of the time,

220

nothing. You'd get a mild flu-like syndrome and three days later you'd be fine. But if you were among the unlucky ten per cent in whom it invaded the nervous system, you could wind up in an iron lung. Or paralyzed for life. Or dead.

And the overwhelming majority of its victims were kids. No reckless behavior, no dirty needle, no tainted transfusion, no unsafe sex involved here. Polio targeted kids, and usually hit them while they were doing normal kid stuff.

Polio epidemics were a summer phenomenon. And since there were no Salk or Sabin vaccines in 1953, no Polio Pioneers yet, the public health departments recommended keeping kids away from crowds. Especially indoor crowds.

Like movie theaters.

My parents had nothing against movies. They took me to Martin & Lewis comedies and all the Disney films, but only in the winter. Summer movies? Uh-uh. You might catch polio.

This was the Holy Writ that was going keep me from seeing *The Beast from 20,000 Fathoms*. Not going to movies in the summer polio season was right up there on a par with not eating meat on Fridays.

But perceiving me as an intelligent child, my folks could not resist trying reason and logic: Come now, Paul. You wouldn't risk paralysis, wasted limbs, life in an iron lung, even death to see some silly make-believe movie monster, would you?

What a question.

Of course I would.

I'd even go back two or three times to see it again. And I told them so every time they asked me. But I'd be reasonable. Just one time will be okay. And don't worry. I won't catch polio. You've seen how long I can hold my breath under water when we go to the beach. I won't breathe while I'm in the theater, okay?

Sorry. No.

1953 was the summer of my discontent. Everyone I

knew – and I do mean *everyone* – had seen or was planning to see *Beast*. Or so they said. Lucky kids. Their parents weren't worried about some silly thing like polio. I remember sneaking off on my bike and pedaling down to Main Street where *Beast* was playing at the Fox Theater. You've seen photos or drawings of starving kids salivating outside the window of a bakery or a restaurant, gazing longingly at the food within, so near yet forever out of reach beyond the glass. That was Li'l F standing before the absolutely neato cool full-color one-sheet poster for *Beast*.

Through June and July I fumed, fussed, and drove my parents nuts. I was relentless. But to no avail. And then one day as we were driving along Route 46, I glanced out the window...

And had a truly brilliant idea.

Immediately I knew how I could get my folks to take me to *Beast*. But it would take planning. Very careful planning.

I was good at that. Because I was always making plans as a kid. I had a rich fantasy life. Always daydreaming. If you ever read *Calvin and Hobbes*, you know me. I never had a stuffed tiger, but I was Calvin. Spaceman Spiff? Me. Calvin even has blond hair, just like Li'l F. It's obvious to anyone who knew me as a kid that Bill Watterson appropriated my childhood for his comic strip.

What I did was lay low for a while; went a whole couple of days without mentioning *Beast* once. I lulled my parents into a false sense of security, let them think the kid had finally lost his obsession with seeing that dumb movie. During that period I was a model child.

And then one night at dinner I brought it up again. I heard my father groan, saw my mother's eyes start to roll back in her head. I leapt to the advantage with a bunch of what-ifs.

What if there was no way I could catch polio seeing *Beast*? Like, what if it was playing in the winter and there was no polio around? Would you take me? Huh, huh? Wouldja?

I guess they figured since there was no way this monster movie was going to be running six months from now, it would be safe to acquiesce. So, finally, to shut me up, they agreed.

Okay. Sure, Paul, if there was no chance of your catching polio, we'd take you to see *The Beast from 20,000 Fathoms*.

I showed them the paper. It was playing at the Route 46 drive-in theater. A *drive-in*. Just me and Dad in the car. No crowds. No polio.

Gotcha!

And then I went into my I'm-going-to-see-*Beast* dance. (I could be an obnoxious kid.) To my folks' credit, they didn't hold it against me. But it wasn't until August, during a two-week stay in a rented bungalow at the Jersey Shore, that my father packed me and my little brother into the family car and took us to the Toms River Drive-In to see *Beast*.

I still remember the almost unbearable anticipation as my father rolled the front wheels onto the mound and set the brake so the car would be parked on a tilt, watching him pull the speaker inside and seat it on the window. He made the obligatory trip to the snack bar, and as the three of us sat in the front seat eating our popcorn and sipping our Cokes, I remember praying for the sky to get dark. Why did it have to stay light so *long?* Whenever I wanted to stay out with my friends, night fell like a steel safe. Where was night when I needed it?

Finally the animated "Ten Minutes to Showtime!" clock appeared on the screen, interrupted by interminable snack bar come-ons with dancing hot dogs and marching Flavo Shrimp Rolls. And then previews of coming attractions – icky romances and war stories – and anything else they could throw on the screen to delay a meaningful cinematic experience.

And then... he Warner Brothers logo, followed by a whirlpool effect and some ominous music.

Is this it? Is this it?

I tell you now, it was worth the wait.

You've seen bugs smashed on your windshield. Well, I was just like one of them, only I was on the *inner* surface, flattened against that glass like I'd hit it at ninety miles an hour.

Beast was everything I'd hoped it would be, from that first glimpse of the eponymous rhedosaurus in the arctic blizzard all the way through to the fiery finale. The film's scenario became the paradigm for all the big monster flicks to follow: A natural or man-made cataclysm (e.g. The Bomb) releases or mutates a huge creature. A lone survivor of said cataclysm or of the monster's first rampage is considered a nut when he describes the perpetrator. Inexplicable occurrences mount until some scientist (inevitably with a lovely daughter/niece/assistant) sees a pattern and figures out what's going on. He too is considered a nut until the monster (of which we've only been allowed glimpses so far) lumbers into the downtown area of a metropolis before millions of witnesses.

Now we get what we bought the ticket for: the chomping and stomping of hundreds of hapless, panicked citizens during scenes of wanton destruction. A special weapon is designed and eventually does the creature in. What science created/unleashed, it can also destroy. By film's end, the genie is back in the bottle but we're left with a warning that there are some aspects of nature with which man was not meant to toy.

Even my father got caught up in the film. He worked for a pharmaceutical firm that had pioneered a number of antibiotics and he was intrigued with the idea that the creature's blood carried an infection from prehistoric times to which we 20th century types were especially susceptible.

Certain scenes are still fresh in my mind: that first

glimpse of the creature through the swirling snow; the scene where it destroys the lighthouse; breaking through the walls of a building in downtown New York. The suspense of the underwater sequence in which the scientist is lowered into one of the Atlantic's off-shore canyons – into the heart of the creature's domain – in a bathysphere is branded on my brain. So deeply branded that I paid homage to the scene in *Nightworld*.

I bought the stop-motion animation – completely. I believed this creature was in the streets of Manhattan. Perhaps because I'd seen those streets in gritty real life on the occasions my father took me to his office when he had to work Saturday mornings. And perhaps because the special effects were the work of Ray Harryhausen. The play of light and shadow along its hide as it moved between the buildings was so real. Bill Warren says (in his indispensable *Keep Watching the Skies*) that it was on *Beast* that Harryhausen developed the techniques he would later perfect for his "Dynamation" process. The seven-year-old kid glued to the inside of the windshield knew nothing of a guy named Harryhausen; he simply *believed*.

Despite its destructiveness, I found myself in sympathy with the rhedosaurus. I was more than a little upset when we killed it with that big magic bullet at the end. The animation was terrific here, and its twisting, turning, tortured death throes were perhaps a bit too real. I felt sorry for it. Finally the dead monster lay curled up within the burning skeleton of an amusement park roller coaster. As the closing credits rolled, my father started the car and we headed back to the bungalow.

I'd done it. I'd seen *The Beast from 20,000 Fathoms*. My life was complete.

But the adventure wasn't finished. We had to cross the Route 37 bridge over Barnegat Bay to get back to Ocean Beach on the barrier island. The bridge at that time was a rickety planked affair no more than a dozen feet above the water. Moonlight was glistening on the bay and I knew at any moment the beast might rear up out of that black water and try to chow down on us. So I cowered and quaked next to my sleeping brother, afraid the rhedosaurus would appear and, I think, almost equally afraid it wouldn't (because I was sure my father could outrun it in our car).

But we made it home without incident. I'd seen my first sci-fi monster movie and I was ecstatic. My folks were almost as happy as I. Finally, I'd stop bugging them about seeing this damn movie. Finally there'd be peace.

And indeed peace reigned in the Wilson house.

Until the trailer for *Them!* started running.

***

The Dirty Dick's Affair

Dirty Dick's Bar
Nassau, Bahamas
March 1963

I'm sixteen years old. I'm wearing a horizontal-stripe boatneck beach shirt over plaid Bermuda shorts, brown loafers, white socks. In my back pocket I've got a creased British Arrow paperback of *More Not at Night* that I picked up in a used bookstall off Bay Street. All topped off by a straw hat with a one-foot crown.

Get the picture?

Total. Geek.

I'm in Nassau on a family vacation. My folks and their good

friends, the Blindts, have flown themselves and all six kids to the Bahamas to escape the New Jersey winter. The daily ritual has become: Beach and touristy stuff all day until 4 o'clock or so when we all traipse down to the famous Dirty Dick's Bar on Bay Street for afternoon libations. The adults hang at the bar in the front room while the kids – three Wilsons and three Blindts, varying in age from 10 to 16 – are relegated to the backroom. Martinis for the adults, cokes or virgin cocktails for the kids. The only good thing about the backroom is the jukebox.

We don't talk much. We've been together all day so there's not a lot left to say. Mostly we listen to the music (if I hear "Yellow Bird" one more time, I will kill) and I read my book. I love the warm weather and the beach, but the bar bores me.

(*"Up and at 'em. We're heading for Dirty Dick's."*
"Aaaaw, again?")

Until...

I don't recall if it's our 2nd or 3rd day there. We usually have the backroom to ourselves at that time of day, but today I look up as three young women enter. They're wearing open blouses over bikinis. They have mocha skin, full, pouty lips, and tons of ebony hair piled atop their heads. They're only a few years older than yours truly, who develops an instant crush on the tall one – but I could have an equal crush on any of the trio.

And then they start to dance to whatever's playing on the jukebox. In their bikinis.

I am mesmerized. Can't take my eyes off them. They are from a different world. They are so cool, so comfortable in their smooth, flawless, bikini'd skin, and they sway so gracefully. I remove my straw hat, but I keep my book out because I can hide my staring by pretending to read. They're totally in their own world and I am wallpaper.

Finally one of our parents announces it's time to go to dinner.

Really? Do we have to leave already?

Next day I'm hanging over my father asking when we're going to Dirty Dick's.

When we return – finally! – the three exotic ladies are already there. Dancing. In their bikinis. (My brother thinks he remembers them doing the limbo. I doubt this. I have no memory of it and am sure beyond question that images of them limboing in their bikinis would have been deeply branded on my still-developing hippocampus.)

Again, I am mesmerized until we're pulled away to attend a dinner-theater restaurant somewhere inland. Little Anthony is going to be singing. The Beatles haven't hit the US yet, but I'm already so over Little Anthony and his ilk. Same with post-Army Elvis. I much prefer what's called R&B. (I don't call it that; don't know if I've even heard the term yet; I just know that Rufus Thomas and Smokey Robinson and Mary Wells have something I like.) But when you're on a family vacation, you go where the family goes.

So we cab inland to this big outdoor restaurant with lots of round tables and a stage. After an indifferent meal, the show starts. But not Little Anthony right away. First we have to sit through an opening act no one has ever heard of: The Ronettes.

I look up and my jaw drops (quite literally) as the three exotic gals from Dirty Dick's step onto the stage. They're dolled up with huge eyelashes and thick eyeliner and squeezed into short slinky dresses, but no question: it's *them*.

And they can *sing!* The lead singer – my second deepest crush of the trio – has this powerful voice with a natural vibrato.

I'm mesmerized all over again. The nameless beauties are nameless no more: They're the Ronettes.

I can't wait to get to Dirty Dick's the next day. I'm determined to screw up my courage and speak to them – tell them I saw them sing and think they're great. But they don't show. On their way to the next stop on Little Anthony's tour, I guess.

Ah, well. We'll always have Nassau.

Fast-forward six months to either shortly before or after Labor Day (not sure) when I'm 17 and have my driver's license. I'm cruising somewhere (or maybe just cruising). As usual I'm listening to my fave Top-40 drive-time DJ Dan Ingram on WABC-AM; he says something about a new song from a group called the Ronettes.

Wait...Ronettes? That name rings a bell. I turn up the volume to hear "Boom...boom-boom-*BAM!* Boom...boom-boom-*BAM!*" (I started drumming for a garage band over the summer so I'm immediately pulled in.) And then that voice from Nassau starts singing, *"The night we met I knew I... needed you so..."*

I damn near drive off the road. It's them! I *know* them! Well, not really, but I feel as if I do. Yeah. I knew them before they were on the radio. I knew them *when*, baby!

I love-love-love the song. And I get this feeling that, even if they never record another tune, I'm a Ronettes fan for life.

THE BEST SONGS

"Be My Baby" – this put the Ronettes on the map. Hal Blaine's iconic drum opening, and then Ronnie kicks in, backed by Phil Spector's famous Wall of Sound. Her fellow Ronettes – sister Estelle and cousin Nedra (the tall one) – aren't on the record. They were back in NYC while all sorts of LA music peeps like Sonny and Cher, Darlene Love, Nino Tempo, and others crowded into Gold Star Studios to sing backup.

"Baby I Love You" – Jeff Barry and Ellie Greenwich, who wrote "Be My Baby," returned to compose the Ronettes' second hit, which is pretty much a redo of "Be My Baby," right down to the "Whoa-ho-ho-ho" that became Ronnie's signature. (Back in the day, when you had a hit with "Up on the Roof," you followed it with "Under the Boardwalk." You followed "It's My Party and I'll Cry if I Want To" with "Judy's Turn to Cry." And so on.)

"(The Best Part of) Breaking Up" – Ronnie's got all pistons firing, especially her sultry "C'mon, beeby" in the outro. (Written by Pete Andreoli and Vincent Poncia.)

"Do I Love You?" – a long intro featuring Carol Kaye's melodic, mesmerizing bass line leading to Spector's thickest Wall of Sound yet. (Also written by Andreoli-Poncia.)

"Walking in the Rain" – written by another married songwriting powerhouse, Barry Mann and Cynthia Weil. The Wall of Sound is downplayed during the verses but comes on strong on the chorus. Nice build at the end of the bridge. Notable for strategic thunder claps.

"You Baby" – by Mann-Weil again; not sure if this was ever a single, but it's a super song, especially Ronnie's moany little "*Ohs*" in the outro.

"I Wonder" – this Barry-Greenwich tune was never a single but a great record with a muscular Wall of Sound (including castanets and Hal Blaine getting all sorts of manic on the toms).

***

Laura Nyro (pronounced like the Roman emperor) was inducted into the Rock and Roll Hall of Fame in 2012. About freakin time.

For those not in the know or too young to remember, Laura

Nyro was a cult phenomenon of the 60s. Find her old Verve and Columbia records and listen to that voice – from her second album onward she did all her own harmonies; listen to those early lyrics and consider that they were written by a teenager. Many of her devotees were other musicians who had hits with her more commercial songs – "Stoned Soul Picnic," "And When I Die," "Stoney End," "Eli's Coming," to name but a few. (Ironically, her biggest single was a cover of Goffin & King's "Up on the Roof.") She dropped out of the scene in the seventies but eventually came back. Sometime in the 90s I caught her show with a quartet at the Bottom Line in Greenwich Village and it brought back a night years and years before when I dropped in on one of her recording sessions.

What follows is true. Mostly. I wrote the piece back in '69 with the old Crawdaddy *or* Creem *in mind as a market. It never sold then, but Kim Newman and Paul McAuley printed it in their* In Dreams *anthology. And later, after her untimely death from ovarian cancer, I offered it to her website and they ran it for years. Might still be running it.*

Here's how that night went down...

Nyro Fiddles

CBS Recording Studios
The New York Tendaberry sessions
July 20, 1969

We were supposed to go to Studio A but there didn't seem to be a Studio A in this building so Mary asks the guard where's the Laura Nyro session and he says it's in Studio B on the second floor. A placard by the guard's desk reminds us that Arthur Godfrey broadcasts from the sixth floor.

We sign in and take the elevator.

The main double door to Studio B opens into a sort of T-shaped vestibule with the sound studio to the right and the engineer's booth to the left. I hesitate outside, not sure we should walk in because it's in use right now and we had been told to go to Studio A in the first place. The guard could be wrong (it's been known to happen) and the studio could be filled with strangers and I'd feel dumb walking in and then just turning around and leaving.

Then through the door window I see Jimmy Haskell walk by from the sound studio to the booth and I know this must be the place. Jimmy's arranging the horns for Laura. He's a sweet, easy-going, middle-aged guy with a salt-and-pepper beard and he's wearing a beanie with propellers sticking out each side. They spin deliriously as he walks.

Laura likes everyone to be happy at her sessions.

We walk into the booth and there's Laura and a friend smoking a little pipe. The friend has longish hair and a mustache, both brown, and is wearing one of those knee-length Indian style coat-shirts, and I think he looks a lot like a guy who used to play lead guitar in my band.

Laura sits by the console in her full-length black dress and black lace shawl and that incredible black hair and I think maybe she's put on a few pounds since I last saw her. There's also this German shepherd running around and it has what looks like an old Sara Lee coffee cake tin in the closet filled with dog food and every so often goes over and chomps some down. Laura tells us the dog's name is Beauty Belle (or did she say Bill?)

It's eight o'clock and the session was supposed to start at seven but the engineers are having trouble setting up the second eight tracks and Laura Nyro, who's usually fairly talkative, is preoccupied tonight. Dallas – could be the city, a guy, or a gal – is on the phone and Laura's telling he, she, or it how stoned she is. The engineer's on another line with someone named Danny explaining that he doesn't see how he can mix the new album this week because his kids are out of school and he's gotta spend some time with them. Indian Coat was trying to persuade him on this point earlier but Indian Coat is now out in the sound studio talking to Twin-

Prop Jimmy while the musicians sit around bullshitting, trying each other's instruments, and getting paid scale for it. Beauty Belle is watching Indian Coat very intently through the glass.

A young photographer approaches the console and waits for the lady to get off the phone. He shows her some shots he took of her a while back and she picks out some she likes and says she doesn't want to give this one or that one to Vogue because they're very personal-type pictures, you know? Indian Coat strolls in and says he wants that one blown up for his wall and Laura says he's got to be kidding. She hates that picture. Well, she doesn't really hate it, it's just that she likes others better and I get the impression she's uncomfortable with the word hate.

Break time rolls around for the musicians so they interrupt their bullshitting in the studio and move it out to the hall where they regroup around the soft drink machine. I go over and hang with one of the trumpets I know who with a couple more years could be old enough to be Laura's father and he tells me it's anarchy, pure and simple anarchy, but wait and see... they'll start to play and she'll point things out and say do this and try that and before you know it everything falls into place and it's beautiful, man. The girl's crazy but she sure as hell knows her music.

Back in the booth they're blasting "Time and Love," the song that's to be re-recorded tonight. The backup tracks were laid down at an earlier session but something didn't click and so they're going to be done again tonight. Laura's tracks with her piano and vocal won't be touched and the band will play off them. After the second run-through of the tape Mary turns to me and says it sounds familiar and I say I guess it does have a few phrases reminiscent of "Flim-Flam Man," especially in the fade.

After more replays the band thinks it's ready and they try it. It's about nine now and Laura wants to finish by ten (definitely no overtime tonight) but the drummer isn't the same one as last time and he's doing some of his own thing (like doubles on the downbeat) and Laura wants to know the drummer's name. Jimmy tells her it's Maurice and she gets on the mike and tells Maurice what she wants. Her speaking voice is soft, almost sibilant, and I can never get used to associating it with the power, range, and clarity that explodes when she gets behind her piano. She tells Maurice to do it like Gary Chester did at the last session, keep it simple and easy and light and happy and no cymbals except for a bam-bam-crash in the chorus and only a one-stroke downbeat, okay?

At first I think the doubles on the downbeat sound better than the singles Laura wants but as the session wears on I come around to agreeing with the lady in black. Many more tries follow and one sounds perfect until Maurice forgets the boom-boom on his bass drum that leads into the fade. It's 9:50 and Laura swears she's not going into overtime again. Everything's going to stop dead at 10:00 whether "Time and Love" is finished or not. Okay now, everybody be happy and light, everybody smile, and one of the percussion men sticks his head out from behind some baffling and flashes Laura this hideous shit-eating grin and everybody laughs.

At 10:15 the musicians take another break and Laura is asking about overtime. At 10:30 all the musicians pile into the engineer's booth to hear the last take. It's crowded and Mary and I have other stops to make tonight so we leave without good-byes because no one could hear us over the replay anyway. Art Garfunkel comes in as we're leaving and asks if the Nyro session is here and I tell him yes. He shakes his head and says he heard it was Studio A.

Outside the moon is high and bright and I remember hearing that somebody might be walking on it tonight. I also hear that Laura Nyro sleeps in a coffin.

I don't know.

***

Published in a 1984 issue of Richard Geis's fanzine, Science Fiction Review, *shortly after the release of the film of* The Keep. *I'm a bit taken aback at the raw emotion and bitter disappointment on display here. How naïve. Robert Bloch read this and dropped me one of his famous postcards:* "You think it's bad when they do it to your novel? Imagine when they do the same to your screenplay!"

Look What They've Done to My Song, Ma

I'd been a knot of tension all day but the liter or so of Freixenet brut under my belt had gone a long way toward untying me by screening time. As the theatre darkened and the screen lightened and the Dolbyized sounds of Tangerine Dream vibrated the seats, I held hands' with my wife and watched. Like Thomas who first wanted to thrust his fingers into Christ's wounds, I'd said all along that until I sat in a theatre and saw it with my own eyes, I wouldn't believe it. But there it was: *The Keep...* "based on the novel by F. Paul Wilson."

Never thought it would happen. The book's slouch toward the screen had been a perfect example of Murphy's Law. A great start: Koch-Kirkwood Productions had generously optioned it for CBS Theatrical films in the summer of '80; *The Keep* was to be part of CBS' big expansion plan. But no one wanted the author to script the movie – he'd never done a screenplay before and couldn't be entrusted to cut his teeth on such a big project. A "pro" was brought in but his screenplay was rejected. Then the screenwriters struck. "Could we have an extension on the first option because of the strike?" Sure. Then Michael Mann was brought on the scene as writer-director – "to ensure a unity of vision on the project." I'd been impressed with *Thief* and *The Jericho Mile* and figured we were cookin' now.

Then CBS went and released a couple of flops and decided to tighten the belt on all future productions. Koch-Kirkwood-Mann said they couldn't make *The Keep* under the new budget restrictions so they went to Paramount and worked a turnaround. Things began to go smoothly for a while: Oscar-winner John Box was signed as production designer, and Wally Veevers, who had worked on all sorts of goodies, from Menzies' *Things to Come* in '35, through Kubrick's 2001, to *Superman*, came on as optical effects director. Principle photography was completed in December, '82 and *The Keep* was scheduled as a summer of '83 release.

Then, tragically, Wally Veevers died before he really got started on the sfx. The early summer release became late summer, then was pushed back to November. Now it was December. Finally, all was ready. I knew it was going to be good. It had to be. Despite the fact that Michael Mann had not deigned to reply to my comments on the first draft of his screenplay nor to my offer of any assistance that he might require, that he had been cool and distant when I visited the set at Shepperton Studios in England, that he had refused to allow me an early screening, that during the entire project he had not sought any advice or opinion from the originator of the characters and concept of the story he was filming, I was sure it was going to be a good film. After all, I'd heard all along how Mann had thrown himself into the project, going so far as to dig out old SS and Wehrmacht manuals to assure a look of utter authenticity; he even brought a linguist to the set to teach the British actors how to speak not with a German accent, but with a German rhythm. He was the movie-maker and I was the book-writer. He was working in his field of expertise. (When I expressed to Whitley Strieber – who had already been down this road twice – my confidence in how well everything was going, he gave me a. small, knowing little smile. I didn't understand that smile then.)

I told myself that in order to protect his own vision, Mann was trying to put some distance between himself and the originator, afraid I'd act like an overprotective parent and harass him to distraction. So despite the rudeness, the rejection, the cavalier attitude, I was sure it was going to be a great movie. Had to be. It had everything going for it. Mann and Paramount knew what they were doing, right? Everything was under control, right?

Imagine a sylvan god creating tree after tree after tree, painstakingly etching each crag in the bark, each vein in every fashioning utterly perfect, unspeakably beautiful trees.
Now imagine him getting lost in his own forest.

The first half of the film was one of the most glorious experiences of my life. (It doesn't compare to hearing that your wife is fine and you're the father of a healthy little girl, but it's up there.) To see scenes you wrote for the page come alive on the screen is an experience every writer should have just once in his life. The photography, the lighting, the sets – all absolutely stunning. I'm a sucker for the expressionistic blend of light and shadow the Germans did so well in the 20s and 30s and much of *The Keep* reminded me of that.

But the narrative...I noticed dangerous little cracks in the narrative. I brushed my fears aside: Michael Mann knows what he's doing; he'll patch them up.

But he didn't patch them up. He let them get wider, becoming fissures, then wide bottomless chasms that eventually swallowed the whole movie. I didn't realize that immediately, but as my post-screening euphoria wore off, I began to question the film objectively.

Silly things – like changing Woermann from the last of a long line of Prussian military men to a street socialist who'd fought the fascists in Spain half a dozen years before. Not only does this rob Woermann of his conflict of loyalties but anyone with a couple of functioning neurons knows that socialist fighters in Spain in 1936 don't wind up Wehrmacht captains in 1941. It is laughable. But not as laughable as Mann's version of Molasar. If he didn't think a human form was visual enough, he could have kept Molasar in a cloud or blurred his outlines or *something!* Anything but that cross between a rubberized Darth Vader and a flayed ape.

He failed to develop a single character to the point where we could care about him or her. He made Glenn/Glaeken into a robot, and added a priest who did almost nothing. Glaeken and Eva (why wasn't "Magda" an acceptable name?) meet on a hill and – *cut!* – they are in bed. Cuza's crisis of faith was gone. The whole point of Cuza being a Jew – other than the irony it lent his position – was to allow Molasar to fake the power of the cross over himself and use that as a lever against Cuza's soul. Without that crisis, the presence of a Jew in the keep smacks of exploitation.

The plot was chopped up into an incomprehensible mishmash. There is no dramatic tension, no catharsis. Molasar's final destruction of the German soldiers takes place off stage as in a Greek drama – we hear a few shots, some screams, and then find everyone charred to a crisp. Glaeken's final battle with Molasar, the confrontation to which the whole movie should have been pointing, is over in a flash. Glaeken's triumph is perfunctory at best, then he too is sucked into the vortex. As in a typical B movie from the 50s, anyone or anything that doesn't quite belong in this place and time cannot be allowed to remain. I avoided that cliché in the book but apparently Mann did not choose to do so in his film.

A parade of missed opportunities. That's what's so frustrating. This wasn't a schlock production. Lots of money, time and talent were involved. What went wrong? I do not know. I can't get a straight answer from anyone. I have production stills of scenes that never made it to the screen, scenes that might have given some of the characters a little depth and explained more of the plot. But they're on the cutting room floor. Why? I don't know.

Maybe Paramount, for its own reasons, made Mann cut the film down to 97 minutes. I'll probably never know. No one tells the author a damn thing.

Whatever the reasons, the story is gone. Nothing is left but a bewildering progression of beautifully lit, wonderfully angled pieces of film. I feel betrayed. Cheated. It angers me to know that millions of people will walk out of the movie thinking that's the way I wrote the book. Some of them will no doubt pick up a copy, but most will not opt for what they'll feel is a more concentrated dose of confusion. And there will be uncounted millions more who will skip the movie *and* the book because of all the scathing reviews from the film critics.

I could have helped. I offered and, God knows, I was willing. If I'd been allowed a little input I could have made it a better picture. Mann the film maker in collaboration with Wilson the storyteller might have come up with a winner. After all, it's my story. I know it best.

As Jeffrey Lyons said on PBS, "It could have been wonderful."

Amen.

***

The FTL Newsfeed Saga

My favorite writing project to work on?

Hands down, *FTL Newsfeed* for the Sci-Fi Channel.

Yes, I know it's Syfy now, but back then it was the Sci-Fi Channel.

FTL was the first – and for a while the only – original programming on the Sci-Fi Channel. An interstitial show, a daily one-minute news blurb from 150 years in the future that ran at various times during the day Monday through Friday, and repeated on the weekends. In fact, an *FTL* was the very first piece of programming broadcast by the channel (introducing *Star Wars*).

Let me give you a little background.

In the summer of '92 I got a call from a guy named Bob Siegal from USA Network saying they were launching the Sci-Fi Channel soon and could I design a world 150 years in the future? I said sure. Then he said he needed it all done and set to go in 6 weeks. I was finishing *The Select* at that time, trying to get it ready for the upcoming Frankfurt Book Fair, and knew I couldn't deliver. Matt Costello and I had shot the bull a few times at various NECons and I'd been impressed with how bright and quick and versatile he was; I'd also gathered that he had a work ethic similar to mine (which is, simply, sit down and do it). Plus he lived only an hour outside the city. (The Sci-Fi Channel was Manhattan based.) So I gave his name to Bob Siegal.

Matt called me back and asked if I was *sure* I didn't want it. I reconsidered and said why don't we split the work? We worked our butts off, meetings, conference calls, faxing, modeming, and finally e-mailing files back and forth – this was cutting edge in 1992. We delivered (on time, I might add) a future scenario detailing the socio-political-economic-technological status of the entire globe and near space for the year 2142 that, quite frankly, blew them away.

We didn't write the actual scripts at first. A fellow named Russ Firestone adapted them from our bible. We'd lay out the story arcs in narrative and in a flow sheet that showed what was happening when and where throughout the year on a month-by-month and week-by-week basis. We'd usually hand that in during the summer, then get called sporadically throughout the year to provide fillers for the newsfeeds. But they let Russ go after two seasons and asked us if we wanted to do the whole thing. We signed in July 1994, and from September '94 onward, scripts as well as story were all ours.

That was when the fun began.

As before, Matt and I would meet a couple of times

a year to map out the large story arcs. But as scripters we'd sit down every quarter and break the arcs into 13-week sections, then block out the 65 individual spots (5 per week for thirteen weeks) that were taped in NYC over a four-day period every three months.

We'd sit in one or the other's kitchen and toss quips back and forth, each taking the topic in question to the next level of possibility, until we started laughing. That was when we knew we'd gone too far, and we'd back up a step.

Matt and I were very well paid for having a lot of fun – hell, we would have done it for free. Plus, we were given carte blanche. The folks from USA Network (the parent company) running the channel weren't sci-fi oriented; *FTL* was a kind a mystery to them, so they let us do what we wanted. The show was surreal in a way: serious, sinister storylines peopled with goofy characters. I remember executives coming up to us and saying, "Is this really science fiction?" We'd nod sagely. "Absolutely." They'd walk away scratching their heads. But we had an insurance policy: We'd cast the head of USA Network, Kay Koplovitz, in a major role as (what else?) the president of the North American Union. Not a Glenn Close by any means, but she was a trouper, learning her lines and hitting her marks.

Not only was it hands-on experience in screenwriting – the equivalent of writing a four-hour-and-twenty-minute movie every year – but we got to work with great people. We had Gilbert Gotfried, Timothy Leary, Peter Straub, Jeffery Lyons, Kreskin and others doing guest spots. Rhonda Shear (remember USA's "Up All Night" movies?) was a regular as Bimbetta Mondaine; so was Tom Monteleone as a (what else?) future mafia capo. Vida Pelletier took over as our producer and we loved her. She was up for anything. We'd make an off-the-wall suggestion and she'd say, "Yeah, we can do that." We got to work with the crazy people at Image Post who did fabulous editing. All those crawls you see on the news stations now? *FTL* had those to the Nth degree back in the early 90s.

In the fall of '96, after a run of a little over 4 years, we received word that this current batch of newsfeeds we were taping would be the last. The network wanted the *FTL* budget for its own movies and such. The last feed aired Christmas week. We wished we'd had enough warning to allow us to tie up some of the storylines, but all in all, no regrets.

FTL launched 9/24/92 and ended 12/20/1996. Where are those 1,106 episodes? I doubt very much anyone has them all – including USA Network. (Or, if USA does have them, I doubt they know where they are). I have most of them, but a gap occurred when the network switched video production companies. So I think I can safely predict that there will never be a complete compilation of *FTL Newsfeed*. And as time goes on, my videotape copies will deteriorate to the point where they are unplayable.

Sic transit Gloria.

***

Written during the 2012 primaries, it's pretty much self-explanatory. Published in a number of places online.

Ron Paul

The Free State Project folks shipped me up to Nashua, NH, last weekend to speak at their annual Liberty Forum. Friday night I was drinking with a couple of the guys when one of them said a friend was having Ron Paul over for a breakfast meeting the next morning and did I want to go. The closest I've ever been to a presidential candidate was my old Georgetown classmate Bill Clinton – we shared the same dorm floor for a year or two - and he'd been running only for class president in those days. Here was a chance to get up close and personal with a guy in the heat of the Big One.

The modest, two-story house sits on a snowy hill

in Limeboro. After trudging up a steep set of not-so-well-shoveled steps, we're welcomed by the owner and offered coffee and homemade muffins and scones. Ron Paul arrives a few minutes later with his wife Carol, his granddaughter, and a couple of aides.

He's anything but physically imposing, and he lacks Bill's room-commanding presence. He looks tired but not fragged. His dark suit is wrinkled and his nose is running a little from the cold outside. As he stands near the center of the room, the dozen or so of us present begin asking him questions and he responds in a measured tone with minimal gesticulation. It doesn't take long to realize that all his opinions – whether on foreign policy or monetary policy or education topics - are linked, all part of a cohesive, philosophical whole that keeps harking back to the "blueprint," the Constitution.

And as the coffee klatch rolls on, I realize that this man hasn't a chance. He speaks to the mind rather than the heart. He promises sweeping reforms in almost every aspect of the government, and though that may resonate with the folks in this room, it's not enough. His opponents are promising varying degrees of a cradle-to-grave nanny state with a chicken in every pot. He's speaking to the adult in us, they're speaking to the child. I have no illusions about whose message will resonate farther and wider.

I just checked last night's New Hampshire primary totals. The Live-Free-or-Die state has chosen the latter.

***

9/3/12 – Spellbinders Conference in Hilton Hawaiian Village in Waikiki

Shelly Berman

So yesterday I'm bitching about the celebrity culture and how I couldn't think of anyone I'd cross the street to meet. Comes Sunday I'm sitting in the hotel bar and in walks Shelly Berman (apparently he's in *a 5-0* episode). I listened to his stand-up comedy records as a kid and can still quote passages. So who must, simply MUST get his photo with the man? He's still funny. Tugs on his toupee, looks Dennis's bald pate, and tells him he should think about getting one; looks at me and says, "Yours is pretty good - almost looks real."

***

Back in 1989 I read some excerpts from Greg Benford's daily journal in a fanzine (I think) and thought I'd try that, just to keep track my increasingly busy life. So I started a digital diary the first day of the new decade and didn't last 6 months. I was writing so much already (and this was before FTL or the interactive work came along) that I couldn't make time for it. I found these entries in the OLDSTUFF file on my hard drive and got exhausted reading them. No wonder I cut the medical practice down to 2 days a week in 1992. I was intrigued by the March 1 entry: I'd forgotten that "When He Was Fab" started as a dream and that my first thought was a teleplay. (Oh, and LISL was the working title for what would become Reprisal.*)*

But let me set the stage: It's 1990. I had a computer – an MS-DOS model using WordPerfect as a word processor and storing my output on 3.5 inch floppy disks. The PCs were discrete systems in those days, in that they were not connected to any other systems. The online world was a bit arcane to the lumpen PC proletariat in those days, so I didn't get online until 1992 when I bought a top-of-the-line 14.4 kb modem and joined an online service called GEnie – General Electric Network for Information Exchange. Got the picture? No email, no cell phones, no texting. You communicated via landline, fax, and the US mail – we wrote letters.

1990

January

1/Mon

A new year and this is the first entry into a new thing for me: A journal.

DeChristmasizing the house today. M and E helping; J working at Rod's. Printed out final draft of "Pelts", will send to Bill Munster tomorrow. Mary couldn't read it; gave J a stomach ache. Maybe I'm onto something.

Mary had a ball doing her New Year's Day rearranging in the house while I started trying to catch up on the on the LISL pages left undone due to last week's holiday activities. I find myself shying away from it because this is the scene where Bill finds the mutilated Danny. This is rough stuff; sometimes I fear I'm going too far; but I've got to present something gut-wrenchingly awful, awful enough to make a man whose whole life is his faith turn away from God and the Church. Believe me, it ain't easy. Even I'm afraid to turn the page. Wonder how the readers will do. I don't want to turn them off before they get to the real heart of the story. Will try to get a through it before the Notre Dame/Colorado game.

2

"Pelts" went off to Bill Munster today.

Tough day in the office. Saw 38 pts. Always a madhouse after a long weekend. Worked on the REBORN flap copy at lunch; have to call Susan about the back cover of the REBORN paperback – it mentions Carol's pregnancy! After all the trouble I went to to misdirect the reader from that, Berkley puts it on the goddam cover. Shit.

Got through the rough stuff in LISL yesterday. Smoother sailing today. Dubbing off some tapes while I write now to watch while I'm gerbiling on the bike: *Hellraiser II, Graveyard Shift, They Live.*

Duke just called and asked if I could help him find a ghostwriter / collaborator for his autobiography. Promised I'd call Al. If he can't help, maybe Jim Frenkel can – I understand he's doing some packaging these days.

Mary saw *Steel Magnolias* with Bernadette tonight. Had a good cry. Glad I missed it.

3

Called Al about Duke but he hasn't got back to me yet.

Very busy in the office today. Had to work the night session to keep up with the appointments. Flu is here. Had to go back for a night session. Saw 36 pts. total.

Managed to knock off 3 pages on LISL before M's b-ball game. Mary had the windows open and it was cold as hell but I stuck it out till 3. M's team played Holmdel and killed them. She did well defensively as usual and I was glad to see her taking some shots. My father came along. It's the first and only game of M's he'll see since he and Ma are leaving for Florida tomorrow. He enjoyed it. Really seemed to enjoy SIBS too; wrote a very nice note. Says Ma hated all the sex in it, which I expected. I told him if Gabor was taking over other people's bodies just to go for carriage rides around Central Park, there wouldn't be much of a story. He wholeheartedly agreed.

J watched *Hellraiser II* before I returned it to Video C. Said it was gross.

4

Ah. A day off from the office. The folks are back in Florida by now. I finished my second 20-min segment of *Hellraiser II* and can see why J thought it was gross. Pretty fucking twisted. I don't feel so bad about that scene in LISL anymore.

Took J out to Tube Steaks for lunch and then over to the Grenville so she could apply for a summer waitressing job. Tried to talk to her about getting on track for her future, about being her own person, independent, etc. I think she was listening. Good kid.

The package from Ed Gorman arrived today: advance proof of UNDER THE GUN (containing "Faces") and a couple of his westerns. His picture is on the back of BLOOD GAME. He looks like he sounds – like a gentle St. Bernard. Also, the signature sheets arrived from Dark Harvest. Oh, joy.

Caught up on LISL (8 pages) and am now back on schedule. Renny is the kind of hardboiled character I can write in my sleep. Even had time to do the flap copy for REBORN (unabashed, backslapping self-promotion, but fun) and do about 3 pages on "Midnight Mass." All in all a pretty satisfying day.

5

One helluva day. S called at 8 a.m. and canceled out for the day. Saw 33 pts. in all.

So the morning was a mess, topped off by a call from Anna McGee saying that Tor didn't have the final draft of "The Barrens" for *Lovecraft's Legacy*. Could I FedEx her a copy? Swell. Signed the sheets for the lettered copies of REBORN between patients. The silver ink pen leaked on a bunch of them but I think there's enough for the 52-copy run. Jocelyn called about reversion of my sf novels from Doubleday. Still not reverted yet.

Came home, Mary was out, did 3 pages on "Mass" then J

& I went up to Belmar to see M play Asbury Park. St. Rose won but Asbury played them tough. M played another excellent defensive game. I rushed back to the office to eat my cold potato and start evening hours. Saw 20 pts. and made a fresh copy of "The Barrens". Didn't get home till 9:40. Bushed.

6

My weekend on call. Had to run to Brick medical records to do a discharge summary on an incomplete chart and then to the office where F and I ran our butts off to keep up with the schedule. Saw 23 pts. this a.m. FedEx picked up "The Barrens" for Tor. Got out at 12:30 carrying the beeper. Picked up new burner for the stove and got home at 1:20. Found a Fed-Ex package from Susan with the *Reborn* page proofs. She needs them back by the 20th. I'm starting to feel overwhelmed. Had some lunch with Mary and then did another three pages on "Mass." Wrote R. Patrick Gates to tell him I won't have time to read his *Grimm Memorials* galleys and blurb it. Not 100% true. I read about a quarter of it and found it very distasteful. Not as offensive as Alan Rogers' *The Children* (at least not so far) but in the same vein. Knocked off another 3 pages on "Mass" before it was time to meet the K&B for dinner at the Draughting Table. Their son B (23) came along; a charming guy.

The beeper didn't go off, I had some John Courage with dinner, and managed not to overeat. Mary and I tried to watch *Physical Evidence* (I liked the Hitchcockian opener) but we fell asleep before it really got started.

7/Sun

Finished *Hellraiser II* while exercising. An impressive piece of surrealist gross-out, a visual killer but nothing lingers on the palate. Saw 10 in the office this a.m. then met Mary and the girls at The Grenville for brunch and this time I did overeat. Back home I did 5 pgs on LISL and signed all 500 sheets for the Dark Harvest REBORN while watching the Giants lose the playoff. Boxed them up for Steve Gervais. Skipped dinner because I wasn't hungry. Gave J SIBS to read. Marty Greenberg called late wanting to know if I'd co-edit an anthology of WWII sf/horror with him. Said no. (Yay! I said no!) Also told me that Fr. Greely vetoed "Be Fruitful" for *Sacred Visions* (and they already paid for the reprint rights) because it was "too strong." I should send him a copy of REBORN. Ha!

8/Mon

Did another 3 pages on LISL, mailed the signature pages off to Gervais. Had a hellish day in the office (39 pts.), came home, had a couple of spritzers, a shower, then collapsed. Ed Gorman wants to trade HPL stories; sent me his ("The Order of Things Unknown"). Ordered a set of Banzai 2000 knives from the TV ad. I'm like Opus when it comes to these offers.

9

A monster day in the office (38 pts.). I'm glad it's not like this all the time. Copied off "The Barrens" for Ed. I'll send him a copy of THE TERY too. Began proofing REBORN during lunch hour. J cooked us chicken marsala tonight – delicious. Did a couple of pages on LISL. B called re: some places in Maui that he'll check out for us over the next 3 weeks.

10

Finished watching *Graveyard Shift* this a.m. Routine formula vampire cum slasher junk movie; knew from the poor continuity of the opening cuts (wet pavement, then dry pavement, then wet again) that it wasn't going to be worth the time. One interesting line: When somebody holds up a cross, the vampire shrugs it off, saying, "That's not real."

A pageless day. Had to work the afternoon for G. The office is still busy as hell; saw 34. Tonight is tennis night. Got out of the office at 5, Mary picked me up, and we were on the court a little after 6. My new racket (Prince CTS 110) is my first oversized and it's super on volleys, gives better control overall, but I think I lose something in groundstroke power, but I've been hitting them long most of the time so all in all it's a beneficial trade. J joined the 6 of us for pizza afterward at the Squan. A good day, even if no writing got done.

11

Have to work the afternoon for G. Another 3 pages on LISL this a.m. (16 this week for a total of 266), then 4 hrs in the office (18 pts), then home. Put my FREAK SHOW notes onto the disk and did 6 pgs on "Mass."

12

The afternoon off. Did some more work on FREAK SHOW presentation and a few more pages on "Mass;" it's coming very well. Dropped some of J's stuff off with Jim B to take to Loyola. Picked up the 8x10 of the girls – looks great. The Squirrel-a-whirl arrived (looked neat in the catalog so I ordered it – yes, another impulse buy). Missed M's game against Pt. Boro tonight. Mary says it was a good one – they were trailing most of the first half but came back to win. J is packing up to leave tomorrow. It was good having her home; gonna miss her.

13

A whole weekend off! Have a headache. Did some work on "Mass" (I'm on pg. 23), went to M's game against Red Bank Regional – somehow they managed to win despite the worst reffing I've ever seen. The Bitch was reffing again. (Good ol' Shannon D managed to get another technical for mouthing off to a ref.) Drove J to Trenton for the train then went to see *Tango & Cash*. Excellent pacing and some inventive action sequences, but I never believed either of those two characters for a minute; a poor man's *Lethal Weapon*.

14

A good day. Did 8 pages on LISL and read about 70 page proofs on REBORN while watching a crushingly dull play-off between the Rams & 49ers. Steve Spruill called about getting us together with the Winters down there for a weekend. Told him about FREAK SHOW and how I want him to join HWA so I can get a story from him; he agreed.

15/Mon

Five more pages on LISL this a.m. M.L. King day so there's no mail. Worked in the office till 9. Saw 37 pts.

16

Another busy day in the office – 36 pts. Ran errands and read REBORN proofs at lunch hour, then rushed out to see M's game against Allentown. They won. J called from Loyola with her new phone number and her new room number. Glad she's settled in. She's been out of touch since Saturday night. Got a card from Dave Schow – wants to get together while he's in NYC. Don't know if I can work it out. Finished the week's 15th pg on LISL today. Unusual to get the quota done by Tuesday night.

17

Have to work tonight to keep up with the demand. Worked on the REBORN piece for *Mystery Scene* and revamped the FREAK SHOW outline. Paul Mikol called; wants very much to do SIBS; apparently everybody who's read it there is very high on it; plans a Jan. 1991 pub date; told him to call Al. Left a message on Schow's machine. Al called; we sold hardcover rights on SIBS to Dark Harvest for a low advance to leave them their cash flow; we'll catch up on the back end. The Berkley contract for SIBS hasn't shown up yet. Finished the REBORN page proofs. Made a few changes that won't be in Dark Harvest; means the Berkley version will be the definitive one. Missed tennis tonight. Saw 37 pts.

18

A day off. Worked on "Mass" most of the day. It's going through a slow section but did about seven pages this morning. Long call from Schow. He talks as much as Gorman. I think he wants me to go to the *Fangoria* convention over the weekend; says Clive and Wm. Friedkin will be there. Could be interesting but he'll probably wander off with Skipp and Spector for bowls of dead baby soup and I'll be left knowing no one in the whole place. Maybe we can get together when he and Lisa pass through on their way to Cape May. Mailed the REBORN page proofs to Susan and wasted time at Jiffy Lube getting the Buick serviced. Got rolling on "Mass" again for another 7 pgs.

19

Finished *They Live* this a.m. Not bad. Carpenter's calling the aliens "free-enterprisers" kind of soured it for me – I mean, if you're enslaving a populace, the enterprise is no longer free. Maybe Carpenter is a crypto-commie...or a crypto jerk. Otherwise it wasn't a bad flick. (Except for that interminable fight scene; had to FF it three times, thinking it was finally over!)

Didn't get much done writingwise today. Stuck in the office till 1, had to run some errands, wrap Dad's birthday gift, pick up the next 4 installments of "Upstairs/ Downstairs for Mary and four movies for me, plus G's tapes of the Joseph Campbell interview. Spruced up the FREAK SHOW proposal and sent it to Steve for comments, then went to the St. Rose-Manasquan game. The Bitch was reffing again. St. Rose outplayed Squan 100% but The Bitch whittled away the starting five until there was only one left; only then did Squan win – in overtime. M was outstanding. And I am pissed. Didn't get out of the office till 9:20. 36 pts. today. I'm drained.

20

Another whole weekend off. Really blazing on "Mass"

today. I think I'm up to page 60 or so. I'm approaching the grand finale. Hope I'm not rushing it. I really love the way it's flowing. One of the vamps just had a meltdown after drinking consecrated wine. Neat stuff! Hope to finish it next weekend.

Mary spent the whole day running the Penance practice down at Epiphany while I dubbed the Campbell tapes plus *Bird*, *StarTrek V*, *Pet Sematary*, and *Farewell to the King* for use in the carrot machine. Got a letter from Pulphouse requesting a novella for their Axolotl imprint. Maybe they'd be interested in "Mass". Have to clear it with Rick & Marty though. They get first dibs. Good ol' Anna McGee sent me the cover proofs of the SOFT pb. I love the quotes but the title lettering is yucky. Maybe I should call her, or FAX her my own design for the title. I mean, shouldn't the title look, well, *soft*? M and E made a pile of Krispy treats and I dove in; haven't had any of that stuff in ages.

Worked out to the first 20 min. of *Star Trek V*. So far, so good. The characters say just what they're expected to say; gives the film a homey feel. Then off to dinner at Jimmy's with J and M. J really liked SIBS; I gave him the page proofs to REBORN along with his sports video gift. We ended the night seeing *Glory* which I liked more than I thought I would, very moving while I was in it, but left me with a flat feeling; they all died charging a fort that was never taken. Futile. I guess this is why I prefer fiction. I see a certain amount of futility every day in the practice; I don't need to pay for more.

21

A rainy day in Bricktown. I got Mary the final 7 episodes of *Upstairs/Downstairs* and she played them while she did her paperwork; I attacked LISL again and found it tough to get back into, but I managed to do 5 pgs. Wrote a letter to Kris Rusch re "Mass" for Axolotl and sent a draft of the FREAK proposal to Marty G. for comment. Started Chet's *Reign* today. Did about 150 pgs. He's got such an easy style.

22/Mon

Did 4 more pgs on LISL. I'm amazed at how I was able to enter Renny's mind and twist all the events of the 2 preceding chapters to make Bill Ryan look guilty as hell when I hadn't set out to do it originally. Read some more of *Reign* – are there two ghosts haunting this theatre? This could be interesting. 36 pts. today.

23

Put the FREAKS and "Mass" proposals in the mail to Greenberg and Rusch respectively. Got the Buick tape player fixed. Got out of the office late. Mary had to work tonight and M was at practice so I had the place to myself. Finished the 15th pg. tonight. This is an emotionally draining segment – Bill is burying Danny alive – and I realized as I'm typing that this is the way I've always thought *Pet Sematary* should have ended; it's a powerful scene in LISL but with King's ability, coming at the end of his book, it would have been utterly devastating; too bad he blew it. This brings me to 296 pgs. Right on schedule. 36 pts. in office.

24

Finished *Star Trek V*; the pleasures of the film were all outside the plot which was hokey. Worked the a.m. only – 18 pts. Things down to a dull roar at the office; called Schow, won't be able to meet him & Lisa in Princeton; maybe on his way back from Cape May on Sun. Went to an Actigall lunch at Winkelman's, stopped at the comic shop to pick up the 4 new *Classics Illustrated* books plus the latest *Cerebus*, then spent the afternoon catching up on correspondence: Steve Jones, Jeff Gelb, Cat Yronwode, John Betancourt, Chizmar. Tor sent me the mechanical for the SOFT cover. What am I going to do with that? After tennis tonight I returned Ed Gorman's call; had a long talk with him. A truly nice guy.

25

A day off. Started *Pet Sematary*. Finished first draft of "Mass" today. Still needs plenty of work but I'm excited about it. Dede's sick so I missed my haircut. Schow called and we managed to get together with him and Lisa in Leed's Point, the birthplace of the Jersey Devil, for dinner. My first time there – it's in the middle of nowhere. The Oyster Creek Inn was yucko but we had a good time. Gave me a copy of *Seeing Red*. Got home and returned a call from McCammon re: "Mass." He thanked me for the Xmas tape and wanted to make sure I was working on the story for him. Then we discovered that the water heater was out. No shower tonight.

26

No shower this a.m. Short schedule in the office due to Dept. of Med. meeting. Home to work on the REBORN piece for *Mystery Scene*; finished it. Finished *Reign*. The water heater's fixed. Great to shower. Missed M's game tonight because of work. 30 pts.

27

Saw 25 in the office this a.m. FAXed the *Reign* blurb to Dark Harvest and mailed a copy to Chet. Sent off the *Mystery Scene* piece to Ed. Worked on revising "Mass" all afternoon. The second draft is hot. Went out to the Draughting Table with Y & J for his birthday. Talked a lot of B-ball. Ended up at his place for a little B&B. A nice evening.

28

Finished *Pet Sematary* – the movie ending was a bigger letdown than the book's, but now I understand the line J always says: "Now I want to play with youuuuuu." Broke my Sunday rule and continued working on "Mass" instead of going back to LISL. Wanted the second draft finished so Mary can read it this week. It came in at 18,600 wds. I'm very pleased. Went for a walk with Mary and discussed it with her. Managed to knock off 3 pages on LISL before E &

S's Super Bowl party. The bowl was a drag but the party was great.

29/Mon

A short morning because I had got to get a haircut, but I managed to knock off 5 pages on LISL. Got a card from Schow and Lisa saying they got lost in the Pine Barrens after we left them at the Parkway; I didn't know there was no southbound on-ramp. I'll have to send Schow a copy of "The Barrens"...so he knows what *could* have happened. Called Spruill; he liked the FREAK SHOW proposal and is cooking a story; told him to keep everything under his hat for now; St. Martin's is jacking him around on a contract on his new book; sounds like his editor's got to kiss McCormick's butt before she can make an offer. Saw 37 pts. in the office.

30

A fairly busy day in the office – 34 pts. Anthony Chase called; H&S took the REBORN trilogy for £45,000; wish it was higher but they do a good job and I'm sure I'll get more on the back end. Mikol called, thanking me for the blurb on *Reign* and asking for a generic blurb for an upcoming Ray Garton collection. Sure. I love Ray's work. Also told me REBORN should be available end of Feb and that he was routing Steve Gervais' originals back to RI via my office so that I could have a look; says they're great. I'm anxious to see them. Saw a list of my latest sales in the new SFC; even I'm impressed at my output. Marty Greenberg called to say how much he liked my FREAK SHOW proposal; he's already FAXed it off to Pocket. He pitched his "Hotel California" idea at me; it might work but I don't know how much time I can afford. Finished up the "Then" section of LISL, then hit the hay.

31

Only had to work the morning today – 14 pts. Finding it tough restarting the "Now" sequence again in Part III of LISL. Mary and I had dinner at The Brothers in Red Bank, then went over to see M's team lose to RBC in OT. Not the refs' fault this time – poor coaching: had the wrong people in during the OT period. Too bad. M was a little down. A message from Chase was on the answering machine when I got back. I'll call him tomorrow.

February

1/Thur

Off today. Started watching *The Seventh Sign*. Chase just wanted to know the delivery dates on the trilogy. Moving on LISL again. Knocked off 4 pgs. – no sweat. Did the Garton blurb and a final polish on "Mass."

2

An easy a.m. in the office. FAXed the Garton blurb to Mikol. Worked on the Lovecraft piece for *Dagon*. Reread "The Thing on the Doorstep" for the first time in 30 years and am absolutely shocked to see such a close parallel between its storyline and SIBS. Scary. Must have been in my subconscious all these years. And to think I've been slapping myself on the back since June for being so clever.

Mailed "Mass" off to Rick, Marty, and Rusch. A busy night in the office. M's team had an easy win tonight over Pinelands without me there. Finished the office with 32 pts. for the day, then watched *White Ghost* on TMC – decent action.

3

My weekend on call. *The Seventh Sign* is getting good. Spent a.m. in the office, saw 16 pts., then home with a bag of bagels from Val. Finished the *Dagon* piece (2100 wds), wrote a letter to Joe about his *By Bizarre Hands* collection. Letter from Munster; wants to publish "Pelts", offering $1.50 royalty per copy, probably a 300-copy run, all of which will go to Friends of Animals. Plans for Sept. publication which will tie in nicely with WFC. Maybe Jill will do the cover.

Out tonight with the Bs to Spike's. Great meal. Ate too much; stomach acting up.

4

Woke up at 5 a.m. and couldn't get back to sleep. Had stomach gripes. Thought about LISL and an idea popped into my head: In the "Then" section, have Martin Spano and Walter Erskine show up as derelicts and confront Bill and/or Renny, thus tying into REBORN and THE TOUCH. I'm going to use it.

Finished *The Seventh Sign*. The Guf idea is pretty hokey but the movie was otherwise well scripted (it left just enough unsaid) and very effectively filmed. I found the end moving.

My Sunday in the office. Saw 7, then went to W's 50th birthday party at the Hyatt. Pretty boring. Only got a couple of pages done on LISL.

5/Mon

Did about 4 pgs on LISL this a.m. Stomach feeling better. Mailed off the *Dagon* piece, then got blitzed in the office. Got PR#1 for the 1990 WFC; nice to see my name as GOH. Mort Castle called about reading some of my stories for cassette release; we'll get together in Chicago at WFC. Heard from Tor: they're remaindering BLACK WIND.

6

Started *Farewell to the King* this a.m. Full day in the office. M's team got killed by Pt. Boro today. I'm glad I missed it. I think the 2 overtime losses in big games plus N's confused, floundering coaching have sapped their spirit. Sad. Talk is that Hoffman may transfer to Vianney next year – that will make an awesome team.

7

Just worked the a.m. Volume seems to be down to normal. The Cipro lady bought lunch for the office. Worked on LISL in the afternoon and got up to page 15 for the week.

Tennis tonight – played lousily. Marty G. called re: "Mass"; liked it very much; I'd asked him to comb it for anything unintentionally offensive to Jews; he thought I used "oy" too much, otherwise nothing.

8

Only had the a.m. off today; kept going on LISL. Returned Mark S's call; he tried to tell me that it's all right that Double Drive-thru is in chapter 11 and tried to convince me that not too much of my money is getting sucked down the black hole of Mt. Ascutney because of the tax write-offs. But I've still got to generate the cash flow to make the payments.

9

Only worked the a.m. Traded tonight for last night so Mary and I could go to a murder dinner at the Art Center with the K&B. Picked up Mary's Valentine gift and cards for the girls. Hit the mall and bought some CDs of the Byrds' *Turn! Turn! Turn!* and *Fifth Dimension*. I still dig the Byrds. "A Toxic Affair" was a lot of fun.

10

A whole weekend off. Finished *Farewell to the King*; my dub was lousy but I liked what I saw. Worked on LISL most of the day; found a good transition to open Part III and really started blazing – did 10 pgs., a total of 30 for the week. Went to a dinner-dance at Mike Doolan's. K&B made me dance; had a good time despite the lousy food.

11

A lazy day. Started Eastwood's *Bird*. Very depressing. Got 5 pgs. done on LISL. Bill Munster called; he thinks he can typeset "Pelts" off the disk and asked me to correct a few typos on disk before I sent it. Says he might contribute part of the proceeds to Greenpeace. Caught the beginning of *Blind Faith*; didn't want to watch it but got hooked and that shot the rest of the night.

12/Mon

Slow going on LISL today. A typically crazy Monday in the office. Packaged the disks for Munster and sent them off.

13

A normal Tuesday in the office. Picked up the latest *Cerebus* at lunch. Ordered flowers to be delivered to Mary at work tomorrow. Suffered through M's grueling game against Manasquan which they lost by 2. No refs to blame this time; they were outplayed from the tip-off.

14

Valentine's Day. A.m. only in the office. Gave Mary her earrings and she was delighted with the flowers. Got some gag gifts (heart-design boxers) from her which I liked. Slogged through a couple of pages on LISL; the Ev section just doesn't want to flow. Dubbed another 4 films for later viewing. Played okay tennis.

15

Off today. Rushed through to the end of *Bird*; couldn't take much more of the self-destructiveness. The music was great, though. I'll have to get the soundtrack. I'm building up a little momentum behind the Ev section. Did a little better than 8 pgs. Gary Raisor called to say how much he liked my Joker story; seemed sincere. Out to Spike's tonight with the B's. Saw pictures of their Orient trip over Xmas. I'd love to do that someday.

16

Started *Lethal Weapon 2*. Finished my 15th page for the week.

17

Out to the Rumson-Lakewood game with Y&J. Rumson made Lakewood play their game in the first half and kept it tied, but Lakewood broke loose in the second half. Went to the Sand Bar for a bite; they need help bad; maybe M...

18

Did 3 pgs. on LISL, then went into NYC to see "Lend Me A Tenor," a fun British farce. Then to dinner with the U's at Garruzzo's – our first time at that restaurant; I broke my resolve to avoid veal and tried one of their specials – excellent.

19/Mon

Finished *Lethal Weapon 2*; Joe Pesci should get a supporting Oscar for his Leo part – damn near stole the movie. Knocked off 6 pgs. on Lisl – really rolling now.

20

Kris Rusch called; she wants "Midnight Mass" for an Axolotl novella. I called Marty; he was leaving for San Antonio for a cable conference (the Sci-Fi channel & all that) and he says it's okay with him if it's okay with Rick & Pocket.

21

Did about 5 pages this afternoon, then worked the p.m. session. Called Rick McCammon when I got home. He said he really likes "Mass" and doesn't care if Axolotl does it first, but he'll have to check with Pocket. Neither of them seems to know what the contract says, but nobody can see how a 900-copy edition costing $10 & up can hurt a mass market paperback.

22

Spent the morning doing my taxes with F (does he ever stop talking?), then worked the afternoon session. Brought my page total up to 20 for the week. Called Rusch and gave her the go-ahead on "Mass". She wants to get it out in time for WFC and I figure if I wait for Pocket, October will come and go before I their okay. So I've decided to present them with a *fait accompli.*

23

    I wrote Marty and informed him of the Axolotl deal; this lets him off the hook when he approaches Pocket.

24

    Worked the a.m. then went to the SCT finals. Two great games – St. J.V. beat TRE and CBA beat Neptune. Then we headed for Baltimore; ran into snow along the way. Picked up J at her dorm, had dinner at Fudrucker's, then turned in early.

25

    Pigged out at the Hyatt brunch then hung around the Gallery while Mary took J shopping. Picked up "My Maillist" program for $16; figure it'll come in handy for the Xmas list. We got back to Brick by 6:45 but I was too bushed to do any writing.

26/Mon

    Finished *Dead Bang* this a.m. Pretty good. Did 4 pgs. on LISL then headed for the office for a meeting with the Roche Labs people. Heard from NEL today via Chase. They're delighted to have me back but hate the title LISL'S LOVE. So do I. I think I'll change the working title to REPRISALS...but not yet.

27

    Didn't get up in time to exercise this a.m. We stopped keeping injectable Valium in the office a while ago – we never used it and had to keep sending it back because it went out of date. Wouldn't you know it? Someone went into status epilpticus in our waiting room today. Life is perverse.

    Picked up the new *Cerebus* (#129) and taped M's first game in the State tourney. St. Rose won handily and M played well. The next game's Friday. I'll have to work on trading it off.

28

Traded off Friday night; it may well turn out to be M's last game; I want to be there. Played tennis fairly well tonight.

March

1/Thu

Was lying half awake at 4 a.m. and had this weird thought-dream about this guy who carries this bucket of slime around with him; he's dull-witted until he sticks his hand in the slime and lets it crawl up his arm and coat his body; then he's bright and suave and debonair. Maybe I should call it "Putting on the Ritz" and pitch it to *Monsters*.

Was way behind for the week so spent the whole day on LISL while dubbing off 5 more films. Did 11+ pgs. Started *Weekend at Bernie's* – funny. M came home and announced that the semi-final was shifted to Saturday – after I'd traded off Friday! Aaargh!

2

Did clean-up-the-study in the afternoon, then Mary & I had dinner at The Draughting Table – love that John Courage on tap. We wandered into the St. Rose - Mater Dei game in time to find out that Tom R had his nose broken and two teeth broken, but as he was taken out on the stretcher he had a bloody fist raised in the air. St. Rose was behind but they were pumped now and went on to win it for the Gipper. There's a certain purity to h.s. basketball. Nobody's thinking about getting a berth in the NCAA finals and how much money that will bring to the athletic program and how many extra applicants to the school; nobody's thinking about scouts from the pros in the audience. For that time, in that place, the game is all that matters. There's heady stuff in the air in those gyms – and it ain't sweat.

Mary & I discussed the definition of "kah" on the way

home. We decided that kah is a more deeply ingrained form of yuck; yuck brought to a professional level; yuck beyond any hope of redemption. Kah is...kah.

We tried to watch *Scandals* (the unrated version) but it was boring. Mary fell asleep; I hung in a while longer but finally turned it off. M called to say E got into a fender-bender with her father's Bronco. Nobody hurt. She was late coming home.

3

Worked the a.m. then took the beeper to the semifinal game. St. Rose won easily, but I was pissed at coach for playing M only 3 minutes. What a shit. She's senior, f'crissake! Anyway, the NJSIAA Parochial B South finals are Tuesday night, with both the St. Rose boys and St. Rose girls playing for their division crowns, which is almost unheard of. We spent a quiet night at home. M was kind of down. She didn't go out.

4

A quiet day on call. Spent an hour or so in the office, then knocked off 8 pgs. on LISL while Mary watched *Troop Beverly Hills*. She thought it was cute but dumb. During and after dinner – some delicious pasta with Mary's hyped-up sauce – we watched *25 X 5*. The Betamax is on the fritz. I'll have to get it fixed.

5/Mon

Finished *Weekend at Bernie's* – very funny. Did 3p on LISL, then left early to take the Beta down for repairs. Not a particularly busy Monday.

6

A rotten day. Started *Dead Calm* but quit it. Slush from the sky, and M's team got crushed by Mater Dei in the finals tonight. A sad end to her H.S. basketball career, but at least they made it to the finals. The boys lost a heartbreaker in double overtime.

7

Started *Road House*; looks good and mindless, perfect for the exercycle. Worked a.m. only. Ordered laptop from DAK; it's a low-end machine – no hard drive, etc. – but perfect for my needs; and the price is super. Did 4p on LISL, then we played tennis. M went to the CBA game – they lost as badly as her team, which made her happy in a way.

Quicken came; looks complicated. I'll have to scope it out before I try to ease Mary into an electronic checkbook.

8

A day off. 7p on LISL. Replaced the o-ring on the bathroom faucet. The Axolotl contract came. Talked to Schnessl about his trip to Hollywood; says Orion is interested in THE TOUCH. Seems very high on the project. Talked to Susan about adding a line to the end of REBORN to let folks know there's more to come; she thought it was a good idea. Liked the new title (REPRISALS) for LISL, too. Installed *Quicken*; looks pretty straightforward.

Called Marty; everything looks cool with Pocket for the 2nd anthology (they have some reservations that I might not be able to pull it off. Hmmph!). Called Rick; he'll be glad to do the intro to "Mass."

9

J flew to my folks' place in FL today; arrived safe & sound. I sent the contracts, revised pgs. and a disk to Rusch today. Bought a new mailbox and installed it. It's a corny-looking barn shape but it's big; we need big.

10

Went with Mary to NYC to be "honored" by the NY Public Library as the author of DYDEETOWN WORLD which is a new addition to its "Books for the Teen Age" list. The novel also made the YA recommended list from ALA.

Strange. I wrote it for adults. Toni Weiskopf took us to lunch at the Palm Court at the Plaza; liked lunch and liked her; reminds me of Lu.

Picked up a carrot cake at Spike's; they said the only reason I got it today is because half the people there are or were patients.

A good day for the ego.

Mary and I discussed giving the Checkfree electronic checking system a try. Why not?

11

A beautiful Sunday, in the 60's, the windows open. Did 10 pp on LISL, watched some b-ball. Didn't eat anything until dinner.

12/Mon

Finished *Road House* – good fights but the Swayze character is so improbable. A bouncer with a philosophy major – really. The ending reminded me of the *In Broad Daylight* murder. Sent off an application for Checkfree. Did another 4pp on LISL, picked up some Beautiful for Mary, then worked the office until 9.

Joe Lansdale called me at the office to remind me about contributing to his dark suspense anthology. Told him I already had a story in mind for him and expected one in return for my FREAKS book. He said it sounded good as long as he had enough lead time.

13

Started *Renegades*; can't believe what an awful actor Kiefer Sutherland is; or maybe it's the part. Looks like a real dumb movie...perfect for the bike. Strobe from the *Press* called about the article – wants to save it for May when the new book is out; fine with me. Says he received bound galley proofs recently from Jove.

Paul Mikol called and said REBORN is in and my copies are on their way. Advance orders are good, especially from

Baker & Taylor. Says the crucifix illo is in the wrong spot in the book, though. The carrying case for the laptop I ordered from DAK arived but the laptop is backordered. Swell. Did 5p on LISL.

14

Called Susan Allison and asked for one of those bound proofs of REBORN; it's the first state of the book. She says booksellers seem very enthusiastic about the novel and she anticipates a good initial order.

The interiors I bought from Steve arrived today via FedEx. He threw in "The Journals" gratis. He's pissed that the crucifixion plate is misplaced, and rightly so. I'm anxious to get these framed and on the wall.

Signed and sent back the Dark Harvest contracts on SIBS. Called Craig Goden of Time Tunnel Books; he wants to feature me and REBORN in his next catalog/newsletter. I'm happy to oblige.

Played tennis (poorly) and came home to find Marty Greenberg had called. Looks like the shit has hit the fan over the Axolotl edition of "Midnight Mass." Pocket Books is all upset. I told Marty that I'd work with him any way I can to smooth things over but that my public stance with Pocket will be to stonewall it.

15

The Ides of March. 21 years since I proposed to Mary. Gave her the rose and Muller's crumb cake I picked up yesterday. I used Auri to polish the Honda, raked the yard, and did 10p on LISL. The Dark Harvest edition of REBORN arrived today. Looks great; the only hitch is that the crucifix illo is misplaced in the text.

16

Dropped the illos off at the Manasquan Gallery for framing; picked up a few poster frames and stuck the DYDEETOWN poster in one. Steve Gervais called, very upset about the misplaced illo and the way the title is placed and colored on the DJ, says it looks like a Marvel comic and that the fetus seems to be wearing a fez. Gee...I sort of liked the package. At least he cares.

A box arrived from Charlie Grant – tip-in sheets for *Obsessions*. Oh joy.

17

Sent my LaNague Federation logo to Toni at Baen; maybe they can use it; can't hurt.

Into NYC with J&M. Was expecting a traffic horror but had one of the smoothest trips ever. Saw "City of Angels" and was disappointed; it's clever, and I liked the set design (esp. the black-and-white sets for scenes from the screenplay) but none of the characters was engaging and none of the music moving or memorable. Penn Gillette, Jack Klugman, and Florence Henderson were seated near us. Ate at Scarlatti; Mary is still talking about her meal; mine was good, but $230 (incl. tip) for 4 meals (no wine) is a bit much.

18

Started chapter 30 this a.m. – hope it will be the last. 78p so far this month; the last chapters always go the fastest; fewer decisions to make. Spent most of the afternoon signing the *Obsessions* sheets while watching Georgetown lose to Xavier; deserved to lose; Xavier wanted it more. Did 4p on LISL.

19/Mon

Finished *Renegades* this a.m. What a piece of junk. I've no idea why the crook stole the Indian lance, no idea why a lot of things went on. How do these things get made? 5p on LISL. Picked up the Beta from the repair shop. Busy day in the office. The Dark Harvest advance on REBORN arrived; sent a copy of the book to Spruill and the tip-in sheets to Al Sarrantonio.

20

Picked up the new *Cerebus* (130) and the latest *Miracleman* (15) today; dropped Sim a line regarding the sudden – and welcome – explosion in the storyline. Another 5p on LISL tonight. An uneventful day.

21

Worked a.m. & p.m., then played tennis. Played better than usual. MHG called while I was out but don't feel like talking to him tonight.

22

It's done – finished the last page of LISL's first draft. Not happy with that last page, though. I've got to get something stronger for a last paragraph. Steve called this a.m. to thank me for the copy of REBORN; says he's going to NYC tomorrow to see his editor; not getting a great advance offer for his follow-up to *Painkiller*. Called Marty tonight. Pocket is standing firm on their opposition to the "Mass" if Axolotl does it first. And since I've already signed with Axolotl, that's that. Too bad they have to be such hardcases. I was on the phone with him when UConn made that fabulous 1-second winning basket. Unreal.

23

Started reading/revising LISL today. Susan Allison called with a super review from *PW* on REBORN. She says advance interest in the book is high; looking for a good initial order.

24

Worked the a.m., then went to K's wedding. Had a great time at the reception. My face hurts from laughing. Don't believe I did the Blues Brothers dance and the Chuck Berry duck walk.

25

Finished *Freddy V* this a.m. Good effects, interesting "origin" story, but the dialog was awful. Did some revising of LISL, then Mary & I went to *Hunt for Red October* which we both liked, although I'd have been more into it if I hadn't read the book.

26/Mon

Started *Horror Show* while on the bike; kind of Elm-Streetish. More revising on LISL; since I've already rewritten the opening sections, it's going smoothly. Called Pulphouse and got Dean Smith; told him the situation with Pocket but that I'd stick with Axolotl.

27

Worked a.m. & p.m. and had the afternoon free for revisions but spent much of it on the phone. Received 2 Charles Fort books and Bloch's old *Night-World* from Craig Goden today, plus copies of some very complimentary pieces on my work he's putting in his newsletter.

28

Lisa Feerick called today. Schow's back in town and they want to get together for dinner in a week or so; sounds fine to me. Someone named Al Corley from something called of Artists Writing for the Screen phoned today; wants to know if I'd like to write a playlet for an off-Broadway Grand Guignol; says Lansdale's in on it. I told him sure. I'll call Joe. Kris Rusch called back and I explained that Rick may not be doing the intro to "Mass" and that we may have to think of someone else.

The laptop arrived today; I love it, but there's no software yet. So I'm charging the batteries and waiting.

After tennis we ate at the Sand Bar because M was on; food's kind of greasy; glad M doesn't work there every Wed.

29

Worked the a.m.; slow. Got a haircut and did some

revisions in the afternoon, then went to Spike's with the Bs. Received a copy of Steve's *Painkiller* with a nice inscription. Sent *Soft* and "Pelts" to that guy Corley.

30

A rainy Friday. Finished *Horror Show*; not very enjoyable; looks like it could have been *Shocker*. Worked on LISL after the Dept of Med and F.P. section meetings, then back to the office.

31

Started *Jigsaw Murders*; do not have high hopes for this. Was on ER call all day but got only one call. Paul Mikol called to say how well REBORN is selling; dropped the bomb that he and Gervais have had a falling out and Gervais has dropped out of the project. I don't believe it. Called Steve, no answer. Shit.

Mary and I lit the fire and stayed home and watched the NCAA semi-finals. My kind of Saturday...except that Duke won.

April

April Fool/Sun

Put in an hour or so at the office, then Mary & I had brunch with the Ks at the Grenville; very nice. Finished revising the first draft of LISL. {YAY!} Called Steve Gervais and talked about his dropping out of the genre; he sounds real down; I guess that what happens when you get no respect.

2/Mon

Finished *Jigsaw Murders* – a turkey. Started entering the LISL revisions onto the disk, then worked the rest of the day.

3

Started *Action Jackson* – great opening, but a Detroit

cop with a Harvard Law degree? Gimme a break! Joe Lansdale called about the *Grand Guignol* thing; he's high on it too; we joked about tuxedo T-shirts on opening night and hanging out at Elaine's waiting for the first reviews. Called Phyllis Weinberg and charged the $325 for the ltd. ed. of *The Stand*; ridiculous price but she says she's already had offers of $700+. Crazy.

4

The first of 5 days off in a row. The *Action Jackson* tape ran out half way through. Started putting the LISL revisions on disk. Spent the whole day at it, then played tennis, then went to Squan.

5

Another full day at the keyboard entering changes. What a drag. DAK called to say they mailed my laptop software out on Mon; should be here soon. Went to Vittorio's; excellent Italian food.

6

And still another full day at the keyboard. Got out for a couple of hours to buy some wine and copy a few things at the office, then back to work. Almost done. The *Checkfree* software came, but no hardware. Al Corley called again. Says his theatre group has chosen its 4 authors for the *Grand Guignol* playlets, and I'm one of them. He was impressed with "Pelts;" I might try to adapt that. He's going to call Al Z. I'm starting to believe in this a little.

Went to the Manor with the bro & sis-in-laws and had a great time. They're good company.

7

Finally finished LISL and printed it out (as REPRISALS). Comes in at 498 pp/110,000 wds. Got Gervais' art back, beautifully framed, and began hanging it. Went out to dinner with Schow and Lisa and an artist named Taylor at the Homestead Inn in Hamilton. The waiters were brusque at best (I hear they're like that with everyone) and the food was only o.k.

8

Separated the REPRISAL pages. Saw *The Kathy & Mo Show* in NYC. Hilarious. Drove past the Astor Place Theatre; it's at the junction of Lafayette, Bowery, & W. 8th. – a crummy neighborhood.

9/Mon

Sent letters to Ed Gorman, and all sorts of stuff to Carolyn Caughey at NEL. Mary took the REPRISAL ms. to be copied. Talked to Al about the play proposal. He said don't expect too much money. That's okay; it's a feather I'd like in my cap.

10

The REPRISAL copies are back. Look good. Boxed them up. Spoke to Steve Spruill about going to Necon X. Got copies of the British BLACK WIND – they look great; better than the TOR pb. Most of the software for the portable arrived from DAK, but not the Turbo Hooker, the crucial item. Spent the night cleaning up the office. Can't believe the accumulation of paper. Started playing with KeyMailer.

11

Schnapps has been losing wt. Thought it was the low-cal cat food for a while but she's bony now. Made a vet appt. for tomorrow a.m. Picked up J this afternoon. She looks good; still tan from Florida.

12

Bad news. Took Schnapps to the vet (she dropped to 6.5 from 10.5 lbs) and he says she's got an abdominal mass and she's juandiced. Not a good prognosis. She's less than 2 yrs. so a tumor is unlikely. We're going to try antibiotics and keep her nutrition up and see if she pulls through. Mary's very upset and I'm down. I'm beginning to understand the term "heavy heart."

Mary mailed out the REPRISAL mss. to Al, Steve, Susan. Al called; he heard from the theatre people. It looks like the real thing. The advance isn't much but neither is the amount of work I'll have to do. Started *To Die For*. Looks like a dopey Dracula-in-LA flick.

Friday the 13th

We've been force-feeding Schnapps some concentrate and milk and Amoxil. Sometimes I think she gets more on her fur than in her stomach. Talked to the vet: her tot. bili is 9, liver enzymes up, CBC normal; got to be an obstruction. If we can't turn her around, I want him to explore her, fix it if he can, and if he can't, don't wake her up.

Caught up on my correspondence and started the precis of the "Pelts" play. Shaping the story to the stage is challenging and keeps my mind off Schnapps. Schow sent a tape of a couple of "Thrillers" + sundries; have to watch it.

14

Finished *To Die For*; pretty awful. Also finished the "Pelts" precis. I think it works well; the only problem is how many sets they'll allow me. Al wrote to say he just received official release of my sf novels from Doubleday, even though it's dated Jan. 30. Al Corly sent some info on the theatre group and on the old Grand Guignol. The production in progress is to be called *Screamplay*. Got the contracts for my *Author's Choice Monthly*. Went out to a Japanese restaurant with the G&W and I pigged out on sushi. Then we saw the Roches at Princeton – they're fabulous.

Schnapps seems to be holding her own. Hasn't lost any more weight. Still 6.5

Easter

Started *Kickboxer*. Looks like Karate Rocky. Caught up on the journal, then went to Coll's for dinner. Great meal but don't feel so hot. I think it's the red wine; doesn't sit well.

16/Mon

Worked 3 sessions today so S could have the end of Passover off. Schnapps holding her own. I pureed some of her dry food with milk but she wants no part of it – tried to bury it!

17

Clinic this a.m., then office the rest of the day. Picked up *Open Space* with "Biosphere" at lunch – no author copies received yet. Hmmph! Called Rick McCammon about the intro to "Mass" and let him off the hook because I know it would put him in an awkward position with Pocket. Talked to Al Z. – we've got an offer for a theatrical movie option on REBORN from a Diane Rosenstein; since people aren't exactly breaking down the door to get it, I said take it. He said the *Screamplay* contract looks adequate so I told Al Corley to watch his FAX tomorrow.

The vet doesn't think Schnapps is doing too well; more dehydrated. Gave her a subcut infusion. We're spooning milk into her and force-feeding high calorie-low volume smelly brown goop.

Saw a preview of *Accomplice*. A devilishly clever play-within-a-play-within-a-play.

18

FAXed the 4-pg., single-spaced precis of the "Pelts" play to Corley this a.m. Spoke to Lansdale who says he's had a similar offer from a West Coast group; he's going to do both.

Strange lab results on Schnapps – bili up to 12, liver enzymes down. Going to recheck her FeLeuk antibodies. I started her on prednisolone today.

Played tennis like a dork but the pizza was good.

19

What a horrible day. Started off okay – I got Wordstar

up and running on the laptop and was happy about that. Then the vet called: Schnapps' elisa for leukemia was positive. No hope; and worse, she's endangering Duffy & Molly. After Mary came home, we said our good-byes and I took her to the vet. As I sat in the exam room with Scnapps on my lap I had to sign a form and answer questions about whether I wanted the body back or if I wanted her cremated and did I want the ashes, and did I want to see her after she was dead. God, no! I could barely speak. I handed her to him and fled. Felt like someone was strangling me. Thank god it wasn't like a movie, with long lingering looks into the cat's puzzled, frightened eyes. I could've cried but wouldn't let myself; scared, I guess; afraid once I start I won't be able to stop.

We decided not to cancel the trip to A.C. with the tennis group. We needed the distraction. And the Taj Mahal was a good distraction. Didn't get home till 2 a.m. I miss her.

20

Feeling down and depressed. Tired. I still can't believe I had Schnapps put away yesterday. Carolyn Caughey called from London to clear up a few things about the NEL edition of REBORN. Worked a little on the *Red Dragon* piece for Scream Factory. Don't feel much like writing.

21

A rainy Saturday; matches my mood. Worked the morning, then cruised into Manhattan to see *Aspects of Love*. A thin, empty play; preaches hedonism, screw whoever's handy; love, honor, fidelity are foreign to the characters. Great sets though.

22

Home all day. Really miss Schnapps bothering me in the morning after my shower. Worked on the fish pond removing the rotten leaves, rearranging rocks, getting the pump going. About a dozen big fish swimming around.

Hooked up the laptop for a test transfer of files. Works beautifully. Did the opening page of "Last Rakosh" for the WFC program book.

23/Mon

Awoke with a back agony – probably from lifting the pond stones yesterday; didn't think I was going to make it to the office but some stretches and 800mg. of Motrin helped. Took Duffy to the vet for a leukemia test and a booster. Mary took Molly later. Let's hope.

24

Picked M & E up from Newark. They look great, had a great time. The Felu tests were negative for both cats. Took the laptop to the office and worked on "Last Rakosh" at dinner hour.

25

Worked the morning, had an office meeting; went to the library for some circus material. Got "Mud Show" which looks good. Picked up *Bone* at the bookstore across the street. Steve returned LISL with some valuable comments. Played tennis well tonight.

26

My day off. Worked some more on "Last," did some yardwork. The SIBS contract finally came through. Very complicated...like a jigsaw, but I signed them and sent them back.

27

Worked on "Last Rakosh" in afternoon; didn't get much done. Had to run down for a haircut before night hours. Article in the *Times* today about "Grand Guignol"...but not my GG. Swell. There's competition out there.

28

Worked in the yard a lot; got something done.

29

Treated the Js to a play for W's 50th. Saw *The Perfect Crime* which was perfectly awful. We decided the perfect crime was taking our money and getting away with it; can't believe it's in its 4th year, even if there are only 100 seats in the theatre. Had a decent meal at Tout Va Bien.

30/Mon

More on "Last Rakosh" this a.m., then worked the rest of the day till 9.

May

1/Tues

Worked the office all day. My copies of DARK VOICES arrived. Worked on revising "Last Rakosh."

2

Worked the a.m. in the office, revised "Last Rakosh" in the afternoon, went to Pegasus with the Js for the Key Pharm. dinner. Had a good time, didn't lose too much money, but racing is *boring!* Missed Ray Garton's call; naturally, he left no number.

3

Mary was gone all day so I got a lot done. Finished revising "Last Rakosh" this a.m. and printed it out. Started on the *Pelts* play and did about 8 pages. Called Alan Ryan who said he'd be delighted to introduce "Midnight Mass."

4

Sent "Mass" off to Ryan; copied "Last Rakosh" to send to the Weinbergs tomorrow. Called Kris Rusch and told her about Ryan's intro and settled some details on ACM #13. My Drabble book arrived.

5

Rainy; worked on the play most of the day. Ray

Garton finally called back; talked to him about a *Freak Show* story; he's agreeable; he'll even join HWA. Went to "Tony & Tina's Wedding" in Philadelphia with the Js and had a ball. Hilarious. A really fun night.

6

Sunny. Finished the first draft of the play this a.m. (4 days – 3 mornings and 2 afternoons – not bad) then worked in the yard all day. Read the play's dialog into a tape recorder for playback in the car.

7/Mon

The dialog tape was lousy but I still managed to pick up some stiff spots. Otherwise, it was work in the office till 9.

8

Worked the office all day; not too ambitious for writing. Did some circus research.

9

Worked the a.m., ran some errands this afternoon. Renewed the circus book. *Hyperion* and *Fall of Hyperion* arrived but apparently Gorman's *Night of Shadows* is o-p already.

10

A fairly unproductive day. Farted around with this and that. Worked on putting the ACC#13 package together for Rusch. Played with the Keymailer and the FREAKS letter, then went to the hospital's medical staff outing: played tennis well, had a so-so lobster dinner, and won $60 at craps in the basement afterward.

11

Al C. called; just keeping in touch. Told him the 1st draft was almost ready. (Don't want him to think I'm too anxious or that it comes too easy.) Called Susan Allison – Berkley's only shipping 300,000 of REBORN. Disappointing.

But she seems to Like LISL a lot. Returned Michael Blumelein's call from yesterday. Seems like he's got his head on straight. I think we're all of the opinion that *Screamplay* is just a little too easy. Where's the hitch?

12

Spent most of the day in the car, riding down and back to Baltimore to pick up J and her things. Happily, we found a home for the cat her roommates had been keeping. The wagon drove well. Mary and I watched *Johnny Handsome* (1st time) and *Body Heat* (again) last night. Not bad.

Mother's Day

Called Mom in FL. Walked the boards with Mary. She didn't like the Gucci watch I ordered; said it wasn't dressy enough. I thought it was. Subs for dinner – that's what she wanted, that's what she got.

14 Mon

Started the new Repairman Jack story for IN COLD BLOOD; think I'll call it "Domestic Problem."

15

Al Z. called. Told him the 1st draft of the play was ready. He said not to send it in until we've got the contracts signed. Okay. Called Quinn re: FREAKS. She had some excellent suggestions. Worked all day so I could be off tomorrow night. Used the laptop to work on "Domestic."

16

Had my blood drawn this a.m. Met with KS computers today. We've got to bite the bullet and computerize the office, especially with Medicare changing its billing rules. $32,000. Oy. Went to M's sports dinner. She got tennis MVP plus plaques for golf, basketball, and bowling. Alan Ryan called re: the intro to "Mass" – not too happy about signing 900 sheets. Hasn't read it yet but turns out he comes to Spring Lake frequently. We'll have to get together.

17

My birthday. #44. Worked the a.m., wrote afternoon. Byron Preiss's office called re: their DRACULA, FRANKENSTEIN, WOLFMAN anniversary books. Said I'd do a FRANKENSTEIN story for them. Already have an idea; should be fun. Took a landscaper thru the back to show him what Mary wants done. My brother called for my birthday, then we went out with the tennis crew to Lon's for dinner & dancing. Mary got me clothes and tickets to "Tru". Got a beer-ball from the S&E and an American Impressionism book from K&B. The band had great 3-part harmonies.

18

Another landscaper this afternoon. Worked on the Jack story but didn't get much done. Tired from last night.

19

Worked the a.m. Got the photos back for ACM. I hope Geo. Barr is feeling generous and creative when he does my portrait. Cleaned up the yard a little. Played singles against M in the wind and beat her the first time in years. She wasn't happy. Went to Princeton to see "Woman in Mind" at the McCarter. It had its moments, but was much too long; almost dozed off twice.

20

Walked the Spring Lake boards with Mary, then spent most of the day working around the yard. Got the pool pump going. Watched *Uncle Buck* and enjoyed it very much; Mary watched *Dad* later but I couldn't get into it.

21/Mon

Worked on the Jack story this a.m., drove J to Rod's for work, then spent the day in the office. Busy. The check for "Last Rakosh" arrived from Bob W. with a note thanking me for dedicating it to Phyllis. Called Marty G. but got his answering machine. Probably out of town.

22

Put the British contracts in the mail to WH and the ACM#13 package on its way to Rusch. Was stuck in the office from 8 a.m. to 9 p.m. Took the laptop so I could get some work done. Knocked off better than 5 pgs. on the Jack story during meal breaks. It's pretty dark; not as dark as LISL, but dark. Had the auto repairman replace the choke release on the Olds while I was in the office. Xeroxed off 20 copies of the FREAKS guidelines.

23

A short day in the office – just the a.m. Transferred the laptop work to the PC. The Diskoptimizer arrived so I spent much of the afternoon fooling with that. Finally got it to work and it has supposedly reorganized and refreshed my hard disk. Hopefully this will eliminate those disk-error messages I was getting when trying to save new work. Played a little tennis at S&E's court, then met K&B at Squan. Watched the last "Twin Peaks" of the season. Unfocussed garbage; bizarreness for its own sake.

24

Had Roland over to powerwash the house – did a great job. The vinyl looks like new. Finished the new Jack story – renamed it "Home Repairs." Just have to check on a Jaguar fact before I send it to Chizmar. Spoke to Al re: LISL. He seems to like it a lot but thinks the chronology should be straight-line and the first "Now" trimmed. I'll have to think about the chronology part. Still no contract for the play. Went to Spike's for dinner and had cajun monk chunks over linguine. Delicious.

25

The girls went to WNEW's summer kick-off at Asbury beach. A marathon day in the office for me. Work-work-work for 3 sessions. Called Marty G. for the FANG list but he's out; Rosalind gave it to me; beautiful voice; you could fall in love with that voice. Started the Jack story for Lansdale on the laptop during the dinner break; think I'll call it "Identities." Came home and collapsed. J's roommate K arrived for the Lacrosse finals at Rutgers.

26

A no-writing day. Worked the office for the a.m., came home and went to PB's wedding, then to the reception until 5. It poured; an inch at least. Then out to dinner at Via Veneto with M & J at 6:30. They gave me "Taboo" for my b-day; we came back from dinner and played it with Kate and J.

27

Worked the Sunday a.m. office hour, then shocked the pool and took the cover off. Worked in the yard most of the day. Had a light dinner and ran off the letters for FREAKS. Bill Munster called about Jill B.'s illo for the "Pelts" chapbook; says it's great; supposedly she's sending me one too. Marty G. called and we discussed the anthology among other things.

Memorial Day

Replaced a couple of rotted boards in the deck, then painted it; vacuumed the pool. M helped. I'm dead. Loyola lost the Lacrosse finals to Syracuse. Stuffed the FREAKS envelopes. Recorded ZZ Top's Memorial Day Blues Bar-B-Q off WNEW. I'll listen to it tomorrow.

29

Had the morning off. Farted around, opened the NIGHTWORLD file; did the first line. Raining like a bitch. Worked till 9.

30

Worked the a.m. Al Corley called; the contracts are ready. Told him the first draft was ready too. Mailed out the FREAKS letters (18 + Quinn). Hit the mall and found REBORN in both the chains, though not in abundant supply;

no dumps. Picked up a copy of DICK TRACY: THE SECRET FILES; *that* had a dump! Worked on the pool most of the afternoon, then did the usual Wed. tennis & pizza.

31

Worked the a.m. for S, then farted around the pool some more. The vacuum hose broke. Borrowed my father's leaf eater which worked great, then hooked up the polaris. Printed out "Home Repairs." Rented 5 films for dubbing.

June

1/Fri

Not getting much writing done. Had a busy a.m. and p.m., plus an office meeting. Mailed off "Home Repairs" to Chizmar. Got the tax info together for F, incl. the English tax exemption form. Spoke to Al Z. and sent him the "Pelts" play to forward to the producers when the contract's in. Picked up a new pool hose, worked on clearing up the water. M got her yearbook today. Joe Lansdale called late and we must've talked for an hour. We started off discussing our plays and got on to raising kids and just about everything else. I pressed him for a FREAKS story and told him to expect the letter any day.

2

I think the pool's finally coming around. J starts her house-sitting job today. I'm not happy about her being alone in that house for a week with only a dog to keep her company at night.

3

Headed for Washington, DC today for the medicine review at Howard University. A smooth trip until I missed the exit to 495, but I found my way to the Spruills anyway. Nancy fixed cajun steaks which Steve charcoaled. We stopped by to see Lynn Winter (Doug had to head back to Detroit for a trial this afternoon), had a little Frexinet, then

Steve led me to the Howard Inn. Called home and found that Gorman had phoned so I returned his call and we had a rambling conversation. I recommended Steve's *Painkiller* and gave him the number to call.

4/Mon

Not much new gleaned from the first day of the course. It's mostly a review; I need more of an update. Strange being one of only a few white faces at the lectures, and to hear so many references to "us" and "our" in a non-white context.

Harlan called my office and Tom Monteleone called home, both re: FREAKS. Harlan can't contribute due to his illness and a professed distaste for "sharecropper" fiction, but offered any technical advice on carny should I need it. Tom was very enthusiastic about the whole idea and wants in; suggested a new writer who contributed to his *Borderlands* anthology (will send a sample story). Tom talked about starting his own small press. Had fried ersatz scallops ("skallops") at Steve & Nancy's, then came back and started integrating Mary's, Steve's, and Al's edits on REPRISALS. Took a break and watched *Hard to Kill* which wasn't bad.

5

About the same as yesterday re: the course. Returned Joe Lansdale's call. He, too, is enthusiastic about FREAKS and it sounds like he's got a great story coming. The painter arrived and Mary says the new green trim looks good. Bought the Spruill's dinner at Theismann's pub, then came back and worked on REPRISALS.

6

Got something out of today's lectures, esp. on office gyn. The new Bethesda classification of Pap smears was explained and the cytobrush demonstrated. Called M and spoke to her before she left for her prom; Mary says she looks beautiful. Wish I was there. Pizza at the Spruills' (they must be getting tired of me by now) and then Steve and I sat around sampling his store of after-dinner liquers. During our conversation we came up with a great idea for a novel. At least it seems great now. (I often drink too much when I'm with Steve; I try to keep up with him, but he's 6-4 with a hollow leg.) Don't know what it'll seem like in the a.m. Came back and did some more work on REPRISALS.

7

Went to the morning lectures, then handed in my ticket and headed for home. It's like I never left. The pool was crystal clear from leaving the pump on for 4 days. Roland was here, finishing up the painting. I vacced the pool, then put Polaris to work. Took my folks out to Portofino's for dinner. Pretty good.

8

Had to work the office today, ran lots of errands in the afternoon, then had a late night in the office. Koontz faxed in a sorry-but-I'm-too-busy but added a lot of useful info about carnivals. Got a story precis from Jill Morgan and a call from Ray Garton – he wants in.

9

Well, M's now a high school graduate. The party went well. Too much food, as usual. Got an excellent story precis from Dan Simmons and sorries from Tanith Lee, Doug Winter, and Schow.

10

Got a draft of a story from Rex Miller by express mail. It's pretty rough, but I think it'll work. Ten days after mailing out the proposal, I've already got 40+% positive response. Only 5 negs, 4 of which I fully expected. I'm getting psyched.

Helped Dad open his pool, then caught up on correspondence. Started putting things together for packing tomorrow.

11/Mon

Packed for Hawaii today, including 7 books.

12-21

In Maui

22

Back from Maui. A fabulous, wondrous place. One of the best trips of my life. Haleakela is definitely going into NIGHTWORLD. Right now I'm tired and suffering from post-Maui depression.

23

Still kinda down but coming around. Went thru the mail. Craig Gardner wants into FREAKS; Rex Miller sent his revision – I've got my first story.

**

I've made many, many trips to the West Coast over the years – book tours, meetings with movie folk, and so many with Matt Costello when we were partnered in inter active media, films, and books. Sometimes I'd write down what was going on.

These are emails home to the family while Matt Costello and I were out in LA doing interactive and film bidness and I was checking with the Beacon folks re: the Repairman Jack film.

L.A. Diary

WEDNESDAY - 1/29/97

60 degrees at 7 a.m. today. Did a 30-minute walk in T-shirt and shorts past the Santa Monica Pier and along the bluffs overlooking the Pacific.

We spent the morning in story conference for *The Dark Half Interactive* with Jed Weintraub and Jeff Leiber at Orion/ MPCA (at the corner of Ocean Avenue and the terminus of Santa Monica Blvd). Had lunch (grilled marinated chicken breast sangwich) in an Argentinean place called Gaucho. More story conference in the afternoon until 4.

Wrote a couple of pages on the novel until Jed picked us up and took us to dinner at Typhoon (a Thai-Korean-Vietnamese restaurant) at the Santa Monica airport. Incredible food...we had crickets fried in fresh garlic and pepper for an appetizer... surprisingly good... you might call them land shrimp. Back to the hotel by 10:30 to sack out.

Early meeting tomorrow. The Santa Ana winds are expected, clearing the air, supposedly bringing the temp to 80.

Why are we living in the northeast?

THURSDAY 1/30

Up at 5 a.m. to work on the novel. Matt called around 7 and I did the shorts / T-shirt walk for 30 min. while he ran. I went up Santa Monica and down Broadway today.

Talked to Barry Rosenbush re: scripters for THE TOMB. Seems they've narrowed the field to 2 – he and Bill Borden favor one (I know him), while Beacon Films favors another. The battle is on. Should know in the next week or two. Says he'd love to see the *Aces* script.

Back to Orion and worked out interaction mechanics most of the a.m., then played *Shadows of the Empire* and *Tomb Raider* to study gameplay and graphics. (Yuh! This is work.) Had lunch at Wolfgang Puck's (had to move to get out of the sun so I wouldn't get burned--AND THIS IS JANUARY 30th!!!!!). Presented our morning's work to the guys, then...

Raced up to ICM HQ in Beverly Hills to meet our interactive agent, Stefanie Henning (who told us she's preggers and due in June). Met the books-to-film agent Alicia Gordon and discussed bringing out DNA WARS during the anticipated hoopla over the *Star Wars* rerelease.

Also met with our film-script agent Doug MacLaren (I like his name because it sounds like a single malt) and discussed what might fly as a spec script. Met ICM's online agent Mark Evans, then discussed detailed of the MSN details with Stef. After that we followed Stef back toward the Pacific to Venice.

Stefanie (and Mark Evans) took us to dinner at World Cafe on Main in Venice (a real bitch finding a parking space) because there was an interactive social thing being held there. Had an excellent dinner of peppered tuna steak very rare with an Australian Merlot that was smooth as silk. Peter Marx stopped by to say hello – we've got an 8:30 with him at the B'Way Deli tomorow). Jed stopped by the table and said he was going to Sushi Hama farther down Main and to stop by after dinner.

So we said goodbye to Stef and Mark and headed that way. Passed Ahhhhnold's *Schatzi's* but didn't care to try it. Went to Sushi Hama and found Jed and Jeanette (also of Orion) and another couple and sat down with them. Wasn't hungry but managed to force down some sushi and Sapporo Draft along with a couple of oyster shooters (raw oyster + soyish sauce + quail egg + scallion slice = DELICIOUS!!!!!). That was enough for the night. Drove back to the Hanoi Hilton here with the windows open and wrote this.

A hard day's night. (Why don't I hear pity noises?)

Alas, tomorrow is another day.

FRIDAY - 1/31

Up at 5:30 to jot down notes on a film idea Matt and I worked out last night, then the a.m. walk (down on the beach this time). The rental car got dinged in the fender while parked overnight. The hotel's reaction was "Duh?" but AmEx said they'd cover everything.

Walked to the Broadway Deli and on the way we worked out what we were going to pitch to MGM Interactive later that a.m. Decided to avoid horror because it might overlap with our MSN project, "Elysium."

Met with Peter Marx (who was set to be the chief programmer of the *Mirage* CD-ROM when it was at TWI) at 8:30 at Broadway Deli to discuss working together on the project we're pitching to MGM; he caught us up on all the interactive gossip. [Learned that Jonathan Wiedeman (who was going to be Propaganda Code's producer of the *Mirage* CD-ROM when it was at TWI) has been hired as a "station manager" at MSN in the area where our "Elysium" project will run.

The MGM meeting with Ken Locher was a dud but we ran into Jonathan Guttentag who gave us copies of *The Ultimate James Bond*, an interactive he'd shepherded to market.

We got invited to an opening night screening of the *Star Wars* rerelease...well, sort of...all the screenings are full until 1:30 a.m. and that's too late if we're catching an 8:00 a.m. flight tomorrow.

***

This is from back in the day when it looked like the Repairman Jack movie was really gonna happen. The dispatches were posted nightly on the RJ website as things went down.

LA Diary – 2002

WEDNESDAY – 11/20/2002

A pleasant, incident-free flight out (had rack of lamb, nice and rare, for lunch in first class); Continental didn't lose my bag and Avis had my car waiting for me. So far so good. But then I had to drive. The 405 was jammed and it took me an hour to make the 16-mile trip from LAX to the Hyatt on Sunset.

It took my niece Emily and her roommate Rebecca 90 minutes to drive up from Hermosa Beach; they made it to the hotel 5 minutes before the limo arrove. The driver's name was Robert and he got us to the Samuel Goldwyn Theater on Wilshire in plenty of time for the world premiere of "The Emperor's Club" (a Beacon film). We walked down the red carpet (zillions of photogs but can you believe it: Not one asked us to stop for a picture).

Barry Rosenbush, one of the two principle producers on the Repairman Jack film (the other, Bill Borden, is in Hong Kong doing retakes on the next Jackie Chan movie), escorted us around. I met Army Bernstein again along with other Beacon people who've been only voices on the phone and names on email before this.

I've been to premieres before and they have their own special ambiance. All the principles in cast and production bring their own group of guests who applaud when their names pop up in the opening credits.

Then the film started. I wish all theaters were like the Goldwyn. The screen is huge, the seats are comfortable, and the sound system and acoustics are first rate.

Since it's a character film, and doesn't need a wide screen to be appreciated, "The Emperor's Club" is not the type of film I'd normally buy a ticket for unless dragged there (as I was dragged to Kevin Kline's last film, "Life as a House," which I wound up enjoying very much). Despite the fact that "The Emperor's Club" doesn't have any explosions or grisly murders, I highly recommend it. Kevin Kline and the rest of the cast are superb in a script that defies expectations. And if you're a teacher, like Emily and Rebecca, you've got to see it. Hell, it made even me want to be a teacher.

A cocktail reception followed with lots of food stations: Indian, Asian, American, etc. Most of the cast was there (although Kevin Kline seemed to fade away pretty quickly) plus a lot of familiar supporting-actor faces. I'm not much when it comes to placing names with faces, but I can tell you there were a lot of familiar faces there. One I did recognize was John Voight. I was standing next to him on line for one of the bars and had an urge to ask him what the hell's up with his daughter, or maybe tap him on the shoulder and say, I think I've seen you before... weren't you in that film... what was it called... oh, yeah: *Anaconda*?

But I counted to ten and the urge passed.

Emily and Rebecca seemed awestruck and I was glad I

could bring them along, but eventually it came time to leave. Our limo was waiting and Robert delivered us safely back to the Hyatt.

Not a bad first day in LA.

THURSDAY

Last time I was at this Hyatt I had a room overlooking Sunset Blvd. That's one busy street, and since the hotel is right across from the House of Blues, it tends to be noisy on that side, especially on Friday and Saturday nights.

Very noisy.

So I asked for something in the rear this time. Wow. The room's writing desk faces the window, and as I type I can look out at all these cool houses, no two alike, clinging like pastel-colored ticks to the flanks of the Hollywood Hills.

Since my body's clock is running 3 hours ahead of LA's, I was up and about early, before the hotel coffee shop opened. But there's a Starbuck's half a block east where I always get my morning coffee when I'm here. I pushed through the hotel's glass doors, reflexively expecting a blast of cold (it's late November, after all) but whoa! 80 degrees.

Did a 30-minute walk up the 45-degree-inclined streets of the Hollywood Hills and then back to the room where I knocked out four pages on GATEWAYS before heading out to lunch with Barry Rosenbush. We had hot (read spicy) dim sum, then hit a screening of "The Ring" in Century City. (He'd heard me mention that I wanted to see it but hadn't had a chance yet, so he got us tickets.)

I loved "The Ring." Just when I thought it was going to have a sweet-but-trite ending a la "Sixth Sense," it turns the tables on you. For me the most unsettling thing was the resemblance between the child Adrian and my grandson Ethan. You must see this dreamlike movie.

Then it was down to Santa Monica to the Beacon offices to talk with Charlie Lyons (the other principle in the company) about the film (discussing He-Who-Shall-Not-Yet-

Be-Named as the lead) and the Repairman Jack video game they'd like to have ready for simultaneous release. Watched the sunset through Army Bernstein's office windows overlooking Santa Monica Bay, looking for the fabled green flash as the sun disappears but nobody saw it. I'm continually amazed at how Army and Charlie and Barry and just about everybody at Beacon demolish all the Hollywood stereotypes.

A little after six we all went around the corner on Ocean Avenue for dinner at Ivy on the Shore. Viki and Jack Thompson (I'm told Jack is the "J" in J. D. Edwards) came along; they're major investors in Beacon and extremely nice, down-to-earth people. I think I love this company. They all seem to like each other (really, genuinely) and they want to do right by Jack.

For dinner I had a variation on Charlie's special risotto (they added lobster) and some excellent margaritas.

Drove most of the way back to the hotel via Santa Monica Blvd.

Day number 2…pretty damn good.

FRIDAY

Up for the day around 5am. Had to wait an hour before I could snag a coffee. My legs are killing me. I'm getting out of my chair like an arthritic 80-year old. Happens to me every time I walk these hills. I exercise – either stationary bike, treadmill, or walking the Spring Lake boardwalk – 5 days a week, plus do weight-training on my quads and hamstrings 3 days a week. My leg muscles are in good shape, but walking up and down 45-degree inclines makes you use them in ways they're not used to, and they're telling me about it this a.m. I think they're ticked off at me.

Between bouts of writing, I work out in the hotel gym this morning, but promise myself another go at those hills tomorrow.

A conference call with Michael Helfant (Santa

Monica) and Brian London (Denver) of Beacon's interactive department. The Repairman Jack game comes down to this: we have 18 months; to get out a game in that time we have to use an existing engine. Michael is going to talk to Black Label (they did "The Thing" game) and the "Grand Theft Auto" developers. Brian and I think those engines will probably work. If it's coded from scratch it will take 2.5 years.

Lunch with Barry Rosenbush and Chris Morgan (who did the fantastic revision on the script) at La Serenata on Pico in Westwood where I pump Chris about how writing gets done – and not done – out here. Barry gives the view from the producer's angle. All in all it's about as efficient as book publishing. They talk about 6-hour meetings on "Repairman Jack" where they go through the script page by page. I'm told that there's been an ongoing dynamic between Army and Barry: Army looks at the novel as a jumping-off point (sort of, Okay, we've got this character – what can we do with him?) while Barry keeps hauling the script back to the book.

During all this I have some of the best Mexican food I've ever had – empanadas with beef tongue. (I kid you not.) Yum.

We talk about He-Who-Must-Not-As-Yet-Be-Named again and I bring up the subject of Gia. I pitch the blonde from "CSI: Miami" (can't remember her name but she is soooo hot). Barry shakes his head. They don't want someone from TV; they want someone who can help "open" the movie on that all-important first weekend.

Barry has been having the same trouble as many of you board walkers: finding copies of THE HAUNTED AIR. He wants to buy a bunch for me to sign to various people at Beacon but is striking out all over LA. He decides to come over to Dark Delicacies on Saturday for the signing. I guarantee him that Del will have a ton of copies.

Back to the Hyatt for more writing. Speak to David Schow for a while and get directions to his house in the hills for a party tomorrow night. Down to the hotel computer to check email and the website. So many posts! I answer what I can. I skip dinner since I ate enough at La Serenata to carry me over.

A quiet night – my only free night on the trip – and I'm taking it easy. I rent "The Bourne Identity" to see how Matt Damon fares as an action star: better than I expected, but he looks more like a graduate student than an assassin.

SATURDAY

Wide awake at 5am again, and that's good. Keeps me on east coast time which will help when I have to get up early tomorrow to catch the 7:30 to Newark out of LAX.

It's a foggy morning. Anywhere else I'd say it looks like rain, but not in Southern CA. The Starbucks doesn't open until 6:30 on Saturdays, so I take my coffee quest to the front desk where I'm told there's an all-night coffee shop half a block away across Sunset in The Standard hotel. Why don't I know about this? Because I never asked. Sort of a guy thing, I guess… like asking a stranger for directions.

Coffee secured, and nothing to do till one-ish, I hit the keys. Between bouts of writing I stare out the window at the hills and realize the big mansion-like building on the far right is Chateau Marmont. One of these trips out here I want to stay there (or at the amazing art-deco Argyle across the street) but I don't want the Belushi cottage. I don't even want to know which one was his.

I get a call from Barry with the sad news that Bill Borden's father died Friday night from long-standing heart disease.

The signing goes well with a good, steady crowd. I'm sitting next to Christa Faust admiring all her new tattoos. I wind up signing whole collections.

Del and Sue of Dark Delicacies are two of the nicest, realest people you could meet. I love coming out here just to hang with them. They say the traffic at all their signings has been declining but they're selling more books per signing due to phone orders. Del says he now gets phone orders for signed books from people who live five miles away. (Must be that LA traffic.) After the official signing, I sign the three stacks of phone orders.

Del and I go to the sports bar down the block for a couple of beers while Sue holds the fort, then we all go out for some meat at Black Angus.

After dinner I head for Schow's place. He lives in one of those neat old stucco houses built into the side of the Hollywood Hills. His place faces the Griffith Observatory and is just about as high. One of the cool things about visiting Dave is that you have to head up Beachwood Blvd which points you straight at the big old "HOLLYWOOD" sign on the hillside.

The party's started by the time I get there. The women are all pretty Goth but most of the guys are dressed in generic clothing you could buy in any Wal-Mart. David, as always, is all in black. I chat with Berni Wrightson and a few others in the kitchen for a while, then Dave and I retire to his office to catch up. He gives me a copy of Hammer's "Plague of Zombies" which I've been hunting for years.

At 11:30 it's time to go. I'm glad I've watched my wine intake. I'd hate to think of driving that downgrade and those hairpin turns with half a load on.

Dave's house is 5 miles at most, probably less, from the Hyatt. Takes me an hour on Sunset. I finally make it back, pack up most of my stuff, set the alarm for 4:30, and rack out.

That's it. Game over. A nice, low-key end to a great trip.

***

Showtime's Masters of Horror *(a series of one-hour horror films directed by "masters" such as John Carpenter, Stuart Gordon, John Landis and others) chose to adapt my short story "Pelts" for its second season. The notorious / infamous and enormously talented Dario Argento chose to direct it. These are dispatches sent to the RJ website from the set.*

Since MoH films all of its features in Vancouver, that's where I went. I couldn't spare the time for the entire two-week shoot, but I could manage a couple-three days.

"Pelts" Shoot – 2006

4/18/2006

A few words about the adaptation: They've kept the basics but altered the ending and added lots of sex. My story held the promise of sex – it fueled one character's actions – but it never happened. (Ah, frustration.) In fact, not one of the people who schemed to gain from the pelts got what they wanted. That was one of the points of the story.

Am I upset? No. Am I about to throw a hissy fit for you? No. Sure, I'd have preferred them to follow my nobody-got-what-they-wanted arc, and preserve the story's symmetry, but when you sell film rights, the operative word is "sell" – which means you no longer own them. They belong to someone else. You hope they'll treat your story with respect, but there's no guarantee. I learned that the hard way with Michael Mann's adaptation of The Keep. But in that case my book was raped. Here, "Pelts" has simply been tarted up without corrupting its essence.

If you're not JK Rowling, with every filmmaker in the world bidding to adapt Harry Potter, thus allowing you to demand cast and script approval, you either take your chances or refuse to sell any rights at all.

So, I arrove in Vancouver late Tuesday night, too late to visit the strip-club shoot. (NB: There's no strip club in my story, but that shoot would have been, um, interesting.)

4/19

Wednesday is a night exterior shoot with crew call at 3pm. Mick Garris – the creator and guiding light of the series

– calls in the morning and invites me to go to the location along with him and director Dario Argento. We all gather in the lobby at 1:30. I've met Mick before. He's a screenwriter, director, producer, novelist, and a gracious, unpretentious, genuine man – about as unHollywood as you can imagine.

He introduces me to the maestro and his translator, Francesca. Dario Argento turns out to be a slight man, about five-eight, with a quick smile and an amiable manner. His heavily accented English is serviceable and Francesca helps him when he gets stuck on a word.

The location for the Jamesons' farm is a historic site about 40km outside of Vancouver. We all make small talk and stroke each other for a while. I try to get him to see that the Jake character shouldn't get it on with the stripper because the motif of the story is that no one involved with the pelts gets what they want. Dario is totally opaque to the idea. So he and Francesca put their heads together over the day's call sheet while Mick and I catch up.

We turn off a country road onto a dirt drive lined with equipment trailers and cranes and generators and the all-important catering truck. Even though it's after 2pm, they're serving breakfast. I have some peppers and eggs and bacon while the other three grab fresh-made grilled-cheese sandwiches.

The house sits 200 yards from the road. It has no power lines running to it so it's perfect for a remote place in the Jersey Pine Barrens. The set designers have wound vines all around the front to give it a more unkempt look.

Beyond that, on a rise behind the bend, they've erected two walls with a roof to serve as an old Piney woman's shack – from the right angle you'd think it was a complete building that had been sitting on the spot for fifty years.

Beyond that the land slopes off to where they've erected the "ruins" Dario requested. In the story there's a species of spleenwort growing in a straight line. It can't grow in the acid soil of the Barrens, so when you see it you can be pretty sure a building (or maybe one of the "lost towns" of the Barrens) used to sit there and the stuff is growing over the limestone of the foundation.

Since this is film, Dario wanted a more visual hint that some other structure preceded the Jameson farm in the area by a long, long time. What they've given him is a couple of piles of worn, broken blocks (styrofoam, but you'd never know) indicating maybe an ancient gateway, and beyond that something that may have been a monolith or temple stone in its heyday. I'm impressed.

A light rain begins as they start the shoot. People grumble but it isn't going to stop them. Today's scenes involve furrier Jake Feldman and his assistant as they find the pelts and what's left of the Jamesons. John Saxon plays Pa Jameson but he's not involved today.

Meat Loaf plays Jake, and Mick introduces me to him as the guy who wrote the original story.

"You dreamed this up?" Mr. Loaf says as we shake hands. "You're one sick guy."

I hear that a lot; I give my standard reply: "Thank you."

Between setups Mick, Meat (his folks named him Michael Aday but he wants to be called Meat -- I kid you not) and I sit and gab in the set's "video village" – a tented area where we can watch monitors and see what the cameras see as they shoot. He's natural and unassuming, and serious about his acting. He wants to know more about Jake and how he feels when he first sees the pelts. I tell him these aren't just pelts, they're uber-pelts and he's seeing his whole future open up before him. He's seeing paradise by the dashboard light.

After hours of lots of activity and very little footage being shot, I'm ready to go. The temperature has dropped, a wind has sprung up, and I'm not dressed for this. Mick is heading back to the hotel to meet with Tobe Hooper about budgeting his upcoming film, and so I hitch a ride.

Back in my room, I write into the night.

4/20

Crew call isn't until 4pm so I spend the day writing. I break to go out and buy a new digital camera since my old Fuji had finally crapped out. All of the photos from yesterday are gone -- or never were. I find a Sony Cyber-shot on sale and snag it. The guy tries to sell me something with more features but if I use a camera four times a year it's a lot.

I'm supposed to ride over with Dario at 2:45. I get there at 2:35 and they've already left. Swell. I call the production office and they say I can ride over with Meat Loaf. So I do. I want to talk about music but he wants to talk about how the film differs from my story. I give him my fiction-imposing-symmetry-on-the-chaos-of-reality theory and why leaving out the homeless woman breaks that symmetry. He says he likes my ending better, but he may simply be polite.

We stop at a convenience store because he likes to drink Diet Coke with ice -- with ice -- and they don't have ice on location. We also have to find a florist so he can buy flowers for a woman he fears he inadvertently insulted yesterday. It's like driving around with an eccentric but lovable uncle.

They drop off Meat at makeup and me at the farm house location. Same as yesterday, they're serving breakfast. I grab some bacon and eggs and head up to the house. Dario is effusively apologetic when I tell him about being left high and dry -- he didn't know I was coming. I reshoot all the photos I took yesterday -- the ruins, the shack, etc., then go to the basement set where all of the day's interiors will be shot.

This is the scene where Larry, the trapper's son, performs a facectomy on himself. Covered with blood after bludgeoning his father to a pulp, he enters, opens a bear trap, and slams his face into it. The bludgeoning is in my story, but the trap is not. It's an AA (Argento addition) -- but I kind of wish I'd thought of it.

The prop is a real bear trap that's had its springs

welded so they can't snap the jaws. Opening the trap takes the most takes because the actor's having a tough time making it look like he's struggling against the springs.

With retakes, lighting changes and different setups for master shots and close ups, it takes almost 4 hours to film a sequence that will run 40 seconds tops on the screen. I look around. Everyone's smiling. They're delighted with the progress we're making.

Meat arrives for the scene where Jake discovers Larry's body with its ruined face (a dummy). He's been on the road doing driving shots for a later sequence. Now, with the interiors, the master shot and close-ups are done in half an hour. He's outta there.

So am I. I say my good-byes and get an Italian left-right double embrace from Dario. I promise to send him the first-edition chapbook of "Pelts." (Hope I have an extra.)

On the way out I meet John Saxon who's playing Pa. No time for more than an introduction and moving on. He'll be shooting scenes with Larry down by the ruins. I'd love to watch but frankly I'm bored.

I drive back to the hotel with Meat. We commiserate about conglomeratization -- he about music, I about publishing. I get him talking about touring for his new album coming in the fall and his early experiences as an actor -- *Rocky Horror* in particular.

I realize how boring acting can be. They picked us up at 3:30 and now they drop us off at 9:30. They've needed him for maybe 90 minutes of those six hours. No wonder some actors get into drugs.

Meat wants to see the original "Pelts" story so I get his email address and promise to send it to him ASAP. He's too tired for a trip to the bar and I don't like to drink alone, so we shake hands and head to our respective rooms.

My Vancouver trip is, for all intents and purposes, over. All that's left is the plane ride home tomorrow morning.

Am I glad I flew 6000 miles roundtrip for this? Yeah.

Very. I met some great people and saw pieces of my story come to life.

Also, it's a wake-up call. Acting has this aura of glamour, but there's nothing glamorous about the nuts and bolts of shooting a movie. It's repetitious and full of empty down time as you wait for your call. What's fascinating to me is the technical end -- the Director of Photography giving orders for the lighting, all these technicians bustling around, knowing exactly what's got to be done. And in short time a dusty old basement becomes an eerie, creepy chamber of horrors.

***

I wasn't sure where to put this. It's sort of a memoir, so...

The Origin of the Signalz

I've never used a writing prompt, never felt the need for one. I've always had the next story (and usually the one after that) gestating in the mental incubator.

So imagine my surprise when, as author Guest of Honor at the 2018 MARcon, I wind up on a panel about writing prompts. A writer named Lorna Woulfe was moderating. She explained how prompts work for her to get the writing juices flowing. It could be the suggestion of a situation, or a kind of person, or even an illustration.

At the annual Borderlands Bootcamp for Writers, the grunts must write a short piece between Friday night and Sunday morning. We assign random prompts – sometimes a first line, sometimes a title, sometimes just a character name. But these have a specific purpose in that they allow us to see what's been learned over the weekend.

As for my personal experience with prompts, I had next to nothing to offer the panel.

Lorna suggested a flash fiction exercise using illustrations. Among those available was this one by Gary

Wedlund (who happened to be on the panel):

I chose it because I was wondering why the smaller child was holding her ears. (Not knowing the title was "Tatum and Her Brother" I wrongly assumed the little one was female.) The possibilities intrigued me. What I came up with in the allotted time will seem familiar to those who've read *The Last Christmas*:

THE SCREAM

"What do you mean, you can't hear it?" Ellie said.

Maura couldn't help but feel her little sister's distress. She was truly bothered by something. Maura strained her ears but heard only the wind sighing through the branches.

"I don't know how else to say it: I don't hear anything. What's it sound like?"

"Like a scream – a long scream that never stops." She stuck her fingers in her ears. "I can't stand it!"

This was strange. Really strange. But not totally surprising. Ellie was the weird sister – the one who believed in Big Foot and UFOs and ghosts, and now she was hearing–

"Make it stop. Please, Maura, you've got to make it stop!"

She wanted to help – really, she did. It killed her to see Ellie like this. But how could she stop a sound she couldn't hear? Only one explanation…

"It's in your head, Ellie."

"No, it's all around. When I put my fingers in my ears it's less but it's still there."

Her face was pale now, and her cheeks... they looked sunken.

"Ellie are you all right?"

"That sound – it's making me sick. I wanna go home!"

"But we're supposed to go to town. Mom needs–"

Ellie retched. "I'm gonna be sick!"

"No, don't!" Maura hated the smell of vomit. It made her want to puke.

Which was what Ellie did right then. Maura had heard the term "projectile vomiting" on TV and that was what Ellie did.

Except she puked blood – bright red blood. A long stream of it.

"Oh, no! Ellie, no!"

And then she dropped to her knees and did it again. So much blood...

Like a chopped tree, she fell onto her side, but never took her fingers out of her ears.

"Make it stop, Maura," she gasped, her face white as a cloud. "Make it stop!"

And then her eyes went blank and lifeless.

Maura screamed. And screamed. And screamed...

Three hundred-plus words flowed pretty quickly and I was sorry I had to stop to read aloud what I'd come up with. Then the panel's slot was done. Time to make room for the next group. I folded up my scribbled sheets and went on to my next panel.

I have a long-standing rule about writing: Never throw anything away. Seemingly useless sentences and passages can come in handy when you least expect it. So on the plane ride home I typed "The Scream" into my laptop's ideas folder and pretty much forgot about it...or tried to.

That noise only Ellie could hear...I sensed a story hiding in there. I simply had to tease it out. What *was* the noise? Let's say a signal of some sort. Okay, but from where?

Outside, of course. The ideas started to cascade: Not one signal but many signals – from the Otherness. They started in the spring of 1941 during some odd goings on in a small castle in the Alps of Transylvania. They're low-frequency electromagnetic impulses that no one should be able to hear, and they change frequencies without rhyme or reason. They must mean *something*, but those who know aren't talking.

Okay, the signals are now a part of the Secret History. But what to do with them? Surely someone would be monitoring them. For the sheer hell of it I name the fellow Burbank; he's *old* and keeps track from an Art Deco apartment building on Central Park West – sort of like the San Remo but with only one tower. Burbank is ensconced in the tower penthouse which is topped by a huge aerial. And because of this fellow's name, it seems only fitting that I call the building The Allard.

The Last Christmas was in its early stages. I had parts to be played but still needed characters to fill them. I knew what they'd do, but I didn't know who they were yet. The private detective started out as an Anasazi named Bernardo and ended up a Mohawk named Tier Hill. But he needed something to fix him in readers' minds. Hey, what if Hill is one of those rare people like Ellie who can hear the signals? I imagine him on a stakeout across CPW from the Allard when he hears a signal start to howl from Central Park. And then this girl begins to scream. He checks it out and learns she can hear the signal too and it's making her sick. I adapt my flash fiction piece to the scene.

That's how stories are pieced together: through careful planning and crazy-ass serendipity.

The signals play a peripheral role in the novel but have a terrific impact on Tier Hill's life. And that should have been that.

But the signals wouldn't let me go. They demanded center stage in a story. So soon after I completed *The Last Christmas*, I started on a prelude to *Nightworld* I'm calling

Signalz. It covers the last few days before *Nightworld* and mixes Ellie's story (you'll see that Central Park Scene from the other side, plus what preceded it and the horrific weirdness that followed) with Hari from the ICE trilogy and characters from the Secret History, some familiar and some new.

Well, well, well...a flash-fiction exercise with a pictorial prompt led to two novels and I'm not finished yet. So thank you Lorna Woulfe and Gary Wedlund. I owe you.

***

John W. Campbell, Jr

One of the questions a writer always gets is "How did you get into writing?" My answer: Via short stories and a fellow named John W. Campbell, Jr. I started out trying to sell short fiction but was receiving those pre-printed "Does not suit our editorial needs at this time" rejection slips with Pavlovian regularity. I wrote "The Cleaning Machine" (now there's a gripping title) and sent it to Analog. *Weeks later I received an envelope from the magazine and expected another form. But no. Inside was a letter from John Campbell himself, the father of modern science fiction, explaining the rejection:*

"It's not a story because it doesn't go anywhere. (The tenants did but the story doesn't!) It's a vignette. A story has a beginning, middle, and end. Send me a story."

So I did. I kept writing and he kept rejecting, but always told me why, and I will forever revere him for that. I'd never taken a writing course – he became my writing course. One day I received a check and no letter. If he couldn't disagree with you, Campbell had nothing to say.

One of my great regrets in life was not going to see him. He invited me to come by the Condé Nast offices when I was in the city but... I kept putting it off. There would always be time. And then one summer morning in 1971 he woke up dead and I'd never have a chance to meet my mentor.

So when Reason *asked me for an obit, I jumped at the chance.*

Requiem for a Giant

At different times during the course of his career he was called a reactionary, a romantic, a fascist, a visionary, a conservative, an Objectivist, a troglodyte, a technocrat, a racist, and other sundry epithets – some more caustic, some more complimentary. He was all of them and none of them.

John W. Campbell, Jr. was an individualist in the truest sense of the word, rejecting all labels and refusing to admit to following any particular philosophy. There will never be another like him. He was the prime mover in shaping science fiction into its present day form and the genre will bear his imprint for as long as it exists. To his monthly editorials in *Analog* he brought a unique combination of prejudice and objectivity which guaranteed the reader an unusual, idiosyncratic approach to any given subject.

He's gone now and *Analog* isn't quite the same. It's still the best s-f magazine on the market, still the largest selling...but something's missing. The editorials don't have quite the same punch, color, incisiveness. He was a giant and a tough act to follow.

BINARY STAR

Campbell was 20 years old when his work first saw print in the January 1930 issue of Hugo Gernsback's *Amazing Stories.* The genre was a natural for an imaginative MIT student who liked to write fiction. Subsequent tales rapidly gained him an ardent following and it wasn't long before s-f editors realized that the John W. Campbell name on the cover meant rapid sales on the newsstand. In a little over four years he was considered to be the most popular science fiction author in America, rivaled only, perhaps, by E. E. Smith.

That position was soon challenged by a new name – Don A. Stuart – whose "Twilight" was published in the November 1934 issue of *Astounding Stories.* This story, a mood piece about man's far-flung future, entranced the science fiction world and further Stuart efforts such as "Atomic Power", "Blindness", "The Escape," and "Night" put Campbell's name in near total eclipse. Stuart's stories were something new to s-f; they were more subdued, more empathetic than Campbell's cosmic-scale romances, and they tolled the death knell for the Bug Eyed Monster – and fantastic invention-riddled space operas which had typified science fiction until then. Stuart's work formed the vanguard in science fiction's coming of age, when mood, plot and characterization began to rate equal time with the scientific aspects of the story.

Stories bearing the Campbell name became few and far between; and after he took over the editorial post of *Astounding Stories* in September 1937, they became virtually extinct. His energies were now totally devoted to reshaping the face of science fiction. Strangely enough, the Don A. Stuart name disappeared, too – but by then most knowledgeable s-f fans knew that Campbell and Stuart were one and the same.

Astounding – which changed its name to *Analog* with the February 1960 issue – became Campbell's life for the next 33-plus years. (It should be mentioned that he also edited the lamented *Unknown Worlds* from 1939 to its demise in 1943.) He decided that it was time for science fiction to move out of its gee-whiz-lookit-that phase and become a more mature medium of expression. Scientific extrapolation is the core of good s-f, yes, but Campbell wanted the writer to put some flesh on his characters: he began demanding personality and motivation, a theretofore rare finding in the field.

A group of young writers who could fill the Campbell

bill began to cluster around *Astounding*. Campbell nurtured the likes of Asimov, van Vogt, Sturgeon and Heinlein, berating them and challenging them – throwing them ideas that he had no time to develop himself. He became the Ezra Pound of science fiction. As Isaac Asimov put it: "Nothing I have ever written, whether he was directly involved or not, whether it was science fiction or not, fails to carry the impress of his influence."

For over 33 years he conducted a continuous search for new talent. If a new author submitted a story that didn't make the grade but showed promise, Campbell would often send it back with a note explaining *why* he rejected it. You have no idea what a buoying effect such a note can have on an author who has previously received only mimeo'd rejection slips from other editors!

If Campbell found a story good enough to be published, however, the author received only a check. This was typical of the man. He loved an argument, loved to inundate an opponent with a flurry of off-beat alternatives; but he quickly lost interest in people who agreed with him.

Wartime paper shortages threatened all the pulp magazines but Campbell's editorial policies had made *Astounding* a leader in the field and it managed to pull through; not so its fantasy-oriented sister, *Unknown Worlds,* which gave up the ghost in October 1943. So Campbell's time was once again exclusively devoted to *Astounding:* he steered it through the so-called "Golden Age" of the Forties and the big boom of the early Fifties, through the slump of the late Fifties and early Sixties which decimated the s-f magazine population until only a handful were left. And he brought the magazine as *Analog* into the present resurgence of the genre.

NEW WAVE

The world changed quite a bit during that period and

so, naturally, did the people who make up s-f fandom. Many of today's younger fans have a mystical/collectivist orientation toward life and non-romantic tastes in literature; consequently, they demand and receive science fiction that suits their inclinations. In other words, pop-philosophy and pop-literary styles caught up to s-f (which many new writers interpret as "speculative fiction").

Thus was science fiction's "new wave" born. Campbell, for the most part, avoided direct personal involvement in the debates, although the antithesis of the "new wave" style was being called Campbellian s-f. *Analog* editorials, however, became more topical, more barbed and the "new wave" folk moved further and further away from Campbell.

What else could they do? Campbell's editorials had a marked tendency to reaffirm the concept that *A is A* and to find value in the sovereignty and efficacy of the individual. He dared to find value in capitalism! ("Capitalism motivates the individual to *be* an individual, and to see just how much he can accomplish in competition with all other individuals." Mystics and collectivists resent such "twaddle."

He rejected stream-of-consciousness and similar pop-styles, insisting on publishing stories with both a beginning and an end and some sort of logical connection between the two:

The major factor that makes an Analog story is a consistency both internally and externally – i.e. the story develops logically from given data in the story, and doesn't violate known science pointlessly and without explanation.

The author, to earn his keep, has to think things out in a direction the reader never considered, or in detail greater than the reader bothers to, or to a logical conclusion the reader shied away from.

He was Aristotelian to the core and a firm believer in what he called the Schwartzberg test: "The measure of the rigor of a Science is the index of its ability to predict." Consequently, he had little faith in psychology (except in some of its applications to the market) and even less in sociology, referring to them as the modern day black arts. He railed against the Scientific Establishment for refusing to take seriously any research into psionics – telepathy, for instance – maintaining that it was probably a dead end, but it shouldn't be dismissed until it had been investigated.

ICONOCLAST

He warred with all Establishments, in fact, believing that the more entrenched and snug and comfortable one became with one's conceits, the more one resisted movement, especially *forward* movement. His editorials challenged everything, spanning the galaxy from esoteric discourses on chemical engineering or the "black holes" of deep space, to the deaths at Kent state or the ecology movement.

The ecology movement... a particular thorny problem for Campbell who was a veteran birdwatcher and all-around nature lover. But he also had a love for man and his works, and a scientist's faith in technology. What brought him into conflict with the ecology movement was the fact that he was an omnivore as far as scientific knowledge was concerned, and consequently he knew a good deal about ecology, something which set him apart from most of the movement's activists. He knew the life cycles of many fauna and flora, both macro- and microscopic, knew the effects of a temperature change on them and which way the population distribution curve would skew in a given situation. He knew that many of the additives in those wonderful lead-free gasolines were carcinogens. You couldn't frighten him with stories of nuclear reactors blowing up because he knew that the uranium in a modern reactor has about as much chance of reaching critical mass as does the uranium hiding in the granite of Manhattan Island.

Campbell did not favor disrupting the ecology of our world, but neither did he favor returning to a pre-industrial type of existence in order to avoid doing so: he put his faith in people's ability to perfect technology to the point of harmony with the environment. He saw the ecology movement as good because it gave impetus to efforts toward this end, but he attacked it for its hysterical, irrational and anti-intellectual overtones.

Read the editorials. They cannot be summarized with any justice, they cannot be broken down. Each must be read as a unit. There are numerous places about the country selling back issues of *Analog*... start with December 1971, the issue with Campbell's last editorial, and move backward. There's the one on the ecology of inner-city rats (5/70) or the one on "freedom of medicine" (10/70). Other topics include public utilities and unionism (5/66), the perfect spacesuit (6/69), the FCC and cigarette commercials (7/69), victimless crimes (8/69), the chemistry of man-made elements (9/69), race and intelligence (10/69), and on and on. Harry Harrison edited a collection of older Campbell editorials for Doubleday which is still in print. I've read in excess of a hundred, concurring with many and vehemently disagreeing with the rest. But I've never found one that bored me.

Most of my correspondence with Campbell occurred during a period in which I was living in rural Missouri. In the spring of 1971 I happened to mention in a letter that I'd be in the New York City area during June; Campbell wrote back and asked me to drop in at the Conde-Nast offices so we could meet face to face. Well, one thing led to another and before I knew it, June was gone and I was back in Missouri without ever having met him. I wasn't too concerned, however, because I was moving back East permanently in 1972 and there'd be plenty of time for us to get together.

In mid-July I received a letter from Kay Tarrant, *Analog's* managing editor at that time, saying that John W. Campbell, Jr. had died in his sleep on July 11, 1971.

The unique individualist who propagated fine science fiction for over 33 years and renovated the entire genre, who acted for so many as both irritant and mentor, was gone. Science fiction and I are so much the poorer for his passing.

***

I wrote this for Mystery Scene *a week after Kay's death in 1993.*

Obituary: Kay Nolte Smith

Kay Nolte Smith died of lung cancer on Saturday, September 25. She was 61. I just heard about it and I'm still in shock. I didn't even know she was sick. She lived about 20 miles north of here in Tinton Falls, NJ. If you quantified the amount of time we spent together you'd have to say we were mere acquaintances, but I considered her a friend. Seems like just yesterday she was on the phone congratulating me because she'd just heard the news about my big advance for *The Select*; she was almost as happy as I. That was the way she was. And never a hint that something was wrong. She sounded fine.

I first met Kay through her work in the early 80's, specifically via her first novel, *The Watcher*. I'd heard it won an Edgar so I picked it up and knew immediately that she was a find. Like most of the best mysteries, *The Watcher* is about something other than its plot. It's a novel of ideas, and it's as timely now as ever. I came to learn that ideas and values were an integral part of Kay's fiction. That figured. She'd been a member of the Rand circle before it disintegrated. Some of the stories could tell...

She was born in Minnesota, grew up in Wisconsin, and received a master's in speech and theater from the University of Utah. Before that first novel she worked as an advertising copywriter and even did some Off-Broadway acting under the name Kay Gillian. Lately, between novels – which were far too infrequent for this reader – she taught speech and writing at the local community college.

Years ago I dropped her a line to the effect that we live too close and have too much in common not to get together at least once to see if we can tolerate each other. Kay agreed and it turned out we got along pretty well. So every now and again Mary and I used to meet Kay and her husband Philip for dinner at one of the shore restaurants. A few years back, Kay and I did a Seton Hall writers workshop together.

A few minutes with Kay and you knew you were in the presence of a keen mind, one so comfortable with its intelligence that it recognized no need to parade it around. She tended to keep her flags furled. The same with her carefully wrought fiction. No flashy surface displays, but all sorts of goings on in the depths.

Among her other novels are *Elegy for a Soprano*, *Mindspell*, and the recent A *Tale of the Wind*. When last we spoke she was enthusiastic about her latest, *Venetian Song*, due soon from Villard. We talked about the future.

On the whole I didn't see her often, sort of took it for granted that she was just a few stops up the Parkway – that she'd *always* but just up the Parkway – writing away, but I will miss her. A great person, a great mind, a fine writer. Knowing she's not there leaves a void to the north. We've just lost one of the good ones.

***

Poul Anderson is beloved by libertarians in general for his mistrust of governments and in particular for his tales of that swashbuckling capitalist, Nicholas Van Rijn. I revere him for introducing me to high fantasy (of a sort). I forget who asked me to do this or where it saw print.

RiP: Poul Anderson

Poul Anderson, one of the most prolific and highly-honored writers in SF and fantasy, died at his home in Orinda, California near midnight 7/31/01. He was 75 years old.

I remember being fifteen years old, very heavily into science fiction – real science fiction, like Heinlein, Pohl, Kornbluth, Clarke, Clement, Wyndham – and a loyal member of the Science Fiction Book Club who sometimes forgot to reply to the monthly mailings (which meant I'd automatically receive both of that month's selections).

After one such lapse in 1961, a novel called *Three Hearts and Three Lions* arrived unbidden to my door. I'd heard of Poul Anderson but had never read him. I knew he wrote SF but this was fantasy. Yuck! No way was I wasting my time on that junk.

But then came a family vacation involving a long ride. With nothing else to read, I slouched in the back seat of the car and reluctantly opened *Three Hearts and Three Lions*.

And had the time of my life. Couldn't put it down; laughed out loud; became a Poul Anderson fan for life.

Through the ensuing decades I watched Poul's career, wondering when he was going to get the big break he so deserved. Despite the number of excellent series he wrote, none of them propelled him to the bestseller lists. When Piers Anthony's Xanth stories started hitting it big in the 80s, I was reminded of *Three Hearts and Three Lions* and realized that all the ingredients fueling Xanth's success – the trolls and ogres, the jokes, the bad puns – had been present in *Three Hearts...*

How Poul felt about that, I don't know. I imagine he'd have shrugged it off with his usual Nordic cool. He was a household name among SF and F fans, and he'd spent his life writing what he wanted to. Maybe that was enough.

He leaves behind a body of great work and no enemies. We should all be so lucky.

PS: David Brin just told me they named an asteroid after Poul (1990 Poulanderson) shortly before he died. Wonderful.

***

Little Richard

That crazy man has always been special to me. He was just a voice on the radio, but what a voice. His "woo-wooo!" was from his soul. In the vocal intro to "Tutti-Frutti" he's (as Paul Williams said) speaking in tongues. "Keep A Knockin" was the first 45 disk I ever bought and, much to the dismay of my Benny Goodman-loving father, I wore the grooves flat. The drum intro made me want to do that and years later I became a drummer in my own garage band.

Through a mixture of synchronicity and serendipity, I finally met the man face to face, one on one. I was out on a book tour – I don't recall the year or the book, but sometime in the early aughts – and staying at the Hyatt on Sunset Boulevard in West Hollywood. It's now the Andaz, but back in the day it was known as "the Riot Hyatt" because of all the rock stars who'd trashed the place. I always stayed there because it was halfway between LAX and Dark Delicacies.

After an afternoon signing at the store, I parked in the lot and walked toward the rear entrance where a white stretch limo idled. Who pops out of the hotel but a guy

I recognized as Little Richard. I'd heard he lived here, but during all my stays I'd never once seen him. Accompanied by two well-dressed, young male aides, he sees me and raises a hand in a casual greeting as he makes a beeline for the limo.

I keep walking too, returning his wave and saying, "Evening, Mister Penniman. Long-time fan."

He stops and looks at me. Only hardcore Little Richard fans know his last name is Penniman. He says something to one of his aides, then gets in the car. The aide intercepts me at the door and says, "Little Richard would like to say hello and give you something."

Well, I'm all for that. I can't think of many celebrities I would cross the street to meet, but this was an exception. So he's seated in the rear of the car. We shake hands, he asks me my name, says he's glad to meet me, and hands me what look like Seventh Day Adventist brochures. He signs one of them and says something like "Go with God" and then he's off to wherever.

Kind of anticlimactic, sure. But he had an impact on my life and I was glad to know he was still alive and up and about. He called himself "The Architect of Rock 'n' Roll" and he was indeed that. (He also called himself "The king and queen of rock 'n' roll" and I supposed he was that too.)

5/9/20 – RiP: Little Richard. "Whop bop b-luma b-lop bam boom"

***

David G. Hartwell – RiP 1/20/16

Lots of people in the field knew David better than I. I'm not sure how many knew him longer. We met somewhere in the late seventies, just before he left Berkeley to start Timescape for S&S. I remember he was the talk of the SFWA writer-editor reception at the time. I was a little younger than David, a newbie with half a dozen short stories and two novels under my belt. I'd be hanging out at the receptions with the likes of Susan Allison, Betsy Mitchell, Shawna McCarthy, and Beth Meacham who were also just getting started. (All of them edited me to varying degrees later on. The term 'networking" hadn't been coined yet, and we weren't doing that anyway. We were all nobodies at the time who simply liked to hang out.) With the Timescape deal, however, David had become one of the movers and shakers in the field.

Over the next few decades David and I got to know each other rather well. Hardly close friends, but we'd intersect at Worldcons and World Fantasy Cons (and Lunacons, maybe?) to share an occasional lunch or protracted bar conversation. After books at Doubleday, Dell, Berkeley-Jove, and Wm. Morrow, I moved to Tor where David had been appointed senior editor. I was contracted there for medical thrillers which were assigned to Harriet McDougal. Harriet left to edit her husband (Robert Jordan) full time just as I was bringing back Repairman Jack, so David became my editor.

We were an odd couple. Here's this guy with a PhD in Comparative Medieval Literature from Columbia editing a self-taught storyteller with an associate degree from Street & Smith. But David showed a guilty appreciation for the pulp traditions I love and we forged an excellent working relationship. I referred to David as the Forester. If a book is a tree, then my beta readers and copy editor Becky Maines made sure the branches were properly pruned and the leaves all green and glossy. David took the long view, keeping an eye on the whole tree and -- as the Repairman Jack series grew in number -- on the forest they created. He'd call me and say something like, "With all Jack's been through to this point, that's probably not the way he'd react to this situation." And he'd be right. I'd so immerse myself in the current story I'd lose perspective on where it stood in the series. David kept me on track.

The last three letters of my car's license plate are "DGK." The mnemonic I use for it? "David G. Kartwell."

And here's the dedication to *Dark City*:

to David G. Hartwell

Many years…

Many books…

Many edits…

Many thanks

Finally…the last time I spent significant face time with David was after the 2013 WFC in Brighton. The northbound trains were screwed up on the day Tom Monteleone and I were heading back to the States, so we hired a car to take us to Heathrow. David was in the same predicament so we told him to hop in. He was in a garrulous mood and regaled us the whole way with tales of all the writers he'd edited, got drunk with, or both. He knew freakin' EVERYBODY. We were all on different airlines, so we separated at Heathrow, and I remember saying to Tom, "I hope to God he writes a memoir someday."

And now he's gone. Ave atque vale, David.

Somebody look for that memoir, okay?

PUFFERY

These are pieces of book promotion in various venues over the years. They exist to prompt a sale, but they also reveal some of the writing process for each. Not every book, certainly, and some that I've done have vanished into the aether. But here's a sampling.

Reborn - 321

Reprisal - 325

Nightworld - 327

Ending the Secret History - 329

Dydeetown World - 331

Sibs - 335

Jack's Myspace blog - 338

The Early Years Trilogy - 342

The ICE Sequence - 362

A bit of puffery from Mystery Scene *#25*

TWENTY YEARS WITH *REBORN*

The Story That Wouldn't Die

Some stories won't, you know. Twenty years with this one. Twenty years of writing it and rewriting it. I think I've got it right now.

Reborn started hounding me in 1970. It began as I was reading an article about a series of biological experiments in Europe on the ova of green and albino frogs. It occurred to me that successful experimentation of this sort on human cells would inevitably lead to an extremely thorny theological question. In trying to answer that question I came up with a very *Rosemary's* Babyish plot. And since I had some confidence as a writer (I'd just made my first short fiction sales), I decided this would be the perfect basis for my first novel. I wrote the book the following summer and sent it to Lurton Blassingame, then my agent. He thought 50,000 words was a bit short and had his doubts about selling it. He was right: Everybody turned it down. There was no market for novels of this sort in 1971; it was horror, and everybody knew that except for aberrations like *Rosemary's Baby* and *The Exorcist,* horror fiction was as dead as HP. Lovecraft. But that wasn't the only reason it failed to find a publisher; I looked back on the old manuscript recently and, frankly, it wasn't very well written.

That should have been that. But the question that strange, bio-theological question wouldn't go away. It kept nagging me. (I'm not trying to be coy by not spelling out exactly what that question is; those of you who know my work are aware that there's a mystery at the heart of almost everything I write; the nature of the question is integral to the mystery at the heart of *Reborn.*) So, after getting two sf novels published, I decided I was ready to tackle *Reborn* again. But I wasn't going to waste time on a rewrite if I didn't have a contract, so in 1978 I spruced up the first three chapters and culled an outline from the rest. The horror market was opening up but still no one was interested.

Now I was really through with *Reborn.* I went on to do another sf novel and then *The Keep.* People occasionally ask me why there was a three-year gap between *The Keep* and *The Tomb.* The answer: another false start on *Reborn.* You see, I hate to admit failure, and after the success of *The Keep* I felt sure I could tackle *Reborn* and finally get it right. Wrong again. In 1982, after many months and many pages, my new agent, Al Zuckerman, gave me his frank opinion: It wasn't working. All the pieces for a good novel were there but they weren't gelling into a living, breathing, functioning organism. Al was right, as he usually is in these matters. I didn't argue with him. I had this character named Repairman Jack hammering on the inner wall of my skull, demanding to be set free. So I went on to do *The Tomb, The Touch, Black Wind,* and the stories that make up *Dydeetown World* and *Soft & Others.* Yet through it all...that nagging bio-theological question.

Won't Get Fooled Again

But I wasn't going to get sucked in again. Thrice burned, twice learned, or however that saying goes. Whenever the temptation to have another go at *Reborn* arose, I'd start singing that song by The Who. But I gave in anyway. It was driving me crazy. So I sat down and tore it apart to see why it wasn't working. That tear-down led me to the answer. And the solution.

The answer was stupidity. In the first three attempts, I'd set *Reborn* in a small town in the Berkshires that was virtually run by a fundamentalist Protestant minister named Preacher Mead. What did I know about Massachusetts? Nothing. What did I know about Protestantism? Nothing. Pretty dumb.

The solution: I moved it out of Massachusetts

altogether and set it closer – physically and emotionally – to where I've spent most of my life: I brought it to New York City.

Suddenly the whole book changed. I kept the original time frame – the winter of 1968 – but the central characters, Jim and Carol Stevens, suddenly became more urbane; the hard-as-nails Preacher Mead became a sympathetic young Jesuit priest named Bill Ryan. From out of nowhere came new characters, all involved with charismatic Pentecostal Catholics who Speak in Tongues. Suddenly I was very excited about *Reborn,* and so was Al.

Write What You Know

It's obvious now why the earlier versions of *Reborn* didn't work. A Jersey boy with an urban, Catholic upbringing had no business setting a supernatural thriller in rural Massachusetts. When you're working in this genre you must be truly comfortable with all the tangs, twangs, tastes, and textures of your characters' real world in order to sell your readers on the otherworldly aspects of your story. I grew up ten minutes over the GW Bridge from New York City; I went to high school in the Chelsea district of Manhattan, a few blocks from Greenwich Village; went to college in Washington, D.C. This is a city boy talking. I don't know diddly about rural towns and it showed in those early versions.

Ken Kesey's front page article in the *New York Times Book Review* on New Year's Eve was titled "Write What You *Don't* Know." He makes a pretty poor case for this bogus advice, so with all due respect to Mr. Kesey: Bullshit, sir. Write what your *readers* don't know – but make sure *you* know what you're talking about or they'll sniff you out in a minute and slam the covers closed.

A Recovering Catholic

Once I set it in its new venue, the book was a joy to

write. It wasn't like rewriting. It was a whole new book. One of the main reasons for that was the new Jesuit character, Father Ryan. I'm the product of a Jesuit education-eight years of it- – and I found myself very much at home with the character.

And slowly, insidiously, the book became Catholic.

You see, you never get away from being a Catholic. George Carlin had a bit called "I used to be an Irish Catholic." But there's no real "used to be" where Catholicism is concerned. You can stop going to church, call the Pope a jerk, become an atheist or an agnostic, refuse to resort to a supreme being for your moral code, never give a thought to the very idea of a god for decades, but if you were raised a Catholic, it's still there inside you. Like being an alcoholic. You're never cured; you may not have had a drink in years but you're still an alcoholic – a recovering alcoholic. It's like that with Catholicism. I'm a recovering Catholic. And Catholicism informs much of *Reborn.* I've long wanted to write a religious horror novel, and this is it. But despite all the Catholic imagery and background In *Reborn,* I wasn't comfortable with that hoary old device of the Antichrist: Satan become flesh to walk the world. Yeah, yeah, so what else is new? Corny as hell (sorry).

But what if I could come up with someone *worse* than the Antichrist?

Beyond Trilogy

Suddenly it hit me: Why not bring back a certain intensely evil character from one of my previous novels? I loved the idea. It added new depth, a whole new resonance to *Reborn.* And like dominoes falling, one idea slammed into another which tipped over another, and another, and when the cascade was over I sat there dazed. I saw that Father Ryan would make a perfect protagonist for an erotic horror novel I had in the planning stages. Father Ryan's presence there would make that novel a sequel of sorts to *Reborn.* Those two novels would require a third volume to tie up all the loose ends. And in that apocalyptic third novel I saw a way to link the *Reborn* trilogy to *The Keep, The Tomb,* and *The Touch.* I would then have a cycle of six thematically linked novels.

A weird, strange trip, this. *Reborn,* twenty years in the making, is finally on its way to the public, to be followed by two more books featuring Father Ryan. (Poor Father Ryan – l have such terrible things planned for him.) Put together, they will tell one long story that spans (ironically) twenty years. I'm half done with the second volume now, and I'm itching to get to the third, the apocalyptic one. That's when all the stops come out.

Yet, after all these years I still haven't come up with an answer to by bio-theological question. But at least I've asked it.

Maybe you can answer it.

***

The Time Tunnel was a mail-order bookstore with a big mailing list. The owner, the late Craig Goden, used to invite me to promote my latest book in his catalog ("From the Tunnel"). How could I say no?

Reprisal

I know I left you hanging at the end of *Reborn.* Sorry about that. But I figured if I had to leave you up in the air, I might as well do it at 30,000 feet. I had no choice. The next book opens 20 years later. A bit of a jump, but I wanted to bypass the growth and development of Carol's son. The Evil Child schtick doesn't interest me – it's been done to death and I don't have anything terribly original to add, so why waste your time and mine with demonic *Bildungsroman*?

Originally the *Reborn* trilogy was not meant to be a trilogy. The idea of *Reborn* germinated in the early 1970s (see *Mystery Scene* #25); *Reprisal* was conceived in the early

1980s as a separate novel in which the underpinnings that give the protagonists life meaning, that make it worth living, are deliberately and violently kicked out from under him one by one. Why? The answer lies in his past, some simple forgotten act has come back to haunt him. I realized *Reprisal* would have greater scope if his *hamartia* occurred in *Reborn*. But if I linked these two novels I'd need a third to tie up all the loose ends. I find most multi-volume works a drag, but I bit the bullet and committed to the trilogy.

So even though *Reprisal*, is the middle of a three-volume *roman-fleuve* flowing from *The Keep*, I constructed it as a separate novel. At its heart, *Reprisal* is a street-level reinterpretation of *The Keep* in that it contrasts two forms of evil – one supernatural, the other purely human – but on a smaller, less political, more intensely personal scale. Once again I leave it up to you to decide which form is more disturbing. On both levels, the target is a character named Will Ryerson. It doesn't take a rocket scientist to figure that he's a fugitive from *Reborn*. He's hiding his true identity from the rest of the world, not the reader.

Reprisal is by far my darkest novel. My wife Mary would barely speak to me for days after she read it, I do some *nasty* things here. One segment – the Christmas Eve scene In Sarah's house – stopped the first draft for nearly a week. I found it so unpleasant to write that I developed an aversion reaction to my keyboard. I wandered around my study adjusting the books on the shelves, shuffling papers, anything but sit down and do what had to be done to a very lovable character. And it *had* to be done. A lot of nasty things had to be done. Part of the purpose of *Reprisal* is to peel back the layers of civility and decorum and peer into the darkness that waits within all of us. Human goodness is not an absence of evil; it is an ability to control that darkness within. Some of us have tighter reins than others. A few of us don't even own a harness. But it is the character whose grip is not so sure and strong, the one who could go either way that interests me.

I do not leave you hanging at the end of *Reprisal*.

(A final note: the third and final volume – working title: *Nightworld* – is completed. It involves characters from *The Tomb* and *The Touch* and ties in all my horror novels and a few shorter works into a six-volume cycle that begins in that remote mountain pass in the Transylvania Alps in 1941 and ends in the 1990s with the destruction of human civilization. Great fun. But more on that some other time.)

***

Another puff piece in the Time Tunnel catalog, this time flogging Nightworld.

All hell breaks loose

The fat lady is about to sing.

Really. This is it. The last volume of the *Reborn* trilogy is done, and that's it for the cycle of six novels that began with *The Keep*. It could have been done as a single, 1,000-page novel, but nobody was going for that idea. So I chopped it into thirds: *Reborn, Reprisal,* and now *Nightworld*.

In *Nightworld* I tie up five previous novels – *The Keep, The Tomb, The Touch, Reborn, and Reprisal* – while continuing to explore the same themes that have run through them. Only this time I've taken it to a grander scale. In *Nightworld*, I dump all of humanity into the crucible and turn up the heat to high. How? By opening huge, bottomless – truly bottomless – holes in the earth. During the day, there's a slight downdraft, but at sunset the flow reverses, bringing with it a foul stench and... things. Big things, little things, flying things, crawling things that attack anything that moves. They rampage through the night hours and return to the holes at dawn. Which would be bad enough, but the days are rapidly growing shorter, and the nights are getting longer. Soon darkness will be complete and permanent, and

the things won't have to return to the holes.

With the laws of man unenforceable, and the laws of nature in disarray, all of humanity is put to the test. You can do little more than hide during the dark hours, but it's during the shrinking light hours, the time when you can come out of your cellar, that you learn who you really are.

As in all the preceding books, there are choices to be made. And what choices you make depend on your values.

Because it's full of monsters, I've dedicated *Nightworld* to Forrest J Ackerman. 4SJ and *Famous Monsters of Filmland* were a rallying point for horror fans in those dreary days in the late 50's and 60's before *Rosemary's Baby* and *The Exorcist* and *'Salem's Lot*. Believe me, there was *nothing* to read. All right, there was Richard Matheson (who wasn't nearly as prolific as we wanted him to be), and old Bradbury (the new Bradbury had switched to SF), and a couple of hard-to-find Lovecraft paperbacks, but that was it. *Famous Monsters of Filmland* filled a void. It was not literary in any sense, contained no fiction, but it *connected* us. You read the letter column and realized that you weren't the only nut in the world who liked this stuff. And if you wrote to Forry, often he wrote back. Most of the major American horror authors under age fifty today were linked in their youth via *FMoF* and can trace some strain of influence back to Forrest J Ackerman's tone of loving respect generously laced with wisecracks. It's time we owned up to it.

Nightworld is a wild book that stands alone pretty well, but you'll get the most out of it if you've read all the others (e.g., Repairman Jack is a major player.) I've included *homages* (that's French for swipes) to the formative monster films of my youth in the 50's, especially *Them, The Beast from 20,000 Fathoms,* and *The Leopard Man.* (See if you can spot the scenes.) I've also got cameos by Flo & Eddie (in disguise) and Joe Bob Briggs' cable TV show. All this and the destruction of human civilization too. (Not only does the fat lady sing, but she brings down the house.)

Really, it's almost a sin to have this much fun and get paid for it.

***

I may have done this for Tor.com (or not). I don't remember. Ends one thing and points to another.

ENDING THE SECRET HISTORY OF THE WORLD
(and pretty much everything else along with it)

Nightworld (2014) ended a lot of things for me.

It opens in mid-May in Manhattan. The days are supposed to be getting longer, but day the sun rises late, and then sets early. It rises even later the next morning, and so on, with each successive day becoming shorter and shorter. Impossible, right? It goes against all we know about how our solar system works – about how *reality* works. Astrophysicists are as baffled as everyone else.

Then, all over the world, holes open in the earth, allowing things to crawl forth; wee beasties at first, then larger and larger. But no matter what the size, each is deadly in its own way. They roam through the dark, wreaking havoc, but return to the holes at dawn, shunning daylight. But the daylight hours are shrinking at an increasing rate. When the sun no longer rises, we'll all be living – well, mostly dying – in a *Nightworld*.

This is my apocalypse, the end of the world I began building with *The Keep* in 1981.

It's also the end of my Repairman Jack series. How many authors do that? End a popular series, I mean, when the publisher would be quite happy to see it keep going? Not enough, as far as I'm concerned. (I won't name names.) But from the start I'd conceived of Jack's story as a closed-end series. Instead of pushing him past his expiration date, I wanted him to go out at the top of his game.

I introduced Jack three decades earlier in 1984 as a one-shot in *The Tomb*. He was so obviously a series character, but I already had my next two books slow-roasting in my head, waiting to be plated and served, and Jack was not a part of them. Besides, a series seemed like a trap, something that would take over my career.

So I waited 14 years to pen a sequel. The success of *Legacies* spurred me to write *Conspiracies*. Then, because I was having so much fun, I gave in and committed to the series. And my prediction proved correct: Jack took over my writing career as I proceeded to add a novel a year (sometimes two when I tackled a middle-grade trilogy about his teen years) until I put him out to pasture with the 23rd installment, *Nightworld*. He'll return now and again when the right story develops, but those entries will take place before *Nightworld*.

It has to be that way. I lay waste to human civilization in *Nightworld*, leaving it in ruins. Up until then, Jack functioned as an urban mercenary, a ghost in society's machine. I break that machine in *Nightworld*, leaving him without a raison d'être. I can still tell Jack stories if I set them before *Nightworld*. But they'll appear when they're ready. The days of delivering a new Jack novel every fall are done.

Nightworld also ended my Secret History of the World.

You see, there are three levels of history. There's the world history you're taught in school, which is largely fiction and varies from country to country, sometimes from state to state, usually reflecting the prejudices and vital lies of the cultures and powers that be. The second level is the objective history – a chronology of the facts as they really went down (which Edward Gibbon calls "the register of the crimes, follies and misfortunes of mankind"). This is hard to suss out because the "facts" have been so polluted by the revisionists. The third level of history is the most intriguing: the *secret* history... the story of the unseen forces that shaped (and are still shaping) the objective history.

The forces shaping my Secret History of the World are somewhat Lovecraftian and Fortean: Nameless, faceless "intellects, vast, cool and unsympathetic," often in cosmic conflict, are manipulating people and events from offstage, much as entomologists might experiment with a beehive or an ant farm. So far I've tied 29 novels and 13 shorter works into it – somewhere in the neighborhood of seven million words.

In *Nightworld* the cosmic conflict stages its Ragnarok on Earth, leaving the place a shambles. It's the end of my Secret History because the curtain has been torn away and the forces working behind it have revealed themselves. The Secret History is secret no longer.

I planned my new novel *Panacea* as a break from the Secret History, but less than a quarter of the way in I found it gravitating to that familiar ground. I resisted at first, then realized my unconscious was pushing me that way for a reason: The novel works better in that milieu.

It seems my Secret History has still got some life in it. We know how it ends, but there remain a lot of areas that need back filling. *Panacea* is the first step in getting that done.

***

A promotional piece in Mystery Scene #20.

Dydeetown World

"*I gathered from the medium-size tyrannosaurus rex running loose in the yard that Jennings discouraged drop-in company.*"

I loved that line from the moment I thought of it,

but I always had something else to write, something more pressing, so it sat unused in my notebook for ten years, an opening hook in search of a story. Finally, in 1984, I decided to put it to use. I'd recently finished *The Tomb* and my mind was still in the private-eye groove. The line gave me no choice – the story had to be science fiction. The line told me things. For instance, it implies a future where genetic engineering and/or cloning are so far advanced that a formerly extinct dinosaur (available in small, medium, and large) patrolling a yard as a watch animal is a ho-hum situation. And if this future can supply clones of famous extinct reptiles, why not clones of famous dead people, too?

And then the wheels began turning.

It was going to be just a short story. Five, maybe six thousand words, tops. A quiet little SF tribute to Raymond Chandler whose work has given me such pleasure over the years. I was, going to use all the clichés – the down-and-out P.I., his seedy friends, the tired, seamy city, the bar hangout, the ruthless mobster, the whore with the heart of gold. But I was going to set it in the far future, in a future I had developed for the SF I was writing during the 70's (three novels, a novella, and a bunch of shorts). But this was going to be different. This story was going to be set on the underbelly of that future. It was going to be grimy and disillusioned rather than bright and full of hope like its predecessors.

The hardboiled P.I. mode of fiction is unequaled in presenting a view of society at street level. The author and the point-of-view character can meld their voices to depict life as they see it. If I were a sociologist in the future studying these times, and I wanted to experience the *Zeitgeist* of the Twentieth Century, wanted to get a feel for the people at street level, their mores, their colors and textures, their *Weltanschauung,* how they spoke and dressed, how the air smelled, I'd read Twentieth Century P.I. fiction. (I believe somebody else has already made this observation, but if not, I'll take credit for it here.)

I wanted to do that in reverse: show my present-day readers a future world from ground level. It would be the same shiny future I'd used in my 70's SF, but it would show the nitty gritty, the social fall-out of the food shortages, the population control measures, the wires into the pleasure centers of the brain – things I'd glossed over or mentioned only in passing before. The future would be ugly. But despite the downbeat milieu, the story would be about freedom, friendship, and self-esteem. And lies.

"Lies." That was the working title. We all revere the truth (or at least say we do), but sometimes a lie can be stronger than the truth, *better* than the truth. There are vital lies – the ones that can give you hope, can give you the strength to keep going when the truth would break you.

And sometimes, under the right circumstances, a lie can *become* truth.

Through trial and error I worked out a punchy, truncated style that dropped lots of pronouns and gave me the rhythm I wanted. The story grew. The projected 5,000 words doubled, then tripled. I managed to tie things up at 18,000 words and was very pleased with everything except the title. So I changed it to "Dydeetown Girl". The voice of the novel, Sigmundo Dreyer, is my first loser protagonist. Years ago his wife emigrated to the settled planets beyond our solar system, taking their only child with them. When we meet him he's a bitter, bigoted, emotional cripple getting by as a private investigator in the east coast megalopolis. He's also a buttonhead – his brain is wired so he can play sensory recordings of fabulous multi-partner sexual encounters directly into his limbic system – which further isolates him from other people as well as the more tender human emotions. Under all of Sig's layers of bravado and delusion and self-loathing, however, sits a stubborn core of integrity. But it's slowly dwindling.

Then a clone of Jean Harlow hires him to find her

lover, and through the course of the story, very much against his will, he changes. Not a big change. In fact, Sig denies there's been any change at all. But it's there. You can sense it Sig and the clone don't ride off toward the outworlds together. Far from it. Sig starts and ends the story alone.

I was delighted with "Dydeetown Girl" and anticipated no trouble selling it. Little did I know. The big three SF mags turned it down, saying it wasn't science-fictiony enough. Too much PI. I didn't agree, but I wasn't worried. Hey, that's what mystery magazines were for, right?

Uh-uh. The two biggies bounced it immediately. Why? You guessed it: Too much SF. I was getting worried now, wondering if I'd written myself an orphan. I decided to give Baen Books' paperback magazine, *Far Frontiers,* a try. About a month later during one of the receptions at the 1985 Nebula Weekend, Betsy Mitchell, then senior editor at Baen (she's with Bantam now), told me they were going to make it their lead story in the Winter '85-'86 issue. I ran into Jim Baen later that night and he told me, "The ending blew me away." Hallelujah.

In 1987, "Dydeetown Girl" was one of the five finalists for the novella Nebula. It didn't win, but seeing it listed as a finalist was vindication enough for me.

And that would have been that if not for Betsy Mitchell. Betsy wanted more from Sigmundo Dreyer. She said if I did two more novellas like "Dydeetown Girl" for *Far Frontiers,* she'd put them all together and publish them in book form. I told her that sounded nice, but I hadn't planned a series and I didn't have any more ideas along that line. She said, "Why don't you do something with those urchins." (The urchins are illegal children living in the abandoned subways under the city-they have no rights, no official existence. They were glimpsed only in passing in the story, but Betsy's instincts had sensed something there.) I said I'd think about it, but since I was deep into BLACK WIND at the time, I promptly forgot about the whole thing.

Not Betsy. This is a very persistent editor. She reminded me at every opportunity that she was still waiting for the next novella. Finally I started thinking about those urchins...

The results were "Wires" and "Kids", both published in *New Destinies.*

So, *Dydeetown World* is a fusion of "Dydeetown Girl", "Wires", and "Kids." But it's not a collection. The two follow-up novellas were written with the idea of continuing the storylines developed in the first, of bringing Sig back to the land of the emotionally able-bodied, and tying everything together at the end. These are not isolated episodes; they are part of a whole. *Dydeetown World* is a *novel.* One I'm very proud of. Beneath its hardboiled voice, its seamy settings, and violent events, I worked at maintaining an element of emotional warmth. Cyber-prive-eye-sci-fi (as Forry Ackerman might call it) – with heart. I think it works.

So, apparently, does Easton Press. As an unexpected lagniappe, they've chosen *Dydeetown World* for their Signed First Editions of Science Fiction series. 3,500 leatherbound hardcovers. I'm looking forward to seeing those, but not to signing all those end papers.

So that's the *Dydeetown World* story. Goes to show that you never know when a 5,000-word tip-of-the-hat to one of the Old Masters will turn into a novel.

Oh. And that neat narrative hook that got the whole process started? The one that was going to open the story? I couldn't use it until page 15. Go figure.

***

A promotional piece in Mystery Scene Magazine.

The Birth of *SIBS*

Yeah, I know. There's a new sitcom on TV this fall with

the same title.

That's the way the year's been going.

But *Sibs* is the title and *Sibs* it's going to stay.

This novel continues to amaze me. I remember how it began. In February 1989 I was down in Baltimore attending a Geriatrics update at John Hopkins Medical Center; after dinner one night I was sitting alone in my room at the Tremont Plaza, going over the opening sixty pages or so of *Reprisal* I'd written during the preceding month. I wasn't happy with them. The whole book needed restructuring and I wasn't up to it at the moment.

So my mind wandered, drifting to an idea that had been roaming the empty spaces in my head for years but had never quite gelled. I'd tested out the plot elements with some success in "Ménage a Trois," a short story I'd sold to *Weird Tales* back in early 1987 for the inaugural issue of that venerable magazine's latest incarnation. "Ménage" is a sexy little horror story involving non-supernatural possession. No demons, no exorcism, no great metaphysical questions about being or free will or any of that. Just a horny, old, wheelchair-bound woman getting her sexual jollies via the young maid she'd hired. I toned it down a little for the *WT* version – my idea, not the editors' – and juiced it up again for the *Hot Blood* reprint.

But after finishing the first draft of "Ménage," I was struck by a kinkier variation on the same theme. That idea was far from ready for development though, so I left "Ménage a Trois" as it was. I did, however, write myself a reminder of the new idea by mentioning in the story that Marta Gati, the antagonist, had a couple of brothers living in New York.

So there I was, years later, sitting in front of the TV, half-watching a UVA basketball game as I mentally doodled with the linchpin character in my half-formed story: Lazlo Gati, Manhattan psychiatrist and voluptuary. Here's what I had:

Kara Wade comes to Manhattan after her twin sister

Kelly takes a nearly-nude plunge to her death from a twelfth-story room in the Plaza Hotel. Kara has a lot of questions. Foremost is why her sister, a dedicated nurse, was dressed (or, rather, *un*dressed) like a hooker when she died. The deeper she digs, the more bizarre her sister's life appears. Kelly's psychiatrist, Dr. Gates, hints at a terrible secret in Kelly's past, something involving both twins. Kara fears that she might be doomed to share her sister's fate.

Anyone familiar with "Ménage a Trois" would guess what's going on, so I wanted to reveal that secret in the first half of the book. But then what did I have after that? The plot as it stood was enough for a novella or perhaps a short novel, and it would have been an okay story but nothing more. Something was missing. I didn't want the entire novel to turn on a single, surprise revelation. I needed to arm myself with a number of surprises before I tackled the book and I didn't have them. It required at least one more piece, one more dollop of characterization or spadeful of plot or whatever to tip the scales over far enough to make me want to write it.

And then out of nowhere it was there. The final nasty twist. Suddenly the story exploded into a thousand pieces, rearranged itself in mid-air (I could *hear* the pieces clicking into place) and fell back to earth in an entirely different shape. A startling sensation to see the tiles of an entire novel laid out before you in a strange new mosaic you don't remember assembling. I turned off the TV and started scribbling an outline.

When I got home I put *Reprisal* aside and jumped into the new book. The working title was *Gemini* and I pounded away on it obsessively. I awoke early every morning knowing what I was going to write. The pages flowed out of me in a steady stream. My usual weekly output on a first draft is fifteen pages a week. Now I was doing as much as fifty. Effortlessly. It was like taking dictation.

I've heard other writers talk about tapping into

something as they're writing but I've always dismissed it as bullshit. I can understand the reluctance to examine one's own creative processes too closely. Let's face it: invariably, the subject of a dissection dies. And nobody wants that. Rationally I tell myself that I'd been thinking about this story for years and it was finally ready to be written. Sounds logical, but I've mulled other books longer and they've never written themselves. That's what happened with *Sibs*. The scariest, most disturbing novel I've ever produced wrote itself in 62 days. One hundred thousand words in nine weeks. I've never written like that before or since. It's like having a manuscript with your name on it dropped into your lap. A gift.

Every writer should have that happen at least once.

***

Remember Myspace? Someone told me what a great place it was to find a new audience for your work. I had this brilliant idea: Why not have Repairman Jack promote himself? Give him his own blog! Have him make fun of me!

Cool, right?

Not really. I barely finished 2 entries before chucking the idea. But I did cannibalize the material for one of the novels. (Never let anything go to waste.)

Repairman Jack's Blog

#1 – September 7, 2006

Okay. This is page one, day one, entry one of my blog. Don't expect it daily. I don't have time and don't have that much to say. I've got stuff to fix. I've got a life.

But what's with this music thing the page is asking me? Do you give a damn what I'm listening to? No offense, but I don't give a damn what you're listening to.

Okay, I have my "Guilty" playlist running. That's the

one with all the songs a supposedly cool guy like me isn't supposed to like. Right now Pete Cetera's "Glory of Love" is playing.

I know, I know it's sappy, but the line, "I am the man who will fight for your honor" speaks to me. Yeah. Honor. How many women these days have ever heard a guy speak the H-word, or even imply it?

Thought so. Too many of us guys – not all of us, but too freakin many of us – are too cool for that. Too many of us are ignorant of what honor is, let alone willing to defend it. Too busy being assholes and playas who think it's all about bling and booty and getting loaded. All show and no go.

So pardon me if I dig a song that mentions the H-word.

Hmmm…I see I've managed to digress before I've begun.

I want to tell you about this fateful trip to a bookstore a while ago. I needed a NY State map and a bookstore seemed like a good place to find one, so I headed over to Broadway.

For those of you who don't know NYC, Broadway runs north-south on the Upper West Side until it hits 79th Street. There it breaks from the grid and starts angling east. It crosses the city on a diagonal all the way down to the East Village where it returns to running due south.

I find a bookstore in the 80s. I snag my map (I have to go upstate on a job) and head for the checkout counter. Along the way I pass a "New Paperback Fiction" rack where a cover catches my eye: *All the Rage*. A pause, a glance, and I'm on my way, but I stop cold when I realize it has a blurb from Stephen King who says he's "President of the Repairman Jack Fan Club."

WTF???

I pick it up and glance through it and it's about me!

Double WTF???

It says it's a "sequel to *The Tomb* by F. Paul Wilson, and I'm thinking, Who the hell is F. Paul Wilson?

I snatch it from its rack and grab a passing employee, a

twenty-something guy with thin hair and thick sideburns.

"What is this?"

The guy looks at me, then the novel, then me.

"We call that a book."

A comedian. Yay.

"I know that. But who's this guy Wilson? How many of these has he written?"

The guy shrugs. "I dunno. You'll have to check with Information."

"But you work here."

"Yeah, but I just put 'em on the shelves. I don't, like, read 'em. Sorry. Check with Information."

Well, obviously this guy Wilson isn't too popular or this wage slave would know him. Or am I being naïve?

I go to information but the kiosk is empty. I find the fiction section and search through the *W* authors where I find one copy of *The Tomb*. I check out the cover and see a quote from Andrew Vachss who says, "Jack is righteous."

Christ! Could these be about me?

The information kiosk is still empty so I head for the checkout area. No line. I walk up to the only cashier, a guy with a shaved head and a black soul patch. I slap the novels on the counter and push them forward.

"What do you know about these?"

He shakes his head. "Nothing."

Swell.

I take them home and start to read. I'm still reading them and don't like what I'm reading. It's like this guy Wilson's got a window on my life.

I'll be back when I finish them.

Don't hold your breath.

Jack

PS: Tell people about this message. I want all Wilson's readers to know what a phony he is.

#2

Well, I've read two of Wilson's damn books and I'm kind of freaked.

What? Oh, first you want to know what music I'm listening to? (WHY?) I'm still on my "Guilty" disk. "Burning Bridges" by the Mike Curb Generation is playing. No, I don't know what it's about. It was the theme from Kelly's Heroes and I liked the movie and so I glommed onto the song.

Mood? How about unsettled?

Why? Because of those two F. Paul Wilson books I read – The Tomb and All the Rage.

First off, let me say that if this Wilson guy is sitting by the phone waiting for the Pulitzer committee to call, he'd better have a good cushion, otherwise he's going to get mad wicked bedsores.

He's no Cheever, let me tell you. It's his style. It's too choppy. Strings of simple declarative sentences, sentence fragments, and maybe, just maybe, once every ten pages, a compound sentence. (Can you tell I paid attention in English class?) Where's the poetry? Where's the imagery? What – I don't deserve imagery? (Hey, Wilson – ever hear of an adverb?) If a writer's got to rip off my life, why can't it be somebody who can do it with a little class? Like John Irving. Or Philip Roth.

No, wait. Not Phillip Roth. Strike that.

And what's with the F. crap? My Uncle Gurney used to say, Never trust a man who won't have a drink with you. Well, I say, never trust a man who won't tell you his first name.

Here's what I'm going to do: I'm going to get in touch with this Wilson guy – maybe through his publisher, maybe by email, whatever it takes. And when I do, I'm going to pretend to be a newspaper reporter who wants to do a feature on him. And then we're going to meet for a face-time interview.

And then...

***

The Early Years Trilogy

After finishing the main cycle of the Repairman Jack series, I went back and told the tale of his first years in NYC and how he became the guy you meet in The Tomb. *One of the online methods of garnering publicity for a new book is known as a blog tour. You write a bunch of pieces that appear in various blogs devoted to reading and reviews. My publisher arranges the appearances and I write the bits. I tried something different to kick off* The Early Years *Trilogy. I'd interview Repairman Jack. The conceit was that the interviews took place after* Nightworld *in a post-apocalyptic NYC.*

The *Cold City* blog tour

PART 1

For *Literally Jen*

If you've read *Nightworld*, you know the world has been left pretty much trashed by the Otherness. If you haven't, no matter. I'm here to talk to Repairman Jack on a wide range of topics, plus I'll throw in some questions asked by readers. He's reluctant to do this, so bear with me if he's not all that cooperative.

He's adamant about no more stories after *Nightworld*, so I've gone back and written a trilogy based on his first years in NYC, before he became That Guy. *Cold City* is the first.

I met up with him at his table in the rear of Julio's – still functioning, though barely. Sunlight filters through the dead plants hanging in the shattered windows, glinting off the *Free Beer Tomorrow...* sign. (Today the beer's free for me since Jack sprang for a couple of Yuenglings.) He's dressed in jeans and work boots and a flannel shirt. His hair's neither long nor short. His mild brown eyes are mostly expressionless; if anything, they're wary. He looks like everybody and nobody.

FPW: First off, for those not familiar, let's establish who you are.

RJ: I am no one.

FPW: A line from *The Exorcist*, right?

RJ: No, I'm *really* no one.

FPW: Okay, I get it. You have no official identity, you carry ID but none of it's genuine, never had a Social Security number, and have never paid taxes. Have I got that right?

RJ: Except about the taxes. I pay taxes every day: sales tax, gas tax, excise tax on imports, sin taxes on these beers we're drinking... it goes on and on. *Ad nauseam* and *ad infinitum*, as they say.

FPW: But you've never filed a 1040, right?

RJ: Don't say that too loud.

FPW: There's no one to hear.

RJ: Still...reflex.

FPW: You make your living fixing situations that aren't amenable to the usual solutions provided by society and its judicial system.

RJ: You ever listen to yourself? That's one helluva mouthful. Why don't we just say I hire out for odd jobs – sometimes very odd – and leave it at that?

FPW: Does that mean you consider yourself a small businessman?

RJ: Very small. Sole proprietorship.

FPW: Repairman Jack, LLC?

RJ: Yeah, right.

FPW: Cash only, I bet.

RJ: Don't take Master Card.

FPW: Someone called you "Batman without tights."

RJ: (makes a face) Christ, you're kidding. Someone's not paying attention.

FPW: What do you mean?"

RJ: Well, first off, Batman's this psycho crime fighter. Most of my friends are criminals. Hell, if he was real he'd be chasing me because I'm a career criminal –

FPW: Can't we call you an "outlaw" instead?

RJ: Why? That's more socially acceptable?

FPW: Well, yeah. More romantic, anyway – in the classical sense of the term.

FPW: I pretty much start breaking laws the moment I get out of bed. No, wait – I'm breaking laws even *in* bed because I've rented my apartment under a false identity. And as for the rest of the day, I earn my living outside the law. I'd say that's a career criminal.

FPW: Can we compromise and just call you an urban mercenary?

RJ: Can we move this thing along?

SIDEBAR

RJ: Do you have Abe in *Cold City*?

FPW: Of course. But you start off thinking he's just Mr. Rosen's weird nephew who sells sporting equipment.

RJ: Right. I didn't suss out his gun-running sideline till a little later. And remember, I didn't meet him in the city. I met him once as a kid.

FPW: I know. In his uncle's store. In *Secret Vengeance*. I don't have Alzheimer's yet.

RJ: But sometimes you mess up.

FPW: I resemble that.

PART 2

for *Fade into Fantasy*

FPW: Okay, so you call yourself a career criminal, and I prefer "outlaw." Can we compromise on urban mercenary? And while we're at it, can we *not* say you're from New Jersey?

RJ: Why? *You're* from Jersey.

FPW: Where I'm from is irrelevant. But you...

RJ: Where would you like me from – Brooklyn?

FPW: No-no. Just as mundane. Something more exotic. Wouldn't it be cool if we could say you were raised in the bayous by crazy mutant Cajuns, or in the Everglades by a bunch of Indians where you honed your fighting skills wrestling crocodiles?

RJ: Alligators in the 'Glades, dumbass.

FPW: Right, right. But – hey! The Jersey Devil! We could say you were raised by–

RJ: Forget it.

FPW: But just being some guy who wanders in from New Jersey and becomes a badass, I mean, that's kind of blah.

It's got no *zing!* Can't we at least say you had some special-forces training – you know, make you an ex-Navy SEAL or Ranger?

RJ: No.

FPW: Ex-cop, then? That would give you connections when you wanted something checked for fingerprints or get car tags run.

RJ: I've somehow managed to get by without all that.

FPW: Yeah, but it would make life so much easier. Wait. How about ex CIA – you know, a specialist in black ops?

RJ: Do I look like Jason Bourne? If you want a Jason Bourne, go get Jason Bourne.

FPW: He's taken. Can I at least call you Jack Bourne?

RJ: Better than Repairman Jack.

FPW: Yeah, I hear you don't like that name. Where'd it come from?

RJ: You know damn well Abe dreamed it up. And once he laid it on me, it stuck.

FPW: What would you prefer?

RJ: Bond... James Bond.

FPW: No, Really.

RJ: Just Jack'll do. Moving on...

FPW: All right, okay. I've got questions from readers–

RJ: You mean people actually buy that bullshit you sling about me?

FPW: No accounting for taste. I put out a call on Twitter and Facebook and the website and got a bunch of responses. So why don't we start with the most oft-asked question–

RJ: Did you just say "oft"?

FPW: I guess I did. The question most asked is, What's your last name?

RJ: You don't know?

FPW: You never told me.

RJ: My last name. Hmmm. I've had so many. Well, to tell you the truth, in all this excitement I kind of lost track myself.

FPW: I know that quote too.

RJ: But you still don't know my surname. Move on.

SIDEBAR

RJ: You've got Julio in *Cold City*, right?

FPW: Absolutely – your first meeting. The place was called The Spot then, as you know.

RJ: And it wasn't his – he was just bartending. And he didn't have the *Free Beer Tomorrow...* sign yet.

FPW: I know that. That was when the window ferns were still alive and well. And the place was in danger of going under.

RJ: (a sardonic tone) Fun times.

PART 3

For *Horror Drive-In*

FPW: Okay. We've talked a little about life, let's talk

some about death. You've piled up quite a body count over the years.

RJ: Whoa! You make me sound like some kind of hit man. A lot of those corpses were the result of someone else pulling the trigger.

FPW: Right, but you arrange situations so that someone else will *want* to pull that trigger – and they often do.

RJ: Sometimes they use a knife. Or a club. But that's my m-o: *Let's you and him fight.* I don't like to get directly involved in the messy stuff.

FPW: But sometimes you do.

RJ: Too often, as far as I'm concerned. But only when there's no other choice. I much prefer to simply step back and let others go at it.

FPW: You split that infinitive.

RJ: How about I split your lip?

FPW: Easy, easy. Back on topic: Rather than simply *letting* it happen, isn't it more accurate to say you *make* it happen?

RJ: (a half smile) I can be accused of manipulating events and circumstances – you know, helping things along in a certain direction – but I don't *make* anybody do anything. They make up their own minds and act on their own.

FPW: Do any of the dead ever come back to haunt you?

RJ: You mean like going bump in the night? Doing a Jacob Marley number on me? You're kidding, right?

FPW: I meant in a more existential way.

RJ: Existential? I think you want another word there.

FPW: (I withhold a familiar hand gesture) Okay, how about a more *emotional* way.

RJ: (shrugs) I'm not much into guilt. Looking back doesn't change anything. What's done is done. You learn from the past (or so you hope) and move on. But I think I can safely say – with maybe the exception of Kusum – that the passing of the people we're discussing tended to improve the gene pool.

FPW: Kusum? Why except him?

RJ: I guess because, beneath it all, he was a stand-up guy, doing what he thought was right, what he felt he had to do. He'd made a vow and he was sticking to it, even when it required him to commit acts he found repulsive. Okay, yeah, he was bug-fuck nuts, but there was something about him...

FPW: What?

RJ: I don't know.

FPW: Yeah, you do. You just don't want to admit it.

RJ: Oh, you're going to psychoanalyze me now?

FPW: Face it: You two were flip sides of the same coin. Under different circumstances you might even have been friends–

RJ: Oh, right. I can see us hanging out here with Lou and Barney and tying one on. Get real, Wilson.

FPW: Okay, let me amend that: You might have found yourselves allies against the Otherness. But his code demanded he do something that your code compelled you to prevent, so–

RJ: So it came down to him or Vicky. I don't consider that a choice.

PART 4

For *Horror World*

FPW: Continuing with dead people: No regrets then about anyone you've done in – or caused to be done in?

RJ: (sighs) Some of my greatest regrets come from *not* eliminating someone when I had the chance.

FPW: Like whom?

RJ: You're writing about him now – in that Early Years thing you're doing.

FPW: Oh...Reggie.

RJ: (shakes his head) Yeah, Reggie. I should've listened to the Mikulski brothers, but... (a shrug) I was early on the learning curve then. And I learned that lesson the hard way, a way that cost the lives of some dear, dear people.

FPW: Any other regrets?

RJ: Yeah. (he stares at his beer bottle as he twists it back and forth – finally, after a deep, shuddering breath) Emma. If I'd got there in time...

FPW: Does Gia still think it was an accident?

RJ: (nods)

FPW: Are you ever going to tell her it was a hit?

RJ: Someday. Maybe. (sighs) Probably not. I'm kind of a coward in that regard.

FPW: Heroes aren't allowed to be cowards.

RJ: Only in your books am I a hero. In real life I can be something of a shmuck.

FPW: Well, the longer you hold off…

RJ: Yeah, yeah, I know. And I think maybe I've already held off too long. It's not as if it's gonna make her feel better.

FPW: But–

RJ: New subject.

FPW: Can I just ask if you and Gia are going to try for another baby?

RJ: Not in this world.

FPW: Okay, here's another question asked by a number of readers: Do you miss the Semmerling LM-4?

RJ: I miss the firepower – most powerful concealed carry I ever had. But I don't miss working the slide after every shot to chamber the next round. It looks semi-auto but it's not a self-loader – it's all manual.

FPW: Then why buy it in the first place?

RJ: Have you ever held one? The smallest .45 ACP ever made and cool as all hell. I was twenty-two when I bought it. What did I know?

FPW: What turned you against it?

RJ: I had to use it to put down that maniac on the 9 train. (author's note: *Hosts*) Too many passengers saw the Semmerling and described it to the cops. Only 600 or so were produced, so if I ever got caught with it, no chance I wouldn't get tagged for killing that guy.

FPW: But you saved a lot of people.

RJ: (snorts) You know how the courts work.

SIDEBAR

RJ: No Otherness – Ally stuff in *Cold City*, right?

FPW: Of course not. You knew nothing about the Conflict back then. But that doesn't mean the Order wasn't at work.

RJ: The Order? Where–?

FPW: Not to worry. You weren't aware of their involvement.

RJ: Then how do you–?

FPW: It's called research, my friend. And we may even see ladies with dogs wandering through now and again.

RJ: (eye roll) Oh, jeez...

PART 5

For *Mind of the Geek*

FPW: On a subject similar to the Semmerling – what about Ralph?

RJ: My old Corvair? Same problem as the Semmerling: too identifiable. Bought it when I was twenty-two and quickly realized it was a dumb ride for a guy who wants to stay under the radar. Everybody noticed it. Imaging trying to tail someone in that thing. Good luck. I wound up keeping it garaged most of the time. Finally got smart and sold it to a collector.

FPW: For cash, of course.

RJ: Of course.

FPW: Okay, here's another one from a reader: "How does he stay off the radar in the post 2001 security environment?"

RJ: Well, that "security environment" is all blown to hell now.

FPW: I'm sure he means between 9/11 and *Nightworld*.

RJ: I was fortunate to have been born before a Social Security number became mandatory as soon as you were born. When I worked as a teen, it was either for myself or off the books. Before 9/11, even if you had your own SSN and wanted to become someone else, it wasn't too hard. You latched onto the number of a dead guy who wasn't in the SSDI –

FPW: The what?

RJ: The Social Security Death Index – it lists upwards of 90% of dead SSNs, but even in this day, lots of deaths go unreported. Especially if you know where the bodies are buried. You use that to establish a credit history by getting a credit card – sooo easy – and paying your bills promptly and to the penny. With money orders, of course.

FPW: Of course.

RJ: Fake ID – a driver license and such – can be purchased without too much hassle, though the better it is, the more it costs.

FPW: But after 9/11?

RJ: After 9/11 the hunt was on for terrorists. Everything got closer scrutiny. If, like me, you had identities established before the attack, you were okay. But after – a whole different story. And things got progressively worse as time went on. DNA technology got better. Cameras started springing up everywhere. You pretty much couldn't make a move without someone recording you. And onboard computers in cop cars made fake licenses of lesser quality highly vulnerable. Big Brother is here and he's ugly as sin.

FPW: Some people think that's a good thing, find it comforting.

RJ: Yeah. The I've-got-nothing-to-hide crowd. Which completely misses the point. "They who can give up essential liberty to obtain a little temporary safety, deserve neither liberty nor safety."

FPW: Jefferson?

RJ: Franklin.

FPW: Here's one you'll love: "Goku or Superman? Post-Crisis."

RJ: (laughs) You do have geeky readers, don't you.

FPW: I love all my readers, especially the geeks. But that's not answering the question.

RJ: Post-crisis? Goku, of course. No question.

FPW: Now who's the geek?

RJ: (shrugs) But ain't I a cool geek?

SIDEBAR

RJ: What about the Mikulski brothers?

FPW: They're in *Cold City* – major players, in fact.

RJ: You didn't give them first names, did you?

FPW: You never told me their names.

RJ: That's because to this day I don't know them.

FPW: You told me they called themselves Deacon Blue and the Reverend Mr. Black. Why would I change them?

RJ: Because you tend to improvise if it suits you.

PART 6

For *Open Book Society*

FPW: Speaking of geeky, many readers consider you an old movie geek.

RJ: Who's old?

FPW: Sorry. I meant a geek for old movies. Here's one: "What was his first Dwight Frye film?"

RJ: Tod Browning's *Dracula*, of course. His amazing Renfield.

FPW: Here's another: "What are his top 5 Universal horror films?"

RJ: In order: *Bride of Frankenstein*, *Creature from the Black Lagoon*, *Werewolf of London*, *The Invisible Man*, and of course, *Abbott and Costello Meet Frankenstein*.

FPW: No *Dracula*?

RJ: Too stagebound. Dwight Frye saves the movie, but his performance can't elevate it into the top five. Wait... am I sounding Maltiny?

FPW: A little.

RJ: Push on, then.

FPW: Okay, here's one I'm going to lay on you but I don't want you to get into any details: "Where did he learn how to fight... take-down techniques with hand-to-hand combat."

RJ: That would be Ishii-san.

FPW: And I get into him in book two of the trilogy, so

let's leave him as just a name for now. Here's one from Feo Amante.

RJ: Eddie!

FPW: Right. "When you think of yourself, what is the engine that keeps you going? I'm not asking about your experiences. I know your history, and I know some of your history impelled your actions. But 30 people with a shared experience will make 30 different choices based on that experience. What engine drives your choices?"

RJ: Wow. All sorts of philosophical.

FPW: Can I say "existential" now?

RJ: Yeah, that too. I guess the drive for autonomy keeps me moving. Which is ironic, seeing as how my life has been manipulated since day one – but I didn't know that way back when. Plus, I derive tremendous satisfaction from solving a problem. Rather than take a sword to the Gordian knot–

FPW: Ooh, Greek mythology reference.

RJ: –I'd rather figure out how to untie it. Or better yet, convince other folks that it's in their own best interest to untie it.

FPW: But sometimes only a sharp blade will do.

RJ: Yeah, sometimes you've got to draw that sword and get 'er done.

FPW: Stephen Bissette asks, "Isn't clean-up a bitch?"

RJ: Hey, Steve. Clean up *is* a bitch. But when you get down to it, if I've done my job, it's not my worry. If my fix goes as planned, someone else makes the mess, and it's up to them to clean up.

FPW: Here's an interesting one: "Is knowing what you

know, and having done what you've had to do, worth it? Or would you rather be ignorant of the Secret History?"

RJ: Worth it? Yeah. I can pretty safely say the Secret History would have had a different end without me.

FPW: Did it end? Is it over?

RJ: Well, after *Nightworld*, the Secret History is no longer secret.

FPW: Oh, right.

RJ: I just wish I'd know about it sooner. Weezy had it sussed out in her teens – not all the details, of course, but she'd known something was moving behind the curtain. I wish I'd taken her seriously back then.

FPW: People should definitely check out *Secret Histories, Secret Circles, Secret Vengeance* to see what you're talking about.

RJ: Must you keep pimping your books?

FPW: Hey, if I don't, who will?

RJ: Move on.

PART 7 (final)

For *Curling Up by the Fire*

We're back for the last time: I'm winding up my talk with Repairman Jack with some questions asked by his readers plus some of my own.

FPW: Here's another from a reader: "What job do you think you might be doing if your parents hadn't been driving under that overpass?"

RJ: (leans back with a sigh) You know, I asked myself

that same question countless times all through those years I considered the incident a case of colossal bad luck, simply a matter of tragically poor timing – if my father's speed had been a few miles an hour faster or slower, that cinderblock would have crashed through another car's windshield, and killed somebody else's mother. But as I came to understand the forces at work, the subtle manipulations all through my life – I'm talking about since my freakin' conception–

FPW: The reason your mother called you her "Miracle Boy" in *Secret Vengeance*.

RJ: (gives me a warning look) You're doing it again. But yeah, exactly. I came to the conclusion that the overpass incident was a setup. The psycho scumbag who dropped the cinderblock was a tool. Yeah, he was going to drop the block anyway because that was his sicko thing, but I can see him standing there ready to do it, watching the cars, going eenie-meenie-miney-moe until he sees ours and something in his head says, *Bingo!*

FPW: So you think it was all part of "a spear has no branches"?

RJ: Absolutely. Act One of that play. And I don't think it was an accident that I found him one night–

FPW: –and turned him into a human piñata for the trucks on the Turnpike.

RJ: Yeah. That screwed up my head. Nothing seemed the same after that. Pushed me to the point where I canceled the old me, closed up shop, and headed to New York to become someone else.

FPW: Which I chronicle in *Cold City*.

RJ: As Abe would say, Enough already!

FPW: Okay, okay. One last question: What's your all-time favorite fix?

RJ: Hmmm. Tough one. I might go with Luther Brady.

FPW: From *Crisscross*–

RJ: You're pimping again.

FPW: Just adding a point of information. Yeah, that was a nice one. Any reason in particular?

RJ: Style points. The successful resolution of a fix is the focus – that's what the customer is paying for – but isn't the whole story. The means to that end matter as well. To make it work for me, the getting there requires a certain élan, an elegance, a symmetry. The fact that the Brady fix also rid the world of Richie Cordova raises it to the next level.

FPW: Cordova's demise was ugly.

RJ: Many of your bloodthirsty readers thought he didn't suffer enough.

FPW: Yep, those are my peeps. Any others?

RJ: Milos Dragovic and Luc Monnet – another two-fer.

FPW: I love biter bitten.

RJ: The expression is "biter bit."

FPW: But that's bad English.

RJ: Don't be such a tight ass. It's the idiom.

FPW: It's also from *All the Rage*.

RJ: Couldn't resist, could you.

FPW: I guess we're done here.

RJ: Ya think?

SIDEBAR

RJ: Please don't tell me you sneaked Gia into *Cold City*.

FPW: How could I? She was still in college in Iowa.

RJ: That doesn't mean you wouldn't find a way for her to visit New York while that whole mess was going down.

FPW: No, it's Cristin all the way. And why would I write something like that if it didn't happen?

RJ: Because of your fetish for tie-ins. "Hmmm... what if Gia was visiting on a trip to MOMA and passed Jack on the street." That kind of crap.

FPW: Hey, not a bad idea. She could—

RJ: Forget it! We're done.

***

The *Fear City* blog tour

I don't recall a blog tour for Dark City, *but the publisher arranged one for* Fear City *to finish off the trilogy. I did mostly Q&A on the tour, but here's a piece I did for Nick Kaufman's blog. I grew so fond of Dr. Moreau that I brought her back for a cameo in* Panacea.

Where in hell did *she* come from?

When the copyedited manuscript of *Fear City* arrived from the publisher six months ago, I set about fine combing the text. My copyeditor for the last dozen-plus years, Rebecca Maines, had done her usual excellent job of flagging inconsistencies and typos and the occasional verbless sentence. I always take extra time at this stage because it's my last chance to sharpen dialog, hone descriptions, and make cuts before the book is typeset.

Things went smoothly until I came to Dr. Moreau.

Yeah, Dr. Moreau. I couldn't resist naming a torturer

known to all the clandestine services and organizations as *La Chirurgienne* after H.G. Wells's vivisectionist. It seemed... right.

You have to realize it had been months since I'd sent off the ms. and she'd kind of faded from my consciousness. But as I reread her passages, I kept thinking, *What dark corner of my hindbrain did I plumb to find this woman?*

The clichéd template of the torturer is Szell from *Marathon Man*. Adèle Moreau, on the other hand, is a cultured, rather brittle French woman with a thick accent. She was trained as a surgeon but developed a sideline of hiring out to extract information from people who don't wish to part with it. She doesn't think of herself as a torturer or a sadist, but rather a pain researcher – a "nociresearcher," to use her term – and sees her interrogations as opportunities for scientific research.

She maintains a certain decorum about her work – e.g., she likes her subjects fully clothed.

"I find proximity to a naked human, how shall we say, distasteful. I can cut away to expose whatever area I wish to explore."

That "explore" got me – and it came from me. Her specialty is the delicate, minimally invasive procedure.

"I abhor brutality – the fists, the truncheons, the waterboarding. And the mutilation of genitalia – *dégoûtant!* So crude. So unnecessary."

Charlot, her pet ferret, stays in her procedure room when she operates and she occasionally feeds him scraps.

What I found most disquieting on the reread was that I had no memory of sitting down and designing this lady from hell. Perhaps I've been turning stereotypes on their heads so long it simply came naturally. If the cliché is an ex-Nazi or an Albanian thug, I'll use a genteel professional – a female instead of a male – and give her a French accent, evoking the culture that gave us the Impressionists. Think Monet's lilies... floating on blood.

Maybe that's all it was...unconscious habit. I took comfort in that.

But then I came to her specialty, known as "IV," and all comfort vanished. "IV" stands for "Infernum Viventes," Latin for "Living Hell." It is, I would say, the nastiest, most diabolically evil thing you can do to a human being. I have no idea where IV came from. Perhaps it exists somewhere in fiction or real life, but I've never seen or heard of anything like it. So I've got nothing to blame for it except my own id. And that's scary.

The key word is "Living." Because in our society, we would not let someone die after they have suffered this procedure. We will keep them alive for as long as modern medical science allows. Prolonging life...it's what we do.

But if you're the victim, the only thing you'd request – *plead* for if you could communicate – is death.

What is IV? Well, that would be a spoiler. And I don't want to spoil one of *Fear City*'s centerpieces for you.

***

The ICE Trilogy

The Panacea *contract was for two books – Panacea and a sequel. When I told my editor I had a third in mind, she prompted me to name the series. One of the background conceits of* Panacea *was the existence of intrusive cosmic entities. So that's how ICE came about.*

Panacea - 363

The God Gene - 385

The Void Protocol - 390

***

PANACEA

I blogged this on the RJ website to promote Panacea. *It also helped me organize my thoughts for the final edit.*

The Fermi Paradox
or
The Great Silence

First we need to gain our bearings and get some perspective.

Our galaxy, a spiral formation of hundreds of billions of stars which we've named the Milky Way because of how it stretches across the night sky, is estimated to be somewhere between 13 and 14 billion years old.

Our home stellar system revolves around a G2 star we call Sol that is approximately 4.6 billion years old. Sol system occupies the Orion arm of the Milky Way's spiral, about 27,000 light years from the supermassive black hole thought to dwell in the galactic hub. If the hub is downtown, we're in the suburbs.

Estimates of the diameter of the Milky Way vary but no one's going to get too upset if I go with 100,000 light years. As for the number of stars in our galaxy, estimates vary from 100 billion to 400 billion; let's be conservative and settle on 100 billion. They all rotate around the galactic hub, making a circuit ever 240 million years, while the galaxy itself is racing through intergalactic space at something like 1.3 million miles an hour.

Of those 100 billion stars, 75% are red dwarves. Sol, however, is a rarer type, one of the so-called yellow dwarves, or G-class stars, that make up 4 to 5% of the 100 billion. Astronomers estimate that the Milky Way contains over 40 billion Earth-size planets occupying the Cinderella zones around red and yellow dwarf stars.

For those not familiar with the terms, Earth-size mean 0.5 to 2.0 times the Earth's diameter. The Goldilocks zone –

also known as the Habitable Zone – is the area around any given star where water can maintain a liquid state. There's also something called the GHZ – the Galactic Habitable Zone, which is estimated to span roughly 22,000 to 30,000 light years from the hub. Earth resides in the Milky Way's GHZ.

So, to sum up: current conservative estimates are for 40 billion habitable Earth-size planets in the Milky Way, most of them circling red dwarves but 2 billion or so circling yellow dwarves.

Think about that: 40 billion potential Earths circling red dwarves, 2 billion circling Sol-type stars. And that's based on just a hundred billion stars in the Milky Way – it's probably twice that number, maybe three times. And most of those stars are much older than Sol – up to 4 billion years older – giving life on them hundreds of millions, maybe even a billion more years to develop. (Consider that the earliest *Australopithicus* appeared just 4 million years ago.)

Which leads to Fermi's question: *Where is everyone?*

Enrico Fermi, the genius Italian physicist, was one of the so-called fathers of the atom bomb. The paradox of his question, posed in 1950, remains unanswered. With billions of habitable planets in our galaxy (I'm not going to touch the unthinkable number of planets in all the billions of galaxies throughout the universe), so many of them older than ours, why haven't we found a trace of sapient life anywhere else? (Notice I'm using "sapient" instead of "intelligent" because intelligence is vulnerable to interpretation and the inevitable wisecracks.)

Human civilization started in Mesopotamia about 8 thousand years ago. Alien civilizations around older stars could easily be millions of years old. Even at non-relativistic speeds, that's plenty of time to colonize the habitable planets in their stellar neighborhood and far beyond.

We've been listening for interstellar soundbites via the various SETI (Search for Extra-Terrestrial Intelligence) groups since the early 1980s, but not hearing a thing. It's called *the Great Silence*, and it leads to an inevitable question: Are we alone in our sapience?

In what might be called the Great Noise, humanity has been beaming electromagnetic waves since the invention of radio. Those waves escape into space and travel at the speed of light in all directions. Estimates say that once they reach the 60-light-year mark (which they have) they won't be distinguishable from background noise. But we're talking a sphere 120 light years in diameter. And since the 80s we've been deliberately beaming messages out there. Any being passing through that space would hear *something*.

And yet...nothing. Like one of my fave Beatles songs: *No Reply*.

A slew of explanations has been offered. The most simplistic: We are the only sapient lifeform in the universe because a Supreme Being (spin the wheel and take your pick) created the universe just for us. This is the obvious favorite of many religions.

So many other theories: We are under quarantine until we mature, we are an experiment and under observation, we simply aren't that interesting, no one has come close enough to be aware of us, we were discovered millennia ago and are viewed as a sort of ant farm to be toyed with. (The Fortean outlook: "The Earth is a farm. We are someone else's property.")

What do I think? Haven't a clue. I'm perfectly happy with saying I don't know what's out there and what they're up to if they are. If pressed, I'll use Occam's Razor and say they simply haven't got around to us yet.

And maybe that's a good thing – not noticing us. Because as Stephen Hawking has said, contact with extraterrestrials carries a significant probability of a bad outcome. To quote the man, the encounter "might be a bit like the original inhabitants of America meeting Columbus. I don't think they were better off for it."

So, have I laid all this before you just to say I don't

know? Truth is, I did it for me. To have my next novel's central conceit – its MacGuffin, if you will – make sense to me and, by extension, to the reader, I needed to reference the Fermi Paradox. This blog is a way of assembling facts and theories and organizing my thoughts, while giving your brains something to chew on.

How do I reference the Paradox? A central character believes that sapience is so rare in the universe that it *draws attention*.

Isn't that a creepy thought? Remember the second part of the Chinese curse? *May you come to the attention of one in authority*. That has always given me a chill. What if we are under the scrutiny of (to quote Wells) "intellects vast, cool and unsympathetic"? I am not a Fortean, but it's a nifty premise to play with in a novel – not center stage, but lurking in the background.

***

The *Panacea* Blog Tour

Some of these interviews will be repetitious in that I have to describe the novel somehow, but they all prose interesting questions – some very interesting – like who would I want to be; and five dinner guests, living or dead, etc.

Tossing Off the Security Blanket

How I Learned to Stop Worrying and Love
Intrusive Cosmic Entities

Books, Bones & Buffy

Cat After Dark

Fiction Fare

Tossing Off the Security Blanket

Wherein **Ann Voss Peterson interviews me for** *The Big Thrill*'s "**Turning Point**" **feature.**

F. Paul Wilson, who has written numerous international bestsellers—from the Repairman Jack urban mercenary series to science thrillers and iconic horror novels like *The Keep*—tells Ann Voss Peterson why he's changing course with his new release PANACEA.

Okay, it seems every time you turn around, someone is starting a new series, and here you've gone and stopped one. Repairman Jack has such a wide and loyal fan base, all I can do is scratch my head and ask why?

Yeah, I know. It seems like a dumb idea. I remember mentioning to Lee Child that I was planning on shutting down the series and he said, "Why would you ever want to do that?"
Good question. I have to admit that on the surface it makes no sense. Not many authors have a security blanket like Repairman Jack, where both the publisher and the readership want another installment every year. But like the man says, "Know when to hold 'em, know when to fold 'em."

What made you decide it was folding time?

Let's go back to *The Tomb*, the first Repairman Jack. That started out as a standalone novel, but by the time I finished I knew I had a series character. I did *not* want to write a series back then. I had other standalone titles pretty much written in my head and I saw a series as a trap, something that would take over my writing career. So I left Jack dying at the end. But *The Tomb* hit the Times paperback list and folks started calling for another Repairman Jack. I ignored them. *The Tomb* remained in print, however, and year after year the fan base grew.
By the late '90s a number of factors created a situation where

a second Repairman Jack novel made sense. So in 1998, fourteen years after *The Tomb*, *Legacies* hit the stands. Its success spurred demand for more so I gave in and committed to the series. But I intended from the get-go that Jack would have a limited run to a predetermined finale.

Eventually I reached a point where I could either let the series follow its course to a natural conclusion or keep pumping out a new installment year after year (or hiring someone to do it for me) simply to collect another paycheck.

You wouldn't be the first.

Don't I know it. We've all seen beloved characters pushed way past their expiration date to the detriment of the series as a whole. I didn't want that to happen with Jack. He's too important to me. Along the way I'd structured each novel to deal with a standalone problem while advancing the backstory. But as time went on, the backstory became the front story, and that was when I knew I had to close the cover.

So instead of a new Repairman Jack you give us PANACEA.

PANACEA is a novel I've been dying to write. The inspiration struck in 2005 but I was so involved with the Repairman Jack books (writing his adult novels as well as his teenage adventures) that I had to put it on the back burner. Which worked to the novel's advantage. All those years of slow roasting helped me hone the backstory to a razor's edge.

Okay, but a panacea is a cure-all, which is scientifically impossible. You have a scientific background. How did you reconcile that?

It wasn't easy. Frankly, if I hadn't left it simmering for so long, I might not have found a way around that wall. PANACEA is Laura Fanning's story: She's approached by a very rich man who's terminally ill and thinks he has a clue to the whereabouts of the legendary panacea. He makes Laura an offer she can't refuse to go find it. The mysterious Rick Hayden is assigned to protect her along the way. All fine and good, but I was having trouble buying my own premise.

That's a real problem. If you can't believe it, how can you convince your readers?

Exactly. Then one morning at 3 a.m.–when I'm often awake in the dark, working out plot problems–Rick started whispering a weird theory in my ear. He nudged me into one of those wonderful and too-rare *eureka!* moments when everything falls into place. Rick's oddball views on the nature of reality altered the story's course in a direction that gave me a way to accept the existence of a panacea (at least within the internal logic of the tale). This was crucial, because now that I'd bought into it, I could sell it.

Care to share Rick's weirdness?

Just a bit of it. He starts with the Fermi Paradox or the Great Silence, which boils down to: *Where is everyone?* With billions of Earth-type planets in our galaxy with the potential for supporting life–many of them much older than ours–why haven't we been contacted? The answer could be that sentience and sapience don't occur very often in the universe. As Rick says, "What if the human level of sapience is so rare that when it occurs it attracts…attention?"

Isn't that a creepy thought? Remember the second part of the Chinese curse? *May you come to the attention of one in authority.* That has always given me a chill. What if we are under the scrutiny of (to quote Wells) "intellects vast, cool and unsympathetic"? Lovecraft and Charles Fort mined that vein, but there's still plenty of ore left in it.

Do you answer the question?

Well…no. I very deliberately sidestep an answer, relegating

it to the background. Because that's not what the novel is about. I'm more concerned with how something like a panacea impacts lives, and what people will do to possess it or suppress it. But Rick's theories supply a nifty premise to play with as a subtext.

Sounds like quite a departure from the Repairman Jack novels.

Not so much as you'd think. Yes, it's a mystery-adventure that hops from continent to continent in its quest, but (surprise!) Rick wound up with a few of Jack's traits. And the whole scenario fits nicely into the Secret History of the World I've been compiling over the years.

Will we ever see another Repairman Jack novel?

I've been in this game a long time, and I've learned never to say never. If a story pops up that's right for Jack (and there's one in the mental Dutch oven now), I'll write it. But I've just completed the sequel to PANACEA with more to come, so Jack will stay on vacation. After 23 novels and a raft of short stories, he's earned a rest, don't you think?

***

I did this piece for Criminal Element

How I Learned to Stop Worrying and Love Intrusive Cosmic Entities

Well, as a writer, that is.

Like the majority of humans, I was raised in one of the Abrahamic religions. (You know: Christianity, Islam, Judaism.) Their numbers are nudging the four billion mark these days. Add another billion Hindus, plus the uncounted belief systems incorporating Intrusive Cosmic Entities, and you've covered a hefty percentage of the human race.

Little wonder the entities are so popular—through history, they've sparked countless tall tales. Go back to the dawn of human history and you'll find the great flood in the Gilgamesh saga was caused by Intrusive Cosmic Entities. A little later, the Abrahamic clans were writing about a similar (or maybe the same) flood caused by their cranky Intrusive Cosmic Entity, Yahweh. Look at the fun the Greeks had with all theirs, and how the Romans continued the tradition.

As a child, and even a preteen, I found Christian dualism comforting. I mean, who couldn't get down with the symmetry of a benign, fatherly Intrusive Cosmic Entity above and a mean, evil entity waiting below? The expression, "God's in His heaven, all's right with the world," was sort of taken for granted. We might have nuclear warheads locked and loaded down here, but everything was A-OK in the cosmos.

Then, H. P. Lovecraft stepped into my world—or should I say *stomped* on my world—with his materialistic Weltanschauung. Without even deigning to dismiss the Abrahamic myths, he described a universe that was indifferent, at best, and—more often than not—casually inimical. I didn't buy into his catalog of interdimensional entities with the tongue-twisting names, but his coldly mechanistic view of the universe...that made a weird sort of sense.

And, that was when I started to—as the Christians say—backslide. I'm now considered a fallen-away Catholic. I prefer the term "recovering Catholic," because you never fully escape the influence of a Catholic school—or a madrasa.

When I started writing, I turned out hard SF—my first sales were to John W. Campbell for *Analog*. But all the while, I was secretly yearning to write about Intrusive Cosmic Entities. (If you paid close attention to HPL, you realized he wasn't writing dark fantasy, he was writing SF.) Finally, I took the plunge with *The Keep* and never looked back.

My Secret History of the World now encompasses 29 novels and 13 shorter works, including the Adversary Cycle, the entire Repairman Jack run, and sundry other tales, all dealing with, to varying degrees, the idea of our civilization, our world, our reality as a marble in a game between Intrusive Cosmic Entities. They don't have names. When you're that big, you don't need a name. (Besides, if we humans know something's name, we tend to pigeonhole it and make it seem safer; the next step is contempt, e.g.: Cthulhu plush slippers.)

When I put Repairman Jack out to pasture after *Nightworld*, I intended to take a break away from the Secret History and its Intrusive Cosmic Entities. Frankly, I worried that I'd become too dependent on them. I was through with all that. I'd had this mystery / adventure / thriller Dutch-ovening in my head for years and was anxious to get to it.

So, I started *Panacea* and immediately began running into a wall. You see, a panacea can't exist. It's impossible. It breaks all the rules of biology and physics. What can cure a MRSA infection can't cure radiation poisoning; what can cure MS can't cure coronary artery disease. I'd stopped believing in my own MacGuffin.

And then, out of the blue (well, seemingly), this character starts spouting a skewed worldview about "intellects, vast, cool, and unsympathetic" (yes, he took it from Wells and knows it) toying around with mankind. If a panacea truly exists, it's these intellects playing games, trying to shake us up. Less Lovecraftian and more Fortean, true, but after all my protestations, here I was back with Intrusive Cosmic Entities. (No, I will *not* quote Michael Corleone.)

I gave up and went with it. And, you know what? Once I'd hurdled that stumbling block, the novel gushed out. The Intrusive Cosmic Entities aren't acknowledged as real in *Panacea*, merely referred to by a fellow who's considered a bit eccentric in his thinking. They play no direct part in the story, but they played a huge part in making it work for its author.

I've come to accept that Intrusive Cosmic Entities are integral to my Goldilocks Zone. So I don't fight them. We have a détente. We even have tea now and again.

***

Books, Bones & Buffy

Welcome to the blog! I'm thrilled to have one of THE legends of speculative fiction visiting!

First of all, please give us the rundown of what *Panacea* is about.

It's a globetrotting mystery-adventure-thriller about a search for the legendary cure-all led by a woman who doesn't believe such a thing can exist. (But she's uniquely suited to the task and has been offered a fee she cannot refuse.) Two ancient cults are working against her. A perfect setup for lots of internal and external conflict, right? ***Panacea*** touches on my recurrent theme of healing (like *Healer, The Fifth Harmonic, The Touch*). Its subtext is Fortean, but it fits surprisingly well into my Secret History of the World.

Panacea deals with the ongoing conflict between science and faith. What do you think it is about this trope that is so intriguing to readers? For me personally, it never gets old!

Same here. A true panacea is impossible; yet, in the novel, miracle cures are happening. So it presents the perfect foil for skeptics such as myself. Researchers say there's a believer gene. If so, I was born without it. But I was raised a Catholic, so I had a childhood filled with indoctrination. In spite of that, by my late teens I'd questioned myself out of any religion.

This isn't my first sortie in the science-faith wars. *The Fifth Harmonic* has a skeptical protagonist with cancer who wants very badly to believe in the cure offered by a new-agey healer but can't. So she puts him through a set of ordeals to break down his resistance. *A Necessary End* (written with Sarah Pinborough) is an apocalyptic novel with an epistemological subtext – about the tension between science and faith and about how we choose to know things.

Panacea has two protags – Laura Fanning and Rick Hayden. Rick's not a skeptic; he's seen some really screwy things in his life and has a warped view of reality. Laura's a medical examiner who firmly believes in the scientific method and that every mystery has a rational solution once you collect the proper data. They make a great pair – conflict sparking all over the place. I loved taking Laura and her hard-nosed view of the world and shoving impossibilities in her face, finally forcing her to emote to a decision.

The action in *Panacea* takes place in some very exotic locales. When you were doing research for the book were you able to do some traveling, or was most of your research

done online?

I've been to some of the places. Haven't been to Israel though. The Dead Sea sounds fascinating, and you don't have to be religious to appreciate how much of western civilization was shaped by events there a couple of millennia ago.

You have published over fifty books! Do you have a favorite, one that is particularly special to you?

A number of books for different reasons. *Black Wind* is my best novel, without a doubt. *The Keep* has sold more than any other title. *The Select* netted me my biggest advance, putting me into the 7-figure club. After thinking about it for 15 years, *Sibs* practically wrote itself in 9 weeks (while I had a full-time job). *The Fifth Harmonic* was the most personal – Will is as close as I've ever brought a character to myself.

You've been a published author since your first novel *Healer* came out in 1976. Have your writing habits changed over the years?

I outline less. I used to do detailed outlines because, as a part-time writer, I was terrified that I'd spend months on a novel and find out I couldn't end it with a satisfying catharsis. You know that clichéd scene where someone wakes up gasping and sweating from a horrible nightmare? That was me at the thought of having to tear up a page of a manuscript. Now I simply do story beats to make sure I have a logical progression and know the most effective places to position the reveals and twists.

I know one of your big literary influences was H.P. Lovecraft, but what about contemporary authors? Who do you love to read, and what have you read lately that you can recommend?

Well, I'm not a fan of HPL's prose or his gods, but I've riffed a lot on his view of the cosmos. Lovecraft is important for his purely materialistic approach to horror fiction. The weenies who found the World Fantasy Convention an unsafe place because of his face on the award (really?) should remember that. In fact, they should genuflect at mention of his name because we might all still be writing about dragons and chain-rattling ghosts without him.

At the moment I'm reading a Victor LaValle novella and quite enjoying it. Lately I've read some good stuff by Peter Clines, Daryl Gregory, Joe Abercrombie, Zoe Sharp. Ann Voss Peterson's Val Ryker series is excellent, and Joe Konrath's Jack Daniels novels are always fun. *Method 15/33* by newcomer Shannon Kirk is quite a ride. I keep collections of short fiction by Elmore Leonard and Dashiell Hammett in my Kindle for emergencies. Just finished an ARC of *Behind Her Eyes* by Sara Pinborough (due 2017) and gotta say, "Wow!" On the non-fiction front *Dark Matter and the Dinosaurs* nearly broke my brain but has some intriguing concepts. I've also read some disappointing fiction by names you know but I won't mention because my dislikes are simply my opinion and I don't put down another author's work unless he or she is bulletproof, and even then I'm not comfortable. J.K. ROWLING, YOUR ADVERBS MAKE ME CRAZY! (There. I did it.)

Tell us three things about you that can't be found on the internet.

I consider myself a skeptic in search of transcendence.
I'm fascinated by "Lazytown."
I hate peaty Scotches.

***

In which I reveal why I'd like to be Willie Dixon and my ultimate dinner-party guest list

Cat After Dark

Please tell us about your upcoming books and their production schedule.

Panacea is out July 5. I'm writing a sequel of sorts, *The God Gene*, now. Not really a sequel, simply another mystery-adventure with the same two lead characters. Lemme tell you, it was with no little trepidation that handed in *Panacea* -- my first non-Repairman Jack novel in many years. It's a significant departure, since the Jack books are noirish crime stories with a fantastic back story. *Panacea* is a continent-hopping mystery adventure in search of the legendary cure-all. But the publisher loved it and even wanted another like it. Thus *The God Gene*.

And sometime this year Tom Monteleone and I will finish *The Silent Ones*, third and last in our YA series, *Nocturnia*.

Who are the authors that have influenced your writing the most?

Tons. In no particular order: H.P. Lovecraft, Richard Matheson, Ray Bradbury, Sax Rohmer, Bill Blatty, Robert Heinlein, Victor Hugo, Robert B. Parker, Poul Anderson, Raymond Chandler, Larry Niven, Dashiell Hammett, Charles Dickens, Fred Pohl, C.M. Kornbluth, Henry Kuttner, Charles Fort, and lots of others whose names escape me at the moment. And I suppose I shouldn't leave out EC Comics, *Captain Video*, The Shadow, *King Kong*, the old Flash Gordon serials. Anyone and anything that grabbed my attention and wouldn't let go.

I'm standing on the shoulders of all of the above, but the one still influencing me thematically (not stylistically), is H. P. Lovecraft. His cosmic horror, his materialistic take on the universe as indifferent at best, but most often malign, shook up my worldview when I was in my teens and has stayed with me since. It echoes all through the Adversary Cycle and Repairman Jack novels, and even into *Panacea*.

If you had the ability to bring one author back from the dead to write one more book, who would it be and why?

I wish Henry Kuttner were around to write more Gallegher stories, and I could do with a couple more Hogben tales.

If you could live in any world, real or imaginary, where would it be and why?

I'd very much like to live in Barry Schenck's Retropolis. You can find it at http://thrilling-tales.webomator.com/ It's sort of the way the present was supposed to look from the perspective of the 1930s (if that makes any sense). Check out the website or check out the 1930 film *Just Imagine*. (Full feature at http://tinyurl.com/h4bomxf – it's awful in the way only early talkies can be, but visually it's a jewel. Watch the first 3 minutes to get an idea of the retrofuture I'm talking about.)

This wouldn't be an interview with you if we didn't talk about Repairman Jack and The Secret History of the World. How far into writing your books did you realize you could convert your stories into one epic world? Were you influenced by anyone? Is there a story behind the story?

Well, the Secret History sort of grew. It starts with Lovecraft's materialist, mechanistic universe – his so-called cosmic horror – amplified by the Fermi Paradox which boils down to: *Where is everyone?* With billions of Earth-type planets in our galaxy with the potential for supporting life – many of them much older than ours – why haven't we been contacted? The answer could be that sentience and sapience don't occur very often in the universe. What if the human level of sapience is so rare that when it occurs it attracts… attention? What if we are under the scrutiny of (to quote Wells) "intellects vast, cool and unsympathetic"? Lovecraft and Charles Fort (who declared "We are property") mined that vein, and I'm following in their footsteps. Those unsympathetic intellects have shaped human history from behind the scenes, that's why it's called the *Secret* History.

Humanity being the plaything of vast, unknowable forces percolates through *The Keep, The Tomb,* and *The Touch* even though they were all intended as stand-alones. I started another completely unrelated novel with the working title *The Chadham Clone.* I meant for it to look like *Rosemary's Baby* or *The Omen* on the surface but actually be something different (just as *The Keep* looks like a vampire novel for a while, but it's not). I wanted to use an evil entity other than the tired old Antichrist, but who? Then I realized I already *had* that entity in Rasalom from *The Keep.* I needed a suburban setting convenient to Manhattan, and realized I already had one in Monroe where *The Touch* took place. I became intrigued by the challenge of tying those two novels, and *The Tomb* as well, into Rasalom's reincarnation, bringing the books full circle. It worked so well that I suspect my subconscious might have been linking them all along.

Things grew from there. The result was an outline for a 1,000+ page novel. Nobody was going to publish that, so I broke it down into a trilogy that became *Reborn, Reprisal,* and *Nightworld.* When I was done I called all 6 novels *The Adversary Cycle,* and that formed the foundation of the Secret History. When I brought Jack back in 1998, he was already part of the Secret History, so I used him to expand on the story.

We also know that you are a medical doctor specializing in family practice. But like Repairman Jack, do you have plans to retire? What will you do when that time comes?

I've been a part-time physician working 2 days a week for quite some time now (I'd never have been able to write all those books had I been full time). I've got a few more practice years left in me. I love my patients, but the government and the insurance companies are conspiring to drive me insane. As for writing, I'll probably keep that up till I die or develop full-blown dementia.

And Jack? He'll be back. I have no doubt that a suitable novel will come along and I'll bring him in from the pasture and put him to work. Can't say just when, though.

If you were able to trade bodies with one person for one day who would it be and why?

Willie Dixon in the late 1950s. I'm writing "Little Red Rooster," "Hoochie Coochie Man," "I Just Wanna Make Love to You," "Spoonful" and other blues classics. I'm doing session work for Chess Records, I'm playing upright bass in Chuck Berry's band. I'm not a household name, but I'm defining the Chicago Blues sound. (Later on, in the 60s, my songs will be covered by the Stones, Led Zep, Cream, the Doors, Hendrix, even Dylan.)

Then again, maybe Kim Kardashian – pre-Kanye, of course. I mean, what's it like to sit on that butt?

What are the next three books you're planning to read?

Just started *Watched Too Long* by Ann Voss Peterson and J.A. Konrath. The books ahead haven't been published yet – ARCs by Norman Spinrad and Charles Stross.

Do you have any guilty pleasure books/authors? You know the ones...stuff you don't let your friends see you reading.

I'll read old pulp novels from time to time, but I'm not guilty about them. The snoots turn up their noses but, y'know, who cares? It's my comfort food. That's why I wrote "Sex Slaves of the Dragon Tong."

I do have guilty music, though. I'm a blues guy, but I have a weakness for good harmony and a catchy tune. My iPod hides an occasional song by the Partridge Family, the Carpenters, Air Supply, and others too uncool to cop to. ("Easy Come, Easy Go" by Bobby Sherman – yoiks!)

If you were to give just one piece of advice aspiring writers, what would it be?

The obvious one is keep writing…write every day. When I started out, writing part time, I found a minimum of 3 first-draft double-spaced pages per day did the trick. That's 21/ week. At that rate you've got over 540 pages in 6 months. That's a decent-sized novel.

In writing those 3 pages per day, avoid tinkering with them. This stalls you by fooling you into thinking you're still writing. You're not. And you're losing momentum. Get those 3 pages down and then leave them alone and go on to the next 3. The time to fix and hone them is after you've finished that all-important first draft – what I call the vomit draft. You'll know your characters better then and can go back and make meaningful edits and additions.

The other is less obvious: Avoid envy. Other writers are going to be more successful than you. Applaud their success rather than begrudge it. Just remember, there's objective success and subjective success. Objective is counted on bestseller lists and dollar signs. Subjective is defined by you: what are your goals in putting those words on paper? Don't lose sight of that.

What five people living or dead would you invite to a

dinner party?

Dorothy Parker, Ambrose Bierce, Ogden Nash, Oscar Wilde, and H. L. Mencken. A veritable torrent of wit. Can you imagine the laughs? The unbridled cynicism?

How do you want the world to remember you?

A stand-up guy who poured a mean gimlet and told lots of good stories.

***

Fiction Fare

Describe PANACEA in 5 words.
Globe-hopping Fortean mystery-adventure-thriller (Ha! Only 3 words since hyphenates count as one.)

How did PANACEA come about, what was your inspiration? What made you think you had to write this story?
I like plots with high stakes. A panacea – a true cure-all – would change the world, and not necessarily in a good way. Yes, it would be wonderful on an individual basis, the curing of the incurable. But healthcare accounts for about 20% of the US economy. Imagine suddenly adding 20% of the population to the unemployed. Plus all the extra people living long lives instead of dying young, having more children, who are having more children...we're talking a global catastrophe.

But the real challenge of the novel was selling something as impossible as a panacea to my readers. I have smart readers, and a panacea breaks all the rules of medicine and biology, even physics. I struggled with that for years until the answer popped out of the dark. (Truly: one of those 3a.m. epiphanies.) Once I had that, PANACEA flowed out.

Can you share (without spoilers) a line or section of

PANACEA that is your favorite?

"You ever think the panacea might exist because we're able to have the opinion that it can't?"

"Can't what?"

"Exist."

Was she hearing right?

"Could you repeat that?"

"Okay. Did you ever think that the panacea might exist because we're able to have the opinion that it can't exist?"

It made even less sense the second time.

Yeah, a WTF question, but the backstory of PANACEA hinges on it. It begins to make sense as the story progresses.

People often say that you should write what you know, did you do that with this story and if so what parts of your life influenced this story?

Writing what you know is all fine until you've run through all your life experiences and pilfered all your friends' and relatives' experiences, then where are you? PANACEA is my 55th book. You can't write 55 books from experience. Ya gotta make up shit.

Healing is a recurrent theme in my work. The title of my first novel is HEALER. THE TOUCH is about healing, so is THE FIFTH HARMONIC. In PANACEA I continue that theme, but from a different perspective. They're all part of my *Secret History of the World*.

When you're not writing, what do you enjoy doing in your spare time?

Reading other folks' thrillers, or thinking about writing. (I have OCD)

Do you have any strange writing habits?

I have an app called Freedom that locks me out of the Internet for a customizable period of time. I lose all sense of time when I go on the Net to look up something. On my way to check the differences between C4 and semtex I look in on my email and FB and Twitter and 20 minutes later I still haven't Googled semtex. I usually set Freedom for 45 minutes at a clip. It helps my productivity enormously.

What are you currently reading?
THE RED RIGHT HAND by J. T. Rogers – a famous murder mystery from the early 1940s that I'm finding massively overwritten (but then, I find almost everything overwritten).

Any advice for aspiring writers?
Don't overwrite. Seriously. It usually comes about as a result of lack of confidence – lack of confidence in yourself and lack of confidence in your reader's ability to "get it." Readers do get it. You don't do any favors for them or yourself by leading them by the hand every step of the way. Better to underwrite a little and leave them some space to make an intuitive leap. They'll be more engaged if they're active participants rather than passive recipients.

What's next for you? Are you working on anything right now that you can tell us about?
A sequel of sorts to PANACEA – same protagonists, different MacGuffin. First draft done, out to beta readers. Still needs work.

Tell us 3 random facts about you.
1) I have a weakness for puns – the worser the betterer.
2) I've decided to live forever. (So far, so good.)
3) I detest defecation. Someday you'll be able to suspend a quantum black hole in your rectum and never again be forced to engage in such an offensive and malodorous enterprise.

Favorites
Favorite Song (right now): I just played "Tried So Hard" by the Flying Burrito Brothers 3 times in a row, so I guess that

qualifies.

Favorite Book (right now): DARK MATTER AND THE DINOSAURS

Favorite TV Show/Movie: "Game of Thrones" (before that: "Justified")

Favorite Word: gallimaufry

Favorite Color: green

Favorite Curse Word: wankerati

***

An interview from ITW's monthly magazine The Big Thrill.

At the Crossroads of Crichton and Lovecraft

F. Paul Wilson on *The God Gene*

Interviewed by Heather Graham

I'm thrilled to interview F. Paul Wilson. I have been in love with his work for years. In his new offering, Paul has given us an incredible work—and, if it shows the same brilliance as novels written by Michael Crichton, it's because F. Paul Wilson is also a medical doctor, a man who has studied every new discovery in the field while compassionately treating patients. There's a note of knowledge and veracity to his story, and those traveling through the scenes this master has created see vividly in the mind's eye the world of Wilson's characters. He kindly answered many questions for me, and so, I'm 'thrilled' to present this interview.

HEATHER GRAHAM: Despite the title, I'm going to assume *The God Gene* **isn't a religious book.**

F. PAUL WILSON: Good assumption. It's best described as a science thriller.

HG: I know it's a sequel to *Panacea***, but is it a direct**

continuation, or something entirely new?

FPW: Both. Rick and Laura are back. After a rocky start in *Panacea*, the two of them are tentatively exploring a relationship. Laura is being sent a dose of the panacea every so often, so that's still on the table, but everything takes a backseat when Rick's older brother drops off the face of the Earth.

HG: So, as they say, "This time it's personal."

FPW: Correct. Rick is estranged from his family – hasn't contacted them in years. When he joined the CIA, he was designated the official Black Sheep of the clan. But he and Laura learn that his brother Keith, an evolutionary zoologist, didn't simply wander off one day. He first destroyed all the genetic sequencing he had done on a mysterious little primate he'd discovered in Mozambique, then liquidated all his assets and transferred them offshore. The mystery primate died suddenly and, on the day before Keith disappeared, he threw its ashes into the Long Island Sound. All coincidence? I don't think so.

HG: Obviously he found something in that primate's genome that he didn't want to share. The "god gene" of the title?

FPW: Let's define "god gene." Two "god genes" exist in the real world: one type is from Dean Hamer's book postulating a genetic basis for spiritual beliefs. The other, the one I adopted, refers to the genes that make us human, that sparked the brain developments that allowed us to leave all the other primates in the intellectual dust.

HG: So there are real "god genes?"

FPW: So-called. Real genes like miR-941, exclusive to the human genome, appeared seemingly out of nowhere a million or two years ago – popped out of our "junk

DNA" and started coding. These pop-ups enhanced our neurotransmitters and brain development. Believers point to a human-exclusive gene like miR-941 as evidence of God affecting evolution. A God Gene.

HG: I'm going to assume – because of your title – that Rick's brother found one of these god genes in that little primate.

FPW: That's what everyone assumes. But it doesn't explain his bizarre behavior. Though startling, the discovery would be a cause for further exploration rather than panicked flight. Keith had to have found something else – something unnerving enough to make him obliterate all evidence of his discovery and disappear. But what? That's the mystery Rick and Laura must solve. Their search takes them to East Africa and Madagascar, and to a place no humans have ever been before. They wind up on the edge of human evolutionary science.

HG: A hard-science mystery-thriller.

FPW: As one of my early readers said, "Very Crichtonish." It hadn't been my intention when I set out, but *The God Gene* edged me into Crichton country.

HG: Not a bad place to be.

FPW: Not a bad place at all. I've always been something of a science geek, and I cut my writer's teeth on SF.

HG: A long time ago.

FPW: Quite. Back when the Permian Extinction was still a fond memory. But the science in *The God Gene* is barely fiction. I make up my own "god gene" – one instrumental in sparking human creativity – but it could very well be real.

HG: The ads say *The God Gene* is part of "the ICE sequence." What does that mean?

FPW: Damned if I know. Okay, seriously, when I told the publisher I was planning a third book with Rick and Laura, they wanted a name for the series. Rick has some strange ideas. He believes that the human level of sapience is so rare that when it occurs it attracts *attention*, and as a result we are all under the scrutiny of (to quote Wells) "intellects vast, cool and unsympathetic." Rick calls them "ICE" – Intrusive Cosmic Entities – and believes they have long meddled with humanity from behind the scenes. ICE never manifest in the books, they're simply posited as a possible explanation for some odd goings on.

HG: Sounds a bit Lovecraftian.

FPW: Because it is. *The God Gene* stands at the crossroads of Crichton and Lovecraft. You'd expect that to be an awkward place, but when you look carefully at Lovecraft's fiction, much of it, deep down, is really SF. Again, not what I consciously set out to do, but now that it's done and I look back, it works. Somehow it works just fine.

***

Another Big Thrill *interview for* The God Gene *that doesn't even mention the book.*

1. Can you give us an understanding of how your writing process works? Do you have a ritual, do you plan out every detail or do you see where the story leads?

I get up 6:30ish, make coffee, run through my fan sites and social media, set my *Freedom* app to keep me off the Net, and get to work. I used to outline a lot more; now I list story beats. But I always know how the story's going to end. You owe the reader a satisfying ending. Sometimes I'll work out a careful chronology of the events that led up to the story and are motivating the characters.

2. It is amazing how your books all tie into a vast

chronology. Was this always your intention or did it evolve over time?

For the SF I started writing in the 70s, I definitely wanted to connect the stories via a Future History a la Heinlein. When I moved on to *The Keep, The Tomb, The Touch, Black Wind,* etc., I never thought of connecting them. They were intended as stand-alones. But when asked to write a sequel to *The Keep,* I started seeing connections that were probably subconscious at the time I wrote them. The Secret History evolved from that and has become huge.

3. What are your thoughts on e-books? Do they help or hinder the modern author?

I love ebooks. That's all I read. I never travel without an overloaded Kindle. For works in public domain – nothing is better. I just downloaded *The Delphi Complete Works of Mark Twain* for $2.99. (I'm not kidding – $2.99.) I've self-published a few titles on my own – stuff that's the wrong length or too politically incorrect for a commercial publisher, or something like my *Ephemerata* which I will keep updating as new material surfaces. (Did you know that about ebooks? If you bought the old edition and a revision comes along, you simply reload the title for the update.)

4. The moral dilemma of controlling something like a panacea is truly daunting. Do you think we would ever be able to handle such responsibility?

The panacea as I have it can be made from a backyard garden – if you know the secrets of success. It couldn't be controlled. Everyone would have it, as everyone should. The social upheavals would be enormous but, as with everything, a new equilibrium would eventually establish itself.

5. If you were given one paragraph to convince people to buy your novel what would it say?

That's a tough one because the ICE novels have so much going on. Everything I like is in them: A weird-ass MacGuffin, extraordinary characters, thrills, chills, violent death, romance, mystery, adventure, exotic locales, hard science, and hints of unwelcome cosmic meddling. A typical Wilson farrago.

6. In between research and writing do you have any time to read? Who do you enjoy most?

I'm looking at my most recent Kindle acquisitions: The Mark Twain edition I mentioned, *Neutrino Drag* by Paul Di Filippo, *Dubliners* by James Joyce, *The Case of William Smith* by Patricia Wentworth, *The Lord of Strange Deaths* (essays about Sax Rohmer), *The Council of Justice* by Edgar Wallace, *The Great Fog* by H. F. Heard, Chaos: *Making a New Science* by James Gleick, *Lovecraft Country* by Matt Ruff. I dip in and out of the story collections; I read old and new, always looking for an author to grab me by the ear and haul me headlong through the story. That recently happened with Seanann McGuire's *Every Heart a Doorway*. Blew me away. Wish it would happen more often.

7. What's next – please say the next book in ICE is coming really soon?

Just this week I finished a draft of *Nadaný*, the third (and possibly last) book in the ICE sequence. Next up is a Repairman Jack novel set between *Infernal* and *Ground Zero*.

***

The Void Protocol timeline

You probably should skip this if you plan to read The Void Protocol *at any time in the future. Spoilers galore.*

This is the timeline for the novel's backstory. It goes all the way back to World War II and traces the origin of the mysterious substance named "melis" which provides the MacGuffin for both The Void Protocol *and* The Last Christmas. *I reworked the timeline many times to get all the events properly aligned. It's a good practice for a novel with a complicated backstory. It helps you keep the events straight and references to the past consistent. An interesting point is that there are many stories here, depending on when you want to start plotting. Just reading through it triggered an idea for a story placed shortly after the Occupant's appearance in the chamber.*

TIMELINE

1944 – A Dusseldorf native, Dr. Maximillian Osterhagen (4/29/10-12/6/96) starts his *Lange-Tür* (Long Door) or *Langen Schritt* (long step) Project deep under the Kronstein in Thunguria (in facilities connected to the Mittelwerk V2 factories there). He's a physicist and has a theoretical basis for a way to move objects – and, hopefully, troops – instantaneously over long distances. Not teleportation, but rather a portal to compress distance and allow something or someone to pass through the opening – a door in the air – onto another locus anywhere on Earth. The military uses are obvious and enormous – a total game changer.

1945 – The project had to be abandoned in April due to Allied bombing of the Kronstein. Osterhagen was rounded up along with rocket scientists like Von Braun by JIOA in Operation Overcast (later Operation Paperclip). At first the US wasn't interested in Osterhagen because he wasn't a rocketeer, but when Army Major Robert B. Staver, Chief of the Jet Propulsion Section of the Research and Intelligence Branch of the US Army Ordinance Corps, interviewed him, he immediately saw the possibilities of the *Lange-Tür* Project. Later in the year, while the rocket scientists are being moved to Fort Bliss, TX, Osterhagen was moved to Fort Dix, NJ and assigned to Captain Duane Horton who oversaw the digging of an underground lab beneath the Lakehurst Naval Air Station.

1947 – *Lange-Tür* construction completed. [Park at a

junkyard on Rte 571. Take elevator down. Golf cart ½ mile to *Lange-Tür* underground bunker, fifty feet below the woods. Pine lights are frequently seen over the area; disappear when people come looking for them, return when they go away. Emergency stairway straight up from bunker. Camouflaged trapdoor in woods with no handle, no way in. No alarm going out.] It includes a cubicle chamber of steel-reinforced ballistic glass 3" thick (just in case they open a portal in the bottom of the ocean or in the heart of a volcano). Trials were finally able to begin. They continued for years. All failed until...

1957 – after a decade of failures and with his funding being siphoned off to projects like MKUltra and HAARP, Dr. Osterhagen was desperate for a breakthrough. Using a high-energy modification of the Casimir effect, he managed to open a portal for a fraction of a second. And in that eyeblink something came through... something not of Earth... something from Out There.

Its passage from Wherever closed the portal and they can't reopen it. The thing glows with a purplish light and shifts from solid to pure energy and back.

1969 – a dozen years with no success at communication and still no way to send the thing back. They're afraid to set it free – imagine the problems it will cause – so they close down Project *Lange-Tür* and leave a skeleton crew to keep watch.

1984 – on one of his irregular visits to the *Lange-Tür*, an aging Osterhagen notices a clear residue on the floor of the chamber. He manages to convince one of the techs to find a way to siphon off a bit. Under strict anti-contamination protocol it's sent to Fort Detrick for analysis.

Dr. Maureen LaVelle at Fort Detrick is approached by Benjamin Greve of DIA and given a sample of the slime.

She mixes it with saline (she calls the mixture "melis" – an anagram of slime) and injects the solution into rats to see if there's any effect. Nothing obvious, except that Dr. LaVelle notes that their offspring become stars at working through mazes and solving other problems.

1986 – Dr. LaVelle has had the same results with primates: a quantum leap in intelligence in the offspring, with enhancements carried on to subsequent generations. Agent Greve wants to take the experiments to the next level.

1988 – after a small number of trials on pregnant federal prisoners showed no adverse fetal effects, Dr. LaVelle uses a mix of legit and black funds to start Operation Synapse which subsumes the *Lange-Tür* Project. The legit part is maintaining the *Lange-Tür*. The real/black purpose of Synapse is totally rogue with goals both altruistic and cynical. They'll set up free OB clinics to serve the lower end of the socioeconomic spectrum. Increasing the intelligence of these children would allow the kids not only to pull themselves out of the economic slums, but perhaps give the US an intellectual edge. Who knows? Melis might produce the next Einstein. The downside? Melis never hurt a single experimental animal, but if it harms one of these kids, well, no big loss – they weren't going anywhere anyway.

Synapse is so hush-hush (messing with the brains of unborn babies!!!) that it was usually not identified by name, only a symbol.

1990 – obstetrician Emily Jacobi, MD (actually Dr. LaVelle operating under a skillfully created legend; her credentials are impeccable, with a string of articles in obstetrical journals.) uses black funds to set up Free OB clinics in the ten poorest inner cities.

1991 – Modern Motherhood free obstetrical clinics

open in Bed-Stuy Brooklyn, NOLA, Atlanta, Anacostia DC, Compton LA, Indianapolis, Chicago, St. Louis, Little Rock, Jackson, MS. The techs think they're administering vitamin infusions instead of melis.

1996 – Osterhagen, heavy smoker, dies of lung cancer, but not before Greve gets hold of The Black Book.

2006 – after 15 years, the kids of the melis-treated mothers were no brighter than their peers – not an iota of increased intelligence. Project Synapse was abandoned as a failure. Dr. Jacobi dropped off the map. Dr. LaVelle reappeared at Detrick where Synapse continued to receive white funds from DIA because the *Lange-Tür* needs ongoing maintenance.

Unknown to Synapse, the melis kids began to manifest odd powers when they hit puberty.

THE BYTE COLUMNS

Sometime very early in 2012, Larry Seltzer, the editor for Byte online whom I've known since he was a kid, asked me if I'd be interested in doing a series of columns about the ever-expanding interface between writing and the digital world. The result was called Random Bursts of Cortical Activity. *For some reason we adopted the conceit of Repairman Jack writing the column as related to him by yours truly.*

The columns cover a brief history of online publishing and online collaboration, touching on working with the likes of Joe Konrath, Blake Crouch, Jeff Strand, and Sarah Pinborough. They came out more autobiographical than intended.

After my 9th column, Byte.com started folding its tents and closed down in 2013. But I had fun while it lasted.

RBCA #1

by F. Paul Wilson (as told to Repairman Jack)

Byte asked has F. Paul Wilson to contribute bits and pieces about the interfaces of technology and writing and, you know...stuff. On the surface, this may strike some as kind of strange. When he mentioned it on Facebook, one of his gay friends posted: *"They asked YOU to write about tech stuff? That's like someone asking me to write a book about banging chicks."*

Not so fast. Let's take a look back at F. Paul Wilson. (Add *!* to his name and it sounds rather pejorative, don't you think?) He could call himself simply "Paul Wilson" – everyone else does – but he feels compelled to add the "F" when he writes. He never could get used to being called Francis.

We met in the early 80s...when he created me.

Jump back to 1980: It's the World Science Fiction convention in Boston where Wilson is talking to Joe Haldeman at a SFWA reception. Joe mentions he's writing his current novel on a computer using something called a "word processor." What the hell is that? When Joe explains what it does, Wilson realizes such a miracle could probably pay for itself with what he'll save on Wite-Out alone. (He was a lousy typist then and, after literally millions of words of published fiction, still uses only two fingers.)

When he received his advance for *The Keep*, Wilson bought an Apple II+ with dual 5.25" floppy drives and 32k RAM. He could have splurged for 64k but who in the world would ever need that? He also bought a word processor called *Apple Writer 1.1* that displayed all-uppercase text in 40 columns on his black-and-white monitor, and broke words wherever it damn well pleased in the wraparound. The rig cost over three grand – a *lot* of Wite-Out.

He wrote *The Tomb*, my debut novel, on that Apple, and I've been riding his cortex ever since.

He stayed loyal to Apple until PCs dominated the installed base to the point where he could no longer trade disks with any of his friends. He switched to a PC.

Wilson tended to be an early adopter when it came to technology. He bought a Motorola bag phone in the early 90s – also called a "mobile phone" or "car phone" back then – with a huge battery that plugged into the car lighter and charged a shocking per-minute rate.

For years he'd been hearing about something called the Internet where people could interact through their computers. In 1992 he took the plunge, bought himself a top-of-the-line 14.4 kb modem, and checked out the bulletin boards. He joined an online service called GEnie – General Electric Network for Information Exchange. This was before the World Wide Web – very crude by modern standards, all text, no graphics (unless you consider ASCII art and smilies graphics).

You had CompuServe, Delphi, and The Source available, but GEnie became *the* hang for all the tech-savvy sf, horror, and fantasy writers of the day. Lots of discussion groups, and something called...email – letters sent at electron speed. Think of all the money he could save on stamps! Then he learned he could attach documents to emails and swap them with other writers.

Dude, talk about *wired*. (And yes, this was before *Wired* the magazine pubbed its first issue.)

The e-letter itself would arrive in seconds, but then he had to download the attachment. Watching the download progress through a 14.4kb modem was excruciating. Imagine sucking a gallon of spackle through a straw.

Wilson was not an early adopter of the mouse, however, preferring to key in DOS commands until the day he agreed to be a beta tester for Windows 95. He needed a mouse for that and immediately realized that the GUI was the wave of the future.

Like many other writers, Wilson landed at AOL during the post-GEnie diaspora in the late 90s. Speedier, prettier, yes – but just not the same.

In 1997, fourteen years after writing *The Tomb*, he started my second novel, *Legacies*. Published in the fall of 1998, it was such a hit that the publisher wanted another. Seeing the writing on the wall, Wilson purchased a domain name. F. Paul Wilson fansites had been around for years, but in March of 1999 he went live with his own: *repairmanjack.com*. Hits peaked at 3.5 million per month from 2008 to 2010, but have slipped to about 2.5 million or so since he started sharing his online time with Twitter and Facebook.

So it's not a mindbending stretch that he'll be contributing to *Byte*. But I warn you: His mind wanders, so these bits and pieces might wander as well. But they'll be filtered through me to keep them honest and keep him in line – so he doesn't waste your time just blowing his own horn (as writers are wont to do).

    Watch this space.

    Jack

RBCA #2

E-publishing: Part 1 – In the beginning.

    Wilson thinks he's a publisher now. Sort of. He's got a bunch of digital titles in print in various formats, and even a couple available as POD (that's Print On Demand for the non-cognoscenti). Even has a name for his company: Wilsongs. Cute, huh?

    I'm not going to attempt anything like a comprehensive history, simply one writer's journey through the e-pub maze. I was along for the ride – an intimate part of it, in fact – so I know.

    Wilson flirted with electronic publishing very early on – like 1993 – when he became involved with the granddaddy of all ebooks, Brad Templeton's ClariNet Library of Tomorrow. But the world wasn't quite ready back then for what ClariNet was offering.

    Through the years, he kept the electronic rights to his fiction whenever he could. Why? Well, just because. No big deal until the aughts. E-rights didn't exist in the 60s and 70s, and when the publisher would add "electronic" to the laundry list of rights it wanted in the 90s, he (via his agent, Al Zuckerman) would cross it out. Never a peep from the publisher. I mean, they were talking books on CD-ROM then. My how things have changed. These days, electronic rights can be a deal breaker.

    Come May 2005, he hears from Simon Lipskar at Writers House (his literary agency) that Amazon is starting a new project, Amazon Shorts, with an eye to making short fiction and nonfiction by established authors available for download. He immediately sees what this means: Amazon.com is getting into the publishing business. Interesting.

Here's the plan: They'll charge $0.49 a pop and are offering a sixty-forty split. It's invitation-only so he's got to keep mum because there's a non-disclosure agreement involved. Does he want in?

Hell, yeah, he wants in. Forty percent of $0.49 is only a hair shy of 20 cents, but it's a *forty-percent royalty*. Whoever heard of a 40% royalty? He knows the future when he sees it. He signs the NDA, then realizes he's too booked up to write something new. No problem. He's got this old story about Yours Truly called "The Long Way Home." He wrote it back in 1992 for Joe and Karen Lansdale's *Dark at Heart*, a small press anthology limited to 400 copies. So at most, 400 people read the story more than a dozen years ago, and it's never been reprinted. Virtually a new story. So he sends it in.

An agent from Writers House emails him the next morning that Amazon is "adamant" about no previously published material. Well, so much for that. Too bad. Would have been nice to get in on something new like that.

Six hours later the agent is back: "Sounds like Amazon realized how ludicrous their position was in regard to your piece, because they've changed their minds. In fact, Jeff Bezos himself said to screw the technicality in this case."

Nice to know Jeff Bezos has even heard of Wilson. Even nicer that after Amazon Shorts is launched in August, "The Long Way Home" becomes the #1 fiction download for 2005 and for all of 2006. (It held the #2 spot in overall downloads, with the #1 spot going to a nonfiction investing piece.) Eventually Shorts was opened to any author who had a backlist on Amazon and the catalogue of stories and articles grew to nearly 2,000.

Truth be told, despite the popularity of his story, Wilson didn't exactly clean up. Amazon Shorts was not a runaway success with the public. But one thing he did notice was a definite uptick in his backlist sales. People who read "The Long Way Home" wanted to read more about Yours Truly, and so they followed the links to Wilson's older Repairman Jack titles. At the time, he figured this was the strategy behind Amazon Shorts. He was probably right to a point, but he was definitely wrong too.

Because in the fall of 2007, just a little more than two years after Amazon became a publisher, it introduced the first Kindle.

And that, as they say, was the game changer.

RBCA #3

E-publishing: Part 2 – Kindle nation

That first Kindle in December of 2007 was a clunky thing. Rocket and SoftBook had been around since the late 90s and the Sony Reader had been released in the US the year before. The Kindle seemed like a me-too product. Wilson wasn't impressed. (But then, he'd also predicted that vampire fiction would die in the mid-90s and thereafter you wouldn't be able to give away vampire novels, so I took that with the proverbial grain of salt.)

Although Amazon was coy about sales numbers, rumor had it that by the end of 2009 the company had sold three million Kindles. *Now* Wilson was impressed. Only avid readers sprung for a Kindle, and that meant three million readers had no access to many of his titles.

Paper editions of his books have always sold well on Amazon, thanks mainly to Barnes & Noble's peculiar reluctance to stock his backlist in any meaningful depth. Via the forum on his website he repeatedly heard from frustrated readers who'd given up on their local B&N and turned to Amazon. So when his editor told him that Amazon wasn't terribly important to overall sales in general, Wilson told him it was to his. Accepting the challenge, his editor went to his computer and called up the figures. After studying the spreadsheets he said, "Well, you're an exception."

The wheels began turning. He'd written SF all through the 70s and had never signed away the e-rights to any of those novels and stories. Why not put them to work on a new platform? Joe Konrath was telling him to do-it-do-it-do-it. Trouble was, they were mostly in .pdf files and he hadn't the faintest idea how to adapt them. His agent provided a contact.

Amazon turned out to be very accommodating for a bestselling author who wanted to e-publish his award-winning LaNague Federation novels with them. Wilson was most concerned about the formatting of one of the books. *Healer, Wheels Within Wheels, The Tery* and *Dydeetown World* contained simple narrative text. But *An Enemy of the State* was peppered with flyers that were crucial to the story. If they could not be properly formatted into the text, the novel would suffer. But the Amazon folks worked it out in return for a one-year exclusive on the e-rights. They offered a 35% royalty, scheduled to rise to 70% during the coming summer. (Are you kidding?) Sold!

So, on St. Patrick's Day, 2010, the complete five volumes of the LaNague Federation series – novels combined with all the short stories – went live on Amazon for a mere $2.99 each. (Why so low? We'll get into pricing when we talk about theft next time.)

Of course, there had to be a glitch, right? The last three chapters of *An Enemy of the State* were missing. But when readers pointed this out, Amazon restored the chapters and zapped replacement copies to the Kindles of all who had purchased the book. Wilson was impressed. (So was I, for that matter.) He was also impressed with the checks Amazon started depositing directly into his bank account every month. On June 1, 2010, Amazon Shorts was terminated, but no one missed it. Amazon Singles replaced it.

Wilson, now a believer, began converting the pre-2000 backlist and putting it online. He's had to learn more HTML than he cares to know, but no biggy. He's had to ask for help now and again (the illustrations in *Sibs* were tricky), but on the whole, he's in control. He could have hired someone to do the conversions, but he's too anal. He wants it just the way he wants it and no one but he knows just the way he wants it. (The guy can be a real pain in the ass, let me tell you.)

So he's now a publisher. Not just an American publisher – he's gone international. He realized that even though his trade publisher owns e-rights to US and Canada and a few other markets, Wilson holds all the others – to *everywhere else*. So now those books are going up for sale on Amazon.uk and .de and .es and .jp and so on.

The 70% royalty checks keep getting bigger and the statements are simple spreadsheets. Really, could it get any better?

Well, certain flies could be removed from the ointment.

RBCA #4

E-publishing, Part 3 – E-looters 101a

So now, with his international publishing empire, Wilson thinks he's F. Paul Hearst or the like. But he's not so smart. When he was publishing his Kindle editions he refused to add DRM. For those of you who don't know – I assume there must be some of you – that stands for Digital Rights Management, which means copy protection. I argued for DRM, but Wilson was adamantly opposed.

His reasoning: Anyone who bought his ebooks should be able to read them on any platform they wish. If you download it to your Kindle, you should be free to use a program like Calibre to switch the format to one compatible with your iPhone. Sounds fair, right? But it makes it way too easy for the looters.

You can call them pirates, if you wish. They like that. Kind of romantic and cool – like Jack Sparrow. But in reality they're looters, pure and simple. What else do you call someone who comes across another person's unprotected property, snatches it up, and takes it home?

Wilson wasn't naïve about the looters, but he thought he could make an end run around them by keeping his ebook price point low at $2.99. You see, a traditional publisher (AKA dead-tree publisher) pays an author a royalty ranging anywhere from 6-10% of the cover price of a paperback. At 8%, a $7.99 paperback nets the author 64¢. At Amazon's 70% royalty, a $2.99 ebook yields a little over $2. The reader saves a fin and the author triples the royalty per copy. Ever hear a more obvious win-win?

But as for stopping the looters: Wrong again, Paulie. They'd already stolen the novels about me from MacMillan and were bundling them in a single zip-file for download. Almost immediately they began swiping Wilson's self-published ebooks.

A twisted part of me loves to watch the moral and ethical contortions the looters go through to justify their actions. My favorite is: "How can you accuse us of stealing when we're only copying? You still have yours." They even formed a looter advocacy group called questioncopyright.org whose motto is: "Copying is not theft." Yeah, you wish, buddy. They went so far as to create a moronic video (chew a couple of Tums before you watch).

This has helped me understand the looters. I thought they were sociopaths or merely morally bankrupt. Well, they're that, but the video makes it clear that they suffer from an incapacity for critical thinking; these lines from the song (written by someone named Nina Paley) make the case:

> *If I steal your bicycle, you'll have to take the bus.*
> *But if I just copy it, there's one for each of us.*

Copy a bicycle? You mean like, scan it? Or download it? If you copy my bike, you'll have to *work*. And even before you copy the bike, you'll have to learn how to weld and how to use tools. And then (get the smelling salts ready) you'll have to *buy* the metal tubing and tires and gears and spend time assembling them maybe even thinking about how to arrange the gears. You may have to sweat, you may get your hands dirty.

And you know what? In the end, you will have created something where there was nothing before. It won't be a copy, it will be *yours*. Then maybe all the clones with all their stolen discs and books at the end of the video won't look so cute.

Sharing ideas with everyone
That's why copying is fuuuuuuun!

Yeah. Tons o' fun when what's being copied would not exist without someone else's intellectual sweat and is the source of that someone's livelihood.

Some looters use the library model: libraries buy one copy and give it to many readers. They claim they're simply doing the same. Think again. Libraries get the book back after each reading. And libraries pay for every copy on their shelves.

Is it okay to go into a sculptor's studio, make casts of his creations, then sell them in your gallery? Of course not. But somehow it's okay to go steal an author's work and duplicate it ad infinitum. The rationale seems to be if it's not a physical object, it can't be owned. But that digital object did not spring de novo from the Internet. It is the result of a lot of physical (typing) and intellectual (thinking) effort by a human being.

The looters even pose as writers. A bonehead named David Shields "wants writers to ignore the laws regarding appropriation and create new forms for the 21st century."

He said this on the Colbert Show. You've got to see it to believe it:

The gall of this clown. But Colbert was the perfect interviewer. One of his comments was a thing of beauty: "Could I create new forms for the 21st century by ignoring property rights and obliterating my neighbor's front door? Because you know what would look good in my house? *Your* things." That pretty much sums it up.

If only simple theft were the limit of the looters' greed. Not satisfied with merely stealing the work, they've been duplicating it and reselling it, becoming Wilson's de facto publisher.

But...I'm running out of room and I'm only getting started.

RBCA #5

E-publishing, Part 4 – E-looters and the leech mindset

Wilson just now – 11:30 a.m. on February 10 – logged off ebookr.com where he found 133 ebook editions of almost everything he's written in almost every ereader format. The site offers unlimited downloads for $14.95 a month. In effect, ebookr.com has declared itself F. Paul Wilson's publisher.

One of many.

The Internet is studded with looter sites that charge *nada* for downloads. (They *do* charge, however, for faster bit rates.) Wilson has been running a Google alert since May '08 and has found hundreds offering his work. He has neither the time nor the treasure to send lawyers after them. It's like playing Whack-A-Mole. And how do you get to servers in Viet Nam?

On a recent visit to a looter site we found dozens of his titles listed in order of downloads. *The Keep* came first with 19,725; *The Tomb* (the first novel with yrs trly) followed with the same number. (Hey, if you're gonna grab one, why not grab them both? They're free, right?) The total downloads of the first five titles came to 92,226. We stopped counting there. Wilson has over 40 titles in print. The grand total would have been monumentally depressing. And that's *just one site*.

Mention this and invariably one of the looter apologists brings up the music model, saying something like, "Look at the Grateful Dead – they let people record them live and share the tapes and it only increased attendance at their shows."

Apples and oranges. The Dead's revenues came from their tours, not their records. Those so-called bootlegs (they can't be real bootlegs if they're sanctioned) advertised their concerts, which were not free. You had to pay to see the Dead live. (That was not intentional. Okay, maybe a little.)

An author's published work, on the other hand, *is* his concert. Giving away a free story or excerpt (and Wilson does this) might draw people in, but if he doesn't make the sale, he doesn't eat. Of course self-pubbed newbie authors with little prospect of sales might offer free downloads of their work in the hope of gaining an audience for their later work, but it's their own work so they can choose to do what they wish with it.

Another apologist mantra we hear ad nauseam: "A torrent download of a book isn't necessarily a lost sale." Whether that's true or not, so what? The book is not the site's to offer for download, free or otherwise.

As for lost sales, have you ever opened an unsolicited email from a torrent site offering downloads of any author's work? Neither has Wilson. He has downloaded his own work from pirate sites to see what kind of quality they were offering but he had to go looking for them. He had to use Google or Bing to find the sites, then had to search out his titles within those sites.

In other words, you've got to go *looking* for that free

download. Do you go to that trouble if you're *not* interested?

So maybe it *is* a lost sale.

"The pirated (their word) downloads will introduce people to your work and generate more sales."

This is the most naive. It happens, sure – guys love to justify their behavior in comment sections by saying an illegal download led to them becoming a faithful fan who now purchases everything said author publishes – but really, how many sales do you think were generated by those 92k downloads of Wilson's 5 titles from that one site?

Once a leech, always a leech. And leeches don't pay for stuff. Our entitlement-addicted society has spawned a horde raised to believe that the world owes them. Owes them what? Everything. Owes them why? Well, because. They have no sense of "mine" and "not mine." Of if they do, their idea of "mine" is in line with Bierce's *The Devil's Dictionary*: "Belonging to me if I can hold or seize it."

Leeches are obligate parasites who take-take-take; the concept of giving something in return is wholly alien. The Internet has exacerbated the leech mindset by offering so much for free for so long that many of us get downright hostile when we're asked to pay for content. I've seen it in Wilson himself: He'd rather buy a dead-tree edition of the *Wall Street Journal* than subscribe online.

People behave in patterns. People who steal with no repercussions will continue to steal. (And "steal" is the proper term – what else do you call appropriating someone's work without permission or compensation?) Do you really think someone who steals *The Tomb* and likes it is going to run to Amazon and pay for *Legacies* and *Conspiracies* and the other dozen or so Repairman Jack ebooks when they can steal them just as easily as the first? Are they going to pay even the measly $2.99 price tag Wilson has put on old titles he's uploaded myself when just about every freaking word he's ever written is available for free download?

I don't know about your planet, but that's not about to

happen on mine.

So what's the solution? My personal preference is a flame thrower or low-yield nuclear devices, but that's not practical. Parasites are a fact of life and part of the cost of doing business. As long as enough stand-up folks pay their own freight to offset them, the producers and innovators will keep on trucking. We hope.

RBCA #6

Cyber-collaboration - THEN

Way back in the first installment I told you about Wilson's initial involvement with the Internet via the online service known as GEnie. He joined for the camaraderie of the other genre writers on board, sure, but he signed up for a more practical reason: access to email. He needed email because he was collaborating with Matt Costello on a project for the nascent Sci-Fi Channel (later renamed, perplexingly, Syfy).

In the summer of 1992 Wilson received a call from a USA Network executive named Bob Siegal saying they were launching the Sci-Fi Channel soon and wanted him involved. USA Network was Manhattan based and looking for a writer (they knew Wilson had written SF) who lived in the northeast. Their plan was to insert daily newscasts from 150 years in the future between their regular programming. Could he design that future? Wilson was all for it until Siegal told him they needed it completed and set to go in six weeks.

Big problem there. He needed to finish a book in time for the upcoming Frankfurt Book Fair, and no way he could do both. He remembered shooting the bull with a writer named Matt Costello at various NECons (http://www.campnecon.com/) (a small annual Rhode Island convention for writers and readers) and had been impressed with how quick and versatile he was. He'd also sensed that

Costello had a work ethic similar to his own (which is, simply, sit down and do it). Plus he lived only an hour outside the city. So he turned down Siegal and gave him Costello's contact info.

A day or two later the grateful Matt called back and asked was Wilson *sure* he didn't want it? How about they split the work? Wilson reconsidered and has never regretted it. The Sci-Fi Channel gig turned out to be one of the best of his career. He and Matt got along swimmingly. They had minds that worked on the same wavelength, plus the network paid them handsomely and did not interfere.

They worked their butts off that summer – meetings in the city at the USA Network offices on Sixth Avenue, in coffee shops, in each other's kitchens, conference calls, and faxing – lots of faxing between the Jersey Shore and Westchester County.

But faxing wasn't working. Both guys were writing on computers but the convenience of a word processor was negated by the limitations of the fax machine: it could deliver only hard copy. That meant editing by hand and faxing back. Cumbersome as all hell. FedExing floppy disks back and forth on a daily basis would be prohibitively expensive. What to do, what to do…?

Matt Costello was the more wired of the two then – he was scripting an interactive CD-ROM called "The 7th Guest" for Trilobyte – and had heard of something called email. Not only were these electronic letters delivered almost instantaneously over the Internet, but digital attachments could hitchhike along – digital attachments like word-processor files. Yikes. Perfect.

They joined GEnie and began swapping files via email. (Wilson gave up his beloved WordStar for WordPerfect for DOS to be compatible with Matt, but no biggy.) Email provided a quantum leap in their writing process. By the end of the summer they delivered a future scenario detailing the sociopolitical-economic- technological status of the planet Earth and near space for the year 2142, including biographies of all world leaders and entertainment personalities, long and short story arcs, one shots, and even commercials. They'd laid out the arcs in narrative form and in a flow sheet that showed what was happening when and where throughout the first year on a month-by-month and week-by-week basis. USA Network was, quite frankly, blown away by their "bible." They offered the guys a retainer to stay on board.

Faster Than Light Newsfeed was born.

The Sci-Fi channel handed the bible to a screenwriter named Russ Firestone who scripted 30-second and later 60-second spots that would play one per day (multiple times), five days a week and repeat all five on weekends. Every so often he'd call them to provide fillers for the feeds.

On September 24, 1992, an *FTL Newsfeed* – their scenario, their characters, their format – launched the Sci-Fi Channel. Wilson and Costello watched from the network's launch party at Madison Square Garden.

In 1994 the network asked Wilson and Costello to take over the scripting duties for a fee they couldn't refuse. The deliverables were 65 one-minute scripts in two-column A-V format every 13 weeks – the equivalent of four hours and twenty minutes of script every year. Now they *really* needed that email.

They pretty much did whatever they wanted with the spots, and maybe drifted a little far out on occasion – like bringing in Professor Irwin Corey to explain the physics behind a new faster-than-light drive. Not just once, but twice, because the press didn't understand him the first time. When one of the USA execs – none of whom seemed to know anything about SF – would ask, "Um, is this really science fiction?" Wilson and Costello would assure him that it was. After all, they were SF writers and who should know better?

With the success of the Costello-scripted interactive CD-ROM "The 7th Guest" (it went on to sell over two million copies), Matt began receiving more interactive offers than he could handle. He asked Wilson to help him out and they formed a partnership. Lots more email collaboration and thousands of air miles produced much vaporware but did lead to Disney's "MathQuest with Aladdin." They also collaborated on two novels, *Mirage* and *Masque* (the latter available now as an ebook under its original title, *DNA Wars*).

When the interactive market imploded along with the dot-com bubble, freelance script-and-design work dried up and Wilson and Costello drifted off to solo projects. Wilson shared credit with Steven Spruill on a thriller called *Nightkill* in 1997 but stayed solo thereafter.

Until now. He's into new collaborative projects, and man, have things changed.

RBCA #7

Cyber-collaboration – NOW (part 1)

With a novel about Repairman Jack (that would be me) due every fall, plus side projects like *Sims*, *The Fifth Harmonic*, and *Midnight Mass*, and later in the decade, a trilogy of novels about my teen years, Wilson had no time during the aughts even to think about a collaboration. And frankly, he wasn't keen on them anyway. For projects like TV and interactive, which by their very nature are collaborative, okay. Directors, artists, code monkeys, etc. are necessary evils that come with the territory. But with novels and stories he likes to be in control. (I know I've mentioned how anal he is.)

So he hesitated when Joe Konrath contacted him in March of 2010 about a four-way collaboration on a novel they'd all self-publish. Whoa. Collaborate with three other people on a novel? And the plot was already set? And he'd simply contribute characters and guide them through a quarter of the word count. Wilson's control alarms were clanging off the wall.

On the plus side, his partners in the venture would be Konrath, Blake Crouch, and Jeff Strand, three writers he knew and liked personally, and respected professionally. So he was willing to listen. Konrath laid out the simple setup: vicious, blood-thirsty vampires running wild and multiplying in an isolated hospital. An enclosed environment where the situation deteriorates and spins out of control before anyone realizes what's happening. The title was *Draculas*.

Okay, definite possibilities there, but four authors? Would their styles mesh? With Matt Costello, and Steven Spruill, Wilson had always done the final polish. (Not out of generosity... the anal thing... the control issues.) With four hands stirring the pot, the stitched-together final product could be a Frankenstein monster with all the scars showing. (Yes, that's a horribly mixed metaphor, but Wilson's the writer half. Deal with it.) Konrath assured him it wouldn't be a problem.

Still Wilson hesitated, so I took him aside and told him to hang loose and go for it. The writing was scheduled to start in the summer. He'd have finished the first draft of *The Dark at the End* by then. He always lets that first draft sit awhile before revising, so he had a window of free time. Why not put it to good use? Besides, Konrath was asking for only fifteen thousand or so words. Let it happen. Wilson took a deep breath and said yes.

Each writer took two characters – a protagonist and a vampire. One of the suggested protagonists: "A gung-ho good ole boy gun-crazy cop (think Kevin Kostner from Silverado) is the boyfriend of the historian. Meets her at the hospital (To propose? Has ring on him?)" I nudged Wilson toward him. We've done tons of research on guns for my books, plus he has a cadre of fans who do lots of shooting. Wilson was getting psyched now. He has a weak spot for gun porn, and now he could write some.

So where does "cyber" (beyond email, of course) enter the collaboration? Konrath said they'd be using something he'd found extremely helpful in other collaborations (and he's done a fair number of them): a service called Dropbox. It's a form of cloud storage locker with a handy share feature. Once you've installed it on your computer, you can create folders in the Dropbox that can be shared with others you designate. Konrath created a folder called DRACULAS with subfolders labeled "Joe," "Paul," "Blake," and "Jeff," and gave them all access.

Dropbox proved crucial to the collaboration. With a loose outline that was little more than a timeline of the novel's major events, everyone agreed to write their characters' parts in a straight-line chronology and upload them to their own Dropbox subfolder as they were finished. This allowed the writers to see what was going on with the other characters as it was happening. Our anal friend Wilson *never* lets anyone see his first drafts, but since momentum was at stake (and because he felt at home with these three), he relented and uploaded his chapters as he wrote them, revising them later.

It worked. One upload made each contributor's latest addition immediately available to the other three. As a result, the pace of the writing increased until the book was expanding at breakneck speed. Everyone went beyond their 15k commitment, amassing 70k words in just five weeks. The final manuscript totaled around 80k.

And as the story progressed, a dynamic of one-upsmanship developed. It started with Konrath's line, "Is that a...flamingo?" If you've read *Draculas*, you haven't forgotten it. If not, you'll appreciate it when you hit it because it epitomizes the novel's unique blend of humor and over-the-top horror. I could hear Wilson thinking, *He's going that far? Hmmm...I could push it a little further.* And so, when Crouch left Wilson's character with a horrifying situation to resolve on the OB floor, Wilson couldn't resist ratcheting it up a notch.

The collaboration was smooth sailing until Wilson

was ready to kill his character. The other authors wouldn't let him. They'd all come to love Deputy Clayton Theel and insisted he survive. They figured out a way to let that happen.

By September *Draculas* was finished and scheduled for Halloween publication. They'd decided from the start that it would be an ebook. The reason? Each of the four authors had publishing contracts containing first-look clauses, but none of those covered collaborations on an indie-published book. The Kindle-exclusive route obviated negotiations with multiple publishers for permissions, etc.

Another advantage to digital publication: They added extras such as interviews, short stories, and excerpts from other novels, plus all the emails exchanged between the writers during the course of creating the novel (an entertaining peek at the personalities of the authors and the creative process of a four-way collaboration). This literally doubled the word count and would have doubled production costs in a dead-tree book. It cost nothing extra in the ebook.

For publicity, copies of the novel were emailed to a horde of bloggers with a request for a review. The blogosphere responded with enormous enthusiasm, and a buzz arose. On Halloween *Draculas* leaped onto Amazon's bestseller list.

NB: throughout the course of planning, plotting, writing, publicizing, and publishing this novel, not a single sheet of paper was used. Not even in payment: Amazon made deposits to Konrath's bank and he distributed the royalties to the contributors' Paypal accounts. No checks have been written. (An audiobook and a trade paperback were published later, but the whole process up to that point had been completely digital.)

RBCA #8

Collaborating in the Cloud (part 2) – Improv with Google

Docs.

Collaborators fall together in different ways. Wilson's current collaboration followed a tortured path. Sarah Pinborough, a Brit writer, was scheduled to be a guest at NECon in 2009. Wilson had never read her and always likes to have tried some of the guest's work. He bought *Tower Hill* and was impressed by the unorthodox choices she made with the plot and the heroine. She had to cancel her NECon trip and so he sent her a complimentary email. A desultory correspondence began.

The following year he was rebuffed by Amazon.uk when he tried to buy the ebook of her new novel, *A Matter of Blood* (US rights had yet to be sold). She emailed him the .pdf which he stuck in his Kindle. He encountered a quantum leap in style, and was intrigued by a character referred to as "the man of flies." The name triggered images and scenarios that ran off at a ninety-degree angle from *Blood*. He knew he'd have to pursue those but felt it only fair to include Pinborough, if she was willing. And frankly, he knew the apocalyptic feel she'd brought to *Blood* would come in very handy.

But Wilson lives down the Jersey Shore and Pinborough's a Londoner. Brits spell funny and have screwed-up punctuation (especially their quotation marks). Could this work?

Wilson opened a Google Doc and committed his nascent ideas to digital paper. The (tongue-in-cheek) working title was "The Flies of the Lord" and he projected novella length. He gave Pinborough access to the doc and asked her if she wanted in. She was game but neither of them would be simultaneously free until late 2011-early 2012. No biggy. They'd keep adding ideas for characters and scenes and plot twists into the doc as they occurred. The other would drop by and comment on the ideas and enhance them or make an alternate suggestion.

The result wasn't an outline, by any stretch; more like the ingredients for a stew without a recipe.

Through a slow process of accretion, the doc grew; by the fall of 2011, when the World Fantasy Convention rolled into San Diego, they had something to talk about. Pinborough had crossed an ocean and a continent to attend, and the two of them sat down for a couple of hours of spitballing.

Now, we've been talking all this cyber and digital stuff, and that's all great, but there's nothing like a face-to-face convo to make things gel in the planning stage. They'd bumped a few times before, but this was their first tête-à-tête, and the ideas flew. They nailed down what the novella would be *about* (beyond the global catastrophe of its plot) but they needed something immediate to involve the journalist protagonist. Pinborough had found something in her research for a YA novel that was deemed too dark for kids, but fit perfectly here. Wilson took that a step further, and suddenly they had a wicked and gruesome twist that delighted them both. The novella was now headed along a path neither could have predicted.

They decided to set it in England (which meant they'd use Brit-style spelling and punctuation) and on a fragmented Dos Passos approach to convey the global scope of what was happening.

Currently they're into the writing process, albeit in a somewhat epileptic fashion since each has other commitments. They're using Dropbox (as in *Draculas*). Pinborough had never heard of it but she's taken to it swimmingly. They've kept the Google Doc as their idea well and are using it as a story map – not a full outline, but rather a progression of story beats a few chapters at a time. This way they won't feel locked down.

But the need for face time is ongoing. For that they use Skype every few weeks. (For the two or three people out there who don't know, Skype provides a sort of audio-visual telephone call via the Internet.) The five-hour time difference between London and New Jersey means Pinborough's finished her morning writing by the time Wilson's making his first cup of coffee. But Skype has proved excellent for planning out their next moves.

Now on to something really exciting.

Two of the point-of-view characters are husband and wife. Oddly enough, Pinborough's been writing the male scenes and Wilson the female. They needed an argument between the two – a blow-up over religion – and the question arose: Who should write it? Wilson suggested they both write it – simultaneously. Make it like improv theater: Wilson, who had to memorize the Catholic catechism growing up, takes the religious wife; and Pinborough, who had a more secular upbringing, takes the skeptical husband. Yeah. Why not?

At a preset date and time, they both showed up at the Google Doc and got into it. Pinborough had written the setup scene a few days before, and they jumped off from there. The result was...electrifying. After some early, slightly barbed back and forth, the heat grew and things were said that seemed to come out of nowhere – things that had nothing to do with religion and everything to do with the crumbling relationship. On looking back, it all sprang from deep in the characters and their marriage as conceived, but neither Wilson nor Pinborough had realized the relationship had deteriorated to this point. (Wilson claims she hurt his feelings during the confrontation.)

Pinborough was delighted with the exchange and Wilson was positively giddy. The argument had reached into areas neither of them would have taken it alone. Beyond the addition of a few dialog tags, they decided to leave it just as it had gone down. They now knew that the answer to the old question of "Can this marriage be saved?" was a big fat *No*.

They resolved to arrange other improv encounters between characters. This can happen only with a collaboration and only with something like Google Docs. (Yes, a chat room would provide the same immediacy, but when they finished here, the dialogue was all formatted and ready for pasting into the manuscript.)

I'll keep you updated from time to time as to how it's going. In the meantime, if you're on Twitter you can follow Pins at @SarahPinborough; she's on Facebook too. But be warned: She occasionally uses language that would make Dorothy Parker blush.

RBCA #9

Collaborating – an Internet tool to help choose a collaborator.

Okay. One more piece on collaborating online. I thought the last entry would tie things up, but then Heide Goody (yeah, that's her name: @HeideGoody on Twitter), one of Wilson's longtime readers, pointed him toward something called Textalyser that analyzes, well, text. She seemed to think it was a good way to decide if your style is compatible with someone who might be a potential collaborator.

I reminded Wilson that a frequent comment about *Draculas* (the novel he wrote with three other guys) was that no one could be sure where one writer left off and another picked up. Part of that was due to the skillful editing by Crouch and Konrath, but compatibility of styles had a lot to do with it. Crouch, Konrath, Strand and, Wilson are all well versed in *thillerese.*

What's *thrillerese?* That's my term for a writing style that emphasizes showing over telling and employs short paragraphs stocked with crisp declarative sentences minimizing passive constructions, all punctuated by sharp, terse dialogue. Noir and detective fiction introduced it, but the modern thriller has made the style its own.

So, to test out Textalyzer, Wilson took a couple of first-draft pages from his collaborators and ran them through the program. The results are tabulated below.

	Crouch	Konrath	Strand	Wilson
Total word count:	356	359	354	357
Number of different words:	271	267	278	252
% Words that are unique:	76.1%	74.4%	78.5%	70.6%
Readability (Gunning-Fog Index): *(6-easy 20-hard)*	5.0	5.3	5.8	3.8
Average Syllables per Word:	1.57	1.7	1.51	1.37
Sentence count:	63	58	51	78
Average sentence length (words):	9.74	11.2	12.6	8.37
Max sentence length (words):	37	45	68	40
Min sentence length	1	1	1	1

(words) :				
Readability (Alternative) beta : *(100-easy 20-hard, optimal 60-70)*	64.5	71	66.4	82.4

NB: in the first readability score (Gunning-Fog), lower is more readable; in the second, the higher the score, the more readable. Note that in the first, all four are under 6.0. In the second, the first three are within 7 points of each other; only Wilson busts the curve, but it's toward greater readability, which is never a bad thing.

Sentence length averages within 4 words. The maximum sentence length is within 8 words except for Strand whose sample passage happened to include a deliberate run-on.

Obviously Crouch, Konrath, Strand, and Wilson were well suited for collaboration. Textalyzer shows why *Draculas* reads so seamlessly.

But that set Wilson to wondering about his current collaborator. Sarah Pinborough is, after all, a Brit. Spelling and punctuation aside, there's the gender difference, plus cultural differences, and she used to teach English. Were they as compatible as he imagined?

So he used Textalyzer for first-draft passages from their contributions to the story. For the hell of it, I suggested Wilson throw in a passage from a writer whose style is the antithesis of thrillerese. He chose the opening paragraphs of Marcel Proust's cure for insomnia, *Remembrance of Things Past.*

Behold the results:

	Wilson	Pinborough	Proust
Total word count :	417	405	415

Number of different words :	325	286	321
% Words that are unique:	77.9 %	70.6%	77.3 %
Readability (Gunning-Fog Index) : *(6-easy 20-hard)*	3.5	5.1	10
Average Syllables per Word:	1.47	1.43	1.51
Sentence count :	101	67	41
Average sentence length (words) :	7.52	10.77	21.05
Max sentence length (words) :	24	34	78
Min sentence length (words) :	1	1	2
Readability (Alternative) beta : *(100-easy 20-hard, optimal 60-70)*	74.8	74.6	57.9

Note the Gunning-Fog readability: Wilson and Pins are under 6.0, Proust is almost twice Pinborough's score and nearly triple Wilson's – and about 17 points lower on the alternate readability score.

Average sentence length is within 3 words for Wilson and Pinborough, whereas Proust is double Pinborough's and almost triple Wilson's.

So it looks like Wilson and Pinborough will do okay on that story. *

But neither should consider collaborating with Proust.

The story kept expanding, reaching 52k words, eventually published as *A Necessary End*.

FICTIONS

Here I present an odd assortment of fictions that don't fit any category, or were published in a very limited venue, or never published at all, including a spontaneous email fiction concocted on the fly by a number of fantasy writers that was never intended for publication.

Style Sheet - 424

Lamont Cranston Is *Not* The Shadow! - 427

The Jan Murray Fan Expo (JanFanEx '97) - 430

The Eisenberg Certainty Principle - 454

Memoirs of the Effster - 465

Pranksters - 473

ICU - 474

Sermon - 476

Unaussprechlichen Kulten - 480

The Whispering Shell - 484

The Tapeworm Letters - 486

The Dozen Days of the Triffids - 488

TZ Terror - 493

F - 498

The Dream - 499

The Glowing Hand - 499

Letter to the Editor of *1963* - 502

Here is the way I used to open my manuscripts when I submitted them...

Style Sheet

I think it started back in the mid-80s with Barry Malzberg's *The Engines of the Night*. As I read through the essays, I noticed a paucity of commas – conspicuous by their absence from introductory clauses and elsewhere in the text. Since Barry was (and is) more conscious than most about style, I figured they were MIA by design. So I paid attention and realized I didn't miss them. In fact the prose flowed more swiftly and surely than it might have with them in place.

Hmmm.

So I began dropping certain commas in my fiction, experimenting with short stories first, then with a novel. I forget which book it was but I remember receiving the copyedited ms and discovering that the editor had added back all the commas I'd left out. Ack. I think it might have been *Black Wind* because I remember referring to the editor as a commakaze (sorry, but it's true). So I had to go through the entire ms and remove those commas.

I was also starting to break out my dialog more – keeping it paragraphed away from narrative. I've discovered there's something about the eye-brain connection that likes white space around text; it allows the mind to grasp meaning more quickly and clearly. Faster comprehension lends a sense of narrative momentum, which leads to the I-couldn't-put-it-down reading experience. Copyeditors (only occasionally, to their credit) would attach my dialog to a preceding or succeeding narrative paragraph. I would have to go back and undo it.

After a couple of novel-length bouts of wasting precious writing time correcting the "corrections," I asked why they couldn't accept the quirks in my deathless prose. I learned that each publisher has its own style sheet that copyeditors must follow; if I wanted exceptions, I simply had to let them know.

Was that all it took? Cool.

So I started adding a note to the beginning of each ms asking the editor not to add commas or fiddle with my dialog paragraphing. As time went on and my idiosyncrasies multiplied, I created a formal style sheet that's now included with every ms.

This is what it looks like nowadays. Feel free to copy and adapt to your own preferences.

TO THE COPY EDITOR

STYLE SHEET for **(title)**

No insult intended if the following appear to be basic common-sense rules to you, but all are raised because of past difficulties.

Commas

I use the serial comma; other than that, I find most commas intrusive and use as few as possible. Please discard all your hard-and-fast rules about commas (i.e. with introductory clauses greater than 9 words, with *if* and *when* clauses, and so on). Add a comma ONLY when you feel it's absolutely necessary for clarity. If it doesn't enhance the sentence, please leave it out.

Who/Whom

I follow Theodore Bernstein's "doom of whom" rule and use *whom* only when it directly follows the preposition; otherwise it's *who* all the way.

The question mark

NO question mark with rhetorical or uninflected questions. ("You're really mad, aren't you." That's a statement.)

Paragraphing

I have my own way of paragraphing dialog – I like to break it out. It's neither terribly unique nor radically unorthodox, but some editors can't resist tacking a line of dialog onto the preceding narrative paragraph. Please don't do that here.

Thank you

I don't want to leave the impression that a writer's relationship with the copyeditor is adversarial – you tugging toward "art" (whatever that is) and the hidebound copyeditor dragging you down to mundanity. Not at all. You both want the same thing: a perfect book. But the copyeditor is paid by the publisher to follow its guidelines... unless guided otherwise.

One thing I've learned: Good copyeditors are gold. They can make you look your best. You see your ms so often you become blind to its errors. A good copyeditor will spot them and flag them. No one's perfect, and errors inevitably slip through, but the two of you are in league to hunt down and kill as many as possible. Typos and grammatical gaffs annoy readers and pull them out of the story. You do not want your reader out of your story.

The nice thing about staying with the same publisher is that you have the opportunity to work with the same copyeditor on subsequent mss. Becky Maines and I have been working together for decades now. She knows my quirks and will even remind me when I deviate from them. But Becky goes beyond that. Not only is she a usage and grammar whiz, she's wise in the ways of the world, especially NYC where Jack roams. She's caught me and called me out on errors regarding subways and hospitals and all manner of city sundries. She never ceases to amaze me with her fact-checking abilities. As long as she's in the business, I want her on my books.

One last thing: If and when you do work up a style sheet, be polite. You're entering a partnership with the copyeditor, and a sure way to sour that relationship is to come off as an arrogant bitch or son of one. As perfect as you might think you are, you have made mistakes and you want them found and corrected before the book hits the shelves.

***

Let's start with my first published piece – evah! They gave me the whole back page for it, but no payment. So, try as I might, I still couldn't think of myself as published author – not until someone paid me for what I'd written.

This appeared in a 1969 issue of Reminiscing Time, *the bimonthly organ of the Nostalgia Book Club. In addition to the club's book offerings, the flyer often included a trip down memory lane by one of the club members. I was 23 years old at the time and had a collection of pulp magazines, especially* The Shadow Magazine. *Tight-ass that I am, it annoyed the hell out of me (still does) to hear people refer to Cranston as the Shadow. So I posed as an old codger and wrote an exposé. In that sense, it's fiction. The data about the Shadow is spot on.*

Lamont Cranston Is *Not* The Shadow!

My number one son, Edward, came ambling into the den holding out a well-thumbed paperback. "Is this the guy you're always talking about?" he asked. It was one of those paperback Shadow novels I had been seeing around town.

I told him that it certainly was and asked him how he liked the old boy. I was shocked at his opinion: 'He stinks.'

Needless to say I was quite dismayed and immediately started thinking of how much the younger generation has lost, suspension of disbelief and all that. I started paging through the volume he had so sneeringly left in front of me and... what's this? Magic cape and hat? Clouding men's minds? Margo Lane? No wonder the boy was disgusted! We had been talking about different characters! These paperbacks were about the Shadow of the old radio programs, an imposter who once went to the Orient and learned the power to cloud men's minds, etc. As kids we used to sit around and laugh at the radio. It was all garbage. We knew about the *real* Shadow because we used to spend a dime twice a month to buy a magazine which contained "A Complete Book-Length Novel from the Private Annals of The Shadow as told to Maxwell Grant." They couldn't fool *us*,

I jumped up, pulled Edward away from his record player and drove him over to my mother's house in the next town. It was in the attic, at least that's where I had left my collection of Street & Smith's magazines when I joined the Army in '43. I had no fear that they might have been thrown out because mothers just don't do things like that after their children have grown up and left home.

Doc Savage, Unknown Worlds, The Avenger, The Whisperer and *The Shadow*, they were all there and in beautiful condition (thank God the attic was insulated). I had loved them all but the Shadow was, and still is, my favorite. And he was never such a milksop that he had to depend on magic powers learned in the Orient as did the imposter on the radio. His very presence, a "blood-chilling" laugh and two glowing eyes peering from a bat-like shape that had suddenly loomed out of the darkness, was a far more effective truth serum than any "clouding of men's minds." I could never understand why the radio insisted on distorting the Shadow's image by dragging in the "supernatural."

However, I *can* understand their using Margo Lane as a romantic interest, even though the printed Shadow had no time for love affairs and only used Margo about once a year when he needed a female undercover agent. Let's face it, radio is a business and you've got to give the female listeners someone to identify with while the guys are waiting for the Shadow to plug a few crooks.

But radio perpetrated one grave injustice against the Shadow legend for which I can find neither reason nor forgiveness. They went too far when they made Lamont Cranston the secret identity of the cloaked avenger. Why, even those recent trivia quizzes have been fooled. Lamont Cranston is *not,* I repeat, NOT the Shadow. Lamont Cranston is Lamont Cranston and is *always* Lamont Cranston. But he travels a lot and, being civic-minded, allows the Shadow to use his identity when he is off to some far corner of the globe. The Shadow also disguises himself as Fritz, the janitor at police headquarters, and a certain character known as Henry Arnaud has also served the purpose of disguising the presence of the cloaked avenger.

Who, then, is the Shadow? Ah, only two human beings on earth possess this information: these are the Xinca Indian servants of the famous aviator, Kent Allard. *He* is the Shadow. Why he devotes his life to a war on crime is never divulged but, when you think about it, what does it matter?

To the police he is an underworld myth, something gangland uses to account for any hard luck that might befall them. But to the crooks, he is quite real and quite lethal. He uses not a revolver but a .45 automatic with full loads and carries *four* of them, giving him 28 shots at his immediate disposal. And you can never tell who's working for him. Cliff Marsland and "Hawkeye" are his contact men in the land of crime. Also working for him are Clyde Burke, a reporter for *The Classic;* Moe Shrevnitz, a cabbie who ferries him around; Harry Vincent, a man who owes his life to the Shadow; and Rutledge Mann, an insurance broker. And of course I must not forget Burbank, the Shadow's contact man, who sits in a dark room somewhere in Manhattan and relays messages from the master of darkness to his henchmen, and vice versa. (For some reason I can't help picturing Burbank as a hunchbacked eunuch.)

Yes, it was good to gaze at the covers and thumb through those untrimmed pages again. That same old hawk-like nose, the gleaming eyes, and the ever-present black cloak and slouch hat were all so familiar. It seemed as if I had stored them away only the day before. I felt at once both young and old.

I also felt very rich, knowing what these are worth today in the nostalgia market. And I also knew that I was kidding myself – I would probably starve to death before I could bring myself to sell a single copy.

***

This qualifies as the epitome of ephemera: a spontaneous email exchange between a number of writer friends via this thing called email that was growing in popularity. I don't know what prompted that first post. I never thought much of Jan Murray as a comedian and he was very much alive in 1997. The date suggests shortly after NECon (always in July); Doug Winter, Steve Spruill, Charlie Grant, Craig Shaw Gardener and I were all regulars at NECon and had become fast friends over the years we attended. I doubt anything would have developed had I not made that Morey Amsterdam crack... and the sad truth is, I had no time for this. (Since it's already long, a few other authors who chimed in here and there with brief comments that didn't much affect the flow wound up on the editing floor.)

Fair warning: It's totally stupid.

The Jan Murray Fan Expo (JanFanEx '97)

Subj: random JM fact
Date: 97-07-28 10:38:21 EDT
From: FPAUL46
CC: DWinter, ChasGrant, CraigS666, Stevory,

Random Jan Murray Fact #1

Of course we all admire and revere Jan Murray as a brilliant, cutting edge comedian, but let us not forget that he was a talented and sensitive actor as well. Who can forget his stand-out performance in "The Vampire" episode of =Kolchak -The Night Stalker=? I can't.

* * *

Subj: JM and synchronicity
Date: 97-07-30 08:55:56 EDT
From: FPAUL46

Certainly it did not happen by accident, fellow Jan-fans. A cosmic force had to be behind it:

The aforementioned "The Vampire" episode of =Kolchak-- The Night Stalker= (starring Jan Murray) aired on October 4, 1974 -- Jan Murray's Birthday!!!

Yes! Can you believe it? The man known and revered around the world as Jan Murray was born Murray Janofsky on October 4, 1917.

And...AND!!!

October 4 is also the birthday of another well-known but lesser comic -- Buster Keaton (who, as you all know, was a major, major Jan-fan).

Cosmic, dude!

* * *

Subj: Re: JM and synchronicity
Date: 97-07-30 19:51:12 EDT
From: DWinter
To: FPAUL46

Breathe deeply and stay by the telephone...

Help is on the way.

* * *

Subj: Jan says NO to the Rat Pack
Date: 97-07-31 09:01:48 EDT
From: FPAUL46

File: 01JAN.JPG (32501 bytes)
DL Time (TCP/IP): < 1 minute

Jan Murray Fact # 3 --

Throughout the 50's and 60's the infamous Rat Pack wooed the multi-talented Jan Murray to join them. Not for his growing recognition as a great actor, or his comic genius, or even his prowess as a game show host, but for his VOICE.

Yes, Jan Murray was a great singer. Frank and Dino were major fans of his vocal talents. Ol' Blue Eyes was once quoted re JM: "That cat's got cool chops." And Dino said, "He'sh the besht." Proof of their respect -- nay, AWE -- is in the attached photo from the early 50's. [apologies to those Jan-fans who don't have MIME-enhanced email -- you won't be able to download the photo, but I can mail you one free on request (please enclose $10 for p&h)]

The photo: That's Jan on the left (hitting C above middle C). Over his shoulder is Frank (notice how he stepped back to let the masterful JM take the lead). To Frank's left is Jackie Gleason on trombone, Jerry Lewis on trumpet, and Dino, snapping his fingers and listening in envy. (Oh, to have been there.)

Yes, Jan-fans, although the Rat Pack put a fraternity rush on Our Man Jan, he demurred, knowing the power of his personality would overwhelm all the other members.

A comment: I've received several calls in response to yesterday's Jan Fact complaining about my mentioning Buster Keaton in the same sentence as Jan Murray. I agree and I apologize: Buster Keaton was funny, but he was no Jan Murray. (Neither was Morey Amsterdam)

* * *

Subj: Going Way Too Far
Date: 97-07-31 10:05:49 EDT
From: DWinter

In a message dated 7/31/97 9:01:48 AM, FPAUL46 wrote:

<<A comment: I've received several responses to yesterday's Jan Fact complaining about my mentioning Buster Keaton in the same sentence as Jan Murray. I agree and I apologize: Buster Keaton was funny, but he was no Jan Murray. (Neither was Morey Amsterdam)>>

Okay, okay, so Dr Wilson can publicly exercise, as he apparently desires, those intense homoerotic fantasies concerning the Mayor of Video Village. I would note that he curiously fails to mention the desperate, short-lived sex-change peccadillo of the late 1970s that saw Mr. Murray record several minor hits, including "Snowbird," under the name "Anne." But nobody, and I do mean nobody, says a word about the late, great Morey Amsterdam (a.k.a. "The Man Who Kept The Secrets"). Just ask 2Pac Shakur.

* * *

Subj: Re: Going Way Too Far
Date: 97-07-31 10:49:16 EDT
From: FPAUL46

In a message dated 97-07-31 10:05:49 EDT, DWinter writes:

<< desperate, short-lived sex-change peccadillo of the late 1970s that saw Mr. Murray record several minor hits, including "Snowbird," under the name "Anne." >>

It wasn't "desperate."

Au contraire. The Jan Man was always on the, er, cutting edge. The important thing is that he =tried= it. And the vile, vicious rumor that he was only half the man he used to be after he changed back is just that: a vile, vicious rumor, spread by a cachinnating claque of cello-humping sycophants devoted to JM's arch rival, Morey "Bore-y" Amsterdam.

* * *

Subj: Re: Jan says NO to the Rat Pack
Date: 97-07-31 10:05:52 EDT
From: DWinter

In a message dated 7/31/97 9:01:48 AM, you wrote:

<<The photo: >>

What is Arnold Schwarzenegger doing in this picture (standing directly behind Jackie G)?

* * *

Subj: Re: Jan says NO to the Rat Pack
Date: 97-07-31 10:49:16 EDT
From: FPAUL46

In a message dated 97-07-31 10:05:52 EDT, you write:

<< What is Arnold Schwarzenegger doing in this picture (standing directly behind Jackie G)? >>

Oops. You weren't supposed to see that. Two men in dark clothing will contact you soon. One of them will ask you to look closely at a pen-like object.

* * *

Subj: JanFanEx '97
Date: 97-08-03 09:16:32 EDT
From: FPAUL46

ANNOUNCING:

Jan Murray Fan Expo '97
October 3-4-5
L.A. Convention Center

Yes, fellow JM devotees, it's coming. This year's JanFanEx will be held over the J-man's 80th birthday weekend. Featured guests will be Patti Page and Kaye Stevens who headlined with Jan at The Sands during the 60's.

The dealer's room will carry audiotapes of his incredible singing and his hilarious stand-up routines. Also available will be videotapes of his dramatic TV appearances. Among the gems: "Killer in a Halloween Mask" from Hunter and "The

Hula Doll Affair" from The Man from U.N.C.L.E, and of course, "The Vampire" from Kolchak-TNS.

Plus – PLUS! – rare kinescopes from Jan's stints as a gameshow host. I know you all have complete runs of "Treasure Hunt," but what about complete (admittedly short) series of "Dollar A Second," "Charge Account," "Go Lucky," "Blind Date," and those two great shows on which JM actually sang: "Songs For Sale" and "Sing It Again"?

All this and...we can't promise, but perhaps A VISIT FROM THE BIRTHDAY BOY HIMSELF!!!

Yes! The Jan Man might make an appearance!

But even if he doesn't show, you don't want to miss JanFanEx '97

* * *

Subj: JanFanEx
Date: 97-08-07 00:49:41 EDT
From: ChasGrant

Dear Sir,

I was moved and, yea, even touched, by your devotion to the wonders of Jan the Man Murray, until... UNTIL you had the nerve, the balls (well... maybe), the gall, the effrontery, the chutzpa (whatever), and the unmitigated cojones to not just once, but twice bash the memory of the greatest cellist/ comedian who ever walked the continents of this fragile planet Earth, Mr (and I say this with the greatest respect) Morey Amsterdam.

You, sir, are a disgrace to the Garden State.

You, sir, are a disgrace to the entire, if not most of the, human race.

Being an ordinarily even-tempered and shy person, I might

have, in the past, let this go. I might have, ordinarily, allowed your delusions and forgiven your trespasses. I might have, ordinarily, prayed for your soul.

That, however, was the Old Me.

The New Me, enraged beyond reason, must doth demand an apology herewith and right damn now, or I will meet you at dawn, on the beach at Seaside Heights, low tide permitting, for satisfaction.

Your choice of weapons.

My second, as soon as I find one, will contact your second (yeah, right, like you've got one) for the details.

Cad, sir. You are a cad.

Meanwhile, I'd like to be on the JM: Borsht or Zen panel, if that's all right with you.

Charles (no "L" (and no cracks)) Grant, Esq.

ps: Steve, I thought we were going to work it out in trade.
pps: Craig, nothing happened at Necon except he fell down a lot trying to look down Yvonne's T-shirt.
ppps: sigh.

* * *

Subj: JanFanEx Progress Report #1
Date: 97-08-07 08:51:07 EDT
From: FPAUL46

Well, we all knew it had to happen. The Amsterdam Acolyte Apocalypse, the Hamas of comedy fandom, has reared its ugly (and shaggy) head.

But let it be known, let the word go far and wide, neither AAA nor MM (the Morey Majority) will disrupt the proceedings. JanFanEx will celebrate Jan Murray, not Morey "Snorey"

Amsterdam.

Attendees are assured that extra security will be posted at the special panel, "Why Morey was dumb and Jan is Cool" (panelists: Melba Moore, Roger Moore, Drew Barrymore; Moderator: Mary Tyler Moore)

(I should note that Ms. M.T.M wanted to call the panel "Why Morey "Lick-the-floory" Amsterdam was such an asshole and Jan is Cool" but we felt that was a tad provocative.)

Keynote Address: "An Insanely Great Guy." Steve Jobs relates how Jan Murray inspired the first Apple computer.

Other panels:
"JM and the other J-Man: Can a Jewish Comedian be a Christ Figure?" (panelists: Nelson Mandela, Wilem Dafoe, Martin Scorsese; Moderator: Father Bruce)

"JM and the Manhattan Project: Fun with Fission" (panelists: Dan Rather, Damon Wayans, and the Spice Girls; Moderator: Frank Perdue)

"JM: The Soul of a Genius" (panelists: Stevie Wonder, Millie Vanilli, NJ Gov. Christine Todd Whitman; Moderator: Kyu Sakamoto)

and that's only the beginning, folks.

Finally...to Mr. Grant:
I will meet you, sir, at 9 p.m. on Saturday, August 16, on the Seaside Heights boardwalk in front of Nasty Nellie's (that's the notorious Heights biker bar – just look for the Harleys lined up outside).

Weapon: since you're one of the Amsterdame (stet) Agelasts, I'll choose a weapon appropriate to your testosterone level: daffodils at close quarters.

Bring your flower and wear your pink tutu. Wait for me

outside the bar. If I'm late, keep waiting. I guarantee that before the night is over, you will have the fight of your miserable life.

* * *

Subj: JanFanEx
Date: 97-08-07 00:49:41 EDT
From: ChasGrant

Dear Sir,
I notice the conspicuous absence of Shecky Green, Myron Cohen, and Joe E Adams at this little lovefest thing. Wuffo?

Seaside Heights. 9. August 16th. Got it. I nominate Craig Shaw Gardner as my second. He'll be the one in the tartan Spandex.

My tutu has studs. Not really pink, though; kind of a nice summery coral. Think it'll make a difference?

Question for the con committee: will Steve and Edie sing the national anthem?

I would like to nominate Sammy Davis Jr. to read all announcements and telegrams. Hell, he could do it with one eye closed.

Morey Lives!

* * *

Subj: JanFanEx replies
Date: 97-08-11 07:03:16 EDT
From: FPAUL46

In a message dated 97-08-08 09:11:59 EDT, Jan Fan Coates wrote:

<< Alas, you may have to find a replacement moderator for the Fission panel--Frank Perdue has since flown to the hen house in the sky. May I suggest Vinny "the Chin" Gigante? >>

Quite inconsiderate of Frankie not to send us word that he couldn't make JanFanEx '97 (unlike the courteous Mr. Gigante – please note, that's =Mr.= Gigante – who did call to explain that he would be tied up over the Oct. 4 weekend and unable to get free). Norman Mailer has been pressing for a high-profile moderator slot. This may be his lucky day.

In a message dated 97-08-09 16:41:57 EDT, ChasGrant writes:

<< I notice the conspicuous absence of Shecky Green, Myron Cohen, and Joe E Adams at this little lovefest thing. Wuffo? >>>

sigh How many times must I repeat this: JanFanEx '97 is run by and for Jan Fans. Shecky's Shekels, Cohen's Cohorts and Adams' Apples are welcome to come, but we will be there to celebrate Jan Murray. Okay?

Sheesh.

<< Question for the con committee: will Steve and Edie sing the national anthem?>>

I don't know how these rumors get started. Since this one is causing such a wave of excitement, I feel I must quash it immediately: NO: Steve and Edie will =not= sing the National Anthem at the opening ceremonies. (Don't despair -- S&E =will= be appearing at the JM Foundation Awards Banquet where they will present the "Murray"™ for Best Dog-in-a-Barroom Joke of the Year.) In deference to our many Gen-X members, and because she really, really, really wanted to give it up for Jan, the National Anthem will be sung by Courtney Love. (I can hardly wait.)

Someone asked: << Surely there must be some news about the Dealer's room!!!
What cool Jan-stuff can we expect!!!?? >>

Please refer to the JanFanEx '97 e-flyer from 8/03. (You DO save these, of course.)

And finally: another someone suggested a panel titled: "Just Who is Jan the Man Murray? Explaining It to the Young'uns" Surely this is a joke. I know – or at least I am relatively sure – that Ms. Navarro is not an Amsterdame mole, but if this is =not= a joke, then I think I speak for everyone here when I say, "Duh."

JanFanEx Progress Report #2 will arrive later in the week. Watch for it. Until then, keep your Jan flags flying.

* * *

Subject: JAN FAN EXPO 97 PROGRESS REPORT #2
Date: 97-08-14
From: FPAUL46

JAN FAN EXPO '97 PROGRESS REPORT #2

PANELISTS NEEDED FOR:

"JM as the Fisher King: Water Imagery in JM's Humor" (Moderator: Sen. Edward "Ted" Kennedy)

"No Man is a Treasure Island: the Game Show as Existential Paradigm" (Moderator: Gerald McBoingBoing)

THE FOLLOWING PANELS ARE CLOSED:

"Noted Political Humorists Deconstruct JM's Stand-up Routines" (Panelists: Strom Thurmond, Harlan Ellison, Richard Gephardt, Pat Buchanan; Moderator: Hillary R. Clinton)

"Illin' an' Chillin' with Jan-Jan the Music Man - A Way Cool Dude Light Years Ahead of his Time" (Panelists: Harlan Ellison, Mickey Dolenz ,the Beastie Boys, Dan Quayle, Hanson; Moderator: Peter Lemongello)

"Digital Jan: the Interactive Adventure Continues" (Panelists: William Gibson, Whitley Strieber, Nicholas Negroponte, Harlan Ellison; Moderator: Matthew J. Costello)

"JM: Borsht or Zen" (Panelists: Brad Pitt, James Redfield, Harlan Ellison, the Dalai Lama; Moderator: Charles Grant) (NB: in the highly likely event that Mr. Grant does not survive the daffodil duel on August 16, the panel will be moderated by the only person who can adequately replace Mr. Grant's grace, wit, and charm - the Rev. Al Sharpton)

I'll have to cut this short because I'm in training for my close-quarter daffodil duel with Charles Grant on Saturday night. (Frankly, my flower-fu is a bit rusty.)

A full report on the duel AND JanFanEx '97 Progress Report #3 next week.

* * *

Subj: Re: JAN FAN EXPO '97 PROGRESS REPORT #2
Date: 97-08-14 14:15:26 EDT
From: CraigS666

In a message dated 8/14/97 11:04:26 AM, FPAUL46 wrote:

<<I'll have to cut this short because I'm in training for my close-quarter daffodil duel with Charles Grant on Saturday night. (Frankly, my flower-fu is a bit rusty.)>>

I'll say...I believe the correct term is Phlo Fu, an ancient and arcane martial art rarely practiced in civilized nations, and which, in the hands of a skilled practitioner, involves hurling the delicate petals with deadly, shuriken-like accuracy. Eye and testicle injuries are common, which is why it was banned from the 1936 Olympics -- Adolf reportedly cringed at the very mention of the latter, having none to spare.

Indeed, is there any truth to the rumor of a similar duel

between JM and Morey "Five Fingers of Death" Amsterdam (long rumored to be a tenth-degree black belt, but he never copped to it) back in 1967, which resulted in JM's fabled glass eye?

* * *

Subj: Re: JAN FAN EXPO '97 PROGRESS REPORT #2
Date: 97-08-14 17:07:42 EDT
From: FPAUL46

In a message dated 97-08-14 14:15:26 EDT, CraigS666 writes:

<< Indeed, is there any truth to the rumor of a similar duel between JM and Morey "Five Fingers of Death" Amsterdam (long rumored to be a tenth-degree black belt, but he never copped to it) back in 1967, which resulted in JM's fabled glass eye? >>

DON'T BELIEVE A WORD OF IT!

This is another example of the AAA's Bureau of Disinformation at work, similar to their tall tale about the incomplete reversal of Jan's sex-change operation. Pure fabrication.

The nature of the injury that led to JM's glass eye in classified. However, I am free to divulge that it most assuredly did not happen at the hands of Morey "Two Limp Wrists And Also A Third Limp Appendage" Amsterdam.

In a message dated 97-08-14 14:43:10 EDT:

<< Re: the duel...Can't we all just get along??? >>

Sounds so easy, doesn't it. But international terrorist organizations such as AAA have no concept of "get along." As you all know, despite my Special Forces and Shiou-Ling flower-fu training, I am a man of peace, much like Jan

Murray. But a challenge was issued by Charles Grant, and I feel compelled to respond on the (flowery) field of honor.

* * *

Subj: NO JanFanEx PR#3
Date: 97-08-18 06:11:51 EDT
From: FPAUL46

JAN FAN EXPO '97 PROGRESS REPORT #3

Hello. This is Bambi, Paul's assistant. I left the header (that was as far as Paul got) but there will be no JanFanEx '97 Progress Reports for a while – and SOME of you know WHY!

For those of you who don't, here's the story as we know it so far:

Saturday night, shortly after 9:00 pm, my dear boss was found unconscious in the alley next to Nasty Nellie's in Seaside Heights. He'd selflessly gone there (not to defend his own honor, but that of the elderly singing comedic/ dramatic/ gameshow god Paul so adores – Jan Murray) in the close-quarter daffodil duel to which Mr. Charles Grant had challenged him.

The Seaside Heights Police force's crack anti-international-terrorist squad and the FBI are still trying to piece together the exact sequence of events, but at this point we don't think there ever =was= a duel. Paul was discovered by a Nasty Nellie's patron who had gone outside to relieve himself (thank goodness for weak bladders – I just wish he'd realized Paul was there =before= he emptied his).

The Seaside Heights Police took one look at my poor Paul and knew immediately what had befallen him. They said the linear green marks across his arms and shoulders and neck were the signature trauma of a vicious flower-flogging.

An emergency request was sent to the FBI Crime lab and

they reported that the pollen found in his hair and nostrils and under his fingernails is found on only one plant – the daffodil.

BUT – the report goes on to say that they found an unusually =large= amount of pollen on Paul, more than should have come from a single daffodil.

AND – other strange linear marks where found across Paul's buttocks; these have yet to be explained or identified. The FBI has taken photos and plaster impressions of Paul's derriere; they are searching their VICAP database for similar injuries.

Because of the severity of the wounds and the suspiciously large amount of daffodil pollen, the Seaside Heights Police force's crack anti-international-terrorist squad and the FBI are looking into the possibility of a second flogger.

They're also checking on the whereabouts of Mr. Grant and his second, Mr. Craig Shaw Gardner (a notorious master of the Wilted-Stamen style of flower-fu), at the estimated time of the assault.

Meanwhile, Paul is still unconscious and on life support. I'm at his side day and night (I'm here now, writing this on his laptop), playing audio dubs of old "Treasure Island" shows (how Paul loved Jan's feisty ad libs) in the hope that the sound of the master's voice will bolster his will to live.

Meanwhile, the investigation continues. I will keep you updated on that, and on Paul's condition as well.

For now, go home, and don't cause trouble – no demonstrations, no burning cellos on the lawns of known members of the Amsterdam Acolyte Apocalypse. Be good for Paul; do what he'd do if positions were reversed. Just sit in the dark, light a candle, nurse a pint of Cuervo Gold, and think Jan thoughts. Do it for Paul.

And please, whatever you do, don't send flowers.

Bambi
Assistant to F. Paul Wilson

* * *

Subj: Re: NO JanFanEx PR#3
Date: 97-08-18 06:31:26 EDT
From: Stevory

What a sad and hilarious end to JanFanEx. I never thought I'd use those two words to describe the same thing.

Or is it the end...?

We're all pollen for you Paul

The Marquis

* * *

Subj: Re: NO JanFanEx PR#3
Date: 97-08-18 11:42:46 EDT
From: FPAUL46

In a message dated 97-08-18 09:41:22 EDT, you write:

<< There's a saint for this, someone to pray to... novenas always help. >>

Dear Steve --

Thank you for your wishes. I read your e-mail to Paul and I thought I saw the trace of a smile around his respirator tube. Have you heard of St. Pistilus, Patron Saint of the Flower-wounded? He himself was martyred by flower-flogging (with carnations, no less!) at Nero's order.

Bambi
Assistant to F. Paul Wilson

* * *

Subj: Where was Spruill????
Date: 97-08-21 10:33:51 EDT
From: FPAUL46
Progress Report on Paul's condition and the Investigation:

Paul is still comatose and on life support, but we have moved him from Meridian Medical Center in Ocean County to a secret private hospital. His location is being kept under wraps in case they make another try on his life.

Who are "they"? We don't know yet, but it is now pretty well accepted that Paul was assaulted with at least two daffodils. I have heard whispers of a two-handed attack. =HA!= Only an elite master can deliver the dreaded two-handed flower-fu attack, and not only are these individuals extremely rare, they are so deadly that they have forsworn fighting.

Therefore I think it is safe to assume that there was a second flogger. The question is: Who was he?

The FBI is searching for a man on a nearby sandy knoll who was seen holding an object up to his face while facing in the general direction of Nasty Nellie's. We can only pray it was a camera.

BUT the other question that nags all of us is: Where was Paul's second? He'd chosen Steven Spruill, and Steve had agreed. But Steve did not show up at the field of honor. I couldn't believe Steve (a renowned master of Fungal Foot-fu) would be so cowardly, so I called him. The story he told me will send chills down your spine.

Steve was about to jump into his car and head north to meet Paul in front of Nastie Nellie's when the Red Phone in his kitchen rang. This is a direct line to the Pentagon, specially installed for his wife, Nancy (who runs the Pentagon). The call said that a DefCon 4 alert was imminent. (For those of you who wonder why Nancy doesn't go to NECon, this is the reason: she's always on alert for that DefCon-4 call, and "NECon" does sound like "DefCon", and you can understand why she wouldn't want to get confused.) So Steve had to drive Nancy to the Pentagon and wait there (actually, hide in the basement) while she got the alert up and running. But after a number of hours, it became clear to Steve and Nancy that the call had been a hoax! And now it was too late for Steve to drive up to Seaside Heights, NJ (he tends to go to bed early). In other words, gentle people, *someone very high up in the government didn't want Paul's second to be present on the boardwalk that fateful night!*

The mystery deepens further: Forensic analysis of the strange linear marks on Paul's buttocks has yielded traces of an as yet unidentified resinous substance.

Keep watch for updates on these mysteries.

Bambi
Assistant to F. Paul Wilson

* * *

Subj: Re: Where was Spruill????
Date: 97-08-22 06:55:58 EDT
From: Stevory

This is Nancy, thanking Bambi for her sympathetic explanation of why my husband Steve did not show up as Paul's second in the daffodil duel. He is so crushed by his failure, (which some people might wrongly think was partly my fault) that he has taken to his own bed and has been napping for the past forty-eight hours. As you know, Steve is as big as several neighborhood citizen's associations, and in his defense I must point out that you can fool part of Steve all of the time, all of Steve part of the time, but you can't fool all of Steve all of the time.

Anyway, Bambi, thanks for your understanding. Steve is no doubt hoping (in his dreams) that Paul enjoys a full recovery, and he is committed to sleeping straight through until this happens.

Best,
Nancy Spruill

* * *

Subj: AmsterDogs!!!!
Date: 97-08-26 05:52:00 EDT
From: FPAUL46

File: AMDOGS.JPG (182612 bytes)
DL Time (TCP/IP): < 1 minute

Hello. Bambi again.

But this time I have wonderful news! Paul is off life support – he's breathing on his own now. He's still not conscious, however, so he can't provide us with the details of the hideous assault and the identity of the second flower flogger (nor the first, for that matter).

Neither can the man on the sandy knoll near the Seaside Heights boardwalk. We were hoping the object he was seen holding up to his face while facing in the general direction of Nasty Nellie's was a camera. Alas, it was only a 7-Eleven Big Gulp cup (filled with Mountain Dew).

But the FBI has not been idle. Its crime lab has finally identified the resinous substance found in the strange linear marks on Paul's buttocks as... bow resin. Yes! The substance commonly applied pre-performance to violin and CELLO BOWS!!!!

This was the clue that broke everything wide open. The FBI then plugged "cello bow" into its VICAP database and guess whose name popped up: Douglas E. ("Cello-cane") Winter, leader of the radical fundamentalist militant wing of the Amsterdam Acolyte Apocalypse – the dreaded AmsterDogs.

While most of the members of the AmsterDogs are experts in flower-fu, Winter's weapon of choice (fundamentalist Morey Amsterdam worshipper that he is) is a cello bow which he usually keeps hidden in a walking stick (hence the moniker).

But all this was circumstantial...until a tourist came forward with a photo of his family taken near Nasty Nellie's that fateful Saturday night. In it are half a dozen AmsterDogs (=half a dozen!=) lurking on the boardwalk. Mr. Winter (cellocane hidden), Mr. Grant, and Mr. Gardner are clearly visible along with three other as-yet-unidentified AmsterDogs. Oh, they appear to be wandering aimlessly, but they aren't. They've got flower-flogging in their rotten hearts (just look at that evil grin on Mr. Gardner's face). Clearly they were =stalking= Paul.

I know all this is hard to believe, so I have attached that photo (with the brave tourist's family members edited out for their own protection) so you can see for yourselves. (For full effect, print it out; those of you who can't download this, please give me a fax number.)

But what was the AmsterDogs' purpose? Merely to beat poor Paul senseless and leave him there to die? Or is there a deeper, more insidious plan?

More developments as they occur.

Bambi
Assistant to F. Paul Wilson

* * *

Subj: the AmsterDogs' plot
Date: 97-08-30 10:13:50 EDT
From: FPAUL46

Hello. Bambi again.

Paul is improving. He's awake, but still too weak to type or even talk. But he's getting better every day. I'm home now, taking a break from keeping watch at his bedside.

But I've been greatly disturbed by some recent communications. I thought they were typical sick stuff, so I ignored him.

But today I got a disturbing letter in the mail. The words were cut from a newspaper and pasted on a sheet of scratch paper from a Hyatt Hotel. It said that Paul was seen with Douglas Winter at an Oriole game in Baltimore on Thursday, October 28. This is impossible. I was at Paul's bedside all that day. But in light of the Schow messages that had preceded this letter, I called the FBI. They told me some frightening news.

The AmsterDogs, the rabid radical wing of the Amsterdam Acolyte Apocalypse, has been linked to secret cloning experiments. The FBI theorizes that the AmsterDogs planned to assassinate Paul and replace him with a doppelganger who would subvert JanFanExpo '97 into a Morey Amsterdam event.

And it fits, doesn't it. Who was the ersatz Paul seen with? None other than Douglas "Cellocane" Winter, a member of the AmsterDogs' central committee.

The FBI said the plot hit a glitch when the clean-up crew that was supposed to dispose of Paul's unconscious body was delayed in Parkway traffic. Another glitch was the inordinate time it took to get the clone's liver conditioned so he could effectively replace Paul. (Apparently, it takes many years to develop what is known to hepatologists as "NECon liver.") There was also a delay in coaching the clone in Paul's vast knowledge of boxed wines (Paul has been called the Robert Parker of wines costing less than $2 per liter.)

So...

Oh, darn. There's the doorbell. I'll send this off now and update you all later.

Bambi
Assistant to F. Paul Wilson

* * *

Subj: No JanFanEx
Date: 97-08-31 12:14:55 EDT
From: FPAUL46

Hey, hello, how are you all, it's me, Paul and I'm out of my coma and feeling just fine and dandy. Feeling better than ever, in fact. Yes, sir, it sure is great to be up and about. Thanks for all the good wishes while I was indisposed.

As for what happened to me, I have no memory. No, sir, can't remember a blessed thing. LOL! I think I just tripped and fell. Yes, that's what it was...an unfortunate accident. Yeah, clumsy ol' me. LOL! But hey, I'm okay now, so let's forget about the whole silly thing.

And speaking of silly things, how about that Jan Murray Fan Expo '97? Whoa, talk about off-the-wall ideas! LOL! Where do I come up with them?

Lemme tell ya, while I was in that coma, I had one of them, whatchacall, epiphanies, and I realized that Jan Murray is a nobody. A schmuck who'd do just about any damn thing to keep his ugly mug before the public. No venue was too small, no gameshow too stupid for that creep. What I ever see in him, huh? LOL!

So JanFanEx'97 is canceled. Fuhgeddaboutit.

But, since I've still got the LA Convention Center rented, I oughta do something with it.

Hmmm...how about, oh, I dunno, another sort of gathering. Maybe a Morey Amsterdam Memorial Concert. Yeah, that's it. A zillion cellos. Cool. And we'll run tapes of the Morey parts

453

of the old "Dick VanDyke Show" (hey – continuous loops of "I Am a Fine Musician"!!!) Right on.

LOL! Tell me what ya think.

Loves and kisses OOOOO + XXXXX :-*

Paul

PS: Thanks to the beautiful and lovely Bambi for helping out. She's gone to visit her folks in Fiji so she won't be returning any messages for a while.

PPS: Hey, how about them O's! Go Birds!

***

I started repairmanjack.com in 1997 to coincide with Jack's return in Legacies. *It quickly gathered a community of readers who became dear friends and who still gather at Grand Unification microcons. This sequence has the same sort of genesis as JanFanEx but not quite so ephemeral. Lisa K threw down the gauntlet with a post on the site's Forum and I took it up. JanFanEx cannot be found anywhere on the Interwebz, but this can. And it's almost as stupid.*

Here in edited form, is...

The Eisenberg Certainty Principle

NEWS: Pepsi Prodigy Cast as Jack
Posted By: Lisa
Tuesday, 30 January 2001, at 2:47 p.m.

January 30, 2001

In a decision that stunned outsiders but surprised no one in the movie industry, up-and-coming actress Hallie Kate Eisenberg has won the coveted role of Repairman Jack. Eisenberg, most famous for playing "World's Most Annoying Child" in the Joy of Cola Pepsi ad campaign, beat out a high-profile group of hopefuls for the part. Rumored to have tried out for the part in vain are Bruce Willis, Nic Cage, Kevin Spacey, Ed Norton, and Kevin Costner.

"Hallie just walked into the audition and stunned everyone," says one insider. "Even though she's female and only 4 feet tall, her presence literally filled the room. She owned the role from the start." Since Eisenberg is only eight years old, producers will have to work around child labor laws. "Luckily with the strike coming up, Hallie will be able to squeeze in an extra year of school and thus be able to concentrate wholly on the film," says her agent. "And with her youth, she'll be able to grow into the role and turn the Repairman Jack character into a real franchise." Eisenberg herself was out at recess and could not be reached for comment.

When informed of the casting choice, author F. Paul Wilson, the creator of the Jack character, exclaimed "Good God and a half," adding as an afterthought, "Who's directing again?" He has not been able to be reached since, and was last seen speeding towards the Jersey Pine Barrens with a cider jug hanging out the window of his car. Authorities are reluctant to follow.

***

Re: NEWS: Pepsi Prodigy Cast as Jack
Posted By: fpw
Tuesday, 30 January 2001, at 4:43 p.m.

from the Pines -- via cellular modem--

The director is Alan Parker. As I understand it, Hallie was

reading for the Vicky part, but the sound of her voice blasted Parker's circuits, convincing him to return to his beloved "Bugsy Malone" motif. All parts will be played by children, all characters will be gender swapped. Gia has already been cast -- Halley Joe What's-his-face from "Sixth Sense." A casting call is out for a plump Hassidic girl to play Abe.

As for me, I'm okay. Spent the day stocking up on ammo and looking for the quickest way west that doesn't involve metal detectors.

Kalifornia, here I come.

More reports from the road when feasible.

FPW

***

Re: NEWS: Pepsi Prodigy Cast as Jack
Posted By: Susan
Tuesday, 30 January 2001, at 7:21 p.m.

May the powers of Light shine upon you during your journey.

Just remember - fire and iron, fire and iron!

Susan

PS: Care package with canned goods, Quisp, and Sour Patch kids on the way.

***

from the road – Zanesville, OH
Posted By: fpw
Wednesday, 31 January 2001, at 7:42 a.m.

Wish I could sleep.

Typing this pre-sunup in the parking lot of a Motel 6. Afraid to get a room. They're looking for me after I ran that roadblock in western PA.

Just downed a bowl of Quisp -- dry -- and a handful of Sour Patch Kids (thanks, Susan).

I'll swap plates with a car in the lot here; that should allow my '60 Studebaker to slip along the interstate unnoticed.

My Merde-lywood mole tells me Jonathan Lipnicki has been tapped for the part of Jack's mother in the cinderblock-from-the-overpass flashback sequence. When I heard the news I got a little reckless and ripped off a bazooka from a sporting goods store off I-80 -- thus the roadblock.

Just a few more of these chocolate-covered coffee beans and I'll hit the road again.

Why can't I sleep?

Must be because I was laughing so hard at the Queen's "The Keep" DVD page. Laughed, that is, until the sobs began. Should have ripped off two bazookas.

Later,
FPW

***

FPW spotted in Ohio!
Posted By: Mike
Wednesday, 31 January 2001, at 1:11 p.m.

Special Report

API Wire Service Wednesday, January 31, 2001 13:10 Hrs

New Jersey, Pennsylvania, and Ohio State Police report a late model Studebaker barreling dangerously along both backroads and the interstate. Thus far they have been unable to apprehend the reckless driver, who, by the latest eyewitness reports, strongly resembles Hollywood Actor and recent father Michael Douglas with a crew cut and wearing 1950's style eye-glasses.

One attempt to run this madman off the road was repelled when the vehicles operated by two Ohio State troopers were forced to exit the interstate after their windshields were rendered unviewable.

Unsubstantiated reports state that this occurrence was brought about by large quantities of a presently unknown children's cereal being ejected from a long, cylindrical, metallic object, bearing a striking resemblance to a WWII issue Army bazooka, being carried by the perpetrator.

Another unsubstantiated report quotes Mobil gas station attendant Fred MacPherson as stating: "He acted kinda funny when I gassed him up. What do I mean by funny? Well he had this strange look in his eye and kept saying he was going to his daughter's birthday party."

At present the suspect is still at large and considered dangerous.

More reports to follow.

***

Re: from the road -- Las Vegas
Posted By: fpw
Thursday, 1 February 2001, at 8:19 a.m.

Sleep? Wuzzat?

Been driving 24 hours straight with pit stops for calls to the mole, gas, food, etc. (straaaange writings on the restroom walls out here).

Blew the Studebaker's trans outside Wichita and had to dump it. Picked up an El Camino. The hardware (if you know what I mean, and I think you do) is under a tarp in the back.

Listened to the radio all night while packing away the Quisp, the Sour Patch families, and of course the chocolate-covered

EPHEMERATA

coffee beans; mostly preachers (now I know where those strange restroom writings come from) who've convinced me that I'm on a mission from God. In fact, God himself has been traveling in the passenger seat since Pueblo, CO. He fades in and out every so often (to answer someone's prayers, I guess) but mostly he's there.

Why do my eyes burn so?

Arrove in Vegas a little while ago and stopped in front of this casino that looks like New York City. For an awful moment I thought I'd got myself turned around but then I realized that NYC doesn't have a roller coaster looping around the Empire State Building. Not yet anyway.

I really need a shower, but I'm denying myself such luxuries until I've completed my mission.

Ate a good breakfast -- steak, eggs Benedict, bagels, hash browns, sausage, bacon, three carafes of coffee -- while I discussed my plans with God. Don't worry. No one was sitting near us. I mean, there were people around when we sat down but they pretty quick moved away. People around here are very considerate that way.

God informed me that Lindsay Lohan, having demonstrated her facility with dual roles in "The Parent Trap" remake, has been hired to play Kusum *and* Kolabati. The revelation prompted a little trip to a munitions fair out in the desert to purchase a Sidewinder missile.

This shall not pass. I cannot fail because the Lord is with me. (At least he was a moment ago. Where'd he go?)

Westward ho.
FPW

***

Re: from the road -- Santa Monica

F. PAUL WILSON

Posted By: fpw
Friday, 2 February 2001, at 7:59 a.m.

Under the Pier. Alone.

My passenger bailed out in Vegas. The El Camino is parked in Venice, near the ballerina clown.

When did I last sleep? Tuesday morning, I think.

Been on an emotional tilt-a-whirl. Good thing I have the Quisp, the Kids, and the chocolate-covered coffee beans to keep me on an even keel.

Most excellent news came round midnight from my Merde-lywood Mole that Alan Parker slipped and tripped on some spilled Skittles at a pre-production cast party and fell out a second-story window. He'll be in traction for months. And I thought, yea, verily, God is on my side.

Of course the production company and Universal immediately began scrambling for a new director, and I thought whoever they get, he or she ain't a-gonna want a gender-swapped cast of prepubescent Merde-lywood brats.

WRONG AGAIN, WILSON!!!!

They found their new director in a matter of hours, and he LOVES the concept. Feels it will allow him to be more creative with the storyline.

The replacement's name is Michael Mann.

.;l,[[e//dl.d]e.a]]-aak763g57fj`` yhwrs;lua

Sorry. A little spasm in the fingers there. But it's gone now.

I'm fine, I'm fine, really, I'm okay. Got this uncontrollable twitch in my right cheek, but otherwise, I'm amazingly cool. Maybe it's because of this PND I've got strapped to my back.

PND? No, it's not post-nasal drip. It's a Personal Nuclear

Device. Picked it up at a street fair in East LA. Forty megatons ought to do it, don't you think?

And those Merde-lywood morons are worried about a Writers Guild strike? HA! Thinking of leaving early to avoid the Friday afternoon rush? HA! NO MORE TRAFFIC JAMS AFTER TODAY, BOZOS!

Those of you east of the Rockies, watch your TVs; those west listen for the boom. Lisa, grab the kids and head for Frisco.

Tomorrow will be a better day. I love ya, tomorrow. Tomorrow Never Knows (ah, but it does). Tomorrow, Tomorrow and the Fairy Chessmen. Will you love me tomorrow. There'll be no tomorrow for Merde-lywood. Tomorrow tomorrow tomorrow tomorrow tomorrow...

Signing off.
FPW

***

Urgent Message for FPW: Change in Plans
Posted By: Susan
Friday, 2 February 2001, at 12:35 p.m.

Im fine, Im fine, really, Im okay. Got this
uncontrollable twitch in my right cheek, but
otherwise, Im amazingly cool. Maybe its because of
this PND Ive got strapped to my back.

I believe you, of course. Still, my intuition tells me you may be a tad upset.

Nuking Los Angeles may sound like a really neat idea right now, but I have a feeling you'll regret it. Rumor has it Mann has booked a flight to Miami this weekend. I'm assuming he was your main target. Mann will be in South Beach tomorrow morning for a brainstorming session on a new flick. Trust me, you don't want to know which one.

I have another thought. I normally do not offer these services, but since it's you I'll make an exception. I'm half Colombian. Think about that for a second.

There are a lot of people in Miami who would like nothing more than to forget that Miami Vice ever happened. You are looking at one of them. I could set you up in a quiet room at The Delano on Collins Avenue under the name Jose Jimenez. My contacts say Mann will be having dinner tomorrow night at the hotel's restaurant, The Blue Door. My paisas and I could arrange everything. You just give me the word. If the Colombians can't help you, there's a large group of Cubans in the Everglades that are just itching for a fight.

You'll have to ditch the El Camino when you get to Miami. I'll have a black Jag waiting for you, so you'll =blend= in with the locals.

Another interesting development - Faith Hill called me today. How do I know her? Long story. Anyway, she was pretty upset. Says she hasn't been feeling right since those Joy of Cola commercials started. You know that hip short haircut she's wearing now? It wasn't a fashion statement. Just a way to cover up the hair she chopped off after spending 3 days on the set of the latest Pepsi commercial.

She wants to help. She NEEDS to help. Faith assured me that she could take Hallie Kate Eisenberg out of the picture (so to speak) until all this blows over. I made Faith promise she would baby sit her for an extended period of time. No harm will come to her. The only torture she'll endure involves a funnel and a liter bottle of Coca Cola. Faith's idea.

If Mann or Eisenberg are not on the set on Monday, maybe production will stop. At the very least it will be interrupted long enough for you to come up with something else.

After the Miami thing, you can lay low at my cottage in the

mountains of Mentone, Alabama. It's a very back to basics house, but I'm sure you'll feel right at home there. People talk funny, drink homemade alcohol out of jugs and the place is surrounded by pine trees. Any supplies you need can be found at the local gas station. Ammo is next to the Moon Pies.

God speed,
Susan

***

In The Wake Of The Pepsi Girl Casting
Posted By: AsMoral
Tuesday, 30 January 2001, at 7:21 p.m.

Los Angeles, CA Associated Press 2001

"SNUBBED AGAIN!"

Spago restaurant became the scene of a violent outrage as pint-sized actor Emanuelle Lewis attempted in vein to turn over the chair in which he sat waiting for his food. His outrage came on the heels of discovering from his agent that he had lost the bid on the role of Repairman Jack. The role was handed to Pepsi lip-sync prodigy Hallie Kate Eisenberg.

"Damn Honky Bitch!" Lewis reportedly cried out as he pulled his booster seat of the chair and kicked it about.

Owner Wolfgang Puck attempted to calm Lewis who in turn bit the renowned chef on the pinky toe.

Lewis and his agent were unreachable for comment.

***

from the road -- coming home
Posted By: fpw
Saturday, 3 February 2001, at 8:24 a.m.

In Response To: Re: from the road -- Santa Monica (fpw)

Well, it's over.

Susan was right about Michael Mann heading to Miami, but now I know the real reason.

There I was, standing outside the Griffith Observatory, left thumb on the button of my forty-megaton PND, right thumb touching my nose, fingers a-waggling toward the smoggy panorama stretching away below, when my cell phone rang. It was my Merde-lywood mole calling from deep within the bowels of Beacon Films.

A change of plans at Beacon: true to their pattern over the past five years, they've decided to can the current script and hire a new writer for an entirely different take on the film. Mann is out, so is the gender-swapped kid cast.

Then my agent called. He's renegotiated the deal – higher option price, higher purchase price.

So I've decided LA's really not so bad. Gotta love those royal palms lining Hollywood Blvd, hmmm?

And what was I so upset about? Beats me. Everything's fine now and I'm on my way back east. Driving, of course. Could have taken the plane but that would mean leaving my PND behind. I'm keeping that. Just in case.

FPW

***

This isn't really a story. Call it "fictional ephemera."

A little background: I'm not sure when – I think it was back in 1990 – and I'm not sure where – maybe at one of Gary Lovisi's annual paperback collector conventions in Manhattan. Anyway, I was listening to Michael Avallone (now departed) discuss his favorite subject (Michael Avallone) and about how he once wrote an entire novel in a day and a half, and how he used to write the entire contents of magazines issue after issue, and so on, all of which I knew. But here's what got me: The hero of these exploits isn't "I" or "me"... it's "the Avo." I listened in awe. Not only is this man referring to himself in the third person, but he's given himself a nickname.

Maybe it was the fumes, but later that day as I was crawling through the Lincoln Tunnel on my way home I began imagining the grandiose exploits of a wildly prolific writer known to one and all (including himself) as the Effster. I typed up a short piece about him for my own amusement, then sent it to Ed Gorman to see if he recognized the inspiration for the character. He not only recognized the Avo immediately, he wanted to publish it in Mystery Scene. *I said go ahead, figuring no one would read it. To my amazement (and consternation), I show up at the 1991 NECon and Rick Hautala and others are calling me "Effster."*

I did a second "memoir" a year or so later, planned others but never got to them. Lucky for you. A little of this guy goes a long way.

The Effster is nothing if not empathetic.

So here they are, the memoirs of the Effster in internal chronological order ("Summer '73" was written first).

Memoirs of the Effster

First Day of Spring '61

So we're sitting around this table near the back door at Gerde's Folk City in the Village, Allen Ginsberg, Jack Kerouac, and the Effster, all recovering from last night's party at LeRoi Jones's apartment, Allen still loaded on psilocybin and Jack already stoked with his own drug of choice (Ripple red), and the two of them engaged in another episode of one of their interminable arguments while I'm scratching out a couple of chapters of the new novel on a yellow legal pad. A warm day for the first of spring, so we've got the door open and the sun's pouring in. Gerde never lets too much sun into Folk

City. Easy to see why. Not too many places more depressing than a night spot at lunch hour.

The Effster's not the only one writing there that afternoon. Some baby-faced kid in blue work shirt and denims with curly light brown hair twisted this way and that like it hasn't been combed since New Year's Eve is sitting on the edge of the stage hitting a few chords on his guitar then stopping to write some lyrics, then hitting the chords again. Allen called him Bobby when we came in, said the kid's been in town only a couple of months and already he's making waves in the folk scene around the Village.

The Effster's not real crazy about folk music.

"I gotta get out of New York," Allen says, scratching his beard. "It's stifling me."

The Effster knows just what he means. I've been here almost a year now and can sense a gradual waning of my literary production. I mean, here it is almost April already and I'm only half a dozen chapters into my third novel of the year (*Stranger in a Strange Land* under my Robert A. Heinlein pseudonym). I've already finished *Ship of Fools* and *A Shade of Difference* (the sequel to my 1960 blockbuster *Advise and Consent* under my Allen Drury pen name), but still have *Failsafe* and *Seven Days in May* to do before June.

By this time last year I'd already finished *The Agony and the Ecstasy*, *A Canticle for Leibowitz*, *Three Hearts and Three Lions*, *Franny and Zooey*, and *Tropic of Cancer*; and the year before that I'd already done *Starship Troopers* (another Heinlein title) and a real fat one called *Hawaii* under the Michener pseud.

Got to get cracking.

"Thank Krishna that Peter and I are heading back to Paris the end of the month," Allen sighs.

"What for?" Jack says with one of his demonic grins. "To meet up with Burroughs? You won't get much out of him these days. All he's doing is that cutting and pasting jive. That's not writing."

The Effster knows Willy B. pretty well. In fact, last time I was in Paris I convinced him to change the title of his novel to *The Naked Lunch* (he wanted to call it *Word Horde*), and finished it for him when he got sick from too much majoun.

"Gonna meet Corso there too," Allen says. "Paris in the spring. It's inspiring."

"Greg's the one who could use some inspiration," Jack says. "Hasn't had much since *The Happy Birthday of Death*."

I agree but keep my comments to myself.

The Effster does not put down other writers. That's reserved for critics and reviewers.

But I've been thinking Allen might be losing his touch as well since he began hanging out with Tim Leary and dipping into mushrooms and meth. He read me his latest poem, "Television Was a Baby Crawling Toward That Deathchamber," and I thought it missed the point. But again I kept my opinions to myself.

The Effster is nothing if not sensitive to other writers' feelings.

"Greg's *Happy Birthday* is truly a fine work," Allen says heatedly. He and Gregory Corso are old friends. "And 'The Bomb' is one of the greatest poems ever written about the nuclear age."

"Nowhere near as good as his 'Marriage'," Kerouac counters, "but who would've noticed 'Bomb' if the old Effster here hadn't suggested Greg have it typeset in the shape of a mushroom cloud?"

"Greg owes the Effster for that one," Allen says. "We all owe the Effster one way or another. You, Jack – what would've happened to *On the Road* if old F. here hadn't convinced Millstein to give it that rave review in the *Times*? You wouldn't be King of the Beats now."

Jack nods. "No argument there. And where'd you be if the Effster hadn't made a few phone calls and got Ferlinghetti arrested for selling 'Howl' in Frisco?"

"Yeah," Allen says somberly. "No obscenity trial, no notoriety." Then grins through his beard. "And no extra printings. You're the greatest, F."

I merely shrug. The Effster has never seen any sense in belaboring the obvious.

Just then the folk singer wanders by, frowning.

"Hey, Bobby," Allen calls. "Why so glum?"

"Lyric troubles," Bobby says, running his fingers through his bed-head hair. "Got a song full of questions but no answers."

"Then you've come to the right place," Allen says, gesturing dramatically. "Myself and my two friends here, Jack and the Effster, are the world's greatest answer men. Aren't we, F.?"

I say, "Sometimes the answers are so obvious you can't hear them. Sometimes they're just blowing in the wind."

Bobby's eyes widen. He snatches paper and pencil from the breast pocket of his work shirt and begins scribbling. "I'm gonna use that, if you don't mind."

I shrug. The Effster is nothing if not generous with his bon mots.

"This is for a folk song, I presume."

"Yeah," he says. "Need some original material for my gigs. Want a real mix. Some standards, some new, some serious, some funny, and some just strange. Don't know how the original stuff'll go over, though."

"Anything original these days is good," I say. "The times they are a-changing."

Bobby jerks like he's been kicked and starts scribbling some more. "Can I use that too?" he says.

I shrug once again. "Why not? It's merely a statement of fact."

"Thanks a lot, F. Thanks a million."

I wave off his thanks. "Don't think twice, it's all right."

He scribbles again. "And that? Can I use <u>that</u>?"

I nod and refrain from saying another word. The

Effster fears this Bobby character will copy down his order for another beer.

"Thanks again, F," he says, heading for the door.

I look at the sky outside and see the gathering thunderheads and figure it should be safe to mention the weather.

"Better hurry," I say. "Looks like a hard rain's gonna fall."

He starts scribbling again as he goes out the back door.

I wish him well.

The Effster is nothing if not generous with his well-wishes for fellow writers, even if they're folk singers. And I have a feeling that with proper guidance from the Effster, this Bobby What's-His-Name might do all right.

Back to work.

Summer '73

So here's the Effster, sitting around the gat-shaped pool (a concrete .45 automatic with steps at the clip end of the grip) at my Left Coast hideaway playing chess with Stevie Spielberg between knocking out chapters of my new horror novel in progress,

"So F," Stevie says, sliding a pawn toward my knight, "what do we do with all those subplots?"

He's talking about *Jaws*, the novel the Effster recently finished under his Peter Benchley pseudonym. Stevie just read it in manuscript and wants to direct it.

"Dump them," I tell him. "They're ballast. I just put them in there to fill out the page count. This is a movie, Stevie. You've got to learn that what works in a book doesn't necessarily work on the screen. Dump the subplots and keep that shark on the screen; and while you're at it, work some sort of basso obbligato into the score whenever the shark's around. You'll have yourself a winner. The Effster guarantees it."

I glance at the board and take his queen with my king's

bishop. "Hey, thanks, F."

"For what? Taking your bishop?"

"No – for the advice."

I smile. The Effster is nothing if not generous with his advice.

Just then Georgie Lucas climbs out of the pool and hangs over the chess board as he dries off.

'I tell you, F," he says, "that computerized camera idea of yours is really working out on the special-effects tests. It's going to take years to do but I think you're going to love the final product."

"I hope so," I tell him as I type another chapter on the new novel. "l mean, you know how 'Star Wars' is the Effster's favorite of all the scripts he's written this year. Didn't want to give it to you if you couldn't make it look right."

"Speaking of writing," Stevie says, obviously trying to distract me as he slides his rook down the right hand side of the board, "you're really taking your time with that new book there."

"Damn right," I say. "It's going to be important, so the Effster's spending a whole day on it, start to finish."

"A whole day!" Georgie says. "You've never spent more than a few hours on a novel!"

"I know that. But it's for Brian."

They both say, "Oh."

I take Stevie's remaining bishop with my queen.

"Yeah, he came to the Effster last week. Wants to do something with teenagers after 'Sisters.' You know DePalma – likes all that red stuff in his movies. I told him the Effster would whip something together for him but I want to do it as a novel first. I mean, you guys know how the Effster has been trying for years to get this horror thing rolling, but it remains dead in the water. I don't know what it is. I thought I'd jump started it with *Rosemary's Baby* under my Levin moniker, but even with a hit movie it never got going. Did I tell you I'm going to do another Levin novel soon? Calling it *The Boys from Brazil.* Anyway, I waited a couple of years and tried again with *The Exorcist* under my Blatty pen name. Another bestseller, but still the horror thing is just sputtering along. I'm hoping this new one will turn the corner."

The Effster is nothing if not persistent.

"If anyone can do it, F," Stevie says, "you can."

"I know. I know. I've just got to set my mind to it."

"Look what you did for international thrillers with your Ludlum books."

Stevie's trying to sneak up on the Effster's queen but I see what he's doing.

"Maybe that's it," I say. "Maybe the Effster should start a new pseudonym and pump a horror novel or two a year into the market under that name. Create a Ludlum of horror. Yeah. That's what I'II do. But what name will I use?"

"Yo, F!" says a new voice.

"Yo, Sly!" I say as Stallone saunters into the backyard. "What's happenin'?"

'Not much. Whatcha workin' on?"

"New novel called *Carrie.*"

He eyes the roll of paper at the rear of the typewriter.

"Slow goin', huh?"

I should explain, for those of you unfamiliar with the Effster Method, that I type on a continuous sheet of paper; it rolls from below the machine and flows onto a take-up roller after the Effster has had his way with it. I call it a Word Processor. (When I get a few minutes I'II work out a way to get this done electronically, but for now this will have to do.) My secretary unrolls it later, cuts it into separate sheets, boxes the manuscript, and sends it off to the publisher.

The Effster never rewrites. He doesn't have to.

Sly says, "I assume this means you finished that screenplay you was doin' for me."

"It certainly does."

I reach under the table and pull a script from the box there. I hand it to him.

"There you go."

He stares at the top sheet. "*Rocky*?"

"It's perfect for you, Sly. Tailor made for you by the Effster. It's gonna make you."

He flashes a lopsided grin. "You're da greatest, F."

"Ain't it da troot," I say In Brooklynese so he can understand better.

The Effster is nothing if not gracious.

"Now," I say as I turn to the chess board and move my queen's bishop three squares, "if I could only think of a catchy pseudonym for my new series of horror novels. Checkmate, by the way."

Stevie gapes as Georgie and Sly laugh.

Stevie says, "Got me again, F," and knocks over his king.

Which gives me an idea.

"Thanks," l say.

"For what?"

"For giving me the surname of my new pseudonym. And for helping me out, I'm going to make the first name Steven – though I might change the spelling a little – in your honor. "

The Effster is nothing if not demonstrative of his gratitude.

"Now get out of here, you guys. The Effster's got too much to do."

They wave and leave.

So much to do. I mean, I'm planning *Slapstick*, a new novel under my Kurt Vonnegut pseud, plus *Ragtime* under my Doctorow name for the snobs, and not one but two Jack Higgins novels, *Storm Warning* and *The Eagle Has Landed*. I'm finishing up *The Forever War* under my Haldeman name, plus Hef's been calling all week, wanting the Effster to do the entire December issue of *Playboy*. Which is okay, but I'd only agreed to do all the fiction. Now he wants the Effster to do all the editorials and non-fiction too. I'm not terribly interested in writing non-fiction, but I agreed.

The Effster is nothing if not accommodating.
Back to work.

***

n 2010 Robert Swartwood put together an anthology called Hint
Fiction. *All stories 25 words or less in the mold of Hemingway's
"Baby Shoes." Rather than simply reprint my piece, here's my
actual work sheet.*

*None of them did it for me until I upped the ante in the last entry
– that was the one I submitted.*

Pranksters

(1) The lawn was the last straw. Who knows a man's breaking
point? Well, they found mine. Nine in the magazine. That'll
do.

(2) The lawn was the last straw. Everybody's got a breaking
point and they found mine. Nine in the magazine. That
oughta do.

(3) Who knows a man's breaking point? The lawn was mine.
Nine in the magazine. That'll do.

(4) I'm a regular guy, but we all have a breaking point. The
lawn was mine. Nine in the magazine. That'll do.

(5) The lawn was the last straw. Why couldn't they just leave
me alone? Well, they asked for it. Nine in the magazine. That
oughta do.

FINAL:
*Bad enough what they did to the flowers, but the cat was the last
straw. Nine in the magazine. That oughta do.*

***

I wrote this for Del and Sue Howison's Framed *– an art book they pubbed in 2003 with a story custom-written for each piece. I believe the story had to be short enough to fit on the page opposite the art. The illo I chose (by Mel Whitlow – who I've been trying to contact but seems to have dropped off the face of the Earth) is below. My first thought was "I See You," but then I did a play on the phrase and the story came together. I've altered it slightly here to give it a tenuous link to the Secret History.*

ICU

They come to look at me in my cell, to give me objects to hold. They present them to me with tongs, then ask me questions and record the answers. They never stay long and they never, ever touch me.

They fear me because I can see – not so much in the literal sense of perceiving objects, colors, movement in my immediate vicinity, but because I can see things they can't.

I can see what was, and I can see what is yet to be. I can touch you or hold something you've held, and see where you've been and everything you've ever done; I can also see what awaits you. At least what awaits you if you continue on your present course. The future is fluid. Shifts in lifestyle, shifts in relationships will change it.

If only I could have seen my own future. But I'm blind to that.

And I can't see the big picture, only the personal. If I could have seen the future of, say, the stock market, I would have been rich enough to control my fate. They wouldn't have dared touch me.

But I feared revealing myself. I thought if people knew of my ability to see their future – really see it – they'd hound me. I imagined myself beseeched on all sides, day and night, with no privacy, no peace, no life. So instead I turned my talent to parlor games, posing as a psychic advisor. I made a good living and was happy enough. I was even happier when I met Maxine. I loved her and trusted her enough to tell her my secret.

I didn't see her betrayal coming because it involved me. Maxine sold me out. Perhaps that's too strong a term. She thought my talent could make us rich. But the wrong people got wind of it. And now Maxine's dead and I'm locked up here with others like me. Every day they bring us things and we read into their future and record what we see. That knowledge is taken and used to make adjustments in policy. Then they bring us other things and ask us again.

At first I told them they didn't need to lock me up. I'd be glad to help my government. And I meant it. But they never answered me. Then I thought they might be hiding me away from other governments who might want to know the future as well, but that's not it. The truth is, they're not the government at all. They're some sort of secret society... I've heard them refer to something called "the Order. What "Order" I don't know.

I *do* know that the reason I'm locked away with the others is because we can also see into the past – *their* pasts. We can tell where they've been, what they've done... all the lies and crimes and betrayals they've been party to. Things they don't want anyone to know.

That's why we'll never leave here alive.

***

I wrote this sometime around the turn of the century. One of those things that come to you out of nowhere and you simply sit at the keyboard and take dictation. I knew it wasn't complete but didn't know where to go with it, so I put it away to marinate. A few years later John B. Ford asked me if I had an incomplete piece or remnant he might finish. I sent him this. He did a good job taking it someplace where I wouldn't have thought to go. That longer version was published in Terror Tales 2 *in 2004 and reprinted in* Evil Entwines *in 2005. But here for you, published for the first time, is the original vignette.*

Sermon

At the sound of the unfamiliar voice, Angela froze. Her hands were in the kitchen sink, scrubbing the big iron skillet. The water running over her fingers was hot, in sharp contrast to the sudden trickle of winter rain down her spine.

She shouldn't be hearing any voice but Stan's. They lived on ten acres bordering and eastern fringe of the Jersey Pine Barrens. No one else around besides Stan and her. And

Tyler, of course, but Tyler didn't –

"Oh my God!"

Angela dropped the skillet and ran to the sliding door that opened onto the rear deck. Outside in the cool spring air she saw her three-year-old son standing on the top tread of the deck steps. He was dressed in his dark blue turtleneck and tan Osh-Kosh overalls. His back was to her, and he was talking to the woods.

Angela clapped her hand over her mouth to trap the emotions bursting within her, to keep them from escaping in a cry of joy. She didn't want to interrupt this moment, couldn't risk distracting Tyler. Tears flooded her eyes as she turned and hurried toward the front of the house where Stan was finishing the annual task of replacing the winter glass in the storm door with a screen.

Her husband's blue eyes widened when he looked up and saw the tears on her cheeks. "What's wrong?"

"It's Tyler!" she managed in a hoarse whisper.

Tall, sandy haired, lean, and agile, Stan was already moving toward the backyard, gathering speed as he passed her. "What? Is he hurt?"

Angela grabbed his arm. "No. Wait. He's..." Again that almost unbearable rush of feeling, and the difficulty of keeping her voice at a whisper instead of a wail. "He's talking!"

Stan wheeled and stared, his voice rising. "Talking? Tyler's *talking*?"

"Shhh! Yes, but don't distract him." She began pulling him toward the deck door. "Just listen."

Their beautiful boy, with his mother's dark hair and eyes, had been classified as autistic a little over a year ago. At first they'd been afraid he was deaf, now they wished that were the case. Tyler didn't laugh, rarely cried, wouldn't look them in the eye, and couldn't – or wouldn't – speak. Not a word. Not even a babble or a burble.

But now...

Angela clung to Stan's arm as they hovered just inside the screen and listened to Tyler's loud clear voice echoing back from the surrounding pines.

"But he's not saying words," Stan whispered against her ear. "It's all garbled."

"I know, but he's vocalizing, he's *articulating*. This is a huge breakthrough."

Angela had read everything available on autism but still couldn't quite grasp it. Why did Tyler hide in his own little world, locked away from his parents, from life? Why would he spend hours watching ants crawl along a board on the deck, but never, never, never look his mother in the eye unless she held his little face between her hands and forced him to meet her gaze? What had made him this way? Who's fault? Hers? Stan's? God's?

They stood there and held each other, mesmerized by the sound of their son's voice.

"You know," Stan said after a moment, "that almost sounds like a language. And listen to his inflection... like he's really saying something."

Angela stiffened as movement at the edge of the trees caught her eye. Something brown and furry was emerging from the underbrush.

"Is that–?"

"Yeah," Stan said. "A groundhog."

She watched as the chubby creature waddled up to the base of the steps and raised to a sitting position on its hind legs, facing Tyler as if listening. And then a fawn emerged from the woods and approached, followed by a bushy-tailed fox, then other deer, and squirrels, raccoons, chipmunks, and more groundhogs. Robins, blue jays, and sparrows arrived, then half a dozen mallards and drakes flapped down from above, followed by long-necked geese. Snakes slithered through the grass, side by side with bounding toads and frogs. Clouds of bees, wasps, mosquitoes, and flies hovered in the air while spiders and beetles mottled the deck posts.

Angela's initial unease surged into panic. It had happened so fast – less than a minute for their backyard to fill with all manner of creatures, all gathered before her son, facing him. She had to get Tyler inside.

Stan grabbed her arm as she reached for the door handle. "Wait."

"But those snakes–"

"Are coiled right next to the frogs. And that fox over there is sitting behind the chipmunks."

She looked up at Stan's tight face, his narrowed eyes. He was as frightened as she.

"What–?"

"Predators and prey...together." His voice trembled with awe. "They seem to be... listening."

Angela stared at the scene, trying to comprehend. Stan was right. The creatures' attention was focused on Tyler. They did seem to be listening.

"I'm scared, Stan. I want him inside."

"Just hold on a sec. Something's happening here. Whatever it is, he doesn't seem to be in any danger. Let's not disturb things by going out there."

Tyler continued speaking his gibberish, his clear, high voice the only sound. No birds cheeping, even the insects had pulled the plug on their chitinous Muzak.

And then he stopped.

Silence struck like a fist. The air lay still, not stirring a leaf. The tableau held for a heartbeat, and then, as if a signal had been given, Tyler and the animals turned from each other, he toward the house, they toward the woods.

Angela slid back the screen and rushed to her little boy. She dropped to her knees before him.

"Tyler? Tyler what just happened?"

He looked at her – of his own accord this time, without his mother's begging or face-holding – and for an instant she saw something in the depths of his pupils, something like sorrow, like anger, like fear. And then his gaze drifted left, and he was gone again.

"Tyler! Tyler, come back to me! Tyler, what were you saying to those animals? What did you tell them?"

But Tyler was through speaking. At least for now.

***

In 2012, Nate Pedersen emailed me about PS Publishing's plan for a very different Lovecraftian anthology. The conceit was that after Providence's Church of Starry Wisdom disbanded in 1877, an auction sale was organized of all the rare, occult tomes in the Church's possession. The auction house catalogued the books and released a catalogue for a private sale. Many the major occult tomes from the sale were accompanied by essays from scholars at Miskatonic University detailing the history of each book. All known copies of the catalogue were lost... until now. Would I be interested in contributing to The Starry Wisdom Library: The Catalogue of the Greatest Occult Book Auction of All Time? *Of course I would.*

For my entry I chose Robert E. Howard's infamous...

Unaussprechlichen Kulten
by
Friedrich Wilhelm von Junzt

This is a copy of the 1839 Dusseldorf German language first edition. Although of more recent vintage than most of the titles in the Church of Starry Wisdom collection, it is exceedingly rare. Said scarcity is the result of a number of factors.

Firstly, the edition was privately printed by Dr. Gottfried Mülder with a limited run of one hundred copies. Among von Junzt's papers, assembled and preserved by Alexis Ladeau after the author's untimely demise, was an array of rather vehement rejection letters from scholarly and university presses across Europe, leaving him no choice but to commission the edition himself at the press of his old friend, Dr. Mülder.

Secondly, many copies of his limited edition were burned by their owners when the circumstances of the author's demise became known.

This volume's provenance is impeccable due to its simplicity. It was discovered among the effects of Alexis Ladeau after his suicide in 1840 (indeed it is inscribed to Ladeau by von Junzt). It remained untouched in a box of miscellaneous books in the possession of Ladeau's sister Colette until her death in 1856. When her children cleaned out her belongings at her small Parisian flat, they found the tome. A French agent of the Church of Starry Wisdom purchased it directly from the estate.

Friedrich Wilhelm von Junzt created a storm of controversy when he published *Unaussprechlichen Kulten*. One of the few scholars of his time to have read the Greek version of the *Necronomicon*, he based *Unaussprechlichen Kulten* not merely on secondary sources (such as the *Al Azif* and other so-called "forbidden books"), but also upon first-hand research among primitive tribes across the globe. *Unaussprechlichen Kulten* is essentially a catalogue of rites and practices in worship of divine or semi-divine entities dating from pre-human times.

Before delving into the deities explored in the work, it might prove instructive to discuss the confusions that have arisen regarding the title. *Unaussprechlichen Kulten* is often referred to in English as *Nameless Cults* or, simply, *The Black Book*. The latter is merely descriptive, since the Dusseldorf edition is bound in black leather. *Nameless Cults*, however, is a misnomer. *Unaussprechlichen* does not translate as "nameless" and the cults described within are indeed named by the author. The confusion arises from the unauthorized edition of an English translation published by Bridewell Press of London in 1845 – some say to profit by the author's bizarre death – titled *Nameless Cults*. It lacks the original Gunther Hasse illustrations, and the text within has been translated with the same care and accuracy as the title – i.e., little or none.

The literal English translation is *Unspeakable Cults*, although some have offered *Unpronounceable Cults* as a possible alternative. Given the names of the various gods worshipped by the cults described within, the latter title is not inappropriate. However, considering the rituals described, *Unspeakable Cults* would appear to be the most apt.

The centerpiece of the text is von Junzt's description of the obscene rites he personally witnessed in worship of the toad god Tsathoggua by the People of the Monolith, near the village of Stregoicavar, in the Kingdom of Hungary. Almost as disturbing is the Cult of Ghatanothoa operating in the South China Seas, purportedly worshipping the first-born of Cthulhu. He gained access to the temple of the Kakureta Kao, the Order of the Hidden Face, in Tokyo and witnessed their rites of self-mutilation. Of more recent vintage is the Cult of Bran in the Scottish Highlands, which worships the Dark Man, an ancient king of the Picts called Bran Mak Morn.

Many of the rites involved the usual human sacrifice – infants and virgins, depending on the cult. But what seemed to have upset von Junzt's contemporaries most were his meditations on the nature of reality and the cosmos in which he leaves no room for the Judeo-Christian deity. According to him, humankind has never been master of this sphere, and its future survival is dubious at best, subject to the whim of vast Elder Entities that ruled here in the past and will return to rule again.

***

Friedrich Wilhelm von Junzt (1795–1840) was a failed poet and eccentric philosopher noted for outré cosmology. He traveled widely and joined nearly every secret society that would have him. *Unaussprechlichen Kulten*, published shortly before his death, was his signature work. Shortly after its publication he was found dead in his locked and bolted apartment. Those are established facts. The bizarre stories that began circulating immediately after his death – and incited the burning of many copies of *Unaussprechlichen Kulten* – have never been substantiated. Some say his throat bore the marks of taloned fingers; others say his throat was torn out; some claim that at the time of his death he had been involved in recreating a sacrificial rite performed by a primitive tribe in the South China Sea. It was rumored that during the post-mortem autopsy his stomach was found to contain the remnants of a partially digested fetus. None of this can be verified because both the police and autopsy reports were sealed and sent to governmental authorities in Berlin, where they languish in a warehouse.

His friend and confidant, Alexis Ladeau, possibly knew the truth. After von Junzt's death he gathered the author's papers and effects, including the early chapters of a new book he had just started. Shortly thereafter Ladeau burned the pages of the new work and slit his own throat with a straight razor.

Physical Description of the Work
- ➤ heavy black leather cover and three iron hasps; 12 x 16 inches
- ➤ 191 unnumbered pages
- ➤ 17 illustrations by Gunther Hasse distributed throughout
- ➤ inscription on the title page:

> *Zu Alexis-*
> *Mein Shipmate auf die dunklen Meere der Unendlichkeit.*
> *Friedrich*
> *22. Mai 1840*

translates to:

> To Alexis –
> My shipmate upon the dark seas of Infinity.
> Friedrich
> May 22, 1840

***

About a decade or so after The Starry Wisdom Library, *Nate Pedersen wrote to invite me to contribute to* The Dagon Collection. *According to the catalog: "It is 1929, shortly after the events in 'The Shadow Over Innsmouth.' The feds have just raided the Esoteric Order of Dagon Lodge. Now they've contracted with Pent & Serenade, Occult Auctioneers, to sell the items secured in the raid. In addition to books, this auction also features weaponry, art, jewelry, nautical items, textiles, and objects both strange and prosaic once owned by the Dagon cult." Here is my entry.*

The Whispering Shell

This lot consists of a fossil *Bolinus brandaris* shell and a water-damaged journal.

At first glance the shell appears to be a battered specimen of the common marine gastropod mollusk popularly known as the spiny sea snail or spiny conch. Malacologists, however, have identified it as a Pliocene fossil of *Bolinus brandaris*.

It was discovered boxed with a water-damaged leather-bound journal in the safe of the late Barnabas Marsh (known as Old Man Marsh) in his office at the rear of the former Masonic Hall that became the headquarters of the Esoteric Order of Dagon.

The accompanying journal appears to be the work of Eliza Orne Williamson, daughter of Alice and Benjamin Orne, granddaughter of the infamous Captain Obed Marsh. Many of the entries therein are indecipherable due to the blurring of the ink caused by water immersion. The front pages suffered the least intrusion, however, and the notebook's earliest entry is a sketch (dated October 7, 1888) of the shell itself, reproduced here.

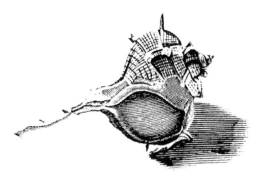

The sketch is labeled, *"The Whispering Shell."*

The first written entry, presumably entered the same day, states that Eliza found the shell while swimming out near Devil's Reef in Innsmouth Harbor. According to the entry, after assuring herself the shell was empty, Eliza held it to her ear to hear the customary sound of the sea. Instead of the amplified ambient noise that passes for the roar of the ocean, Eliza swore she heard a whispering voice. She said the whisper was too faint to make out the words, but she had no doubt it was a voice. However, when she showed it to her husband James, he said he heard only the dull roar that he'd heard in every other shell he'd ever held to his ear.

Other early entries make it clear that Eliza started the journal for the sole purpose of transcribing the whispers. After the sketch and a description of her methods (to amplify the sounds within the prehistoric shell, she employed a hearing trumpet once used by her grandfather, Obed Marsh), the water damage becomes extensive, the ink blurred and indecipherable but for an occasional isolated word that does not belong to any known language. *Y'ha-nthlei... R'lyeh... Cthulhu fhtagn... Pth'thya-l'yi.* These at least are transcribed in letters of the Latin alphabet. Later entries are not, e.g.:

In true journal style, Eliza appears to have made daily entries starting in the fall of 1888, faithfully dating each one until the spring of 1902. Then the dating becomes sporadic and the Latin alphabet gives way to scribbled runelike characters in a language no one has been able to identify.

Sometime in the early twentieth century she fell into a depression after the suicide of her eldest son, Douglas. Why he shot himself, no one knows, but soon afterward, Eliza wandered off, leaving everything behind, and was never seen again.

After her disappearance, the Whispering Shell and the journal came to reside with Barnabas Marsh. Rumor has it that Barnabas kept the shell with him at all times and used it to identify what he termed "the Deep Trait." He would ask random individuals to listen to the shell. If they heard whispered words instead of the "ocean," he told them they carried "the Deep Trait" and would invite them to join the Esoteric Order of Dagon. He left no explanation of "the Deep Trait" other than to say that it was far more widespread than he or anyone had imagined. Since he did not survive the Bureau of Investigation's raid on the EoD, he is not available for clarification.

Certain knowledgeable individuals within the Bureau have advised that the Whispering Shell be filled with cement before being put up for bid. They have been overruled but, in way of compromise, the Whispering Shell comes with a warning: *Listen at your own risk.*

***

Back in 2004, Garrett Peck and Keith Gouveia were editing an anthology of short-shorts of less than 500 words called Small Bites. *The book is virtually impossible to find so I'm reprinting my contribution here. The title and epistolary format is a nod to C. S. Lewis. I'm pretty sure only a tiny fraction of the people who read it made the connection.*

The Tapeworm Letters

Dear Tape (we've been together so long I feel I can use

your first name) -

This will be my last letter. Of course I don't know if you read the others. Like them I'm printing this very small on a scrap of paper which I'll swallow. NB ~~you dirty~~ THIS IS MY LAST SCRAP!!!

So, if you're reading this, Tape, old buddy, take heed: YOU'RE KILLING US!!!

Yeah, that's right, ~~you lousy~~ I said US!!!!

We both know you sank your hooks into my gut and been sucking my blood since soon after I washed up here. One of your eggs must have been on a piece of fruit or in one of those crabs I caught and had to eat raw, or something like that. Doesn't matter how. You're here.

That's okay up to a point. I've always been a live-and-let-live kind of guy. And anyway, you were here on the atoll first. At least your egg was. So I'm cool with you being in me - UP TO A POINT!!!

What I'm not cool with is you taking advantage of the situation and bleeding me dry ~~you greedy little fucker~~.

God, it's hot today. No shade since the storm knocked down all the trees. Feels like the sun's cooking my brain. NOT THAT YOU CARE!!! Always pretty much the same temperature where you are.

But here's my point ~~you goddamn bloodsucking~~ You're taking too much, especially now that the trees are dead. All I've got is berries and whatever crabs and fish I can catch. And with the way I'm losing weight and strength, I'm catching less and less.

But do you care? OBVIOUSLY NOT!!! But listen up ~~you dirty, shit-dwelling~~ Here's a newsflash: If I die, YOU die. Get it? You can't live without me ~~because you're a fucking parasi~~

Just thought I saw someone walking down the beach but it was just my imagination. Been seeing a lot of strange things lately. Hearing voices too.

God, I'm so hungry.

So here's the deal, Tape: You take a little less and leave

me a little more. That's all I'm asking. It's reasonable, don't you think? Because I don't want to die and neither do you.

But if you won't listen to reason, ~~motherfu~~ I'll have to get drastic. "Get medieval on yo ass." That's a line from a movie. Must have watched it a million times but for the life of me I can't remember its name. God, will I ever see another movie?

Anyway, if I don't see some improvement, you're going to get a gasoline bath. Yeah, that's right. The raft's ruined and the motor's dead, but there's still gas in the tank. You don't straighten up, ~~you little cocksu~~ I'm going to have to chug some. Then I'll light it with a signal flare. THEN YOU'LL BE SORRY!!!!

So be reasonable, Tape. We need each other.

Your friend,
Sam

***

Back in 2009, when I first joined Twitter, I experimented with a brief, episodic tale of my triffids revolting, told in the requisite 140-character increments. By 2016, when they revolted again, I was much more comfortable with the format and the result was a more elaborate and detailed telling. Forty-plus tweets totaling a mere 1000 words over 12 days.

The Dozen Days of the Triffids

WED – 2/24/16
The crazy temperature swings in the NE have confused my triffids. Usually dormant in Feb, they're presently moving about and...agitated.

Really high winds tonight, but the triffids seem to be

relishing it...milling about. Not to worry -- they're penned.

THUR – 2/25
Raining again. The triffids are loving the moisture. Getting awful big, and there seems to be more of them. The pen's getting crowded.

Strange...usually the gentle clicking of the triffids is like white noise...lulling. Tonight it's really loud, and setting me on edge

FRI – 2/26
Hmmm...a part of the fence on the triffids' pen was blown down last night. I hope none got out. Damn, I wish I'd counted them recently.

Checked the woods and found a trail of turned-up leaves. No deer did that. Have to face it: One of the triffids got out. Maybe more. Crap.

still no sign of the missing triffid (triffids?). Can't report it...illegal here to raise them in NJ. Worried...this is just like 2009.

keeping News12NJ on for reports of triffid sightings. None so far. Maybe I dodged a bullet and none escaped.

SAT – 2/27
Triffid pen okay this AM. No reports of sightings. Shaken by the triffid kill (dead rabbit) on my front porch. An offering? Or a warning?

found a decomposing deer in the woods about 250 ft from the house. Signs of multiple triffid feedings. Crap. This means big trouble. CRAP!

time for a triffid hunt. Got my Benelli Super Black Eagle II autoloading 12-gauge packed with 3.5-inch double-0 magnums. Wish me luck.

Of course, a flamethrower would be better, but I'm holding that in reserve. Don't want to set the woods ablaze...yet.

came up empty on the hunt. Damn triffids are eluding me. News-12-NJ has no reports of sightings. This is still manageable.

SUN – 2/28
Yesterday I waited with the Benelli near the dead deer, figuring the triffids would come back to feed. They didn't. Today I go after them.

spent the whole damn day hunting the escaped triffids - not a sign of them. Like they're avoiding me. But triffids can't think. Right?

can't sleep due to the noise from the remaining triffids in the pen. They're clicking like demented castanets. What the hell is going on?

MON – 2/29
was awakened by =silence= this AM. No triffid clicking. Looked out and they're gone - ALL of them. Somehow they opened the pen's gate.

Roamed the woods with the Benelli all day but no sign of triffids. I'm a little worried. More than a little. What's going on?

Checked the yard and found the flower beds torn up. Vandalized by triffids? Is that possible? This is getting creepy now.

quiet tonight without the triffids. The pen is empty. Where could they have gone? Not the state park, I hope. If so, I'm screwed.

TUE – 3/1
the yard is completely torn up – triffid tracks all over. A big

hole in the chain-link fence by the reservoir. They've broken into the state park.

Gonna be even harder to find them now. And...wait... 3 shapes moving away thru the reservoir water. OMG! TRIFFIDS CAN SWIM!

I wish triffids would attack each other, but what's the point? They're carnivores. Be like offering broccoli to Venus flytraps

Yikes! Came home tonight and ran over a triffid in my driveway. Stepped out in front of me. I dumped its crushed remains in the reservoir.

WED – 3/2
I'll have to spend the morning sweeping up. The triffid I killed was somehow thrown thru the picture window. They're mad and I'm worried.

Looked to see a tangent of triffids surrounding the house - everywhere except the pen... standing around...clicking...waiting?

The phone is out. Triffids dug up the land-line. How do I explain this to the phone company? I think I'll just let it be and use my cell.

Tried to drive out to a motel but found the garage door dented just enough to keep it from lifting. The triffids did it. I'm trapped here.

THUR – 3/3
Didn't sleep all night due to the triffids' incessant clicking. They're all around the house, just milling about. I'm going nuts.

Someone suggested driving them away with bad music. Worth a try. I've got the B-52s' "Rock Lobster" looped and blasting.

OK, the triffids are still here, so B-52s not working. Gonna blast out some Kanye and see how they like that.

Gah! Kanye made the triffids insane! They smashed thru the porch to attack the speakers. I'm barricaded in the study while they run amok!

Triffids back in the yard now...waiting for dark? I'm trapped. The place is a shambles. And they stole my cell phone. Can they think? WTF?

The triffids have me cut off from the outside world. My only contact is my laptop via an Optimum hotspot. Could be worse. At least no Kanye

The triffids are still in the yard, digging out by the transformer. You don't think they're trying to cut the pow

FRI – 3/4
Sneaked out at dawn and flipped on the generator. Along the way I blasted a whole bunch of triffids with the Benelli. I've had it!

The triffids have retreated. Licking their wounds? Regrouping? It's not over yet. Didn't get them all. May have to take it to them.

So I've got power again and managed to do some real damage to the triffids. Now I've got to deal with the carcasses. Blech.

The dead triffids are in the compost heap...gotta take it to the survivors and go hunting at first light. Maybe half a dozen left.

Sat – 3/5
1/2 - Woke up this AM and found all the surviving triffids back in their plot. WTF???? But they've stomped the fence flat.

2/2 - Was that the point of all this? Don't fence me in? They could've sung me the song instead. I don't trust them...MY TRIFFIDS MUST DIE!

Went out to the triffids 3 times with the shotgun today. Couldn't blast them. My cuties look so happy rooted there. Seems like murder.

SUN – 3/6
All quiet here with the triffids nestled in their fenceless plot. I see they killed a careless rabbit. (Bon appetit.) Everywhere else in the US it's Remember the Alamo day. Around here it's Remember the Days of the Triffids. (Aren't they cute?)

***

I'm going to call this fiction, because it sort of is. It evolved out of my keynote address to the Twilight Zone Magazine *Dimension Awards ceremony in 1985. (The first, last, and only Dimension Awards, held in the Tower Suite of the Time-Life Building.) Two of the winners were newcomers whose work I admired: John Skipp and David J. Schow; we've remained friends ever since. The crowd expected some serious remarks about the state of weird fiction and where it was going. Instead they heard...this. Afterward,* TZ *editor Michael Blaine asked me to write it up for publication in the mag, and so here you have it. (Trust me – I was funnier live.)*

TZ Terror

Writing horror is a scary business. And it's getting scarier. Mainly because it's getting harder and harder to scare people.

Even the famous horror writer's handbook, *Neat and Scary Stuff to Write,* is hard pressed to come up with new ideas. In fact, for the first time in modern, memory, *Neat and Scary Stuff to Write* is late. And let me tell you, that's really scary!

For those of you who don't know, *Neat and Scary Stuff to Write* (NASSTW or "Nastoo" to us insiders) is the fantasy-horror writer's source-book published annually by the Miskatonic University Press in Arkham, Massachusetts. It is analogous to, but *long* predates, the mysterious post office box in Schenectady used by science fiction writers. NASSTW is even more mysterious. As soon as a subscriber uses one of the story ideas listed in its pages, that particular idea disappears from all other existing copies.

All copies are sent out first-class mail on January 2nd of each year. Consider that fact for a moment and you have the answer to the oft asked question as to why so many famous horror writers hail from New England. Now you know why Peter Straub moved from Britain to Connecticut. And why Stephen King, who could buy most of the Lesser Antilles, still resides in Maine.

They get their copies first! Yes! Living in the same postal zone as Arkham, MA, gives them first dibs on the best ideas in the book. That's why they're the best-selling horror writers in the world.

Many feel Stephen King has taken unfair advantage of his geographical position – has been downright piggy, in fact – with his early access to NASSTW. But word has come down from Miskatonic U. that he has been severely reprimanded. And you don't ignore a reprimand from those eldritch quarters. (If I remember correctly, the last writer to ignore a reprimand was a fellow named Ambrose Bierce.)

But all that aside, the fact remains that the 1985 edition of *Neat and Scary Stuff to Write* is late. And I can't help but think that it's because even the folks at ol' MU are strapped for new topics to scare people.

A little perspective, if you will: Consider how easy it used to be to scare people. Fifty years ago women fainted in the theaters at the sight of Boris Karloff as that patchwork quilt of human flesh in *Frankenstein*. My mother tells me that back in the '30s when she was a teenager, she heard about this new creepy movie called *Dracula,* so she got the Stoker novel out of the library and read it. The book so terrified her that she slept with a rosary around her neck for months and refused to see the movie when it came to town.

Traditional things-that-go-bump-in-the-night like werewolves and vampires and man-made monsters were potent horrors half a century ago.

Things have changed. We live in a different world now. We've seen extermination camps and atom bombs. For the last thirty years we've had the power to turn our planet into a sterile dirt bomb lofting through space.

Of course, we haven't done so yet and hopefully won't, but in the face of that sort of stuff – which is very scary but not at *all* neat – vampires and Frankenstein creatures are nothing. In fact, they've become so trivialized that they're now used to hawk cereal to little kids.

Frankenberry!

County Chocula!

Booberry!

Oy!

Fifty – hell, *fifteen* – years *ago,* that kind of ad campaign would have been unthinkable. Which wasn't fair. I mean, I would have *loved* any one of those cereals when I was a kid. Other kids might have been put off, but I wasn't like other kids. While they were building Revell plastic battleships and bombers, I was building an Aurora plastic Frankenstein monster with the glow-in-the-dark face. I know I'd've thought Frankenberry was neat. Of course, my folks never would've let me have any. Just like they wouldn't let me read EC Comics. But I found ways to buy and read *Weird Science* and *Tales from the Crypt,* so I imagine I'd have found a way to get a daily fix of Count Chocula.

But what I'm getting at is that it's pretty damn hard to scare people who grow up starting off every morning with a bowl of Booberry while watching a videotape of *Friday the 13th* for the ninety-second time!

I mean, what's next? And what will *their* kids eat for breakfast?

Can you see it? A guy in a hockey mask with a bloody' machete across his shoulder and a box of cereal in his hand: "New vitamin-fortified JASONBERRY! Delicious little puffs of wheat in the shapes of eight different sharp-edged farm tools, with just the right touch of sugary red, Jasonberry-flavored coating on each delicious little point! JASONBERRY! Get it... before he gets you!" Spare me.

Another trend potentially inimical to the future of horror fiction is the recent academic interest shown toward the genre. This could be the true kiss of death.

What if horror fiction becomes, like, I mean, totally respectable? If there comes a day when you can actually be seen reading it in public? When you no longer have to tear the cover off a sleazy porno novel and wrap it around your most recent horror purchase so you can read it on the bus or the subway without feeling like some sort of deviant?

This is not a groundless fear. Look at science fiction – it was almost *ruined* by respectability! The same fate could befall horror fiction. Horror writers are particularly vulnerable to the seductive call of academic acceptance.

Imagine: The college professor seeks, finds, and corners the horror writer at the bar in the hotel where the fantasy convention is being held. He tells him how impressed he was with the crucial scene in his last novel, *The Necrodancer,* in which the reanimated corpse of the nameless wino plucks out the eyes of the rich industrialist and serves them in martinis to the cocktail party guests. What a blistering political statement! What a monumentally scathing commentary on the social and economic dichotomies intrinsic to western culture! And would you care to lecture my class at Columbia on modern novelists?

Now, the horror writer is not a terribly political person. In fact, he assumes Carter is still president. He was up until four in the morning and is already on his third Jack Daniels before breakfast; he dimly remembers that he wrote that scene because he thought it was a neat-o gross-out, and vaguely hoped it might catch the eye (sorry!) of a producer-director of low budget splatter films.

But does he say so? Does he deflate such praise – *diminish* himself – by telling the truth?

Hell, no!

"Yeah, those damn dichotomies," he says. *"Damn* those dichotomies! Always did tick me off!"

Don't be too hard on the fellow. He's been accused for years of (God forbid) entertaining his readers. Now he's being praised for relevance, social significance, and maybe even (oh, lord) *literature!*

What's so wrong with that? you say.

Plenty!

Think about it. The next time he sits down at the trusty old word processor he might be thinking about writing something that will please and engender more praise from fellows like the one in the bar, or something that might coax some kind words from Christopher Lehmann-Haupt of the *New York Times.* And if he succeeds, others will follow. Pretty soon there will be a whole crew of horror authors writing to please the academicians and the *Times* and everybody but the reader.

And before you know it, they won't be writing horror anymore.

Which may be the best thing for them. Because we're all pretty well stuck without our annual copies of NASSTW. And don't think the top names in horror fiction don't

F. PAUL WILSON

know it. The smart ones have been planning ahead for the day when they won't be able to scare people anymore. As I'm sure you all know, in lieu of royalties for his last two books, Stephen King accepted controlling interest in the Ralston-Purina company.

It's true! He's already got two new products in line for distribution. Cujo Kibble – in the shape of little bats and Volkswagens; and Church Chow, for those cat lovers who want their pet to keep coming back... and back... and back.

The rest of us aren't so fortunate. We keep sitting at our desks before our lifeless word processors as we stare out of our windows and wait for the postman – not hoping he has a check from the publisher, but praying he'll bring the new *Neat and Scary Stuff to Write.* For without that, there'll be *no* checks from any publishers.

If any writers out there have received their 1985 copy of NASSTW, *please* contact me immediately care of *TZ.*

Until then, I'll have to make do writing westerns and (ugh) romances. And articles like this one.

Help.

***

Done in 2001 for Del and Sue Howison's charity anthology, The Altruistic Alphabet. *Of course I picked* **F**. *(And committed poetry. I don't do poetry, so this might be the only poem of mine you'll ever see.) The first was a trial run; the second was published.*

F

F is for FRUMCRUNCH, a hideous beast,
A nuveau rich monster, a real arriviste.
He'll dress like a yuppie, and smile like a priest,
Then crack your skull open and make you its feast.

F is for FEAR that waits in the night,

That lurks 'neath the bed where it's hidden from sight.
It's small in the day, a smidgen in height,
But swells zillionfold when you turn out the light.

***

Back in 1996, Nicholas Royle polled a zillion writers about their dreams and published them in The Tiger Garden. *Here's mine. I can't see any hidden meaning here.*

The Dream

This dream has recurred throughout my life, but *only* when I have a fever. I finding myself running atop rainbows of colors that are moving under me like a giant treadmill. The colors stretch from horizon to horizon and they're rolling *fast*. I have no destination...I'm simply running like crazy to maintain my position as the colors move under me. The sky is blindingly bright and I'm hot because I've got to keep running and running atop these moving colors.

***

In 1996, Stephen Jones polled his writer friends for any supernatural experiences they might have had. The intended collection was to be called Ghostly Encounters *but that changed to* Dancing with the Dark. *Hidebound skeptic that I am, I've never had something I could call a supernatural experience. Not wanting to be left out, however, I related a story my mother used to tell us.*

The Glowing Hand

This is a third-hand supernatural experience. It happened to my aunt, and as a child I heard it from my mother. Ours was an Irish Catholic household. My father may have been born in Glasgow and raised in Liverpool, but my mother was Mary Elizabeth Sullivan from rural New England. Trust me, it was an Irish Catholic home, where we believed that prayer worked, that statues of the Virgin could weep real tears, that holy people could develop the Stigmata, and that a miracle could be just around the corner.

So I was well primed at age five to experience my first true *frisson* during my mother's recounting of Aunt Margaret's vision of the glowing hand.

***

Aunt Margaret had been sleeping peacefully when she awoke in the dead of night. She opened her eyes and noticed a glow from the hall outside their bedroom door. At first she thought her husband had left the living room light on, but it wasn't that kind of light. This was much paler...almost white.

And it seemed to be growing brighter.

No...not brighter. Closer.

The light was coming down the hall...toward their bedroom door. She was just reaching for Uncle Bill, to wake him, when she saw it: a hand, glowing as white and pale as the moon, floating down the hall outside her bedroom. The sight of it, and the possibility that it was going to float into the bedroom, paralyzed her.

But the hand didn't turn. Instead, it continued its slow pace down the hall, and soon after passing from sight, the glow faded, leaving the house in darkness.

Margaret woke Bill and together they searched the house, waking twelve-year-old Billy in the process. He'd seen nothing either, and the apparition was laid off as a nightmare.

But the next night Margaret awoke and once again saw the glowing hand making its way down the hall. This time, after it passed her door, she leaped from bed and ran out into the hall just in time to see it fading from view...outside Billy's door. She looked in on her son and found him sleeping peacefully. Still, the sight of that hand hovering outside his door had filled her with a terrible foreboding.

The next night she didn't have to wake up because she hadn't been able to sleep a wink. And then it happened again. Shortly after two a.m., the glow began at the far end of the hall. But this time Margaret wasn't going to sit in bed and wait for it. She got up and went to the bedroom door. And there, drifting through the air not two feet from her, was the hand, glowing brighter than ever. But this time – saints preserve us –*clutched in its glowing fingers was a long, sharp knife!*

Margaret almost fainted, but she hung on and stumbled after the apparition as it continued down the hall, *and passed right through the door to Billy's room!*

She lunged forward, burst into the room, just in time to see the hand plunge its knife into Billy's abdomen!

Billy didn't stir. He seemed completely unaware that anything was happening –until he and his father were awakened by Margaret's scream.

But the hand and its knife were gone, and once again the whole experience was written off as a nightmare.

But not for long. Billy doubled over with acute abdominal pain the next day and had to have an emergency appendectomy.

—

No one ever offered an explanation, or even a supernatural rationale for these "warnings" that Billy would soon be going "under the knife." It was one of those things that just happen. And that's probably why the story chilled me so. Something like that could *just happen.*

Of course I had my mother tell it and retell it until she was sick of the story. But every time she came to the part where the ghostly knife plunged into Cousin Billy's belly....*Brrr!*

I never forgot the story, and even had a character retell it in one of my novels.

***

1963 was an absolutely wonderful 6-issue comic book series from Image in 1993. Written by Alan Moore and drawn by Steve Bissette and Rick Veitch, it parodied the Marvel Comics of, well, 1963. When I gushed about it to Steve at a NECon, he said they were looking for people to write letters to "Affable Al," the editor (Alan Moore). So I did. It appeared in The Tomorrow Syndicate *(December 1993). (It's also the first appearance of a character from the Secret History: the hack writer P. Frank Winslow, who mentions this very letter in* Bloodline.*) Alan's hilarious response follows.*

(NB: I placed this under "Fiction" because it's a made-up person writing a made-up editor about a made-up malady.)

Letter to the Editor of *1963*

P. Frank Winslow
662 Rolling Dune Way
Blech, N.J.

Dear Mr. Al,

Your writing is making me sick! Don't get me wrong! I LOVE your wonderful comics! But for the last few months or so, I've noticed strange symptoms while reading certain titles. The first occurred during *The Tomorrow Syndicate* #8 when I began to itch while reading "Fear Is A Fossilized Fiend." During "The Thrall of the Threatening Three" in *The Fury* #11, I developed my first hive. An ugly bumpy itchy rash broke out all over my body while reading "Where Wait the Writhing Wraiths of War" in *Mystery Inc* #20. But the very worst happened in the first paragraph of "Al's Amphitheatre" in the latest *Tales From Beyond*. After reading the first 95 words – 55 of which began with the letter M – I began to wheeze, my entire body began to swell until my throat closed! I had to be rushed to the hospital where they performed an emergency tracheotomy and placed me on a respirator! Only after I was filled with cortisone for days did I begin to breathe on my own again!!! The doctors diagnosed my condition as a rare allergy – to alliteration!!!! They warned me that I had to give up Sixty-Three comics or the next S-pager could be my last!!!! So please, AI! Stop the alliteration!!! Or at least limit it to three- and four-word runs. I've started desensitization therapy and I can handle those now. But if you go on longer than that, gosh knows what'll happen. I might die!!!! Don't let this True Believer down!

Awaiting your reply,

Reply:

Well, wobbly one, we wouldn't want Whimpering Winslow to wane and weaken woefully when wounded by the wit, wisdom and wizardry whipped out weekly by our whacky wazir of wonderment! Wayfarer, we'd weep, wail and whine like women at such wicked and wanton wastage! We'd wheeze, waver and whiten worryingly! Why, we wouldn't wonder if we warranted a whipping for willingly warping the wigs of warm-hearted, worthy whipper-snappers the world over!! Does that answer your question, quivering one?

REVIEWS

I'm not a good reviewer. I hate to say anything bad about a fellow author's work because I know what goes into writing a novel. Okay, I'll make an exception with a household name who's bulletproof and I think is phoning it in.

Over the years I did occasional book reviews for the Asbury Park Press, Reason Magazine, Science Fiction Review, SF & Fantasy Book Review, Invictus, *and* The Intergalactic Reporter. *I did a few movie reviews for* Yucsnuc *and comic book reviews for Orson Scott Card's* Short Form. *I can find only a few of these. Just as well, I suppose.*

BEMs & Such - 505

That Comic Book Stuff - 508

Alongside Night - 530

The Number of the Beast – 534

Red Dragon - 540

Thought Probes - 542

For Us, the Living - 544

The Mandalorian - 549

The *Fringe* Rip-off - 550

Fast-Forward Movie Reviews - 552

BEMs & Such

Back in 1973 I had the temerity to (briefly) author a review column (BEMs & Such) *in a libertarian fanzine called* Invictus. *The first is an introductory note (sadly, both the SFBC and Dick Witter are gone) and the second is the only review I could find. I may have done others. If I find them, I'll add them here.*

from *Invictus* #27, April-May 1973

This is the first installment of a continuing column dealing specifically with science fiction – there will be occasional tangents into noteworthy fantasy, but as a rule I'll stick to the real thing.

Science fiction is experiencing one of its cyclic surges of popularity and simultaneously undergoing significant changes. The old romantic, man-against-the-universe, rugged individualist, pro-technology prototype is being challenged by a more cynical, collectivist, anti-technology mood. There's good reading on both sides, and this column will attempt to help *Invictus* readers sift through the junk that takes up a discouraging amount of space on the current sf bookshelves. And besides discussing individual books of interest, I'll occasionally give an overview of an author with a good track record.

But first you've got to know where to get good sf without going broke and without running all over town. Here are two suggestions:

1) The Science Fiction Book Club -- probably the only book club in the world in which the reader actually comes out ahead. In the current offer (on the back of any sf magazine) you get four hardcover books for a dime and the promise to buy four more in the next year. For your dime, I would suggest you pick the collections – The Foundation Trilogy, A Treasury of Great SF, The SF Hall of Fame, The Hugo Winners, etc. The monthly selections run in the neighborhood of $1:50 to $2.50, and each bulletin gives you ten choices, most of which are excellent. So, for less than ten bucks you can wind up with eight hardcover books with nice dust jackets (often by artists like Frazetta). And after you've fulfilled your contract, you just quit and join again.

2) The F. & S.F. Book Co., PO Box 415, Staten Island, N.Y. 10302 is run by Dick Witter, with whom I have deal for over a decade but have never met. He carries a full line of in-print hard- and softcover sf along with some used editions and old magazines. A 10% discount is given on orders over $10; 20% off orders over $25. Your order is usually on its way the same day it's received and he sends you a separate note informing you of same. A quarterly catalogue is free on request.

from *Invictus* #28, June 1973

Four by Gerrold

I bought *When HARLIE Was* One through the Science Fiction Book Club on a whim; I'd never heard of David Gerrold, but the synopsis sounded good. It turned out to be one of the most enjoyable reads I've had in a long time. HARLIE (a Human Analog Robot Life Input Equivalents) is a supercomputer at a quasi-adolescent stage of development who – and Gerrold soon has you thinking of the computer as a *who* rather than an *it* – is trying to identify with humans while existing in a subculture of other computers. This is one of the story's more interesting concepts: HARLIE can link to other machines in all parts of the globe, communicate with them, outwit them and get desired feedback. His goals are his own and in their pursuit he mixes with human frailties and interdepartmental politics; some of the results are outrageous. His greatest desire, however, is to construct a computer superior to himself in all ways – a Graphic Omniscient Device – G.O.D. (The imagery is certainly Nietzschean.) The G.O.D. proposal and HARLIE's struggle to justify the continuing expense of his existence to the company's accounting department make for science-fiction at its best. I recommend it without reservation. (It's also available from Ballantine in paper.)

Incidentally, the technical background for *HARLIE* was handled in such a deft, matter-of-fact manner that I assumed David Gerrold to be a full-timer in the computer field and an s-f moonlighter. Not a chance. He's a professional writer in his late twenties with a B. A. in theatre arts from USC. His first piece of writing to hit the public eye was "The Trouble with Tribbles," Star Trek's most delightful episode. Ballantine recently released two Star Trek books by Gerrold: *The Trouble with Tribbles* traces the screenplay from inception to production and covers all the problems and personalities in between; an interesting look at what goes into a single episode of a TV series. The other is *The World of Star Trek*, which is mainly for dedicated Trekkies.

The Man Who Folded Himself lacks *HARLIE*'s touch of whimsy but is no less interesting. Heinlein, Asimov and Silverberg have done some fascinating things with the time travel concept and with the paradoxes which might ensue should it ever become a reality. Well, Gerrold outdoes them all paradox-wise in this one. Danny Eakins thought that his uncle would leave him a huge fortune but wound up instead with a simple black leather belt. Not so simple, really – the belt is a highly complex instrument that will move the wearer through time. Danny immediately begins hopping all over the space-time continuum, doubling back on himself and causing myriad branchings in the time stream. Piling paradox upon paradox, he's constantly bumping into other versions of himself; inevitably, a couple of the Dannies get around to the ultimate onanism. It's all very well handled, however, and Gerrold manages to keep things moving. *The Man Who Folded Himself* is more personal than *HARLIE* but of equal quality.

Start reading David Gerrold now. I have a feeling he'll be around for a long time and his novels will probably be reprinted time and time again; but read them now before future imitators steal their originality.

That Comic Book Stuff

Back in the late 80s I did a few review columns for Scott Card's Short Form *reviewzine. They appeared in the first two issues and then, although I had submitted a column, he didn't include it in the third issue (which he listed as a combo of issues 3 & 4). No explanation. No one else was covering comic books, so maybe he decided to stick strictly to prose reviews. Whatever. Here are the two that were published. I have no copy of the third column that was never pubbed, but I've included a partial column (the start of #4) plus a best of 1987 list that was to go along with #3.*

Keep in mind that comic books were just on the cusp of being appreciated as more than kids' stuff. I began writing the column in 1987, the year Watchmen *first saw print. I sensed something big happening and I wanted to talk about it.*

Column #1 (Winter 1987)

Yes, I'm going to be talking about comic books here. Now, now... take your nose out of the air and listen: About half a dozen years ago, after a two-decade hiatus, I started reading comic books again. No, I did not suffer an acute personality regression or a mental-critical breakdown. I merely kept an open mind and found some exciting, well-crafted, worthwhile entertainment. If you can do the same, you might be in for some enjoyable experiences.

This column is not for the active comic fan or aficionado – they will find nothing new here but my personal opinions. It will be geared to those of you interested enough in imaginative fiction and storytelling to put aside those preconceived notions and reservations – most of them well founded – and take a look at what's going on in a much maligned and misunderstood field that had been coming of age right under our noses.

I hope to provide you with an overview of who and what is worthwhile in current comics.

Why Me?

Why not? At age six I began reading *Uncle Scrooge* and the EC horror titles, and continued reading comics into the early 60s. I stopped when the comics went superhero crazy. (There's one of my prejudices: Superpowered guys and gals flying around in skintight suits with no rational means of propulsion turn me off.). I thought I had outgrown comics. I had and I hadn't. I had certainly outgrown superhero comics.

I wrote a few scripts for Warren's *Creepy* and *Eerie* in the 70s when I was between novels and stories, and kept an eye on the field without really reading much. Mainly because nothing in comics interested me. But comics began to change in the late 70s. What I call the "Independent Age" began then, and it has changed the face of comics.

Capsule History

First there was the Golden Age. This is generally accepted as the period from the birth of the comic book in the 30s to the anti-comics controversy in the early 50s generated by Dr. Frederic Wertham's book, *Seduction of the Innocent.*

The Silver Age is said to have started when the revamped *Flash* appeared in Showcase #4 in 1956. A new age, the Independent Age, began with the publication of the first issue of *Cerebus* in early 1978. (More on *Cerebus* at another time.)

Through the late 60s and most of the 70s, comic books were published by either a shrinking number of major companies, or tiny underground publishers (and underground comics are most definitely an acquired taste). But with the advent of specialty shops and comic shops, smaller publishers (called "groundlevel" at first but now known as "independents") with no newsstand distribution found an outlet for their wares. These titles were generally grittier, riskier, and more imaginative than the moribund superheroes.

The majors, of which only Marvel and DC remain today, began to publish more mature comics and sell them directly to the comic and specialty shops. The overall result has been a revitalization of the entire industry. The past year has seen an explosion of titles from new independent publishers.

With few exceptions, the comic books reviewed here will be either from independent publishers or direct sale issues from the majors. They cost more because of smaller press runs and higher grade paper, which gives color quality you could never get on newsprint.

Skintight

That doesn't mean I won't mention a worthy newsstand comic when it pops up. One comes to mind right now.

BATMAN (DC, color, $0.75) is one of the few skintight costumed heroes I can tolerate. Maybe that's because he doesn't fly, doesn't have X-ray vision, can't climb walls like a spider, and so on. He's just a very capable man who is maybe a little bit mad. He has been given new life of late by writer-artist Frank Miller.

It took a long time for the Batman to recover from the indignities of the TV series, but now he's back with (if you'll pardon me) a vengeance. Earlier in the year we had a 4-issue limited series called *The Dark Knight Returns*, written and illustrated by Frank Miller, which is now available for $12.95 in a single large-size trade paperback in places like B. Dalton and Waldenbooks as well as your friendly neighborhood comic shop.

It takes place in a Gotham that no longer wants him. It's densely written and illustrated (you have to *read* this one, chillun – looking at the pictures alone won't do) and like good sf, what's going on in the background is as important as the main action. Buy a copy, settle back, and take your time with it. You won't regret it.

Miller has also written a Batman flashback being serialized in the current newsstand issues. It's called *Year One*, and it chronicles Batman's first year in costume, not 100 percent sure of himself, feeling his way along as he challenges all of Gotham's thugs – the ones on the street and the ones in city hall. As illustrated by David Mazzucceli, it's wonderfully dark and brooding.

The storyline started with issue 404. I've just read the second installment and it's everything you could ask for. Back issues can easily be obtained. Renew your acquaintance with this old friend. You may not recognize him.

Reid Gets His MTV

On the other end of the spectrum, we have REID FLEMING, WORLD'S TOUGHEST MILKMAN (Eclipse, b&w, $2.00). David Boswell invented Reid for *The Georgia Straight*, a Vancouver underground paper. He self-printed a collection in 1980 and Eclipse Comics has picked up Reid as a regular. It reprinted the original collection as a "special" and now has the first official issue in the shops. (Get that? Issue 1 is really the second issue. The "special" is also numbered 1.)

Reid Fleming is easily the most belligerent being in comics. He will pick a fight with anyone, anywhere, at the slightest provocation. If it happens to be time for his favorite soap opera ("The Dangers of Ivan"), he will walk into a stranger's home and change the TV channel. But he can be very funny at times. The best laughs are in the first ("special") issue; the second issue (#1) has superior pen work but fewer punchlines since it is only an installment in a longer story. Try it. How far wrong can you go with a title like that?

Hot Series

ELECTRA: ASSASSIN (Epic, $1.50; Frank Miller scripting again, this time with the inimitable Bill Sienkiewicz doing the art. The 6th installment of an 8-issue series is currently in the stores.) It's about a dazzlingly beautiful long-legged human killing machine named Electra. It has sardonic humor, kinky sex, and ultraviolence.

The writing is fragmented, disjointed, even psychotic at times. It can be hard going but -worth every ounce of effort.

The accompanying art is indescribable, painted rather than drawn and idiosyncratic as the script. It has to be seen to be appreciated or believed! This one would have been impossible to do on newsprint. I love it. I pounce on every issue. The only comic I search out with greater anticipation is...

WATCHMEN – (DC. $1.50). I must mention this series of comic books. It will run 12 issues. Issue 7 is out now (early December). I don't want to say too much about the story because it's only half published, but I can't say enough about the quality here. The script is by Alan Moore, an Englishman who has been gradually setting new standards of quality for comic book writing; the art is by Dave Gibbons.

Story and art mesh perfectly. The covers are low key, serving also as the first panel of the story. The cover of #1 is already a classic: a bright yellow smiley-face button marred by a single splotch of blood. The premise: An alternate America where costumed superheroes really existed. Only one of them had super powers, the others were just masked avengers – some nice guys, some psychotic, some profit-oriented.

But their day is past – they have been outlawed as vigilantes. They are in retirement... and someone is killing them off one by one. It's a murder mystery, it's alternate-world SF, it's character study, it's violent, sexy, and excellent. If Moore and Gibbons can maintain the quality, I'll be recommending *Watchmen* for a Nebula. Start buying the back issues and reading them now. This is a milestone.

Short Takes

THE QUESTION (DC, color, $1.50). A revival of Ditko's backup series for his *Blue Beetle* issues from Charleton in 1967. I've read only the first issue so far. It's got a violent ending in which our faceless, crime-fighting hero is beaten to a pulp, shot through the head, and thrown in the river. Maybe this will be a one-shot. I'm looking for #2.

NEMO, THE CLASSIC COMICS LIBRARY #23 (Fantagraphics, b&w, $3.50). This is a bimonthly magazine devoted to newspaper comic strips. I mention this issue because it contains the fanciful 14-week *Little Orphan Annie* sequence from 1937 in which Annie meets God. Yes, God. Who else could the bearded, ageless, kindly, omnipotent, omniscient Mr. Am be but "I Am that I Am"? The sequence also features the Asp, my favorite character in the series. It was previously reprinted in *Arf! The Life and Hard Times of Little Orphan Annie* (Arlington House, 1970). I'll do a whole column on *LOA* sometime soon.

THE FACE #1 (Ace, b&w, $1.75). I bought this because Steve Ditko did the pencils, but found it unimaginative and grossly overpriced. This is a modernization of a crime-fighter character who appeared in the 1940s. He wears a scary mask to frighten his criminal foes. He wasn't very interesting back then and neither is he now. Skip this one unless you're a Ditko completist.

Homework

There. That ought to give you something to chew on for the next three months. Use the time to pick up on some of the titles I've mentioned. Start with the first three issues of WATCHMEN; if you like them, buy the rest; if not, try REID FLEMING or BATMAN, or get in on THE QUESTION early. From there you can graduate to THE DARK KNIGHT RETURNS. If you're really feeling adventurous after that, try ELECTRA: ASSASSIN. These are mostly limited series and are your best bet because they are fully developed stories with a beginning, middle, and end contained in a set number of issues.

You might also try the Comics Buyer's Guide. This weekly newspaper, edited by long- time sf fans Don and Maggie Thompson, is the *Publishers Weekly* of the comic book field. It carries the latest news and loads of ads from dealers and distributors. If here's no comic shop near you, you can get what you want through CBG.

We've had a start here. In future installments I'll take in-depth looks at individual titles, creators, and trends in the field. Along the road, I'll be hacking my way toward a set of critical principles for use in reviewing comic books as short fiction without losing sight of their history, their intent, and their primary nature: dramatic graphic entertainment. Maybe we'll all learn something.

In the Future The 3-D revival. THE SPIRIT lives on. CEREBUS TBE AARDVARK. Reprint comics: oldies but goodies. SHATTER: the MacIntosh comic. Ditko. THE ROCKETEER. The British Invasion.

Column #2 (February 1988)

OF AARDVARKS AND MEN

Cerebus (Aardvark-Vanaheim - b&w - $1.70) Hard to believe that the 100th issue approaches as I write this. And each and every issue written and drawn by its creator. In a field where artists switch from title to title faster than sf editors switch publishers, that has to be a record.

How do I explain this comic? How do I describe it so you won't dismiss it out of hand as I did for many years? What can I say about a run of comic books that started off as a clunky Conan parody starring a sword-wielding barbarian aardvark in a mythical past, and somewhere along the way turned into a satiric masterpiece that skewers love, war, peace, politics, religion, and even comic books?

It began in the winter of 1977-78 as *Cerebus the*

Aardvark, written, drawn, and published by a twenty-one year old Canadian high school drop-out named Dave Sim. The art was relatively crude, but the writing was witty, barbed, and surprisingly self-assured. Issue by bi-monthly issue it got better and better, becoming a critical and commercial success. With issue #11 it became simply, *Cerebus*. To my mind, it is largely responsible for the renaissance of the comic book and the start of the independent renaissance.

But for years I ignored all the good things I was hearing about *Cerebus*. Just somebody else trying to cash in on the Robert E. Howard craze. An aardvark playing Conan? Spare me! I'll pass, thank you veddy much. Then in 1985 something called *Cerebus Jam* appeared with Dave Sim collaborating ("jamming") with other artists. One of those artists was Will Eisner, creator of *The Spirit.* I bought it for the Eisner section. I was, as they say, blown away, especially by the Popeye pastiche. ("Cerebusk" – really!) I was hooked, caught, roped in, tied up, captivated.

But who is this Cerebus the Aardvark?

Hard to say. Physically, he's a gray-furred fellow, about three feet tall with thick legs, a thick tail, and a thick snout that was long in the early issues but quickly became short and stubby. He usually wears a ticked-off expression and refers to himself only in the third person. ("Cerebus is thirsty. Bring Cerebus some ale.") Oh yes – he drinks a lot.

I've long since stopped thinking of Cerebus as a walking, talking earth-pig, the only one of his kind (at least that we see) in a world of humans. I think that's a comment on Sim's writing ability. (The only time you're reminded of his non-human origin is when his fur gets wet – its odor sends people running from the room.) Cerebus is a person, a complex one, and that's why his character is so difficult to describe. He can be brash, macho, self-centered, cold-blooded, childish, and petty, yet at times he is capable of warmth and possesses a mordant wit. His moral code seems

515

utilitarian, yet he is loyal to a fault. He is both Everyman and an Innocent Abroad.

And the artwork, the wonderful pictures that go with this story – the highest compliment I can pay the penwork of Sim and his partner Gerhard (who does the magnificent backgrounds) is that I no longer think of *Cerebus* as a black and white comic. The inking, the crosshatching, the many shades of gray are all so well done and so damn *right* for the settings, that as far as I'm concerned, this *is* a color comic. I can't see it any other way. Color would be worse than superfluous – it would ruin the art.

The early issues are fascinating in retrospect as you watch Dave Sim progress as an artist. Crude at the start, Sim gradually develops a functional yet ornate style that takes on new dimensions when Gerhard joins up. Sim can do amazing things with word balloons. He puts big trembling letters in a big balloon for an angry shout and tiny letters dripping icicles for cold contempt. And Cerebus's eyes – they are immensely expressive. The little aardvark's face is mostly snout – not much room for expression there – so all his emotions are reflected in his eyes.

With issue #100, Dave Sim will have completed one third of the Cerebus story. Yes. That's right. Three hundred issues are planned. Sim seems quite sincere about staying with *Cerebus* until he is 46 years old. Fifteen more years to go.

Book I is called, simply, *Cerebus* and comprises the first 25 issues. The comic is no longer sword and sorcery, but it started off that way, and had great fun with the clichés of S&S. With characters named Red Sophia and Bran Mac Muffin and Elrod of Melvinbone, the humor is broad and full of laughs. After the first dozen issues, though, as Cerebus's wit and intelligence come to the fore, his sword becomes less and less important. Dave Sim really begins hitting his stride with "The Palnu Trilogy" (issues #14-16) and the introduction of Lord Julius, whose appearance and pattern of speech bear a remarkable resemblance to those of Groucho

Marx (whose first name happened to be Julius). Cerebus is introduced to Lord Julius's peculiarly loony brand of politics and we get the first inklings of a change in the wind. The stories become less and less self-contained. You start to get the feeling that there's a bigger picture behind all this. Sim begins changing the milieu. Gradually we lose the feeling that we're in a parody of the Hyborean age.

With the start of Book II, *High Society* (issues 26-51), we sense that we're in an alternate 18th Century Europe as Cerebus enters the world of politics. This is not *Mr. Smith Goes to Washington*, folks. Cerebus is almost immediately corrupted. He meets a politically savvy woman named Astoria who becomes his guide through the labyrinthine bureaucracy of Iest. Stylistically, it's interesting to note that somewhere along the way in "High Society," Sim drops that time-honored narrative voice of the comic book, the caption. For the last fifty issues or so, *Cerebus* has been told entirely through picture and dialogue. When you think of it, that's the way it should be. I mean, if you've got a picture of a slump-shouldered guy walking through a downpour past a road sign pointing to the right toward "Iest," you don't need a caption saying: "He trudged through the deluge toward Iest."

High Society is too layered, too complex, too damn long to summarize with any justice. Not every issue in the sequence can be called funny. Some are not meant to be. But the ones that are are hilarious. I think of "The Deciding Vote" chapter and just the memory makes me laugh. Then there's "PetuniaCon" – a political convention in the form of a comics/sf convention, with panels, fans, the works. A wealth of good reading.

Book III, *Church and State*, began with #51 and is still in progress. As of this writing, Cerebus is Pope.

I could go on and on. The series is loaded with good and great moments, ones that make you laugh out loud or shake your head in wonder as Cerebus graduates from chief of the kitchen to Prime minister to Most Holy, head of the

Church of Tarim. Along the way he runs into incarnations of the Marx Brothers, Foghorn Leghorn, Yosemite Sam (in the form of twins), and the Rolling Stones, to name a few. And then there's Artemis, the schizophrenic costumed avenger whose thought balloons are hilarious and who undergoes a metamorphosis every dozen or so issues – from Cockroach to Moonroach to Wolveroach and ever onward. And so many other characters, all well drawn (pictorially and verbally) and memorable.

So. Get into *Cerebus*. But not with the current issue. I fear you will be totally baffled if you begin there. Your best bet is to start at the beginning. Issue #1, however, now sells in the $200-300 range. Don't worry. There's a way out. The first 25 issues were collected into a massive single-volume called *Cerebus*. When you finish that, I'm sure you'll want to move on to "High Society," another 500+ page volume.

I don't want to sound like a shill for this book, but I'm completely taken with it. It makes me laugh out loud. I gave packages of the first three volumes of SWORDS OF CEREBUS as Christmas gifts last year. They went over big. The only caveat I must offer is to stay away from Cerebus if you're a fan of Michael Moorcock's Elric stories. You see, there's this recurring albino character called Elrod of Melvinbone. He talks just – "Ah say, just" – like Foghorn Leghorn, the rooster from the old Warner Brothers cartoons. Years ago, I used to like Moorcock's tales of the oh-so-dour and tragic Elric, but now I can't even see Moorcock's name without hearing Foghorn Leghorn's voice ("Son – Ah say – son, are you listenin', son? Do Ah hafta use subtitles? Ah'm talkin' about a trunk, son – suitcase, that is!") and cracking up.

Two Mini-series End

Batman #404-407 (DC, color, $.75)

Elektra: Assassin #1-8 (Epic, color, $1.50)

YEAR ONE is over and I'm sad to see it finished. Unlike THE DARK KNIGHT RETURNS, Frank Miller tells this tale in straight-line traditional comic book form. David Mazzucchelli's art is perfect for the story. My only complaint is that visually the story appears to take place today rather than back in Year One. A small point, but I wish someone had caught it and fixed it.

The script is excellent. Miller keeps getting better and better. As in THE DARK KNIGHT, Miller spends a lot of time on James Gordon (a lieutenant at this time) of the Gotham Police. Gordon is developed as a family man, a courageous individual of incorruptible integrity and sense of duty. But he's not made of iron. He has his weaknesses and he winds up being blackmailed for one of them.

Even spear carriers in YEAR ONE gain a third dimension from Miller. Bruce Wayne's butler, Alfred, for instance. He obviously thinks his employer is nuts for spending the night roaming Gotham in a skin tight suit and cape. He remains loyal, but is not averse to trying a bit of barbed reality therapy on his boss. Witness the following exchange which occurs over a number panels as Bruce Wayne does one-handed push-ups while Alfred sits and reads from the paper:

ALFRED: Master Bruce – I've just come across a fascinating piece in the Times. Concerns the effects of lack of sleep among the marginally sane...

WAYNE: Quiet, Alfred.

ALFRED: ... "marked increase in paranoia" ... hmmm ... "tendency toward aberrant, even violent behavior."

(Wayne gets up and heads for the door.)

ALFRED: Off again, sir? Shall I fetch your tights?

WAYNE: Never during the day, Alfred.

You've got to admit, this is a long way from Bob Kane. Bruce Wayne, however, is left largely unexplored. Wisely so. It serves no constructive purpose to probe too deeply the psyches of our masked avengers. Better they remain enigmatic, primordial, atavistic. *Batman* 408 will be scripted by Max Allan Collins, who writes hardboiled P-I novels and scripts the current Dick Track strip and Ms Tree comic book. Should be good. Batman – Year Two will begin in Detective Comics with issue 575. We live in wondrous times.

Elektra: Assassin is over too. As mentioned last column, Frank Miller strikes again, this time with Bill Sienkiewicz doing his unique thing with the art. Whatever faculty it is that we use to suspend disbelief will have to work overtime in the finale issue.

This is truly a unique work. All the scenes are filtered through the minds of characters, consequently, you have criss-crossing first-person viewpoints, identifiable only by the colors of the caption-balloons. And with Miller's frenetic quick-cut style, often with multiple viewpoints in each illustrated panel, believe me, you need those colors!

And the artwork – sheesh! Nobody does it like Sienkiewicz. Yet its bizarreness perfectly reflects the surrealism of the script without overwhelming it. (Just to gaze on page 25 of the last issue is worth the cost of the whole series – it should be a poster.)

But you simply cannot divide script and art in *Elektra: Assassin*. This is without a doubt the most demanding comics I have ever read. You can't just glance at the pictures, pick up a few words, and turn the page as in the old days of comic books. Here you've got to study the illos, read *all* the words, and then make something of both. The whole of the thing is far more than its parts would indicate, and I can't think of any medium besides the comic book where this story could have been told half so well.

In the process, *Elektra: Assassin* has raised a lot of hackles. It's been called too violent, too sexy, too cold, too cruel, and too damn offensive to too many people.

Yeah, well, it's all those things and more. I've come to see it as a sort of Rorcharch test with words. Never can tell what you're going to find in those pages. Might even find a piece of yourself. By the way, the ending is ingenious, ironic, as whacked out as the rest of the book, but totally satisfying. I loved this mini-series. And I hear Bill Sienkiewicz is doing The Shadow next. I can hardly wait.

Computerized
Shatter (First, color, $1.75)

This is the world's first computerized comic, done entirely (except for the color) on a MacIntosh LaserWriter system. The first printing of the first issue (SHATTER SPECIAL) is something of a collector's item. Seems the computer hackers' world got wind of it and the issue sold out almost immediately. I remember thinking when I first heard of a computer-generated comic that it might dehumanize comic art by sucking the individuality out of it, that the MacIntosh would be the Great Leveler – the microchip Franklin D. Roosevelt, as it were – of comic book artists. I was dead wrong.

Michael Saenz did the art for the Special and the first two issues; the next six were done by Steve Erwin and Bob Dienethal and were definitely inferior. The latest issues (#9) has a new artist, Charlie Athanas, who's as good as Saenz. So it does matter who's at the console. And it's amazing what they can turn out. You have to see it yourself to judge. I am impressed, but I don't see its widespread use in the near future. One interesting point, though: There's no "original art" for Shatter. It's all on disk.

As for the story: *Shatter* is a cop for hire who stumbles onto a scheme to kill talented people and sell the RNA extracted from their brains so that second-raters can co-opt the victims' talents/skills/whatever. Sort of like those old flatworm experiments (discredited now, I believe) where they ran a planarian through a maze until it got it right, then ground it up and fed it to another worm which, lo and behold, knew how to run the maze on its first trip! I find Shatter's central plot premise hard to swallow (sorry) but writer Peter B. Gillis does find some interesting twists. Not a great sf comic, but you could do worse.

Questions, Claws, and Paranoia
The Question #1-5 (DC, color, $1.50)
Wolverine (Marvel, color,$4.95)
The Silent Invasion #1-6 (Renegade, b&w, $2.(0)

   In the last column I mentioned that the first issue of *The Question* left its hero lying on the bottom of a river with a crushed skull and a bullet in the head. Somehow he survived. (No way! After the beating I saw him get in #1, his brain would have looked like a glob of currant jelly.) But we suspend our disbelief and press on with this supposedly "reality-based" comic. The villain is that new cliché, the corrupt, politically ambitious Fundamentalist tv preacher, only this fellow feels he can best serve God by serving Satan. None of it was very engaging, but there was a thread running through the first four issues that pulled me along. The Question is still an intriguing character; nowhere near as interesting as Ditko's original, who never hesitated to question other characters' – or even the reader's – values, but there was enough of a sense that writer Dennis O'Neil was striving for an added dimension to make me pick up issue #5. I was pleasantly surprised. The story within is CITYSCAPE, a montage of a city sliding into anarchy. It is far better than the extended plot in the first four issues. Which means it's getting better. A good sign. I'll buy #6.

   Wolverine is just out as I write this, a reprint of the 1982 4-issue mini-series in a single volume on high-quality stock. I don't know if this was the first mini-series, but it was the first one I ever picked up. Excellent color, excellent script by Chris Claremont, excellent story by Frank Miller (yes, him again). Wolverine is one of the later additions to the X-Men, Marvel's band of mutants. A hirsute, homicidal, cheroot - smoking fellow who can pop three long adamantium claws out of the dorsum of each hand at will (snickt!). Better you shouldn't ask how he moves his wrists when they're retracted, just enjoy the ride as Wolverine follows the woman he loves to Japan and runs into a bunch of folks almost as nasty as he. Told in the first person with lots of violent action, lots of corpses, but lots of inner conflict, too, as Wolverine confronts the bloodlust that bubbles continually just below his skin. Claremont's script is textured and layered in ways you don't expect in a comic book. After reading this mini-series five years ago, I realized that the American comic book was growing up. So buy it for its historical as well as its intrinsic value. It's a bargain at five bucks considering what the original issues go for on the collector's market, and the reproduction is better by a factor of at least eight.

The Silent Invasion is another expensive black and white that's worth the money. Truly unique in art, story, and concept. A combination of "I Led Three Lives," "Invasion of the Body Snatchers," and "Earth vs. the Flying Saucers." The art is on the expressionistic side, using very black blacks, and eccentric figures, settings, and perspectives. I'm reminded of those air-brushed covers that graced the old Pocket Books and Popular Library paperbacks in the 40s. The introductory story is complete in the first six issues. It's all about Matt Sinkage, a reporter in Union City in 1952, who has had a close encounter with flying saucers and can't get anyone to believe him. In fact, someone seems intent on suppressing the story. And then there's his neighbor, Mr. Ivan Kalashnikov, who's very secretive. Is that a short wave radio in his apartment? Is Matt's fiancee, Peggy, really the person he thinks she is? Events progress in a serpentine fashion, coiling upon themselves until we're as entangled as Matt. What's real and what's not? Who can be trusted? Is Matt crazy? It's a marvelous evocation of 1950s paranoia, blending flying saucers with the communist menace. I don't know where Larry Hancock and Michael Cherkas came up with this off-the-wall concept, but it works, and Renegade should be congratulated for seeing its worth and publishing it. Its only drawback IS its bimonthly publishing schedule – I tended to forget certain characters and plot elements during the interludes. But you won't have that problem if you're starting now. You can buy all SIX Issues and read them in one sitting. Lucky you!

Short Takes

First Six-Pack (First, b&w, $.50) A good idea. For half a buck you get black and white samples of half a dozen color titles from First Comics. Take advantage of it.

Luger #1-3 (Eclipse, color, $1.75) A three-part mini-series with excellent art by Bo Hampton, Thomas Yeats, and Steve Oliff. Kinky sex, nudity, gore. About a guy with a pistol built into his right hand – it fires through the tip of his index finger, Well, the art IS nice.

Possibleman #1 (Blackthorne, b&w, $1.75) An "origin issue" in which Dexter Smeal gains the power to possibly become Possibleman ("...an invincible, grade A four star foe basher deluxe!") just by blowing his nose, and meets the dreaded Zit Queen. I say "possibly" because the nose-blowing doesn't always result in "a big jaw – bold layouts – regulation muscles – the works!" The law of chance prevails. On one desperate occasion, a honk turns him into a bowl of chopped liver. A delightful book, written and drawn by William van Horn in a style reminiscent of George Herriman's Krazy Kat in its later years. There aren't many black-and-white comics worth $1.75, but this is definitely one of them.

Uncle Scrooge Comics Digest #3 (Gladstone color $1.50) See if you can find a copy of this left over anywhere. It contains a reprint of "Tralla La," my favorite Uncle Scrooge story of all time. Although the small digest-size pages diminish (literally and figuratively) the art, nothing can diminish the outstanding quality of the quintessential duck story by Carl Barks in which Uncle Scrooge finds a Shangri-La of sorts where he can escape the pressures of the financial world. But a simple bottle cap threatens to destroy this agrarian paradise. The story is an ingenious lesson in economics. After reading it, no one – either eight years old or eighty – can fail to grasp the concept of supply and demand.

COLUMN #3...

THE BEST COMICS OF 1987

1) *Electra: Assassin* (Epic - 8-issue miniseries)
    Artist: Bill Sienkiewicz
    Writer: Frank Miller

2) *Watchmen* (DC - 12-issue series/ Warner trade paperback)
    Artist: Dave Gibbons
    Writer: Alan Moore

3) "Hunger" in *Hellblazer* (DC - issues #1-2)
    Artist: John Ridgway
    Writer: Jamie Delano

4) "Year One" in *Batman* (DC - issues #404-407)
    Artist: David Mazzuchelli
    Writer: Frank Miller

5) *The Silent Invasion* (Renegade - issues #1-6)
    Artist: Larry Hancock
    Writer: Michael Cherkas

6) "The 3rd Mission" in *Airboy* (Eclipse - issues #17-18)
    Artist: Bo Hampton & Willie Blyberg
    Writer: Charles Dixon

7) "Cityscape" in *The Question* (DC - issue #5)
    Artist: Denys Cowan & Rick Magyar
    Writer: Dennis O'Neil

8) *Scout* (Eclipse - issue #19)
    Artist - Writer - Guitarist: Timothy Truman

9) "A.T.M." in *Mr. Monster* (Eclipse - issue #8)
      Artist: Michael T. Gilbert & Mark Pacella
      Writer: Michael T. Gilbert

10) "Earnest Nonsense" in *Cerebus* (Aardvark-Vanaheim - issue #107)
      Artist: Dave Sim & Gerhard
      Writer: Dave Sim

COMMENT

The choices above are very personal and pertain only to comics I've *read*. I'm sure there were other works published during 1987 that would have made the list had I seen them, but there has been a marked increase in the number of comics published over the past few years with no concomitant increase in the hours in a day. I'm sure I missed a lot of good stuff.

I tried to be somewhat objective, paying special attention to the *gestalt* of the work – the meshing of art, dialog and story. Emotional impact played a big part, as well.

I juggled *Electra: Assassin* and *Watchmen* back and forth between first and second place. Finally, I gave the Miller-Sienkiewicz piece the top spot because of its strong use of the visual medium: the story could *not* be told in any form other than a comic book. I did not feel I could say the same of *Watchmen*.

1) *Electra: Assassin* – a Rorcharch Test with words. Bizarre story, psychotic art, idiosyncratic execution. Love, death, and madness. If you haven't read it, pick up the single volume graphic novel due soon. It's not for everyone, but the good stuff never is.

2) *Watchmen* – the graphic novel against which all future graphic novels will be measured. You've read about it in *Time, Newsweek,* and *Rolling Stone,* and it largely deserves

all the ink it's been getting. I must tell you, though, that the one-man conspiracy at the heart of the involved plot turns out to be a hoary old sf cliché familiar to all sf fans and even *Outer Limits* viewers. But don't let that put you off. It's the getting there that counts. Alan Moore's characters and wonderfully detailed alternate America make it a very worthwhile trip.

3) "Hunger" – the inaugural story in *Hellblazer*. Street-level supernatural horror with seamy, seedy, violent art and script about a lord of the flies. Very British. The Barker influence is strong. It looks as if we've finally got a real horror comic, one that breaks from the EC straitjacket.

4) "Year One" – a fledgling Batman learning the ropes with no one to teach him, making mistakes, finding allies. Moody, evocative art (despite its careless anachronisms) and excellent script.

5) *The Silent Invasion* – a skillful evocation of 1950's paranoia blending UFO scares with the communist menace. The eccentric, expressionistic black and white art perfectly complements the story. This too is due to be released in a single-volume reprint.

6) "The 3rd Mission" – a clever braiding of fantasy and WWII history in *Airboy*. The premise: the Hiroshima and Nagasaki atomic bombings were only two of three missions. A third B-29, the Yankee Babe, was destined for Moscow (wouldn't *that* have changed the world as we know it!) but disappeared over Siberia. Now, in the 1980's, the plane reappears in Soviet airspace, on route to complete its mission. The art by Bo Hampton and Willy Blyberg is superb. The ending is unexpectedly moving.

7) "Cityscape" – from *The Question*, the highpoint in this retreaded character's run. An excellent montage of a city slipping into anarchy, with damnation for some and a chance

at redemption for others. Too bad the rest of the series isn't up to this hardboiled quality. Too bad the title character has strayed so far from the source material – the Ditko version was much more provocative.

8) *Scout* #19 – I have to list this because of the way the flexidisc recording that comes with the issue is integrated into the script. It's decent hard blues done up by the writer-artist and some musician friends. High marks for originality, derring-do, and because I'm a blues fan.

9) "A.T.M." – a typical *Mr. Monster* story by Michael T. Gilbert, which is to say it is head and shoulders above most other comic book attempts at humor. Only Mr. Monster could witness an old woman being sucked through the card slot of an automatic teller machine – amid appropriate sprays of gore – and conclude that "Something was amiss."

10) "Earnest Nonsense" – in which Cerebus the Aardvark meets the Flaming Carrot and Sponge Boy in outer space. (Don't ask.)

COLUMN #4

(started but the column was cancelled)

ECLIPSE COMICS

This has become my favorite comic book publisher. There's no one reason for that position. Take any one of its many titles -- permanent and transient, derivative and *sui generis* alike -- and you will find that each has its share of flaws. But when you step back and look at the whole picture, you see quality and depth in a young independent publisher that is not afraid to take chances on some truly off-beat modern material, yet manages to retain a fond awareness and respect for what has gone before. Eclipse has a sense of history, and a true collegial awareness of the comics field.

Most of all, Eclipse is eclectic: Funny animals, Japanese and British reprints, 3-D, superheroes, horror, sf, action-adventure, nostalgia, and just plain weird. Here are a few titles I've bought and read in runs of varying length. Like everything else you read in this column, it's extremely personal.

Let's get the mediocrities out of the way first.

Derivative Stuff

DNAgents (color - $.95) This is the first Eclipse comic I ever saw. It first appeared in late 1982 and is a cross between *Teen Titans* and *Fantastic Four*. For some reason I was on the mailing list for this title (maybe because I'd ordered the eventually aborted Steve Ditko special from Eclipse Books), but although the art was attractive, I found the stories so uninteresting I wrote the company and asked them to stop sending the freebies. Don't get me wrong. The first half dozen issues weren't bad for the subgenre of teenage mutant superhumans, they simply didn't take me anyplace I hadn't been many, many times before. And besides, they wore skin tight costumes and flew around shooting power beams out of their fingertips. Enough already.

Adolescent Radioactive Black Belt Hamsters (b&w - $1.50) One of the seemingly limitless variations on the parodic subgenre created by *Teenage Mutant Ninja Turtles*. Cute funny animal stuff but hardly worth the price.

Superhero

The flagship title of the Eclipse line is, I would say, *Miracleman*. Besides *DNAgents*, it's the company's only other skintight-suited superhero title. If it had been a reprint of the original British books from the fifties, it would belong in the previous category -- in spades. But this is a new Miracleman, reborn with Alan Moore as midwife. It's something special despite chronic delays and seismic fluctuations in the quality of the art,

A little history: *Miracleman* got his start in 1954 in Britain as a character named Marvelman who was a blatant rip-off of America's Captain Marvel. He even had a magic word that could turn him from ordinary boy Micky Moran into the superhuman adult known as Marvelman. No, it wasn't "SHAZAM!" it was "KIMOTA!" (That's "atomic" phonetically backwards.) The series was killed in 1963 and remained buried until the March, 1982 premier issue of *Warrior*, when the new adventures of Marvelman began serialization. So why the name change? Simple. Eclipse Comics didn't want to be hassled by Marvel Comics over the title, so they chose a similar name that fit the double-M logo on Marvelman's costume. Thus was Miracleman born.

But a very different kid now. These are the '80's. Micky Moran is a middle-aged man who has forgotten who he was, forgotten the magic word. Just an everyday Brit with a wife and child...and strange dreams. How he relearns who he is makes for fascinating reading.

***

I believe this appeared in Reason *in 1979.*

Alongside Night

L. Neil Schulman.
New York: Crown Publishers. 1979.
181pp. $8.95.

Let's not call this science fiction.

After all, the publisher isn't, despite the fact that it follows the best "If this goes on..." tradition of the genre. Let's call it near-future fiction and leave it at that, although it's also a coming-of-age novel, a Utopian/dystopian novel, and a novel of ideas. It's also a first novel, and it's full of surprises, not all of them confined to the plot.

Briefly, *Alongside Night* concerns Elliot Vreeland, the 17-year-old son of a Nobel Prize-winning economist –

one whose theories seem to jibe nicely with the Chicago School. (The Author's Note disclaims any intentional similarities between the economist character and Milton Friedman.)

COLLECTIVIST TROUBLES

Elliot Vreeland's world is Manhattan in the not-too-distant future, in an America that is falling apart. Decades of fiscal mismanagement and irresponsibility have finally brought the country to the brink of economic collapse. The inflation rate is through the roof, the cost-of-living index was 2,012 percent for the last quarter of the previous year, a taxi ride costs 2,000 blues (New Dollars). Businesses are failing hourly, strikes are rampant, and Elliot, a high school senior, is not even sure there will be any colleges left to attend come September.

But these are merely background problems, a part of everyday life. Elliot's trials begin in earnest when his father, mother, and sister disappear, kidnapped – possibly murdered – by forces of the State. Armed with a .38-caliber Peking revolver and a money belt full of Mexican 50-peso gold pieces, he begins a trek through a future Manhattan on the verge of social collapse.

At first look, the cityscape Schulman presents is a nightmare, totally alien to anything on earth; yet the more you see, the more you realize how uncomfortably close it is to Mayor Koch's town. There are bright spots, however – pockets of civilization made safe by merchant groups who have hired security forces to protect their customers. Eventually, Elliot connects with the Revolutionary Agorist Cadre, a laissez-faire underground group that has been labeled "terrorist" and "gangster" by the government, and outlawed. Within one of the cadre's safe areas he meets Lorimer, a girl his age who, like most cadre members, goes by a pseudonym and who is more than she seems.

The agorists dine in places like the Tanstaafl Cafe, fly

the Gadsden flag, and say things like "A is A." The author has put a lot of effort and ingenuity into little things among the agorists, especially the names of their businesses: *NoState Insurance, Anarchobank* (which issues the Bank Anarchocard to qualified customers), the *Black Supermarket,* and so on.

Some will be tempted to compare *Alongside Night* to *Atlas Shrugged:* both works deal with America on the brink and with a libertarian group that has retreated to a secret enclave. But the resemblance stops there. Ayn Rand's book puts forth a set of carefully derived principles and expounds on the philosophy derived from those principles. Schulman takes a completely different approach – his characters make no speeches. Aside from excerpts from a few fictitious books, there is little discussion of principles. Instead, he lets the social and economic chaos of Elliot Vreeland's world speak for itself. The thrust *of Alongside Night* is entirely empirical. The message is clear in everything we are shown: *collectivism doesn't work.* And if we continue with our current fiscal and social policies, Elliot's world is what we must expect.

Do not let the above lead you to think that there are no ideas here. There are. Plenty of them. None entirely unique to libertarian thought, but many that are potentially shocking to the uninitiated – those who still believe in municipal bonds, the stock market, the FCC, urban renewal, and on and on.

But most important of all, I think, is Schulman's emphasis on, and insistent use of, the term *agora*. It's from the Greek, meaning marketplace, and is, as far as the reading public is concerned, a neutral term. Unlike "capitalism" and even "libertarianism" ("What's that you say? He's a libertine?"}, agora engenders no knee-jerk responses. It's not even an official *ism.*

FIRST NOVEL TROUBLES

As with any first novel, *Alongside Night* is not without

its flaws. Any novel of ideas must walk a tightrope. The ideas are the raison d'etre for the work, yet it must remain a novel: there must be emotional involvement of sufficient intensity to counterbalance the intellectual content. This isn't easy. It requires an expert sense of balance. Schulman does well for the most part, but after a tense beginning, the adrenalin fades as we move into the middle chapters. There's intellectual stimulation aplenty as we explore the Revolutionary Agorist Cadre and meet the mysterious Lorimer, but emotionally it's a trough.

It could be, however, that I found these sections emotionally flat because of my familiarity with libertarian thought; outsiders, seeing laissez-faire economics put to practical use for the first time, may well find the middle chapters riveting. A strong emotional component here might only prove distracting.

The main characters could use further development. Do not misunderstand: they are not stereotypes; none of the major characters is a stereotype. But Elliot is a bit too cool for a teenager whose family has been kidnapped, his father possibly murdered by the State. And Lorimer/ Deanne, considering her developmental environment – how did she ever manage to become a libertarian? Neither of them seems to have much of a life outside the plot. Elliot obviously likes science fiction – but is it a mere reading preference, or does he have a passion for it? He plays chess well – a passion, or something for idle hours? I didn't feel I knew him too much better at the end of the book than I did at the beginning. Again, this may be a calculated effect on the author's part, but in a novel involving coming of age, I like to be pushed a little deeper under that character's skin.

NO COMPROMISES

These are minor points. The story picks up again in the second half, and there are so many good moments all the way through. Schulman's writing is at its best when he's moving his characters through the streets of Manhattan-to-be, where virtually everyone is a criminal: there are the moral criminals – the muggers, the thieves, the bureaucrats – and there are the statutory criminals – gun owners, gold owners, black marketeers. You get *the feel* of social breakdown. It's unsettling.

Yet it's not all bleak and chaotic. There are touches of humor and glimmers of hope amid the gloom. There is a truly startling moment in part one in which Elliot asks a porn shop counterman who has been hiding gold for his father why he hadn't stolen the gold and run off. The man's reply: "I didn't steal the gold 'cause it don't belong to me." After seeing what is going on in the rest of the city, the simple integrity of that statement hits you right between the eyes... and stays with you for the rest of the book.

This is a radical novel. It pulls no punches, offers no compromises. It effectively presents a social, moral, and political point of view without polemic, without stridency. Without hysteria, it projects a bleak future for us all, but not without hope, for there's a deep affection for humanity despite all its foibles underlying every sentence. I understand J. Neil Schulman is only 26; I foresee a long and successful writing career ahead of him. I don't know him, but after reading this, his first novel, I'd like to.

Alongside Night offers the libertarian reader a great deal of pleasure, but holds so much more for the nonlibertarian. It will shock those who are unprepared for it. Who knows? – It may even wake a few people up. I hope it sells 20 million copies.

***

Reviewed for Reason *in their December 1980 issue.*

The Number of the Beast
Robert A. Heinlein

The trouble with Bob Heinlein is that he doesn't need to write. When I want a story from him, the first thing I have to do is think up something he would like to have, like a swimming pool. The second thing is to sell him on the idea of having it. The third thing is to convince him he should write a story to get the money to pay for it, instead of building it himself. – John W. Campbell, Jr.

It began in 1939. Robert Anson Heinlein was 32, a Naval Academy graduate who, because of tuberculosis, had been retired long before his time. He was looking for something to do. As a lark, and because he thought he might get a little money out of it (the Depression was still on), he wrote a short story called "Lifeline" and sent it to a pulp magazine called *Astounding Stories.* John W. Campbell, Jr. had been in the editor's chair there for two years and was looking for writers capable of creating a new kind of science fiction. This unknown named Heinlein must have showed promise, because Campbell bought that first story and started a relationship that would change the face of science fiction.

With Campbell's prodding and encouragement, Robert A. Heinlein began producing stories about the future peopled with characters who *lived* in that future. Gone were the long, expository passages describing social and political orders of the day or explaining in detail the technological marvels on all sides. Instead, the reader was experiencing the future through the eyes of an inhabitant of that future, and that inhabitant took it all for granted – just as all readers take their own surroundings for granted. Nowadays, this approach to writing sf is *de rigueur;* in 1939 it was something new. But it caught on. Readers liked the challenge of piecing a future world via innuendo and insinuation from a character's casual observations. It heightened the feeling of *being there* and added to the sense of wonder so necessary to successful science fiction.

Over the next few years, many other stories in the same mold began to sprout up, most notably by Anson MacDonald, but also by Lyle Monroe, Caleb Saunders, and John Riverside. They weren't imitating Heinlein – they *were* Heinlein, who was cranking out stories, good stories, so fast that he had to use pseudonyms to keep his name from appearing two or three times on *Astounding's* contents page. What has come to be known as the Golden Age of Science Fiction had been launched.

After the war, Heinlein wrote *Rocketship Galileo,* which was eventually made into George Pal's *Destination Moon,* and which began a train of juvenile sf novels that has seldom been equaled in quality. Everything he wrote sold well. He became known as the Dean of Science Fiction and could have gone on doing endless variations on his favorite theme of the competent man, with predictable financial and critical success for the rest of his days.

Instead, he chose to experiment, much to the alternating delight, concern, and fury of his legion of fans. *Starship Troopers* won him a Hugo award in 1960 and a reputation as some sort of cryptofascist. Two years later, after *Stranger in a Strange Land* brought another Hugo, people were calling him a heretic and a sex nut. *The Moon is a Harsh Mistress* earned him still another Hugo and endeared him to libertarians for its rational anarchist philosophy and the famous acronym *tanstaafl.* After reading / *Will Fear No Evil,* some people thought he was a pervert, and with *Time Enough for Love,* a number of critics said it was all over for Robert A. Heinlein, despite his Grand Master Award from the Science Fiction Writers of America. But it's not all over. At age 73, 41 years and 41 books after "Life-line," he has given us *The Number of the Beast,* a long rambling book not at all like what he was writing in the '40s and '50s, but more in line with the style he has developed over the past decade.

For most of its length, *The Number of the Beast* dwells almost exclusively on its four protagonists: Jake Burroughs;

his wife, Hilda; Jake's daughter, Dejah Thoris ("Deety"); and her husband, Zebadiah John Carter. All four are exceptionally bright people, ranging in age from 26 to 49. All have science-oriented backgrounds. The book concerns their flight from one alternate universe to another in search of a new home safe from the aliens pursuing them.

Why are aliens pursuing them? That is never really clear, but it is assumed that the aliens want to prevent dissemination of Dr. Jake Burroughs's latest discovery. Jake, a mathematical genius, has come to the conclusion that all existence is made up of not four but *six* dimensions – three spatial and three temporal. By his calculations, the number of possible universes along these axes, accessible either by translation or rotation, is 6^{6^6} (that's six to the sixth power to the sixth power). And according to the Book of Revelations in the Bible, 666 is the Number of the Beast – hence the title of the book. But not only has Jake Burroughs discerned the existence of the two extra axes, he has devised a way to move along any and all of them, to any alternate universe he chooses. (Frankly, I find Jake's theory and his translation/ rotation device easier to swallow than a man with a middle name of John and a last name of Carter meeting and marrying someone named Dejah Thoris Burroughs.)

The four protagonists hop from universe to universe looking for a safe and suitable place to settle, arguing all the way and alternating command of their vocalizing, computerized craft, Gay Deceiver. At first the alternate universes appear to be simply that – variations on the world we live in. For instance, they hop to a world almost identical to ours except for the fact that there is no letter / in the alphabet there. They visit a Mars (remember, they can travel along spatial as well as temporal axes) that has a breathable atmosphere and has become a penal colony for the Russian and British Empires. (The United States is still a British colony.) And then there's a strange, inverted universe, almost like a Klein bottle. No *real* surprises yet.

Then they arrive in the Land of Oz. No, not someplace *like* Oz, but L. Frank Baum's Oz, complete with Glinda, Scarecrow, Pumpkinhead, and the rest. This was my favorite sequence in the book, and all too brief. I was as moved as Deety when she learned that all the Oz characters knew her because of all the time she had spent reading the books. And an especially nice touch was the instant friendship that developed between the computerized Gay Deceiver and – who else? – Tik-Tok.

From there they hop to Lilliput, then to an English-style countryside where they watch a white rabbit in coat and tails rush by, followed by a little blonde girl in a pinafore. Then they jump to interstellar space and run into one of E.E. Smith's Lensmen, and so on.

Eventually they come to the realization that many of the more than 1.03×10^{28} universes of Jake's theory are inhabited by fictional characters to whom their own world is *the* real world. Which leads to the unsettling question: Are our travelers fictional characters in a book in one of the universes they've yet to visit? (Heinlein slips you the answer, but you've got to be alert to catch it.) Eventually they arrive in Heinlein's own future history and meet up with the infamous Lazarus Long.

WHO WILL LIKE IT?

Heinlein is obviously having a ball with *The Number of the Beast,* and if you're in no great hurry you can catch a scenic ride with him. On a deeper level, he is exploring the qualities of leadership – the duties, drawbacks, and responsibilities of taking command of a group of people. But I have a caveat, and it's a major one: you're going to have trouble with this book if you're not a science fiction fan. And by "fan" I don't mean someone who has read some Bradbury, seen *Star Wars* twice, and catches all the reruns of *Star Trek;* I mean someone who has a solid grounding in science fiction, who reads *lots* of it. Otherwise you're going to miss innumerable puns and in-jokes, and the epilogue will leave you completely baffled.

I also have a gripe: the dialogue. One of the author's own characters sums it up best. Near the middle of the book, Zeb Carter says, "Yack, yack, yack, argue, fuss and jabber – a cross between a Hyde Park open forum and a high school debating society." At the slightest provocation, anyone – or all four – of the characters will run off at the mouth. I tend to like books with lots of dialogue, especially the terse, bare-bones style Gregory McDonald uses in his Fletch books; but this... this is too much to take at times.

The narrative style may give a few readers pause. Heinlein tells everything in the first person but shifts from character to character; so you have to reorient yourself to the narrative / as you move from section to section. Fortunately, the publisher has headed each page with the name of the current point-of-view character, and this helps a lot.

A word about the artwork. When I heard that Richard Powers was going to be illustrating the book, I thought it was a terrible choice – too surreal; okay for a cover, but not for a bunch of black and whites. I was wrong. Powers has done over 50 illustrations for *The Number of the Beast,* and they are *perfect!* The human figures are lush and full of character, and the background surrealism is just right for the text it reflects.

All in all, an excellent value for $6.95. A classy package. If you're one of those who say that Robert A. Heinlein hasn't written anything decent since *The Moon is a Harsh Mistress* (and there are a fair number of those), you'll think any price too high. But if you liked *Time Enough for Love,* you'll love *The Number of the Beast.*

***

In 1991, Scream Factory, *a fanzine, was doing retrospective reviews of the great horror novels of the 80s. I chose* Red Dragon. *This appeared in issue #7.*

Red Dragon
Thomas Harris

Where to begin? I was impressed from the first chapter. No teaser, no bloody opener that's become almost *de rigueur* if you want to catch the interest of the TV generation. Harris starts with his characters and deftly delineates them with fine, quick strokes. This flowed into the reconstruction- reenactment of the mass murder of the Leeds family within Will Graham's mind as he investigates the scene. The tiny pieces of mirror over the victims' eyes grabbed me by the throat. A bizarre touch that works beautifully. Suddenly the killer is more than a mere perpetrator. He's someone with a very sick agenda.

When we finally get to meet the killer, yellow-eyed Francis Dolarhyde, he's at once fearsome and pathetic, as deformed within as without. Not just a killer; more than a serial killer; he's a serial mass murderer. And nutty as a fruitcake. But this is no one-note villain. As Harris leads us along, we come to appreciate the wellsprings of Dolarhyde's madness. We don't understand that madness – you'd have to be a psychopath yourself to make sense of such monstrous crimes – but we do follow to some extent his Gordian logic.

And then there's Harris' style. It's fast, smooth, and seemingly effortless. He's the perfect storyteller. His characters are real because he sinks beneath their skins and lets us see them from the inside out. He's utterly transparent within his fiction, knows how to remove himself completely from the space between the reader and the story. I've read three of his novels, yet do not feel I know a thing about the author himself. That's storytelling in its purest form.

And yet all of the above would not be enough to make my Top Ten of the Eighties list. It took Hannibal "The Cannibal" Lecter, the psychopathic psychiatrist, confined for life to a hospital cell (the irony!), to put *Red Dragon* over the top. Lecter's presence adds an extraordinary dimension to the novel, lifting it from the procedural-thriller genre onto a level all its own, a level that provides an unobstructed view deep into the very heart of human evil.

Throughout the novel Harris confronts us with two species of evil. One, Dolarhyde's, though appalling in scope, is all too human, born out of rage and madness. The other is, however... something else. Lecter's evil is a distilled essence, an evil of such hideous purity that it seems almost supernatural. It transcends madness. It feeds on pain. When people in the world outside the Chesapeake Hospital for the Criminally Insane are faced with a horror they cannot comprehend, they seek insight from Lecter, the font of evil. They petition him like supplicants before a dark god. And he bargains with them – for petty privileges, for a taste of their pain. We watch him through the supplicants' eyes as he sits in his cell and reaches between the bars to lacerate their minds and hearts with his verbal scalpels. We are nothing to him- another genus, a lower lifeform to be toyed with and disposed of at his whim. Fortunately we've gained the upper hand; we've bottled this evil djinn... for now. Although cast in a supporting role here, Lecter's influence is pervasive. Each page is goosefleshed with the chill of his presence. The result is unforgettable.

Red Dragon. A nightmare journey across the dark side of the human soul, the high-water mark of dark suspense in the Eighties.

***

For a while I was Reason Magazine's *go-to guy for SF-related matters. They commissioned this review back in 1982*

Thought Probes
Edited by Fred D. Miller, Jr. and Nicholas D. Smith.
Prentice-Hall. 1981

Imaginative Philosophy

Whoever heard of discussing time travel paradoxes in philosophy class? I mean, really! Philosophy courses as I remember them seemed more interested in the philosophers themselves and in the schools of thought with which they were identified than with actually analyzing their ideas. Just one more course full of dull facts and names to be memorized and regurgitated on command.

Fortunately, that is not the case with *Thought Probes.* This text focuses on *ideas.* Through deft questioning, it encourages its readers to use their analytical abilities and put concepts to work, testing limits, finding strengths and weaknesses – in short: *to think.*

I freely admit that much of my enthusiasm is due to the text's use of science fiction stories to illustrate philosophical points. This is a legitimate academic use of science fiction, unlike the literary approach that tends to pull the stories apart and examine them with respect to plot devices, means of character development, narrative techniques, and so on; the result is the equivalent of a dissected frog – all its workings are exposed, but the damned thing doesn't jump anymore.

The editors of *Thought Probes* have found a better use. They give a brief overview of an area of philosophy, followed by a story ("conceptual experiment," as they like to call it) concerned with that area, followed by a philosophical essay ("analysis") in the same area, winding up with questions ("probes") geared to stretch the mind. They make you analyze the content of the story. What was it about? What was the author trying to say? Do his concepts hold up under close scrutiny? Fitting treatment for a body of writing called "the literature of ideas." For that's what draws people to science fiction. Not cutesy writing styles and literary tricks – *ideas.* Ideas are also what draw minds to philosophy. And because so much science fiction begins with "What if…" and goes on from there, it is ideally equipped to probing matters of morals, ethics, metaphysics, and epistemology. The two are made for each other.

Fred Miller and Nicholas Smith appear to be no strangers to the two fields they bring together in their text. The length and breadth of their knowledge of science fiction is impressive. They are familiar not only with the Big Name masters but with the Lesser Lights as well, giving numerous examples in the recommended reading sections at the close of each section. Many of the stories included in the text as "conceptual experiments" are among the most provocative ever written in a highly provocative field: Clarke's "The Star," Heinlein's "All You Zombies–," Godwin's "The Cold Equations," Niven's "Cloak of Anarchy," plus a couple of stories that are seeing print for the first time.

The editors appear to recognize no taboos. In discussing the question of God and the problem of evil, they give considerable time to atheism. On the subject of politics, they give full measure to the anarchist viewpoint, questioning the necessity of any government at all.

Of special interest to *Reason* readers will be the respect – almost deference, I might say – accorded the libertarian point of view, not merely in the political context (the political "analysis" segment is an excerpt from Robert Nozick's *Anarchy, State, and Utopia),* but in the areas of free will versus determinism, morals, and values as well.

But most important, it's geared to make you think about things you wouldn't ordinarily think about. It starts the mental juices flowing. It sparks the mind. It makes thoughts, ideas, and concepts exciting. That's what a philosophy text should do but, as many of us know, too often does not. That's why *Thought Probes* is so special.

I never thought I could be enthusiastic about a philosophy text, but this is a wonderful book, a marvelous book. If you're a student or a faculty member, do your very damnedest to get *Thought Probes* into the curriculum. I truly wish it had been around in the mid-60s when I was required to take Introductory Philosophy at Georgetown University. And if you're not a student or faculty member, well, you just might like your thoughts probed anyway.

***

David Hartwell sent this to me for review. It appeared in his NY Review of SF #187 (3/04). I think he was taken aback by my vehemence and so he commissioned a more sympathetic companion review from Spider Robinson as counterpoint.

For Us, the Living
Robert A. Heinlein

I'm sitting alone in the House of Blues on Sunset – it's an easy walk from my hotel and I don't want to brave the Friday night LA traffic – with a Sapphire gimlet (straight up), a Cajun sirloin (medium rare), and Robert A. Heinlein's *For Us, the Living* before me. I'm on Chapter 4 and having the damnedest time making sense of it. It's not the gimlet (I've had only two sips), it's the book. What the hell is going on? Until today I'd have considered the phrase "unreadable Heinlein" an oxymoron. (Okay, his last couple of novels were tough sledding in parts, but they were a walk in the park compared to this.) Now I'm not so sure.

I wanted to like this book, wanted to love it. But reading it, I'm sad to say, is a bloody awful chore.

I don't say that lightly, especially since the book is dedicated to me. (Well, the dedication page says, *for*

Heinlein's Children, and I count myself in that number.) I never knew Robert A. Heinlein personally, so I have no opinion of him as a man, but I'm intimate with his work: I grew up reading his juveniles, then graduated to his more adult fare. I genuflect before his oeuvre. If not for him I doubt I would have written science fiction. And when I did start writing, I made my first sale to John W. Campbell, just as he did. I feel *connected* to this man.

With those bona fides, I believe I have the right to tell you that *For Us, The Living* should not have been published. Heinlein did not want it published. Near the end of his life he and his wife destroyed what they thought were the last existing copies. I see only one way to interpret that: The author did not want that manuscript made public. And with good reason. It's more a series of Socratic dialogues – including multi-page monologues – than a novel. It even has an appendix and footnotes – some with algebraic equations.

Imagine a utopian novel with all the character development and narrative drive of *When the Sleeper Wakes,* but with less plot, and you're approaching *For Us, The Living.*

Let's go back to the beginning – in more ways than one. Heinlein always told us that he wrote his first piece of fiction, "Lifeline," in 1939 and sold it to *Astounding* on his first try.

Not wholly true. "Lifeline" was not his first stab at fiction. A year or so earlier he'd written a novel-length book called *For Us, The Living* (hereafter: *FUTL*). This "Comedy of Customs" (the handwritten subtitle Heinlein added a to the first page of the manuscript) concerns a naval pilot named Perry Nelson who is killed in a 1939 car accident and wakes up a century and a half later wandering around in another body. A beautiful nude dancer named Diana takes Perry in and begins teaching him about the world of 2086. They fall in love, but when one of Diana's old beaus comes around, Perry gets jealous and cold cocks him. This is unacceptable behavior in 2086, so Perry has to choose between banishment to Coventry or deprogramming / reprogramming. He chooses the latter and eventually regains Diana's heart. Along the way he has an affair with a woman named Olga and becomes fascinated with rocketships. The book closes with Perry entering a ship for a twenty-four-hour circumlunar flight.

That's pretty much the whole plot: Boy meets girl, boy almost loses girl, boy gets girl back in a ménage à trois, boy rockets off to the moon.

All the rest is talk-talk-talk.

Which is the apparent reason Heinlein wrote *FUTL*: To lecture the world of 1939 on the errors of its ways, and how it could evolve into the utopia he describes if only it will heed him.

The clear, effortless Heinlein prose is there – no doubt about it, the man was a natural – but the style is a long, long way from "The door irised open." They're still saying "Oh, bother" in 2086, and everything from stoves to TVs is too often described in excessive detail (five-and-a-half pages on the gizmos in a flying car), as if their façades are as important as their function.

As for his characters, they exist simply to ask and answer questions. Perry is a supposedly generic pale male from the 1930s who, within hours after being taken it, is lounging around nude with a beautiful and equally nude woman. Is he aroused? Not so anyone could tell. Is Heinlein kidding? Not so anyone could tell. And Perry's jealous rage at Diana's old lover is out of character with whatever we've been able to gather about him: It's merely a vehicle to slip him into the legal and medical systems of 2086. (The deprogramming / reprogramming, by the way, is laughable.)

Throughout the book Diana arranges for a series of experts to lecture Perry (and thereby the reader) on how the utopia of 2086 came to be. Much of this future history – not *the* Future History – is fascinating. The new US Constitution and especially its 27th Amendment (the war referendum amendment wherein only people eligible for military service may vote as to whether or not the country should to go to war) are intriguing, but the economics Q&A sessions are snoozers. Worse, they're *naïve* snoozers. The banking system, even in 1939, was far too complex for the fixes Heinlein proposes. But every once in a while your drooping lids are popped open with a passage like the following, in which Perry is talking to an economist named Davis.

Perry: "Everything may look rosy right now, but I believe that I see the seeds of decay in this system. Doesn't it encourage the reproduction of the unfit in unlimited numbers? Wasn't Malthus right in the long run? Aren't you steadily weakening the race by making life too easy?"

Davis: "I don't believe so. I think your fears are groundless. The pathologically unfit are inhibited from breeding by a combination of special economic inducements and the mild coercion of the threat of Coventry."

Heinlein tries to dress it up throughout the rest of the passage, but no matter how you spin it, he's talking about state-sanctioned eugenics, a notion that had a lot of popular support (Edgar Rice Burroughs was a notable advocate) in the 1930s.

The international stance of the US in 2086 is unwaveringly isolationist, and domestic policies are an odd mix: libertarian in the "private sphere," and authoritarian and utilitarian in the "public sphere." Heinlein proposes a benign Big Brother government that controls the banking system and doles out a monthly welfare check to every citizen.

But if you gird your loins and wade through the monologues, you'll wonder how he predicted FDR's third term and the EU, and be chilled by his description of an attack on the US in 2003 that leveled Manhattan. You'll also find yourself nodding and grinning as you recognize the social, sexual, political, and technological underpinnings of many of his subsequent stories. The free love, the feminism, the sense of duty and loyalty are all there. Many of the roots of Heinlein's Future History are tucked away in *FUTL*. You'll recognize bits and ideas that led to everything from "The Roads Must Roll" and "The Man Who Sold the Moon" to *Beyond This Horizon,* and *Stranger in a Strange Land.*

Does that mean you should run out and buy it? Probably not.

If you're someone who has read a fair amount of Heinlein, you won't find much new here – at least not much you will like. If you're someone who harbors fond memories and good feelings about his work, this won't enhance them; it may even tarnish them. And if you've never read Heinlein, please, please, *please* do not start here.

In his introduction Spider Robinson does a heroic job of looking on the bright side and subtly coaching you that what you're about to read isn't really as bad as you'll think it is. The afterword by Robert James is fascinating, giving us a look at 1930s politics and the events in Heinlein's life that influenced the utopia of *FUTL.* Easily the best part of the book.

But all this is moot. I say again: A deceased author's wishes concerning his unpublished work should be respected. Destroying all the known copies of a manuscript makes Heinlein's intent unmistakably clear: He did not want *For Us, The Living* to see the light of day. To go against those wishes is an affront to his right to privacy. To dig up a copy and publish it is literary grave robbing. What the hell was the Heinlein estate thinking?

Perhaps I'm overly sensitive about the issue. I have my reasons. My own first novel, *The Accidental Patriot,* was a book-length political diatribe, a near-future libertarian manifesto. A book not unlike *For Us, The Living.* And like *FUTL,* no one wanted it. I was sure the only reason the publishers were rejecting it was because of its radical political content. Years later I found the manuscript in a box in my cellar. A quick browse of a few chapters and the real reason for its universal rejection was obvious: The damn thing was unreadable. While trudging through *FUTL* I had a frisson, not from the text, but from thought of someone publishing *The Accidental Patriot* after my death. I know that the only existing copy was consigned to the flames – literally – many years ago, but the thought still caused a shudder.

Maybe you could make a case for a small print run by a university press as a reference for academics and Heinlein completists – this is, after all, the unborn fetus of his Future History – but for Scribner's to publish it as a major release... inexcusable. That's thumbing your nose at a dead author's dying wish.

Robert A. Heinlein did not want you to read this book. If you honor the man, honor his wish.

***

The Mandalorian (Season One)

Back in the day, when I was a new member of SFWA, we issued the *SFWA Handbook*, and in it we advised all writers to avoid the "space western." It might be popular on TV (*Star Trek* was called "*Wagon Train* in space") but the genre's print editors weren't interested.

It's still popular on TV as evidenced by the acclaim for *The Mandalorian* on Disney+. John Favreau, the writer and showrunner, has dipped into both the western bounty-hunter genre and the Japanese ronin films for inspiration. The title character is a masked bounty hunter who does a good imitation of Clint Eastwood's voice and wears a cape instead of a serape.

In season one's first three of the eight episodes we're treated to a saloon shootout, some alien bronco busting, a desert town shootout, and the successful capture of the objective: a fifty year-old alien child you have no recourse but to call "Baby Yoda" (he's not) who is terminally cute. By the end of chapter 3 the Mandalorian has decided to take the child under his wing, which lands a price on his head and sets all the other bounty hunters after him. (*John Wick*, anyone?) I watched him stride along with the floating basinet beside him and said, "*Lone Wolf and Cub.*" My daughter and grandson were watching with me but had no idea what I was talking about.

Episode 4 is a cut-down version of *The Magnificent 7* (or *Seven Samurai*). I say "cut down" because there are only two gunslingers (*The Magnificent Duo?*) – the Mandalorian and the hot but very scary Gina Carano. I could go on but I won't. I must, however, mention the arrival of Gus Fring in the guise of Mof Gideon, and the very cool salute to the finale of *The Wild Bunch* in episode 8.

I'm not complaining about the homages (?) because I had fun identifying them, but going forward I hope for more original plotting. I do see a problem with the Mandalorian religion forbidding him to show his face to another human being. It's a big drawback in that it's so distancing. This character is carrying the series but the helmet makes it very difficult to engage with him. Even old Mount Rushmore Eastwood gave us *something* as the Man with No Name (he could do a lot with a squint).

***

The *Fringe* Rip-off

2011 – Ripped off by my favorite TV show

So I'm sitting there watching the November 4 episode of *Fringe* (title: "Novation" written by J.R. Orci and Graham Roland) and slowly my jaw drops as I realize how much of it is stolen...from Matt Costello and me.

In case you missed it, *Fringe* is developing a story line about beings called shapeshifters from alternate Earth who possess a special cellular structure. With the help of an implanted disc, they can sample anyone's DNA and become a perfect copy (down to the base-pair level) of that other person. The disk stores the various genomes and can switch between them.

Flashback to 1998: Warner Aspect publishes a novel by Matt Costello and me called *Masque*. It centers around secret agents called "mimes" who have a special mimetic DNA (mDNA) that can be programmed to copy anyone else's DNA. All they have to do is slip in a template disk encoded with that genome and their bodies change into a perfect copy of that person down to the molecular level. They also have blank programmable disks that can copy a DNA sample, allowing them to "steal" anyone's genome on the fly.

Notice any similarity? Come on. Just a little?

They say you can't copyright an idea. Fine. But this is a lot more than a mere idea, this is a process, this is a whole *technology*. It's also the same plot – using these beings to infiltrate a rival group.

And it's not as if Hollywood has never seen *Masque*. It's been floating around since Tom Cruise's production company (Cruise-Wagner) optioned it for Polygram Pictures immediately after publication. When Polygram folded, so did the deal, but numerous game companies have been interested in adapting it to interactive form (which was how we'd originally conceived it).

Am I angry? Sadly, no. I say sadly because this seems to be the way writers work these days. Disheartened is more like it. Where I come from, writers honor each other's work. But the second-raters are always with us. They'll rip you off without so much as a by-your-leave because odds are they'll get away with it. (Not always: Just last week Little, Brown yanked the Q. R. Markham novel, "Assassin of Secrets," for plagiarizing dozens of writers, including Robert Ludlum.)

Since TV is such a collaborative process, the writers of this particular script might well be clueless as to the origin of the technology. But whoever introduced it into the story conferences had to have read *Masque*. It's too...damn... close. And then there's the fact that producer Roberto Orci (older brother of the co-writer) is no stranger to charges of plagiarism (see *The Island* vs *The Clonus Horror* suit).

I'm not the litigious sort, and don't keep lawyers on retainer like Fox, but, you know, a little tip of the hat would be nice.

If you want to check out what I'm talking about, the episode, "Novation," is out there; and the novel is available as an ebook under its preferred title, *DNA Wars*.

***

Fast-Forward Movie Reviews

Over the years I've done, quite literally, hundreds upon hundreds of brief movie reviews, published in my monthly newsletter, "The F Files." They certainly qualify as ephemerata, but they've already got their own website where they're catalogued by title and FF rating, so I'm not going to waste space replicating them here. If you're interested, go to: https://fpaulwilson.blog/about/

OPINION

I'm a contrarian and a skeptic by nature. I mean, I was born this way. If it's part of the zeitgeist, some lobe of my brain wants to come about and take a different tack. So I warn you: If you have sensitive triggers, you might be better off skipping this section.

I learned in college that I didn't think like other people (see "The Prometheus Award" below). I got along fine with the SDS radicals when we'd discuss legalizing pot and abolishing the draft, but when I'd talk about laissez-faire capitalism as the only moral economic system, it was "Get outa here!" And I got along fine with the Young Republicans until I mentioned legalizing drugs and prostitution and busting Lenny Bruce out of jail. Then they'd hold up figurative crosses to ward me off.

You see, I believe everyone owns their own life, and all my positions flow from that one simple premise. Too many people seem anxious to surrender that ownership to the state or the collective, so I've found it easier to keep my opinions to myself. But sometimes ya gotta speak up.

But opinions change and some of these pieces are a little bit out there for me these days. Whatever. I embraced them at the time, so…

Literary Darwinism - 555

Ad Statum Perspicuum - 558

The Prometheus Award - 562

F. PAUL WILSON

Galt's eGulch - 566

JFK Rant - 569

Dark Matter and the Dinosaurs - 573

Universal Prose Care - 574

And Now, From the People Who Brought You Vietnam and Watergate... - 578

Off-Shore Healthcare - 586

There Ain't No Such Thing as a Right to Healthcare - 588

In 1984 I submitted this to Charles Platt's Patchin Review. *Typical of Platt, his reply was quintessential Platt: "I vehemently disagree with every word of this, so I see no choice but to publish it." It appeared in issue #4.*

Literary Darwinism

Droids to the left of you, unicorns to the right, thick-thewed barbarians behind, and a daunting array of gleaming hardware ahead. Where else could you be but in the science-fiction and fantasy section of your friendly neighborhood bookstore?

A superficial survey is discouraging – everything appears formularized, packaged to start the browser salivating in response to his personal Pavlovian dinner bells.

Awful, no?

No. Not in the least.

Many people loathe surprises in their reading. Publishers know this, and so a tacit code is developed: a young, night-clothed woman fleeing a mansion dark but for a single lighted window guarantees gothic fans their money's worth; Conan-type warriors are another kind of promise, as are unicorns and hardware. What's wrong with that? They sell. A market has been established for these genres and subgenres. A demand exists; the publishers supply it. Both groups are happy. A perfect symbiosis has been established.

But what of those who don't mind surprises? Who pursue them, in fact?

Fear not. A careful look reveals that all is not lost. Beneath the veneer of sameness there lies surprising variety. Between the latest installment of the Pirates of Io Saga and the fifth volume of the Feathered Behemoth Trilogy wait unheralded gems.

Their Majesties' Bucketeers by L. Neil Smith comes to mind as a recent example. I defy anyone to categorize this delightful novel, completely devoid of human beings, in which a trilaterally symmetrical alien detective living in the equivalent of Earth's Victorian era solves a locked-room murder. The cant of Victorian prose is seamlessly reconstructed, and the intellectual excitement of an era in which technological advances are being made not in far-off government and corporate labs but down the street and around the corner in lofts and garages, is perfectly rendered

This book is a find. But it fits no subgenre – unless there's a group of alien detective fans hiding out there. It's a mutant, yet it appears to be finding an audience. Not a pre-fab audience, but a custom-made, word-of-mouth audience. Del Rey took a chance on this one and so far the reviews are pretty good; I see it disappearing from shelves so I must assume sales are, too. So there's something around for the adventurous types.

But what about those dour, tight-lipped, finger-wagging neo-Puritan biddies who moan constantly about Literary SF (a subgenre in itself, as formularized and predictable as space opera), to whom any book that's uplifting, positive about the human spirit, or in any way enjoyable, is either regressive or trivial? Is there anything for them?

Yes, even for them, although you'd never believe it to listen to their incessant whining. Admittedly, there's not much for them, but then, there aren't too many of their kind. They make a lot of noise, and have a fair number of camp-followers who mouth the proper buzzwords to keep themselves in the good graces of this vocal minority (just as conservative politicos invoke the Almighty whenever they can to stay on the good side of the Moral Majority, and liberals sing hymns to FDR and JFK to keep their A.D.A. ratings) but the hardcore numbers in the seri-lit camp are few.

Despite all the wailing and gnashing of teeth, there is something for just about everyone. According to *Locus*, a total of 1843 new science-fiction books were published in

1978, 1979, and 1980; and 1798 reprints in the same period. That's damned near a free market. With over 3600 titles to choose from, I can't see too many tastes going unsatisfied. You've got Disch and Burroughs and Norman and Varley and Malzberg and E.E. Smith in there. Something for everyone...

...but not in equal proportions. And there's the rub.

Let's all agree on something (please?): Books are published to be read. Not to boost the short leg of an end table or to start fires. To be *read*. Let us also agree that publishers must make a profit in order to pay their editors, typesetters, and printers, in order to stay in the business of publishing books (...to be read). Therefore it is counterproductive to print and distribute in the mass market quantities of a book that only a very select minority wants to read. Eighty percent returns means the publisher loses money, which means he has to make up that deficit elsewhere in the line, inevitably at another author's expense (one that more people might want to read), either through a smaller advance or a rejection slip.

Certainly no one should stop a publisher from putting anything he damn well pleases into print; and just as certainly, no publisher should be raked over the coals for rejecting books that won't sell. You might be able to make a case for affirmative action in real life, but not in publishing.

Laissez-faire, I say. Let literary Darwinism be the order of the day. There is no sane reason why publishers should not produce lots of the types of books that lots of people want to read, and very few of the books that very few people want to read. Authors whose works have a readership of 40 or 50 can self-publish or find a patron to finance minuscule print runs for their fans, thereby saving lots of trees.

The result is sterility, you say? Wrong. There will always be mutations. The viable ones will renew and rejuvenate the field; the mistakes will either spontaneously abort, be stillborn, or fail to procreate. There is a natural progression going on, continuous, unstoppable, leading I don't know where. Look back: the tenor of science fiction in any single decade is different from that in any other. For instance, 1940s science fiction was quite unlike that of the 1930s or 1950s. 1980s science fiction will be different from the last decade's. It will change in response to its environment.

Literary Darwinism. Natural selection. You'll have to resort to fascistic measures to alter the situation. So accept it. It encourages innovation, but not merely for the sake of innovation. Mutations are welcome, but they've got to hold their own. Writers must find an audience or move over and make room for someone else.

So it goes.

***

The title of this 1990 piece is also the title of Author's Choice Monthly #13, the issue devoted to yours truly. I wrote it as an introduction but I think it belongs with the opinion pieces. I'm a proponent of transparent prose for storytelling, and the title is Latin for "Toward Invisibility."

Ad Statum Perspicuum

The pink subscription renewal slip for one of the genre's more intelligent and challenging fanzines is sitting on my desk here and I'm wondering whether I should resubscribe. It's a thought-provoking little journal, and that's why I hesitate. It makes you think about writing, about schools of writing, about your place among other writers, about what all these critical minds will think about the next piece of your work they happen to read.

I wonder if too much of that sort of thinking is a good thing. Maybe it isn't wise for a writer to put what he does under a microscope.

That sounds anti-intellectual. I don't mean it that way. But I confess to being more than a little afraid to peer too deeply into the workings of my own writing process. It might prove dangerous... might kill the magic.

I'm not turning New Age on you. By magic I don't mean that writers are guided by some sort of muse or are tapping into a mystical realm for their output. I mean the mystery of the writing process itself – how it gets from nowhere onto paper, how it gets *done.* It's the mystery that makes the process seem magic, so I'm afraid the magic will go away if I solve the mystery.

In other words, I fear self-consciousness. I fear what it will do to the flow. I want to be conscious only of my story and of getting it across most effectively. I don't want to worry about whether I'm following all the rules of a given school, don't want to cast myself as, say, a post-modernist and be damned if I'll write anything but post-modem stories. I'd prefer to hunt about for whatever seems to work best, whatever style offers the story the neatest fit, whatever sounds right, *feels* right for a particular piece.

The only thing I'm self-conscious about is invisibility. I strive for it in every sentence. I want to be the invisible writer, a master of disguise, forever changing his style to blend with his surroundings. A trompe l'oeil writer.

I'm not there yet. It's a lot more difficult than it sounds. You've got to learn to sing in a variety of keys. Point-of-view becomes all important. You must merge yourself completely with the characters, sublimate your thought processes to theirs, and not only perceive the world through their senses, but respond to it within their own frames of reference.

This can be tough on the ego at times. It means subordinating everything you know to what the character knows, or thinks he knows. And there will be times when, if you're going to do it right, you will be required to toss out all those years of hard-won education.

For instance, if the p-o-v character of the moment is a truck driver who dropped out of school on the day he got his driver's license, hardly read when he was in school, and hasn't picked up a book since he left, you can't have allusions to "The Miller's Tale" wafting through his mind as he hurtles down the open road. Hell, you can't even have the word "waft" waft through his mind. You've got to think like a high-school drop-out, even if it means throwing out a few hoary clichés now and again. Not exactly fertile ground for evocative prose.

Some writers aren't cut out for this, can't stifle their egos long enough to bring it off. After all, the main reason some of us write is it's the only way we can get people to notice us. I'm sure a few names have come to mind already. The last thing they want in life is invisibility, even for the length of a short story. They prefer to put on a literary Fourth of July, filling the page with explosions of awe-inspiring descriptions and bursts of dazzling metaphor, no matter how inappropriate to the p-o-v character. This is literary booga-booga, it's waving a red flag to be sure the reader doesn't forget who's writing this wonderful stuff. And that's fine for them. It can be great to read, and I'm as awed as the next guy. But it's not what I'm after.

But into what school does this invisibility thing fall?

Who cares? As far as I know, it doesn't have a school or a name (please let's leave it that way) although I imagine most of us who strive for invisibility within our fiction fall into the storyteller category. I believe I prefer that term to writer or author. A writer or author might produce technical manuals or essays or political speeches or scientific articles or even greeting cards. Storytellers do only one thing.

But invisibility has serious pitfalls too. Top of the list is colorless prose. So you've got to sweat some if you want to keep things lively without showing your hand. And I suppose the major criticism of this sort of writing is that it isn't "challenging." The critics aren't talking about the content of the story, which in the best fiction is where the real challenge lies, but the prose. Yet what exactly do they mean by "challenging prose"? Prose that requires deciphering? Maybe I'm thick, but I don't understand that. Why should I set up barriers between the reader and my story? I want to clear a path between the two. I want reader and story to meet and fall in love. (If love isn't in the cards, I'll settle for a one-night stand.) And to prevent my presence from inhibiting their relationship, I try to become invisible.

But if I'm out to minimalize my auctorial presence, does that make me a minimalist?

Here we go. Another subset, another "school" of writing, another labeled pin to transfix you squirming to your proper place in the Great Design.

Too many writers hunger to slap a label on themselves. Maybe it's the literary equivalent of L.A. gangs strutting their colors, flashing their secret hand signs so they can recognize each other. Why do you have to belong to a gang? The publishers and booksellers do more than enough segregating. Why create further subdivisions? Aren't we fragmented enough?

No, I'm not a minimalist. I doubt I could be if I tried. If I've got it right, minimalism is characterized by flat, affectless prose that dwells on the superficial levels of everyday events, arranging them so the reader can experience little epiphanies. It proposes to challenge the reader to delve beneath the prose and root around until he or she digs out the meaning. And if the reader comes up empty-handed, it seems implicit that it's the reader's fault.

Sorry. I can't buy that. Don't bring a slab of raw meat, a pile of vegetables, some red wine, and a fistful of seasonings to the table and tell me it's *boef bourguignon*. And when I say cook it up for me, don't tell me it's minimalist cuisine – the diner is supposed to do the rest because that makes it more "challenging."

Pardon me, but I've always thought that simmering the ingredients into a flavorful stew was the author's job. That's why most readers come to the restaurant.

A reader never should be afraid to question how much a writer is bringing to the table. In too much of the minimalist fiction I've read, the answer is: not much. Don't be taken in by self-proclaimed authorities or the hot new writer touting the latest literary nouvelle cuisine, elegantly arranged on plain white china, as Real Writing that only those with discriminating palates can appreciate. Ask them what they're bringing to the table.

Don't get me wrong. I think plurality is wonderful. I'm happy for every style, old or new, that finds an audience. I just don't understand the chauvinism.

As for the stories included here, I've picked them because I feel I've been most successful in disappearing into their separate woods. If you find no coherent style to link them, if each seems as if it was written by a different author, then I've done my job. There's no school here, just storytelling. If you want to stick me with an *-ism* or an *-ist*, go ahead and try. You've got to find me first.

***

I presented the Prometheus Award at the 1983 World Science

Fiction Convention in Baltimore. I was asked to make some prefatory remarks.

The Prometheus Award

I suppose I should first answer the burning question uppermost in all your minds: What the hell is a libertarian? (Please note I use a lower case "l.")

Trouble is, there isn't any single universally accepted definition. Ask a thousand libertarians and you'll get 1022 definitions. And I hate definitions – they're straight-jackets. But strip away all the rhetoric and what you've got is an unshakable reverence for and commitment to the individual's right to self-determination. And it logically follows that if all individuals have the right to their own lives, then no single individual or group of individuals – no matter how large – has the right to use force against another individual. As a song went in the Sixties when I was in college: "Go where you wanna go, do what you wanna do, with whoever you want, Babe"...as long as that "whoever" wants to do and go with you. Put more crudely: Swing your fist any way you please, just don't hit anyone's nose. Or more succinctly: Laissez-faire.

You are free. If you are able, you can accumulate three cubic acres of cash, put it all in one big building, install a diving board and swim in it; or you can give it all to the poor (or better yet, build some factories and give those poor jobs); or eschew all wealth and live with some like-minded people on a farm in pure agrarian communism. No other social system – or non-system, as we like to say – allows you such latitude. You are free. You can explore all the possibilities of human existence, just as long as you don't apply force to others in order to make them share your vision. That is the ideal libertarian world.

Which right now can only live in fiction. The Prometheus Award was born to honor works of fiction which most closely approximate that ideal in their pages. The reason I have the mike in my hand at this moment is that my second novel, *Wheels Within Wheels,* won the first Prometheus Award in 1979. My third novel, *An Enemy of the State,* was a finalist for the second. A novella I named "The Tery," which was published in Jim Frenkel's *Binary Star* #2, has become a libertarian favorite. All of which prompted a fan at a Lunacon a few years ago to introduce me to his girlfriend as "F. Paul Wilson – he writes libertarian sf."

As I've said, I don't like labels. I don't even like to be called a libertarian – but "libertarian sf writer"! I vowed that my next book would be neither sf nor libertarian. It turned out to be a horror fantasy called *The Keep* and I did my damnedest to keep libertarianism out of it. The protagonist's moneybelt full of gold coins snuck in there, but for the most part I succeeded. Wasn't easy though. Libertarianism is not a suit of clothes you can put on and take off. It's ingrained in the heart and in the mind. It's in your cells. It's a worldview and it colors all your perceptions.

But it's not as much fun being a libertarian anymore. In the Sixties, a libertarian was a complete oddball. You didn't have the name "libertarian" to hold up. You didn't know how many others there were like you – or IF there were any others like you. You were a freak. No one knew what to do with you. But you could have FUN! You could blow people's minds by being anti-draft and pro-gold, anti-social security and pro-Lenny Bruce. You were a scandal to everyone in the middle of the road; the John Birchers didn't want you 'cause you didn't see anything wrong with legalizing the smoking of a certain weed; the New Left thought you were groovy until you started talking up laissez-faire capitalism as the only truly moral economic system... stopping their poor little Marxist hearts in mid-beat. You gave them ALL a rash.

Look what's happened since then. Everyone now knows that the social security system is nothing more than a giant chain letter. Richard Pryor plays the Hollywood Bowl and every other word is one of the ones Lenny Bruce used to get busted for; and the draft is gone and will stay gone unless certain elected officials – most notably, my favorite fascist Ted Kennedy – have their way and bring it back. And gold is legal.

Did I ever have fun with gold in the mid-Seventies.

"Hey, Paul.' What are you putting your money into?"

"Uh, mostly my mortgage payments, but I'm using whatever's left over to buy gold."

"GOLD!"

"Yeah. It's only $102 an ounce."

"$102 an ounce? You jerk! It's only worth $35! Aw, you're kidding me! Hey Tony! Wilson says he's buying gold! Whatta clown!"

I just smiled. I knew. All libertarians knew where gold was going.

But back to how things have changed. Would you believe there's even a Libertarian Party now? A decade ago, some of us thought that was impossible. (Some of us still think it's impossible. But I won't open that can of worms...)

Being a libertarian these days is almost – ugh – respectable. I can't stand it.

I remember when Neil Smith called me in the summer of '79 to tell me *Wheels Within Wheels* had won the Award – $2500 in gold at the time – I wasn't sure of my feelings. I was naturally elated to have been chosen, but had reservations about accepting an award from a political party. I hesitated. Neil wasn't aware of my hesitation because it's hard for the human mind to appreciate a nanosecond. During that nanosecond, a still small voice spoke from the back of my brain. It said, "Hey! Schmuck! It's 2500 bucks – in gold!" So I said, "Thank you Mr. Smith, I'd be proud to accept the award."

The year, as last year, the award is being presented by the Libertarian Futurist Society, which maintains a certain discreet distance from the party. (A libertarian futurist, in case you didn't know, is someone who, when you tell him that nothing is certain in this world but death and taxes, will differ with you on both counts.)

The envelope please...

(It went to James Hogan's *Voyage from Yesteryear*)

***

Here's one of those pieces you write because the urge/idea hits and then realize you have no idea where to publish it. I don't think I ever did. Since writing it in 2014, I've used bits of it in keynote addresses to aspiring writers and such, but I can't recall ever committing it to print. Until now.

Welcome to Galt's eGulch

If you're a capitalist and you know it, clap your hands.

That means you, all you self-published statists, collectivists, progressives, communists, anarchists, Democrats, Republicans*, syndicalists, and self-styled nihilists. How does it feel being a capitalist? Because that's who you are when you self-publish: You're investing time, talent, and money in creating a product and bringing it to market, then trying to drum up demand for it; or you're seeing a demand and creating a product to fill it. Either way: capitalism, baby.

Just to be clear: Capitalism is an economic system in which trade, industry and the means of production are controlled by private owners with the goal of making profits in a market economy.

That description fits the self-publishing ebook industry to the proverbial T. The writers own the means of production – i.e., themselves – with the goal of making profits in one of the last market economies on the planet.

Pretty cool, huh?

I'll bet only a few of you had any idea that's what you were into. Probably because you were educated to think of a capitalist as someone who looks like the Monopoly man, who exploits workers in his factories, who sells junk bonds on Wall Street, who buys politicians (even though public unions probably own more politicians than anybody) so he can suck up corporate welfare. You were presented with straw men like crony capitalism (e.g., Halliburton in the Bush era and Solyndra in the Obama regime), and told it was the real deal. But those were never the real deal. They fall into the farrago known as state capitalism, which is something else entirely.

Were you never told that true capitalism depends on free minds and free markets?

In short, you've been given the distinct impression that capitalism is baaaad – unless tempered by enlightened elected officials (which ignores P. J. O'Rourke's maxim: "When buying and selling are controlled by legislation, the first things to be bought and sold are legislators.")

You want to know what a capitalist looks like? Check the mirror.

Lots of folks with vested interests in the publishing machine status quo (and it's not just publishers and booksellers) decry the lack of gatekeepers in the indie publishing boom, and the tsunami of dreck being marketed by the lumpen proletariat. It's freakin' anarchy out there, man.

I say, Yay.

In traditional publishing and bookselling, shelf space and shelf time are limited, so money talks, losers walk. If the publisher decides it wants to make you a bestseller, it buys space on the stores' front tables.

The ebook world is more egalitarian: shelf space is unlimited, as is shelf time (because, as Konrath tells us, ebooks are forever). You don't need a printing press, you don't need a warehouse, you don't need delivery trucks... you simply need a book.

I happen to have my feet in both worlds (what Bob Mayer calls a hybrid author). I love my trade publisher. Truly. He's a salt-of-the-earth type whose employees love him as well.

He runs his company like a family. I've known my editor for longer than many of you have been alive. But writing is an obsessive-compulsive disorder for me, and my publisher can't handle all my output (and, frankly, doesn't want to). I'm not one of those writers who writes for moi. I'm not an artiste. I write to be read. And that means that sometimes I go the DIY route.

When I have something that's not right for my trade publisher (due to length, subject matter, market considerations) I cross the line into the world of self-publishing. As you've probably already discovered on your own, it's work. You thought capitalists sat in their offices and smoked cigars with their feet up on the desk, didn't you. This is what real capitalism is like. There's no welfare – corporate or otherwise – in self-publishing; no safety net, no nanny forcing readers to buy one book of Harry's for every book they buy by Dick and Jane, because Harry's self-esteem will be wounded if he doesn't sell any books. (Never mind that he can't write a coherent sentence, you owe him sales.)

Everybody's welcome in the marketplace. You want to take the ebook world by storm and be number one on all the lists? Welcome. You want to earn a little extra cash to buy some extras for the kids? Welcome. You want to publish that one very personal memoir so you can give it to friends and family at Christmas? Welcome.

I use etailers like Amazon, Nook, and Kobo to manage my sales; I love to see their checks hit my bank account every month. I gladly hand over 30% for a table at their flea markets. But I don't need them. I could keep 100% by selling directly through my own website (as I do with signed dead-tree books), but that's even more work. (Subcontracting leaves me more time to write.)

Just remember: Not everybody wins. (Not everybody even cares about winning.) No one's going to send you a check just for showing up. You need talent, you need drive, and y'gotta wanna. It's not a zero-sum game. Millions of

Kindles and Nooks and Kobos are waiting out there in the hands of millions of voracious readers, looking for that next book they'll love to death.

Welcome, fellow capitalist, as we search for the best way to write that book and get it into their download queues.

A warning, though. This level of freedom might not last forever. I believe the indie ebook market is as close to laissez-faire** as we'll ever see again, but I'm worried about what happens after our Commerce Department gives up control of the DNS next year. The US has done a pretty good job protecting Internet free speech across the globe*** (not 100% of course -- what's ever 100%?), but once we're no longer minding the store, things will (slowly, inevitably) change for the worse. Not so much in this country, but I can see the dictatorships (autocratic and theocratic-- I'm looking at you, China, Russia, and Iran) wanting to deny domain names to certain schools of thought or rendering pesky websites nameless, making them virtually impossible to find. And once those dominoes start falling...

But for now, we can publish whatever we wish. So write that book and become a published author... and a capitalist.

*(I hope you don't think they believe in capitalism)
** (certain etailers may not accept your book extolling the virtues of child molestation, and they have every right to choose what goes on their servers; you, however, have the right to sell it on your own.)
*** (how things changed in the 10 years since this was written)

***

Sent to Timothy Lane, editor of Fosfax, *a fanzine. I don't recall if he published it.*

JFK Rant

1/30/92

Dear Editors:

I've just suffered through the fourth TV interview in as many weeks watching the hilarious Oliver Stone shamelessly promote his *JFK* and feel compelled to say something about it. Maybe scream is more like it. Mary is tired of hearing me rant. *Fosfax* falls victim.

Where to begin? I remember JFK's assassination because it screwed up my senior prom night in high school. (Oswald had to pick *that* day to kill him.) I first heard about it at the InterCity station in the Washington Heights section of Manhattan while waiting for a bus back to New Jersey. People on the old #35 were talking about the president being shot in Dallas. I didn't believe it. When I got off the bus I ran home and found out he was dead.

Since that time I've seen a monumental whitewash job done on JFK's memory. The expatriates from the Camelot claque got together with the rest of the liberal establishment and its Northeast literary epigones (talk about conspiracy) and expunged their master's record of any blot of anticommunism, any hint of bellicosity, any profession of belief in the Domino Theory. He rose from the ashes as Shining John, the Dove of Doves, the man who would have withdrawn all our troops and "military advisors" from Vietnam, fed the hungry, clothed the naked, and sheltered the homeless if only he'd had the chance.

So when Oliver Stone asks: Who was to gain from the death of JFK? The logical answer is: The Military-Industrial Complex.

As we say around here: Bullshit.

JFK believed the communist threat from the USSR and Red China was very real; he was a professed believer in the Domino Theory. And if I may quote from his press conference on September 10, 1963 (ten weeks before he was killed); a passage which, by the way, seems to have got lost when the Camelot claque reprinted excerpts from JFK press conferences in their innumerable post-assassination encomiums – evidence of the whitewash mentioned above:

> *We want the war to be won, the Communists to be contained, and the Americans to go home. That is our policy. I am sure it is the policy of the people of Vietnam. But we are not there to see a war lost, and we will follow the policy which I've indicated today in advancing those causes and issues which help win the war.*

Are those the words of a president the Military Industrial Complex would want to assassinate?

Pardon me, but I don't think so. (Another expression we use around here.)

Stone's *JFK* would be a better film if retitled *Monte Python's JFK*. Really. It's perfect for them. You take a murdered, anti-Communist, Domino-Theory-believing president who didn't blink when Khrushchev moved missiles into Cuba, you posthumously doublethink him into a dove, then you blame his murder on the very folks who were sympathetic to his anti-Communist, Domino-believing ways in the first place.

In other words, folks, the JFK killed in Stone's film is a revised, expurgated, double-thought person who never existed.

I wish Philip K. Dick were alive. He'd have loved this.

But even if you've been totally suckered into the JFK-as-dove fiction, how can you swallow this: We have the CIA, the FBI, Army Intelligence, the Cubans, the Vietnamese, and sundry other Politically Correct villains conspiring and succeeding in killing a U.S. president (and, according to Stone, RFK and MLK too) and somehow, with all those people involved, keeping it secret for almost 30 years.

Pardon me again, but I don't think so. There's an old Spanish saying that goes, *Three may keep a secret if two are dead.* Stone's ungainly Grand Unified Politically Correct

Assassination Conspiracy Theory requires *lots* of very busy folks.

Consider further: This same many-tentacled combine presumably would be in *favor* of keeping someone like old Tricky Dick in office, yet with all its supposed power and influence – enough, remember, to kill a president, a senator/presidential candidate, and the most visible and influential black political figure in the nation's history, and cover it up for decades – it can't quite put the lid on a simple break-in involving a Washington, DC hotel suite.

Pardon me yet again, but I don't think so.

Has the JFK assassination ever been explained to anybody's satisfaction? Hardly. Has this film shed any light on the question? Hardly. Will it get people thinking about it? Yes, but in the wrong direction. If there was a conspiracy, it was small and tightly organized by pros. Your best bet would be the Chicago mob:

1) JFK was literally and figuratively in bed with one of the Chicago families;

2) the mob was more powerful and better organized then, with the balls, the personnel and the logistical ability to pull it off;

3) it has the tradition of *omerta* that might conceivably bury a secret this long.

Why would the mob kill JFK?

Fact: JFK's victory in Cook County swung all the Illinois electoral votes to the Democrats, the very votes that provided JFK with the narrow majority he received to win the election.

Speculation: Mayor Daley usually gets the credit for delivering Cook County, but maybe he had help. And maybe JFK (or his father) welshed when it came time for payback.

Just a thought. Far out, but a more likely scenario, I think, than the sprawling offspring of Stone's Politically Correct Paranoia being shown in the theatres. But promoting the mob theory would not make Stone the darling of the

Right People in Hollywood and might even get him in trouble with the Wrong People elsewhere in the country. Let's face it: Stone's Grand Unified Politically Correct Assassination Conspiracy Theory is safer. Definitely safer.

So I tell you, if I were part of the *real* conspiracy – whoever it was – to kill JFK, I would heartily applaud the release of Monte Python's – excuse me – Philip K. Dick's – excuse me – Oliver Stone's *JFK*.

***

*Another one of those things that occur to you (this in late winter 2017) and you write out with no idea what to do with it. I read a book on dark matter (*Dark Matter and the Dinosaurs*) and realized at the end I didn't understand any more than I had at the beginning. I felt like I was back in Catechism class at Our Lady Queen of Peace grammar school, trying to get a straight answer.*

Don't take this too seriously. Just having a little fun.

God & Dark Matter

Our galaxy is spinning like a pinwheel. What keeps all those stars from flying off into intergalactic space?
Priest: God
Scientist: Dark matter

Where is God?
Priest: Everywhere.

Where is dark matter?
Scientist: Everywhere.

Can we see God?
Priest: No, but we know He's there.

Can we see dark matter?
Scientist: No, but we know it's there.

Can we touch God?
Priest: No.

Can we touch dark matter?
Scientist: No.

Is God here now?
Priest: God is in us and all around us.

Is dark matter here now?
Scientist: Dark matter is in us and all around us.

So God hasn't normal flesh.
Priest: Correct.

So dark matter isn't normal matter.
Scientist: Correct.

Where did God come from?
Priest: It's a mystery.

Where did dark matter come from?
Scientist: It's a mystery.

How do we know God exists?
Priest: Without him the galaxies would fly apart.

How do we know dark matter exists?
Scientist: Without it the galaxies would fly apart.

***

I wrote this satire to help promote The Select. *It appeared in the 2/20/94 issue of* The New York Times Book Review *shortly after Hillary Clinton's hilarious health care plan (with all its intricate and arcane provider-patient alliances) was made public, and must be viewed in that context. For about six months Hill's plan was the wonder of the country. Everyone wanted to know how, after spending all that time and all those millions, she could come up with such an unfeasible disaster? Bill quickly swept it under the rug.*

Universal Prose Care: A Modest Proposal

Given the reforms recently proposed for other areas of endeavor that impact society on the macro and micro level, the publishing industry is now in line for restructuring. Using the innovative principles of managed publishing, the National Literary Realignment Act will undertake said restructuring. The basic triad of author, publisher, and bookseller that makes up the current system will not be altered; their interrelationships, however, will be realigned.

In order to more precisely specify the respective functions of the groups involved, Step One will be Designation Modification. Henceforth, authors shall be designated as prose providers; publishers shall be print producers; booksellers shall be tome dispensers. The three entities shall be realigned into discreet interactive alliances.

The Prose Provider - Tome Producer Alliance

Since it is a given that every prose provider has a basic human right to be published, it is obvious that the current methodology of print production requires top-to-bottom restructuring. The present system of print producers wading through redundant piles of manuscripts – often as many as a dozen print producers reading the same multiply- or serially-submitted manuscripts – is extremely wasteful of editorial time and corporate resources. Quite simply, this system of choosing manuscripts on the basis of subjective quality and/or salability is a dinosaur. It has not only outlived its usefulness, it is inherently unfair. It must go.

The solution is the Prose Provider-Print Producer Alliance. In the managed publishing system under the

National Literary Realignment Act, Regional Boards of the Literary Security Agency will assign each print producer a variable number of novelists, essayists, biographers, and poets, based on the pool of available talent and the print producer's size and past history of production. The prose providers of each alliance will submit only to their designated print producer, and that print producer in turn will receive submissions only from prose providers within their alliance. The benefits of this arrangement to the print producers are immediately apparent. The alliances will streamline the submission process, shrink the slush pile, drastically shorten reply lag time, and eliminate wasteful duplication of effort. Print producers will be relieved of the tiresome burden of weighing the relative merits of submissions to decide which will be accepted. *Every* manuscript will be accepted, then edited and published in a timely fashion. The benefits to the prose provider also are obvious. No longer will they waste valuable time pondering which print producer should first receive their manuscript. Under the alliance system, they'll know exactly where to send their work. They will also be spared the anxiety of wondering whether or not their work will be accepted for publication. No worry here. It is always accepted. (And since stress is well known to be deleterious to health, the Prose Provider - Print Producer Alliances will contribute significantly to improving the national health as well.)

The specter of overutilization has been raised. To deter this, safeguards will be in place from the outset. Each prose provider will be assured an annual publishing allotment of one short story, and a triennial allotment of one novel. If there is undue public demand for more of a particular prose provider's work than his or her backlist will satisfy, said prose provider will be allowed (only after submission of Extraordinary Demand Requisition Forms A73 through F29 and not before issuance of an Excess Verbiage Authorization Number by the Literary Security

Administration Regional Board) to publish one extra short story per year and one extra novel (not to exceed 100,000 words) during every triennial novel allotment period. This will prevent undue quantities of literary resources from being gobbled up by a few excessively prolix individuals.

The Print Producer - Tome Dispenser Alliance

Month after month, tome dispensers are inundated with brochures and advance reading copies of forthcoming titles, are harassed by armies of salesmen from the print producers. Month after month, they must sift through thousands of titles and decide which to order, how many to order, weigh discounts against co-op advertising budgets and myriad other variables. This system is blatantly wasteful, squandering both tome dispensers' time and print producers' resources.

The National Literary Realignment Act will resolve such waste. Literary Security Administration Regional Boards will set up Print Producer - Tome Dispenser Alliances by assigning each tome dispenser a fixed number of print producers to supply it with books. Each dispenser will order a fixed number of copies of each title from each print producer in its alliance. This number will be determined by Literary Security Administration Regional Boards in accordance with the local area's population density, average socio-economic status, and literacy level.

With a single stroke, this simple measure will reduce overhead for tome dispensers by cutting untold personhours per week. In addition, it will save print producers the high cost of over-runs and unexpectedly heavy returns (thus saving innumerable trees); the resources now devoted to advertising, sales, and promotion can be redirected toward the editorial departments and toward lowering the unit price of their products.

And the consumer? Literary consumers will do what they have always done: Go to stores and buy books.

But under the National Literary Realignment Act they will benefit not only from reduced unit cost, but also from exposure to countless new prose providers who would not have seen print under the present outmoded system.

With lower costs all around, greater variety of literature, positive impact on both the environment and the national health, it is clear that the National Literary Realignment Act is a win-win proposition, and is sure to be met enthusiastic approval by both the public and the impacted parties.

***

My guest editorial in the April, 1975 Analog. *At fifty years old, the piece is definitely dated, but I'm reprinting it here as proof that the debate did not start with the Obama administration.*

The title is a play on adman Jerry Della Femina's memoir, From Those Wonderful Folks Who Gave You Pearl Harbor. *Being a libertarian, I was all for letting the free market handle things. But with Medicare and Medicaid already seasoning the pot, a free market in healthcare can't exist. (Don't forget that the money mentioned here is in 1975 dollars, and even so were astronomically naïve as to what even a partial system like ACA costs.) This is how things looked in the mid-70s. I return to the subject 20 years later in the next piece. But first…*

And Now, From the People Who Brought You Vietnam and Watergate…

…health care.

The men and women, elected and otherwise, who run our government have decided to overhaul the way health care is delivered in this country. Having demonstrated over the past decade and a half their expertise in foreign relations, political ethics and economic management, they have somehow come to the conclusion that their talents are needed in the field of medicine. After all, there is a health care crisis in the United States, isn't there?

There is if you read the major wire services or the *Times* or the *Post,* or watch the news and special reports on CBS and NBC, or listen to politicians like Kennedy and Mills, *et al.* These information dispensers and opinion-makers have so efficiently inundated the mass media with negative medical propaganda over the past few years that fully 75 percent of the people in this country are convinced that they are in the middle of a health care crisis.

However, in a University of Chicago national probability sample poll which asked "Are you dissatisfied with your own health care?" the affirmative response amounted to a mere 10 percent.

In no conceivable analysis of these percentages can one honestly construe a groundswell of public opinion behind the words and actions of our elected officials.

Statistics are boring, but there's quite a contrast between what is being disseminated through the media and what is really going on. For instance, we're told that health care is not sufficiently available to the people under the auspices of the current chaotic private non-system. But 90 percent of the population feels satisfied with the non-system that has put a doctor 17 minutes from the average doorstep and somehow manages to see 2,300,000 patients a day (over 50,000 of those through house calls!). And as for emergency rooms, the average wait is less than 29 minutes with an appointment and less than 37 minutes without.

So much for availability. On to those frightening mortality figures. Our political leaders and editorialists seem to take great relish in telling us that the United States ranks number 22 in life expectancy for men; but they neglect to fill you in on the fact that a staggering number of us die from causes unrelated to disease. In fact, accidents are the most common cause of death through middle age in the United States – 50,000 of us are done in yearly on our highways alone; add to that the deaths from personal violence, accidents around the home and work-related trauma and you've shortened the lives of a sizable number of Americans without the help of disease.

The infant mortality issue carries the same brand of misrepresentation even further. The favorite ploy is to take statistics from countries that are relatively genetically homogenous and compare them disparagingly to the US melting pot. But if you look at a genetic "mixture of European countries along with another melting pot called the USSR – nearly all of which have some form of government controlled medicine – the results are quite edifying:

Infant deaths/1000

USSR..28.0
European Free Trade Association......22.5
Common Market Countries................21.6
United States of America.................19.8

The death of even one potentially rational human mind is, of course, one too many; but the figures show that government programs do nothing to improve the situation.

The cost of healthcare in America, however, seems to be the most overburdened issue. We're told that medical costs rose 50 percent in the decade between 1960 and 1970. But no one mentions that this rise compares favorably with the rise in cost of other services over the same period; nor is it mentioned that it was during this period that intensive care units and coronary care units came into their own and medical technological sophistication advanced at an unprecedented rate. And of course the politicians are loath to remind the consumer that the decade in question was the one in which the Federal Government made its first intrusion on private medicine (Medicare and Medicaid became law in 1965) for an obvious reason: some savvy voters might infer a cause-effect relationship.

Health care, like any other service, is expensive.

There's no getting around that, despite a recent Louis Harris poll showing that the average American family spends $133 a year on health care, less than the average car annually burns up in gasoline. But don't expect a government National Health Insurance plan (NHI) to cut that cost. A Rand Corporation survey estimates that NHI will *add* up to 16 million dollars a year to health care expenditures. The money will have to come from somewhere, either from increased taxes (which leave you less to spend on other things) or increased deficit spending (which ultimately makes what you have worth less) or both.

In spite of this, most Americans, if pressed, will say that they wouldn't mind seeing the US adopt a program of free medical care similar to the one in England.

The key word here, of course, is *free.*

OK, the government pays for it, but Heinlein's acronym, TANSTAAFL, is never truer than when applied to government action. Governments produce no income; they can only appropriate money from productive individuals, run it through a bureaucratic grinder and return but a small fraction to those who earned it. No government has ever truly saved its citizens money by getting involved in health care.

England is a good case in point. The famous British National Health Service, when inaugurated, estimated its annual cost at 170 million pounds. Expenditures are now running at 2.6 *billion* pounds a year.

Why the incredible overrun? Besides the usual mismanagement, duplication of effort and blatant wastage that attends any bureaucratic endeavor, the primary reason is overutilization – an inevitability once the financial link between a consumer and a commodity or service is removed. Everyone wants to "get his due" and consequently there are waiting lists, some years long, for elective surgery. The uncomplicated inguinal hernia, nose job, cataract, et cetera, is forced to wait until space is available. So patients are sent scurrying around the countryside looking for empty hospital beds and available surgeons.

Outpatient care is even more chaotic. Patients who are genuinely ill are crammed into crowded waiting rooms for hours alongside hordes of malingerers looking for a sick slip for work, hypochondriacs in for one of their thrice-weekly visits, lonely senior citizens with nothing better to do. People with minor complaints that would formerly have been handled by over-the-counter preparations (but which, under the British system, can be had for a fraction of the cost if prescribed by a physician) while the doctor in the back rips through twenty patients an hour.

It's hardly surprising that Prime Minister Wilson, long a vocal supporter of the National Health Service, has a private, non-participating physician to tend to his own health needs.

The vaunted Swedish system is no better. There are some 15,000 people on waiting lists in Stockholm alone. It can take three years to get a gallbladder to the operating table and a patient can look forward to a seven-year wait for plastic work. There's even a wait of nearly a year and a half to get a hearing-aid repaired!

And the above is only a small part of the price Americans will be forced to pay for "free" medical care. One of the grimmest portents of things to come can be found in Senator Bennett's amendment to the 1972 Social Security Act which calls for the establishment of "Professional Standards Review Organizations" (PSRO). As explained to the public, PSRO boards will be composed of local physicians who will monitor hospital admissions of patients participating in government programs (this means Medicare and Medicaid now, but will cover virtually all US citizens under NHI) to guard against unnecessary procedures and to insure that patient care meets certain standards.

Sounds reasonable, doesn't it?

What you're not told is that the law provides for the establishment of regional and national codes of health care to which physicians and patients will be subject.

For instance: Assuming no complications, a patient will be allowed "x" number of days in a hospital for gallbladder surgery and no more. A local PSRO board of physician-bureaucrats (made up primarily of doctors who are either re-tired or couldn't make it in practice) will consult the code book and send the patient home on day "x" despite the protestations of the attending physician who knows that she has five children and will not be able to convalesce properly at home. Two extra days as an in-patient could make a significant difference as far as wound healing is concerned. But the board doesn't know the patient; it knows only what the code book of regional standards says.

The local PSRO board is also empowered to block a patient's admission to a health care facility if the case does not meet certain norms. Appeals can be made, of course, but a favorable decision might come too late.

If complications should ensue – wound dehiscence from an early discharge or death from a denied admission – the patient or his family must grin and bear it. The Federal Government has anticipated such occurrences and has made PSRO members immune from prosecution.

However, the most frightening aspect of the PSRO amendment (and remember: this is not pending legislature – this is already law) is that it gives the local boards, which are funded by, and answerable to the Federal Government via the Department of HEW, the right to inspect a physician's medical records. What has been traditionally privileged information is now available to local, regional and Federal PSRO boards. Records that a physician would formerly release only with the patient's written permission are now up for grabs without the benefit of a court order or a search warrant.

Thus a "plumber's squad" is no longer necessary to gain access to the medical records of someone like Daniel Ellsberg-all that's needed is a little pressure on the local PSRO board.

Another Louis Harris poll demonstrated that of all professions and institutions, medicine ranks *first* in the confidence of American citizens; politicians place a poor *last.* On those terms alone, the Bennett PSRO amendment is a blatant absurdity: the institution last in public confidence has arrogantly and unilaterally decided to police the first in public confidence, purportedly for the public good.

There is most certainly a health care crisis in America. Not the one propagated by members of Congress and their mouthpieces in the media in a startling modern day vindication of Goebbels' thesis that if a big lie is repeated often enough, it soon becomes accepted as common fact. No, the true crisis is the threatened intrusion of brazen and ludicrously unqualified bureaucratic minds upon a vital area of human endeavor that has historically served, and is currently serving, the health needs of this country with efficiency, privacy and compassion.

Remembering that the poor and the elderly are already covered by Medicare and Medicaid (so don't get taken in by tales of destitute people wracked by disease – programs are available to pay for *all* of their health care expenses), the American consumer must ask himself what he will gain by further extension of the government into private medicine. Answer: nothing. A glance at the European experience and at the PSRO law amply shows what he stands to lose.

Another question: Is there any way NHI can be stopped? Only one – all physicians and hospitals in this country must unite, refuse to participate in the plan and repudiate the validity of PSRO authority over their patients and their medical records.

But now we're into speculative fiction. Doctors are a maverick breed and notoriously unorganized; the AMA, which is run by the same breed who will volunteer for PSRO positions, has virtually jumped on the NHI bandwagon over the protestations of its membership.

We will have NHI, maybe not this year, and perhaps not next year, but Congress will eventually get where it wants to go. We will have NHI not because we need it, but because the people in Washington want it. And don't be lulled into false security by thinking that the power of the vote will save you. A passage from Panshin's *Starwell* is appropriate here: "Celebrities... meet only fools, creeps, panhandlers and climbers. People they would truly like to meet never have the bad taste to present themselves. The quality that makes them worth meeting automatically determines that they will never be met."

Substitute "voters" for "celebrities" and you have an oblique indictment of even the most democratic system of government. The man who is not of an interventionist mentality, who is satisfied with self-domain and does not seek domain over others, who is not drawn to the seat of power like a moth to a flame, rarely has the time, inclination or plain bad taste to run for public office. And should' he do so, he's rarely elected.

This viewpoint may prove too cynical for you...at present. A few years under NHI, PSRO and the rest of the Federal alphabet soup may well change your mind. The Federal machinery is gearing up to institute a health care system that has been proven time and time again to be more costly and less efficient than the current one. The current system is hardly faultless and it is unquestionably expensive, but it will only be hindered and debased by Federal intervention.

We shall have NHI and therefore I wish you good health in the coming years.

You're going to need it.

***

I don't know if this was ever published. I'm thinking not. Obviously written around 1994 when Hillary Clinton was seeking to take over US healthcare a la the British NHS, so maybe I intended it as a companion piece to "Managed Publishing" to help promote The Select. *This eventually became the basis of my story "Offshore."*

You've Heard of Offshore Oil Rigs --
Here Comes Offshore Healthcare

There's a dark side to the Clinton health care reform package: Any plan that caps spending, whether through price controls or a flat-out dollar ceiling, must involve rationing of services. One leads to the other like night follows day.

Health care rationing is a dirty word in this country, however, so beware the various euphemisms being floated our way. "Queuing" is one. It means you get in line and wait your turn. (In the United Kingdom they don't mince words, they simply turn you down -- to the tune of 12,000 cancer chemotherapy patients, 9,000 renal dialysis patients, and anywhere from 4,000 to 17,000 coronary artery bypass patients *per year*.)

With "queuing," however, you're told that you're not being denied that coronary artery bypass, or that hip replacement, you're simply waiting your turn.

You could die waiting your turn.

In fact, twenty-four people in British Columbia in the queue for coronary artery bypasses did just that in 1989 under the Canadian system. And in Newfoundland, waiting your turn for that hip replacement routinely takes 18 to 24 months.

And then there's the problem of keeping your place in line. If you don't have political connections or can't pay off the right people, you'll find yourself bumped back time after time. Let's face it: Our duly elected senators, congressmen, governors, and other public servants with political clout are not going to sit around and wait among the hoi polloi for their number to come up. Their names are going to appear magically at the top of the lists. And if one of their wives needs a hysterectomy, well, you don't really expect a Washington doyenne to get at the end of the queue and wait her turn, do you?

The new ways in the U.S. may well begin to resemble the good old days in the U.S.S.R. where the commissars and their friends and families got the best apartments and the highest food rations while the rest of their comrades got the leftovers.

This explains why the hospitals along our northern border, in Seattle, Detroit, Buffalo, Cleveland, and Rochester, are loaded with Canadians. We're Canada's safety valve.

But when we have a national health plan with spending caps and long, long queues for treatment like they do, where will *we* go?

Just as Canadians cannot legally pay for their medical services, it's very possible that hospitals on the U.S. mainland may not be allowed under the new plan to operate on a fee-for-service basis. So what about that gallbladder or arthritic hip that's making your life miserable? Or those clogged coronary arteries that are a ticking time bomb in your chest? What do you do when the local health alliance administrator tells you to get in line and wait the six, twelve, or eighteen months it's going to take to get definitive treatment? You've worked all your life, you've got money saved, and you're willing to spend it on your health. Where do you go?

Off shore, most likely.

That's not as far-fetched as it sounds. There are unused oil rigs off shore in the Gulf of Mexico that are beyond the twelve-mile limit. I foresee a day when some of them will be converted to hospitals. The same with luxury liners. The

Love Boat will become the Health Boat, staffed with defiant medical personnel, cruising the coastline, stopping and anchoring beyond the twelve mile limit until patients can be ferried out from the shore for the surgeries and medical treatments denied them on the mainland, and then moving on to pick up the next batch.

These off-shore hospitals will be equipped with the cutting-edge medical technology unavailable on the mainland due to the very same spending caps that will limit access to medical care.

It's a strange paradox. Nowadays we're told of the 37 million Americans who supposedly don't have health insurance. But lack of health insurance doesn't mean lack of access to health care. Any one of those uninsured can walk into any emergency room and be treated for whatever ails them. Under universal coverage, we'll all have health insurance but, because of the queues, we won't have universal access to health care.

Go figure.

Universal coverage and spending caps are ideas whose time has come. They promise a new era of national health. Fine. Tip your hat to the new revolution. But save your money and stock up on seasick pills. You may need them for those trips off shore.

***

Originally written for my column on the now defunct True/ Slant *site where I mostly posted science news with occasional comments. Here was a true opinion piece. Need I say it raised lots of hackles?*

There Ain't No Such Thing as a Right to Healthcare

The acronym for that would be TANSTAARTHC. Nowhere near as euphonious as TANSTAAFL, but...

"Health care is a human right."

The phrase has entered the zeitgeist. Google it and you'll get 25k hits. Google "right to health care" and you get 200k. Maybe I'm not listening hard enough, but I hear no one questioning its validity.

A right is intrinsic. It's not given to you, it's something you're born with. Its existence is not dependent on the actions of others. In fact, only by the actions of others can it be taken from you.

I find the stranded-alone-on-a-desert-island rule a convenient way to differentiate genuine human rights from the poseurs.

Let's start with the basics: life, liberty, and the pursuit of happiness. You've still got those on a desert island. You may not be happy there, but you don't have a right to happiness, only to seek it out.

On a desert island, you still have the right to free speech. And freedom of religion. And freedom of sexual expression. You also have the freedom to smoke or inject whatever available substances you care to.

But the island does not provide three squares a day because there are no farmers to provide them; you do, however, have a right to grow or forage whatever you can. You don't have a right to a roof over your head because there are no carpenters on the island, but you do have a right to erect one.

And you don't have a right to health care because there are no doctors and nurses and drugstores on the island.

No point in belaboring this. Genuine human rights do not require the participation of anyone outside the individual. Anything that does require the aid or intervention of another party is something else. I'm not sure what it is, but it's not a human right.

Challenging health care as a human right, inevitably and unfortunately, casts one as a heartless person, blind to human suffering, who wants sick people to go untreated.

Nothing could be further from the truth.

The question asked here is not whether our fellow human beings should receive the health care they need, but whether it is a human right.

Why is this important? Because health care as a human right is newspeak. It redefines a term to fit a given political or social agenda. Philip K. Dick said, "If you can control the meaning of words, you can control the people who must use the words."

Wishing doesn't make it so. No matter how badly you want it to, "Human right" does not translate into "You owe me."

Nobody owes you health care. You have the right to negotiate for the services of someone who knows more about health than you do, but you don't have a right to that person's knowledge and effort.

If your society decides that all its members should have free access to health care, then you are the fortunate recipient of a gift or a mandated benefit or whatever society wants to call it. But it's not a human right.

TANSTAARTHC.

TIMELINE: THE SECRET HISTORY

The Secret History of the World recounts the events that remain undiscovered, unexplored, and unknown to most of humanity – the goings on behind the scenes, hidden from the workaday world. It stretches from the Oligocene epoch to the end of civilization as we know it. ("Year Zero" recounts those terminal events; "Year Zero Minus One" is the year preceding it, etc.)

30 mya – the Squatter uses enhanced primates to create an "Archimedes" device connected to a cavern in the then-temperate Antarctica

25 mya – the Drake Passage forms, cutting S. America off from Antarctica and the Archimedes device

600 kya – the Ally modifies adapiform primates to transfer hsa-mir-3998 to *H. sapiens*

15-16 kya – THE FIRST AGE
Glaeken and Rasalom square off in Elder cavern
Glaeken causes Rasalom's first death
But Rasalom, paladin of the Otherness, manages a return
Srem compiles her *Compendium*
The Great Cataclysm ends the First Age and resets human civilization

4200 BCE – The rakoshi are created by the Otherness in the Indus Valley

452 BCE – Q'qret, a Septimus colony established in the Pine Barrens, includes a pyramidal structure built to house the last q'qr. Q'qret eventually became a palimpsest town, built over and renamed Quakerton during Colonial times

1317 BC – the Gaijin Masamune katana forged in Japan after Glaeken requests a heavy dirk to be refashioned into a kodachi. The dirk's metal had fallen from the sky in a blaze of light

1476 – Glaeken traps Rasalom in the Keep he built in the Dinu Pass

1498 – the *Compedium* is rescued from Torquemada and the Inquisition

1579 – the first appearance of the Kuroikaze on Honshu's Noto Peninsula

1847 – Glaeken seals the *Compendium* and other books during one of his inspections of the keep

1857 – Captain Sir Albert Westphalen sacks the Temple-in-the-Hills in West Bengal, killing the high priest and his wife, but their children survive

1860 – Rudolph Drexler born 4/7

1874 – noting that Joseph Wharton was buying up large areas of the NJ Pine Barrens, Glaeken stepped in as "Mr. Foster" and bought a tract of woodland in order to isolate an area that had been frequented in ancient times by devotees of the Otherness.

1878 -- President Andrew Johnson spends 3 nights in Quakerton, NJ.In his honor, the town renames itself Johnsonville, which is eventually shortened to Johnson, NJ

1890 – Ernst Drexler Sr born

1906 – Tesla's Wardenclyffe tower breaches Veil, causes 'Frisco quake; Rudolph Drexler disappears at Wardenclyffe

1912 – Madame de Medici vs Sherlock Holmes ("The Adventure of the Abu Qir Sapphire")

1923 – Ernst Drexler Sr diverts Karl Stehr's shot during Munich putsch ("Aryans and Absinthe")

1926-45 – *Black Wind*

1927 – Jonah Stevens loses his left eye in Great Lower Mississippi Valley Flood

1930 – Jack's father born

1931 – Jack's mother born

1938 – After wandering the globe for millennia, Glaeken moves to Tavira, Portugal, where he crews for a fisherman named Sanchez

1940 – 11/28: U-104 reported missing NW of Ireland, all hands presumed lost December: U-104 arrives Fimbulisen

1941 – early April – Jasmine "Jazzy" Cordeau impregnated
        with a human clone;
April 22: German soldiers occupy the Keep
April 23, 8:56 PM EST – the signals start
May 3 – Glaeken slays Rasalom for the 2nd time.
        Rasalom invades the clone in Jazzy's womb
        Glaeken, no longer immortal, begins aging.
        Jonah begins visions of "the Vessel" in his blind eye
June – Glaeken moves to Bucharest of be with Magda
July – Alexandru sells *Compedium* & other books to a Bucharest dealer
September – Prof. Cuza dies from complications of scleroderma
December – Glaeken and Magda marry

1942 – Jan 6: the Vessel (Hanley's clone) is born to Jazzy
 Rasalom remains a helpless prisoner in its body
Feb: Jonah and Emma Stevens adopt the Vessel from St. Francis Orphanage and name him James
March – the Twins are born

1946 – Walter Erskine born in Chillicothe, MO

1947 – the *Lange-Tür* project begins

1949 – a Bucharest book dealer sells the *Compendium* to an American collector

1950 – Korean War: Jack's father trained as a US Army sniper by Sgt. Nacht

1951 – Ernst Drexler II born

1955 – the Gaijin Masamune stolen from the Peace Memorial Museum in Hiroshima

1959 – Tom Jr born

1961 – Kate born

1962 – Jack's father gets a vasectomy

1968 – Feb 11: Rasalom is freed from "the Vessel" when James
 Stevens fathers a child with his wife Carol. Rasalom
 becomes the child – agency at last
 The conception causes a burst of Otherness, triggering
 a slew of birth defects in the local unborn that become
 known as "the Monroe cluster."
  Dr. Hanley's plane crashes
  All the signals stabilize
Mar – *Dat Tay Vao* enters Walt Erskine in Viet Nam
April – Jack conceived
Sept – Weezy Connell born
Oct – the first of the "Monroe Cluster" is born
Nov 7 – Rasalom reborn in Hickory Hill, AK to Carol Stevens.

She calls him "Jimmy."

1969 – Jan – Jack born
Feb – Mrs. Clevenger moves into Johnson, NJ
Oct – Eddie Connell born

SOMETIME IN THE EARLY 1970s – Jonah Stevens's kids: Hank born in January; Jeremy in December; Moonglow / Christy born the following December.

1970 – 24-yr-old Walt Erskine gets medical discharge from Army after treated for a mental condition at Northport V.A. Hospital. Diagnosed as a paranoid schizophrenic. Thought he could heal people.

1972 – Walt joins a faith-healing tent show in the South

1974 – After being kicked off tent show tour because he was never sober,
Walt comes to live with sister Adelle in Johnson, NJ

1975 – American collector robbed of the *Compendium* by Jonah Stevens

1976 – Luther Brady mysteriously gifted the *Compendium* after college

1979 – Jonah Stevens killed in an elevator "accident"

1981 – Tom starts Seton Hall Law
Kate spends Junior Year abroad in France.
Walt Erskine in DC for Vietnam Veterans dedication

1983 – Aug: Jack and Weezy find a corpse and a strange pyramid in the Barrens (*Secret Histories*)
Sept: Jack starts South Burlington County Regional High School
Kate starts UMDNJ in Stratford.
Jack hired by Ernst Drexler II to mow the Lodge lawn
Jack discovers buried town below

Jack finds a missing boy and has brush with last q'qr.

Jack sees six-foot sigil he will need later (*Secret Circles*)
Oct: Walt cures Miriam's child.

Jack and Piney kids confront mob in the Barrens ("Piney Power")

Starts a vendetta against Carson Toliver for assaulting Weezy;

Abe Grossman stops by Used and meets Jack (*Secret Vengeance*)

1985 – melis discovered at *Lange-Tür*

DIA Agent Benjamin Greve gives melis to Maureen LaVelle at Ft. Detrick (*The Void Protocol*)

1986 – Operation Synapse initiated via Agent Greve

1987 –Jack grads South Burlington County Regional High School, starts Rutgers

1988 – Walt Erskine moves to New York; meets Martin Spano

1990 – Jan: Jack's mother killed by a thrown block
Feb: Jack kills Ed
June: Jack moves to NYC at age 21; connects with Abe

Jack meets Julio at The Spot, starts affair with Cristin Ott

Jack and the Mikulskis break up a child trafficking ring (*Cold City*)

1991 – Jack sets up Neil Zalesky and Vinny Donuts kills him
Julio inherits The Spot, Jack buys the Semmerling and his Corvair
Jack rents the UWS apartment (*Dark City*)
Horace B. Gilmartin Foundation opens the Modern Motherhood clinics

1993 – Arabs build WTC bomb in a Jersey City garage
Jack avenges Cristin via *infernum viventes*

Feb. 26: Jack and Burkes fail to stop WTC bomb. (*Fear City*)

2001 – Feb: Agent Greve delivers melis sample to Plum Island researchers

2004 – Jack meets Chandler. ("Fix")

2006 – Modern Motherhood clinics close

YEAR ZERO (minus) FIVE:
Dec: Bill Ryan buries Danny in St. Ann's cemetery (*Reprisal*)

YEAR ZERO (minus) FOUR:
Jan: Bill Ryan ends up on West End in Bahamas
May: Department R3A ("the Troika") formed in NSA
June: the Düsseldorf atrocity

YEAR ZERO (minus) THREE:
Feb: Dr. Lazlo Gates kills himself in Times Square. (*Sibs*)
Mar: Professor Sal Roma forms SESOUP
         Jack meets Gia DiLauro via Burkes
Summer: Jack encounters the rakoshi (*The Tomb*)
         The Facelift killer strikes: ("Faces")
Sept: Disturbance in the Veil ("The Barrens")
Oct: "A Day in the Life"
         Ilya Medved joins SESOUP
Nov: "The Long Way Home"
Dec: "Santa Jack" / *Legacies*

YEAR ZERO (minus) TWO:
Bill Ryan returns to US as Will Ryerson
April: the Ehler house disappears in Monroe; the Twins (who've been managing the yeniçeri) disappear with it (*Conspiracies*)
May: tire and crankcase oil drop in Long Island.
         Scar-Lip escapes into the Barrens (*All the Rage*)
June: subway massacre stopped by "Subway Savior;"
         Jack reconnects with his sister Kate.
         The Lady re-enters his life when the Unity virus infects

Kate.
> Kate dies in an explosion at the Jersey Shore (*Hosts*)
> the Atlantic City Upwelling. (*The Upwelling*)
Aug: strangeness at Menalaus Manor in Queens (*The Haunted Air*)
> the Catskill Cataclysm. (*The Upwelling*)
> German U-104 discovered in iceberg D-31a (*Lexie*)
> The end of Scar-lip (*Scar-Lip Redux*)
Sept: Hurricane Elvis
> The Achimetes Lever activated; Earth's axis increases (*Lexie*)
> The Lady suffers her first death (*Gateways*)
Oct: on Plum Island, Hess and Monaco dose David Quinnell with melis
Nov: Dormentalism / Luther Brady scandal. (*Crisscross*)
Dec: LaGuardia massacre. (*Infernal*)

YEAR ZERO (minus) ONE:
Jan: Jack and Madame de Medici in NOLA ("Infernal Night")
> Oculus murdered in Red Hook warehouse HQ (*Harbingers*)
April: early – Dawn Pickering conceives
> *The Fifth Harmonic*
> *Panacea*
> Advent of the Kickers / Hank Thompson / *Kick!* (*Bloodline*)
> Alan Bulmer meets Dat-Tay-Vao; Walter Erskine dies. (*The Touch*)
May: Jack meets Glaeken (*By the Sword*)
> Massacre on Staten Island; kuroikaze redux. (*By the Sword*)
> *The God Gene*
> Sylvia's sculptures on display in NYC
July: Alan Bulmer's house burns (*The Touch*)
> Mount Sinai hospital shootout; Lady dies 2nd time (*Ground Zero*)

Aug: Rasalom settles in Pendleton, NC as Rafe
The signals (stable since 2/11/68) start to change, moving inchmeal up or down toward a common frequency.
Sept: another disturbance in the Barrens. ("TPOTC&OE")
Weirdness at Lakehurst (*The Void Protocol*)
"Tenants"
October - December: The Order develops the Jihad virus. (*Fatal Error*)
Rafe/Rasalom in Pendleton, NC; targets Lisl.
Dec: Madame de Medici and Snowpocalypse
(*The Last Christmas*)

YEAR ZERO:
Jan: "Pelts"
Dawn's baby boy is late
Feb: Rasalom – in Pendleton, NC setting up Ev and Lisl.
Renny Augustino – in NC tracking Bill
Glaeken and Bill dig up Danny Gordon in St. Ann's
Rasalom learns Glaeken mortal since the Keep
(*Reprisal*)
Internet collapse. (*Fatal Error*)
The Duad forms (*Double Threat*)
Mar: Imperial Valley / Salton Sea quakes/flood (*Double Dose*)
Explosive destruction in Nuckateague, LI.
Rasalom kills Eddie, Weeze, the Lady and the baby
(*The Dark at the End*)
May: all signals match the Sheep Meadow signal (*Signalz*)
Nightworld begins

Thus ends the Secret History (because
the story is secret no more)

Also by F. Paul Wilson

Repairman Jack*
The Tomb
Legacies
Conspiracies
All the Rage
Hosts
The Haunted Air
Scar-Lip Redux (graphic novel)
Gateways
Crisscross
Infernal
Harbingers
Bloodline
By the Sword
Ground Zero
The Last Christmas
Fatal Error
The Dark at the End
Nightworld
Quick Fixes – Tales of Repairman Jack

The Teen Trilogy*
Jack: Secret Histories
Jack: Secret Circles
Jack: Secret Vengeance

The Early Years Trilogy*
Cold City
Dark City
Fear City

The Adversary Cycle*
The Keep
The Tomb
The Touch

Reborn
Reprisal
Signalz
Nightworld

The ICE Trilogy*
Panacea
The God Gene
The Void Protocol

Graphic Novels
The Keep
Scar-Lip Redux

The LaNague Federation
Healer
Wheels within Wheels
An Enemy of the State
Dydeetown World
The Tery

Other Novels
*Black Wind**
*Sibs**
The Select
Virgin
Implant
Deep as the Marrow
Sims
*The Fifth Harmonic**
Midnight Mass

The Duad Novels*
Double Threat
Double Dose

The Hidden*
The Upwelling

Lexie

as Nina Abbott
Rx Murder
Rx Mayhem

Novellas
"*The Peabody-Ozymandias Traveling Circus & Oddity Emporium*"*
"*Wardenclyffe*"*
"*Signalz*"*

Collaborations
Mirage (with Matthew J. Costello)
Nightkill (with Steven Spruill)
Masque (with Matthew J. Costello)
Draculas (with Crouch, Konrath, Strand)
The Proteus Cure (with Tracy L. Carbone)
A Necessary End (with Sarah Pinborough)
"*Fix*"* (with J. A. Konrath & Ann Voss Peterson)
Three Films and a Play (with Matthew J. Costello)
Faster Than Light – Vols. 1 & 2
(with Matthew J. Costello)

The Nocturnia Chronicles
(with Thomas F. Monteleone)
Definitely Not Kansas
Family Secrets
The Silent Ones

Short Fiction
Soft & Others
Ad Statum Perspicuum
The Barrens & Others
Aftershock & Others
A Little Beige Book of Nondescript Stories
The Christmas Thingy
*Quick Fixes – Tales of Repairman Jack**

Sex Slaves of the Dragon Tong
*The Compendium of Srem**
Ephemerata
*Secret Stories**
Other Sandboxes
The Compendium of F – 50 Years
of F. Paul Wilson (Vols. 1-3)

Editor
Freak Show
Diagnosis: Terminal
The Hogben Chronicles (with Pierce Watters)

Omnibus Editions
The Complete LaNague
Calling Dr. Death (3 medical thrillers)
*Scenes from the Secret History**
Ephemerata
Three Films and a Play (with Matthew J. Costello)

Printed in Great Britain
by Amazon

39537985R00341